MW01132399

# The Cut of Women's Clothes
## 1600–1930

*by the same author*

THE CUT OF MEN'S CLOTHES 1600–1900

1612. Portrait. Artist unknown. *Private collection*

# The Cut of Women's Clothes
## 1600–1930

NORAH WAUGH

*with line diagrams by Margaret Woodward*

A Theatre Arts Book
Routledge
New York

A Theatre Arts Book
First Published in 1968 by
Theatre Arts Books
29 West 35th Street
New York, NY 10001
www.routledge-ny.com

Theatre Arts Books is an imprint of the Taylor & Francis Group.

Printed in the United States of America on acid-free paper.

Library of Congress Catalog Card Number 68-13408

ISBN 0-87830-026

# Editor's Note

I have completed, and seen this book through the press, out of a deep personal affection and respect for the work of my colleague the late Miss Norah Waugh, who died suddenly, at Easter 1966. I hope that this has been achieved in the way she would have wished.

Margaret Woodward

# Acknowledgments

For permission to use extracts in the 'Quotations from Contemporary Sources' sections, grateful acknowledgments are due to:

His Grace The Duke of Northumberland for two extracts from *The Diaries of a Duchess*: Elizabeth Duchess of Northumberland, published by Hodder & Stoughton;

Sir Harold Nicolson for an extract from *The Diary of Lady Anne Clifford*, published by William Heinemann;

Miss Ilka Chase for passages from *Always in Vogue* by Edna Woolman and Ilka Chase, published by Victor Gollancz;

The Directors of Punch Publications for two verse extracts from *Punch* of 1909.

Also to the authors and editors, or their executors, and to the publishers of the following books:

*Remember and Be Glad* by Cynthia Asquith (Barrie & Rockliff);
*Edwardian Hey-Days* by George Cornwallis-West (Putnam & Co.);
*Sophie in London* by Sophie de la Roche (Jonathan Cape);
*Georgiana Duchess of Devonshire*: Extracts from Correspondence (John Murray);
*The Farington Diary* (The Hutchinson Publishing Group);
*Discretions and Indiscretions* by Lady Duff Gordon (The Hutchinson Publishing Group);
*With Dearest Love to All*: The Life and Letters of Lady Jebb, edited by Mary Reed Bobbitt (Faber and Faber);
*Edwardian Daughter* by Sonia Keppel (Hamish Hamilton);
*Women's Dress in the Jazz Age* by James Laver (Hamish Hamilton);
*Betsy Sheridan's Journal* edited by William Le Fanu (Eyre & Spottiswood);
*Goodbye Piccadilly* by W. Macqueen-Pope (Michael Joseph);
*Champagne from My Slipper* by Ruby Miller (Herbert Jenkins);
*Memoirs of Susan Sibbald*, edited by Francis Paget (The Bodley Head);

*En Habillant l'Epoque* by Paul Poiret (Editions Bernard Grasset). The quotation is from the English edition published by Victor Gollancz under the title *My First Fifty Years*.

*Period Piece* by Gwen Raverat (Faber and Faber);

*The Russells in Bloomsbury* by Gladys Scott Thomson (Jonathan Cape);

*More Letters from Martha Wilmot*: Vienna 1819–1829 (Macmillan);

*A Century of Fashion* by Jean-Philippe Worth, translated by Ruth Scott Miller (Little, Brown & Co., Boston, U.S.A.);

*My Two Worlds* by Nora Wydenbruck (Longmans, Green & Co.).

Grateful acknowledgments are also made to the following: Mrs. P. Anthony; M. Parguez; Major Ralph Verney; The Victoria and Albert Museum; The London Museum; The Gallery of English Costume, Manchester; The Museum of Costume, Bath; The British Museum; The Metropolitan Museum, New York; The Kungl, Livrustkammaren, Stockholm; Leeds City Art Galleries; Centre de Documentation du Costume, Paris; Cheltenham Museum; The Central School of Art and Design, London; *The Tailor and Cutter; The Lady; Weldons; Vogue.*

# Contents

9

# Cutting Diagrams and Tailors' Patterns

## CUTTING DIAGRAMS

### Part One: 1600–1680

### Part Two: 1680–1795

## Part Three: 1795–1890

## Part Four 1890—1930

## TAILORS' PATTERNS

# Plates

1612. Portrait. Artist unknown. *Private collection*        *colour frontispiece*

*plates 1 to 17 between pages 32 and 33*

1.   *c.* 1605. Anne of Denmark, wife of James I. Engraving. *Victoria and Albert Museum*
2.   1623. Duchess of Richmond and Lennox. Engraving. *Victoria and Albert Museum*
3a, b.   *c.* 1600. Embroidered jackets. *Victoria and Albert Museum*
4.   *c.* 1610. Hip rolls. Caricature by I. de Vos and Galle. From a Dutch Engraving
5.   1607. Lady in Grey. Artist unknown. *By courtesy of the Hon. M. L. Astor*
6.   *c.* 1628. Countess of Southampton. Artist unknown. Ham House, Richmond
7.   1634. Henrietta of Lorraine by Van Dyck. Kenwood House, Highgate, London
8a, b.   1639. Two ladies from the well-known engravings by Hollar
9.   *c.* 1640. Marchioness of Winchester. Artist unknown
10.   1645. Corset of cherry red satin, bound with turquoise ribbon. *E. Wilson Filmer Collection. Art Gallery, Hull*
11.   1660–5. Bodice of ivory silk. *Verney collection, Claydon House, Bucks*
12.   *c.* 1650. La Toilette. G. Ter Borch. *Rijksmuseum, Amsterdam*
13.   *c.* 1660. Frances Courtenay, Countess of Andover. Artist unknown. *By courtesy of the Earl of Aylesford*
14.   *c.* 1670. Monument, Sir Richard and Lady Atkins. *St. Paul's Church, Clapham, London*
15.   1660–70. From The Seasons. Artist unknown. *Museo del Prado, Madrid*
16.   *c.* 1670. Katerina Agatha von Rappolstein by T. Roos. *By courtesy of the Earl of Southesk*
17.   1670–80. Lady in town dress. I. D. de St. Jean

17

# Introduction

Until the middle of the nineteenth century there was a certain similarity in design and proportion between men's and women's costume. The style of men's clothes was repeated in women's dress with, however, much greater exaggeration and much greater variety. The leisurely life of the lady of fashion, her more malleable body and the much wider choice of materials at her disposal, gave her a greater freedom of interpretation of the fashionable line.

Each century, with short transition periods between, has produced its own distinctive style, the fundamental cut remaining constant over a number of years. Changes in details, such as trimmings, draping, accessories, etc., followed one another incessantly. They were used to emphasize the fashion line and to give variety, and they reflected personal taste and the social and artistic background of the period. Changes in cut were much slower, each one evolving from the previous style, and were influenced to a great extent by new textures in materials.

The diagrams given here have been chosen as far as possible from existing specimens in order to show a sequence of cut. Dresses also have been selected which give a good period shape and are not too overburdened with decoration; in this way the slowly developing changes of cut can be readily observed. The illustrations show the dresses as they would have been worn, with the trimmings, hair styles and accessories essential for the complete picture of a well-dressed woman.

PART ONE

Seventeenth Century
1600-1680

Engravings by Jacques Callot. *c.* 1630

# 1600-1625

W omen's fashions of the last years of Queen Elizabeth's reign continued to be worn for a time after James I came to the throne; yet during the first quarter of the seventeenth century there came a period of transition bringing with it a gradual elimination of the earlier extravagances.

At the beginning of the century there were, in addition to the formal dress with its wide farthingale and high standing ruff, several rather more informal types, a loose gown with petticoat, a loose gown with jacket and petticoat, or sometimes simply a jacket and petticoat. These were worn with a modified version of the wheel farthingale or, more usually, with the french farthingale (cul postiche or bum roll). This was a roll padded with cotton or horsehair which was tied round the waist over the hips. It might consist of a single roll, large or small, or several narrow rolls held together with tapes and arranged to form a circle whose outside rim was strengthened by a strip of cane or whalebone. After about 1615 the large wheel farthingale began to be discarded, though it lingered on into the 1620's. Small hip rolls, however, continued to be worn. No farthingales or farthingale dresses seem to have survived until the present day but fortunately there are a few gowns and jackets still, from which the cut of seventeenth-century clothes can be deduced.

## FORMAL DRESS

The farthingale dress worn on formal occasions consisted of a separate bodice and skirt. The bodice of this dress had a circular basque which spread out horizontally over the wheel farthingale, and the skirt was worn open in front to show the underskirt. In the seventeenth century the bodice was called a 'body' or 'pair of bodies'. The underskirt retained its name of 'kirtle' for a while, but later became 'petticoat', a name which was also used until the end of the eighteenth century for any skirt closed all round. During the first part of the century, the large padded sleeves of the earlier bodice were replaced by simple straight sleeves with additional long hanging sleeves, over the top of which were set epaulettes (wings). The early bodice had usually been worn open in front, each side being attached to a long central triangular piece of

23

material known as the 'stomacher'. The stomacher was discarded and the front bodice was now cut in one with a low U-shaped neckline. The skirt, which now hung straighter than the earlier one, was not so open in front and was often closed all round. As a rule the dress would be carried out in one material only, the same trimmings being used for bodice and skirt. The low-necked bodice could be cut from two pieces of material, front and back, joined together towards the back by two side seams running from the armhole down to the waist with a very slight inward slope, like a man's doublet. The back was always cut high to the neck, where a small stiffened collar would support the ruff. If the front of the bodice was to be worn high to the neck, extra seaming was necessary. There would have to be either a centre front seam shaped to take the bust, or two side seams that followed the line of the earlier front worn with the stomacher, that is, running from the shoulders over the bust and inclined inwards to the waist centre front. (On a large woman the low necked bodice might also require front seams.)

The sleeves were cut in two pieces like those in a man's doublet. The bodice always had a strong interlining and was worn over a heavily stiffened under-bodice–'the whalebone body'. This also was cut from two pieces of material with two side seams shaped into the waist with a long pointed front. The sides were cut two or three inches longer than the waist, and were slit up into tabs to allow for the curve of the hips, or separate tabs were added from the waist to which the farthingale was tied.

Unlike the earlier skirt which was circular in cut, the skirt accompanying this bodice would have been made from several widths of material, each unshaped, or only slightly gored on each side, and gathered or pleated on to the waistband. The skirt fullness could also have been attached to a small circular yoke fitting over the top of the farthingale.

About 1615 the waistline began to rise. If the bodice had front-side seams, these now moved down from the shoulders to start from the armhole, and sloped in towards the centre front, which was slightly pointed. The back seams also moved towards the centre back at the waist; the shoulder seams widened, and the basque was discarded. This bodice could be cut from four pieces: front, back and two underarm pieces. Sleeves were unchanged, though occasionally the front seam was left open. The skirt, whether open or closed, hung rather straight over small hip pads. This was the style of dress worn in England until *c.* 1625. See frontispiece and plates 1, 2.

## JACKETS

Jackets, known as 'waistcoats' throughout the seventeenth century, were informal wear for ladies of quality and the habitual costume of other classes. The early specimens which have survived are the beautifully embroidered ones dating from the end of the sixteenth century to *c.* 1630. These jackets are a distinctive English fashion, and reflect the Englishwoman's skill in embroidery and her love of gardens. Most of them are of white linen and embroidered all over. The early designs, worked in black or coloured silks, are coiling stems enclosing conventionalized flower and fruit motifs, sometimes with birds and insects in addition. Later designs are more fluid, and in one colour only. In the more elaborate jackets, gold and silver threads are used, as well as sequins, and they are edged with gold lace.

The basic cut is the same throughout. The two front pieces, with centre front shaping, are joined to the back by two side back seams. The jacket is cut a few inches below waist level to form a basque which is achieved by slitting the bottom and inserting triangular gussets. In the earlier jackets the back seams run from high in the armhole slightly in to the waist; there is one gusset centre back, and three or more each side, set to a low waist; usually there is a collar. The sleeves are cut from two similarly shaped pieces, straight to the elbow and then curved forward to take the bend of the arm, with a front seam set well forward and inserted at a point high into the armhole. The sleeves are wrist length, with a small cuff. Later jackets follow the broader fashion line; that is, the shoulder seams widen, and the back seams, set lower in the armhole, slope in and are from two to three inches apart at waist level. The gussets are set to the higher waistline, and the collar is omitted. The sleeves are often very wide, cut from one piece of material and gathered top and bottom. The neckline may be quite high or very low.

One jacket only has been preserved with an accompanying petticoat. This is also white, but of heavy cotton, and the design is larger in scale and more coarsely worked. It is cut straight, gathered to the waist, and embroidered all over except for a few inches round the top which is covered by the jacket-basque. In portraits and miniatures of the period these jackets are shown worn with long loose gowns, the petticoat being of a different material.

Skirts, or petticoats, for simpler styles of dress were cut from several unshaped widths of material and gathered or pleated into the waist. For a more elegant line both back and front would be cut slightly circular; that is, with the waist curving upwards each side and with gored side seams. They were ground length, without trains. The skirts given in the Spanish books are of this type (pages 48–51). See plates 3, 5.

## GOWNS

From mediaeval times a garment that hung loose from the shoulders was called a gown, and in France a *robe*, a distinction which lasted until the gown became incorporated with the dress in about the middle of the seventeenth century. Women's gowns were ground length, sometimes with a slight train. They were cut without a waist seam and were worn loose or held in to the waist by a sash or ornamental girdle. Usually they were sleeveless, but sometimes they had long hanging sleeves, and they always had epaulettes. Earlier gowns were often worn closed in front from neck to waist, but in the seventeenth century this had become a fashion for older women or merchant's wives. The gown was cut with two fronts and one back piece, with side seam towards the back. When worn open, the fronts were narrow at the top and the width round the bottom was arranged by having extra fullness pleated into the armhole under the arm. The sides were straight or gored. The back was cut wide, and the fullness was pleated into the neck and shoulders. A small stiffened collar at the back of the neck supported the ruff. Loose gowns were also worn as what we now term dressing-gowns but which then were called 'night-gowns'. This is a somewhat misleading term as it was also used for informal dress worn during the day. The French were more logical–they called a dressing-gown a *robe de nuit* and an informal dress a *robe de chambre*. See plate 5; Diagram I.

## MATERIALS, DECORATIONS, ETC.

The best silks, velvets, damasks, cloth of silver and gold, etc., also lace, came from Italy and were very expensive. In both England and France laws were continually being passed prohibiting their import. Very little silk was made in England and French silks were not of a high quality. They were therefore often enriched by slashing, pinking, embroidery, etc. As with the men's doublets of this date, all the bodice seams might be outlined with two or more rows of narrow braid, the same trimming being repeated on the skirt. Skirts worn with elaborately embroidered jackets often had a deep border of rich embroidery as well as having the hem edged with lace or fringe. The borders of the gown and epaulettes were edged with braid or embroidery, but very often just scalloped.

All dresses had some form of neck wear. The farthingale low-necked bodice had the high standing fan-shaped ruff which needed to be supported by a frame made from wire or buckram. The closed Elizabethan ruff was still worn, usually with high-necked bodices. The standing band was a semi-circular collar, also with a wire frame. The falling ruff–several goffered layers attached to the top of a deep neck band–was more customary with informal dress. 'Band' was the contemporary name for a collar. Collars were often attached to the 'partlet': this was a false front, or chemisette, which filled in the low neck of the bodice. Ruffs and collars were made from fine linen, lawn or lace, or lawn edged with lace. The laces used were heavy needlepoint such as *reticella*, *point de Venise*, and by the end of the period bobbin laces were also worn. Long aprons of gauze or of fine lawn, often beautifully embroidered, were fashionable informal wear. These were at first worn under the basque or the jacket, and later over it, to give the higher waistline. Short circular capes, and longer ones for travelling, were worn throughout the century. The 'safeguard' was an extra skirt, or part of a skirt, which protected the dress when the wearer was travelling or on horseback.

# 1625-1645

Although there is always a great similarity between English and French modes, the simplicity that English clothes had achieved by the early 1620's was not evident in France. At the beginning of the seventeenth century the French bourgeoises wore the jacket, petticoat and gown like their English contemporaries, but the farthingale dress continued for formal and Court wear into the 1620's. Here also the neck became very low but was more V-shaped. Sleeves continued very full but they began to be set in a series of puffs all down the arm, the puffs often being slashed. By the mid 1620's these puffs had been reduced to two, one on the upper and one on the lower arm. They were plain or slashed, and required a padded and whaleboned or caned inner sleeve to balloon them out. These sleeves (*manches ballonnées*) were worn with the new fashion of fitted gown, which appeared *c.* 1625 when, as in England, the waistline had risen and the silhouette broadened—a fashion that was probably introduced into England when the French princess, Henrietta Maria, became Queen of England in 1625. See plate 6.

## THE GOWN

The fronts of the new gown were cut in one piece, usually without a waist seam. The back, however, was now always separated at the high waistline and a very full trained skirt added. The bodice was cut with wide shoulder seams and wide neckline; the back side seams, which almost met at the waist centre back, ran out to the armhole to continue in an unbroken line over the shoulder. The very full sleeves were set into this line, thus giving a very deep armhole to allow for the large under-sleeves. The gown sleeve was a half sleeve, usually slit in front and caught at the elbow. The shoulder line was emphasized by the narrow epaulettes placed over it. This setting of the sleeve far into the back was continued throughout the seventeenth century and, with some modification, during the eighteenth century as well. The early style of jacket worn under the gown was now replaced by a bodice fitting tightly over the boned body, or the boned body itself might be worn when it would be covered with a rich material. It retained its original shape—that is, the long stomacher front and side tabs. The full balloon double sleeves might be attached to this bodice; they were often cut as one long sleeve, slashed, or if plain

27

usually with open front seam, and caught to the arm above the elbow. The fronts of the gown were pinned each side of the bodice down to the high waistline, or were caught across by narrow ribbon ties or straps. This type of gown continued to be worn for some time, but eventually, by the mid 1640's the bodice was cut separately from the skirt all round and was boned, a separate stomacher piece filling in the open front. The sleeves lost their bulk, and various styles of under-sleeve were added. See plate 7.

## BASQUED BODICE

Another style which developed in the late 1620's was a more fashionable version of the jacket. Here again, the man's doublet may have been the inspiration. The short high-waisted bodice was cut like that of the new gown, but the skirt was replaced by a basque. The basques varied. They might still be cut like those of the embroidered jacket – with triangular gussets – but more frequently they were made from several wedge-shaped pieces called tabs, or *tassets*, which either hung separately or were joined together. This bodice also was open in front, the sides being pinned or laced across the stomacher. Sleeves were very full, and were cut either in one straight piece, or from two pieces slightly curved. In both cases the front sleeve seam was placed well forward, and was inserted into the bodice high in the armhole. It was fashionable to leave this seam open to show the undergarment. There was emphasis and variety in sleeves; many were ballooned above and below the elbow, being either plain or slashed. Others were simply gathered into the armhole and again halfway down the forearm into a wide band, which was loose enough to show the full chemise sleeve which hung below. For formal wear the bodice matched the skirt.

In the 1630's a short bodice without basques was also worn. The centre front was usually cut in one piece, without a stomacher and with a very low neck and slightly pointed waist. This style as a rule had voluminous sleeves.

This period had a very characteristic neckline. It was cut very low and narrow in front, and the side pieces sloped out to give a broad neckline. This, together with the wide shoulder seams, large sleeves, epaulettes and high waistline all emphasized the fashionable trend towards breadth, which reached its peak 1630–1640. After 1630, although there was no change in cut, there was a lessening of rigidity in construction. The boned body was discarded, the boning being transferred to the lining of the short bodice or gown bodice. The stiffening from the sleeves and stomacher was reduced. This was especially noticeable in England, where the whole interpretation of the fashionable silhouette was softer and more fluid. See plates 8, 9.

## SKIRT

The full skirt, worn over hip pads, was cut either unshaped as before, or, for more formal wear, the front slightly circular with gored sides, deep pleats being set each side centre front to simulate the side skirts of the gown. This style would have a slight train. The petticoat of the gown would be cut unshaped, and the fullness kept to sides and back. See plates 6, 7, 8, 9.

## MATERIALS, DECORATIONS, ETC.

The 1625 gown was made from damask, velvet, silk, etc., and seems invariably to have been black, with the under-bodice, sleeves and petticoat made usually of a light-coloured contrasting material. At the beginning silks and satins were still pinked and slashed. Trimmings and embroidery were being less used. Ribbons were not so lavishly applied as they were on men's clothes, though bows, rosettes, and ribbon ties round the sleeves and high waist gave touches of bright colour. In the 1630's the fashionable Englishwoman began to wear her formal dress, of basqued bodice and skirt of plain silk or satin, completely untrimmed, though quite often the neckline, the edges of the basque, and the bottom of the skirt were scalloped. Collars, etc., were often discarded and only a narrow fold of fine lawn, or the chemise frill, softened the neckline. The full chemise sleeves of fine lawn ending in a frill appeared below the bodice sleeves; sometimes the frill was replaced by ruffles, that is, several layers of lawn or lace frills mounted together and sewn to the bottom of the bodice sleeves. This simplicity was an admirable foil to the only decoration used, the glowing colours of jewelled pieces made from a single precious stone or groups of stones with pearls. One piece was worn centre front, or jewelled buckles replaced the stomacher lacing, and the open sleeves were caught together at intervals with jewels. This new design in jewellery was the result of the discovery of rose-cutting early in the seventeenth century; the faceting of precious stones so enhanced their beauty that they were set with very little metal work. A string of pearls and pearl ear-rings were invariably worn.

The low-necked bodice meant, of course, that a great variety of neckwear was still worn. With the 1625 gown it was either the large closed falling ruff, or a standing collar, now narrower but of greater length, adjusted to follow the broad neckline. By the 1630's this collar had collapsed and lay flat round the back of the bodice, just coming over the shoulders to the front. When made of lawn it was cut straight and shaped to a slight curve with pin tucks, and frequently bordered with lace; the matching turn-back cuffs were also shaped with pin tucks. For humbler wear the chemise itself filled in the neck; otherwise there were partlets with collars attached, closed to the throat or opening into a V-shape. This style might be worn inside or outside the bodice. The neckerchief, either a square or oval-shape, was folded diagonally and worn round the shoulders open or caught at the throat. The neckline and bottom of the sleeves were frequently edged with a lace border over which a transparent lawn collar, or a neckerchief–or both–and cuffs, were worn.

# 1645-1680

During the 1640's the change of silhouette back to a slender line reduced the volume of material used and lengthened the waist.

## BODICES, JACKETS

By 1650 the waist was quite low and in order to balance the design the tabs or basque became smaller. The stomacher was still worn, but bodices with plain fronts were becoming more usual. Although still cut on the same principles, these longer bodices required more fitting. The back was shaped as before with two back side seams starting at the armhole, curving to within an inch each side centre back and continuing in parallel lines down to the waist. The front might be cut with a centre front seam shaped in to the waist and with an underarm seam; more frequently, this bodice also had two side front seams starting from the armhole and curving over the bust to run in two parallel lines ending in a blunt point which by 1660 was very long. This cut also frequently had an underarm seam. The neckline was now oval, running round the outside edge of the shoulders straight across the back and dipping slightly in front. To ensure a good fit round the top of the bodice the shoulder pieces were cut separately, from straight pieces of material, with a seam in front and a low diagonal seam at the back. The sleeve was cut from one piece, or from two shaped pieces, the fullness being reduced and set top and bottom in small regular pleats or with pin tucks taken from inside. The fashionable sleeve, was gradually moving up the arm, and by the mid 1670's was quite short. The fashionable bodice was always mounted on a very heavy boned lining whose seams, in order to facilitate this boning, were always straighter than the more subtly shaped ones of the covering material. When worn with matching skirt, the bodice was cut longer than the waist and the sides were slit into tabs. These side tabs went under the skirt waistband, with the long centre front point outside, and the bodice was closed by centre back lacing. Sometimes the boned bodice stopped at the waist, when small tabs or a short basque would be added. The latter style was more usual in informal bodices and in continental dresses. These informal bodices were more lightly boned with a centre front

30

lacing. During the transition period 1670–1680, when the bodice was worn underneath the mantua, the lines of the bodice seams straightened; sometimes there were two or more seams each side centre front and the same each side centre back. See plates 10–17; Diagrams V, VI.

## SKIRT

For formal wear the skirt matched the bodice. It was cut like the earlier one but with less fullness and was set in very regular pleats round the waist. In the 1660's formal dress began to have an additional overskirt, slit up the centre front and falling into a long train at the back. A little later the front skirts were slightly draped on each side, eventually being arranged in folds round the hips and caught up to the centre back. The underskirt was always called a petticoat. See plates 14, 16, 17.

## GOWN

The fitted gown with stomacher had gone out of fashion but the looser gown, the *robe de chambre*, was being worn for informal wear more often. (In this connection it must be remembered that during the seventeenth and eighteenth centuries the room where a person slept was also used as a reception room.)

## RIDING HABIT

Some women adopted the man's doublet for riding. When in the 1660's the man's riding coat was becoming fashionable wear, women also began to appear in it. It was worn for hunting but also sometimes for travelling by coach.

## MATERIALS, DECORATIONS, ETC.

Colbert, Louis XIV's astute minister, satisfied his young monarch's love of magnificence by developing industry and commerce in France, and towards the end of the seventeenth century Italy lost her long supremacy in the production of luxury dress materials and accessories. The new French silks, laces, etc., lavishly displayed at the French Court established a high standard for fashion which was to be copied throughout Europe. In England also, largely owing to the influx of French Protestant weavers, a flourishing silk industry was being developed.

Although there was little change in cut during the third quarter of the seventeenth century, the increasing richness of materials and trimmings transformed the simplicity of the 1650's. At that time the bodice and skirt, worn as formal or Court dress, was still made from plain silks or satins and was untrimmed except by jewelled pieces. The long centre front might be worn, like the sleeves of the bodice, open to show the chemise, the sides being caught at intervals with jewels. The shoulder seams, too, might be left unstitched. Later these dresses were carried out in figured silks, brocades, etc. Exquisite lace collars were worn, or the neckline might be draped with transparent gauze caught at intervals with tassels of pearls or jewels. Strings of pearls or precious stones were looped round the neckline, draped across or laid down the seams and round the waist. The bodice seams were also outlined by lace borders or embroidery, sometimes the same decoration being repeated on the petticoat up the centre front and round the hem. The overskirt was caught up with jewels. For less formal wear ribbon bows and rosettes replaced the jewels.

The chemise sleeve, now less voluminous, was trimmed with lace ruffles and ribbons, the fullness being caught round the arm with ribbon ties. Simpler bodices had the plain chemise visible above the neckline and below the bodice sleeves, or were worn with collars, neckerchiefs and cuffs, the quality of the linen varying according to the status of the wearer.

1.   *c.*1605. Anne of Denmark, wife of James I. Engraving. *Victoria and Albert Museum*
This dress shows the extension of Elizabethan modes into the early years of the seventeenth century, modified only in detail by such items as the low U-shaped neck line, the narrow sleeves, and the slightly higher waist with its simple closed bodice

2. 1623. Duchess of Richmond and Lennox. Engraving. *Victoria and Albert Museum*
The drum-shaped farthingale has been discarded, and the skirt is now held out at the hips by means of a padded hip roll

3a.  *c.* 1600. Jacket (back view). Embroidered in silver thread and plaited silk braid with sequins

3b.  *c.* 1660. Jacket. Pink silk, embroidered blue thread

Two examples of the informal jackets worn at the turn of the century, they are embroidered in an allover pattern and left unboned. *Both from the Victoria and Albert Museum*

4.  *c.* 1610. Caricature. From a Dutch engraving
Ladies bolstering out their skirts with hip rolls

6. c. 1628. Countess of Southampton. Artist unknown.
*Ham House, Richmond*
The full slashed sleeves (manches ballonnees) and the widening lace collar all emphasize the width across the upper part of the body. In this formal dress the bodice with its higher waist still retains its stiffness, and the basque has become divided into tabs

5. 1607. Lady in Grey. Artist unknown.
*By courtesy of the Hon. M. L. Astor*
Lady wearing an informal jacket very similar to Plate 3a. A gauze apron covers her petticoat and the gown she wears resembles Cutting Diagram I

7.  1634. Henrietta of Lorraine. By Van Dyck. *Kenwood House, Highgate, London*
The gown is still being worn over a bodice and petticoat, the long hanging sleeves of
its predecessor in Plate 5 seemingly cut short and the corners held together with
rosettes. At this date, though usually darker in colour than the underlying dress, the
gown is of a lighter textured silk

8. 1639. Two ladies from the well-known engravings by Hollar.
Although the cut remains the same as the dress shown in Plate 6, these two prints show the softer and more fluid line already becoming apparent in Plate 7. The waist is even higher and each sleeve has become a single puff.

9. *c.* 1640. Marchioness of Winchester. Artist unknown.
A new lightness has evolved both in colour and texture. The rigidly-boned
corset has temporarily been discarded and some of its boning transferred to the
lining of the bodice

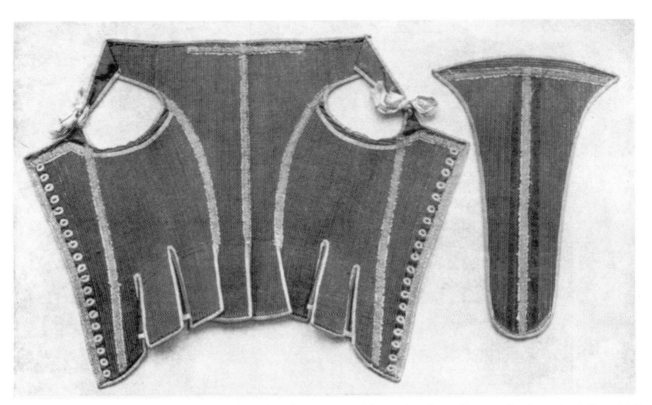

10.   1645. Corset of cherry red satin, bound with turquoise ribbon. El Wilson Filmer collection. *Art Gallery, Hull*
This corset shows the low horizontal neck line as seen in the back view on Plate 12.

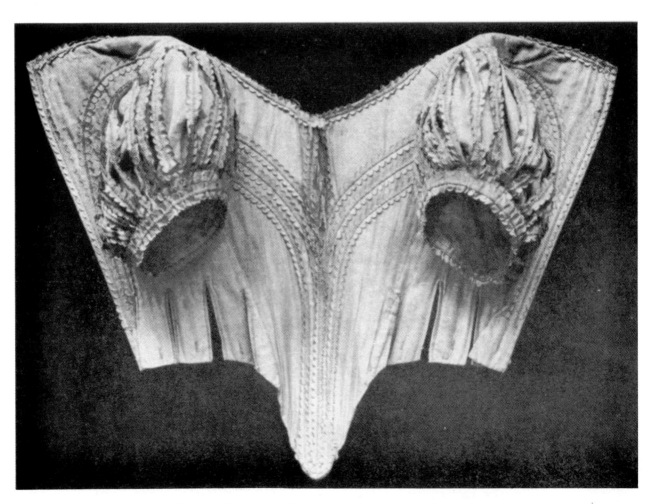

11.   1660–1665. Bodice of ivory silk. *Verney collection. Claydon House, Bucks.*
The dress bodice is now mounted directly on to the stiffly-boned corset. The waist has begun to descend again and the side tabs are now worn inside the petticoat. See Cutting Diagram VI

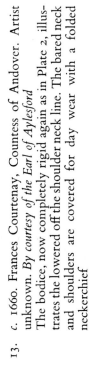

13. c. 1660. Frances Courtenay, Countess of Andover. Artist unknown. *By courtesy of the Earl of Aylesford*
The bodice, now completely rigid again as in Plate 2, illustrates the lowered off the shoulder neck line. The bared neck and shoulders are covered for day wear with a folded neckerchief

12. c. 1650. La Toilette. G. Ter Borch. *Rijksmuseum, Amsterdam*
Dresses of this date are usually laced up the centre back, and the full sleeves are gathered into an arm scye cut deeply into the back of the bodice

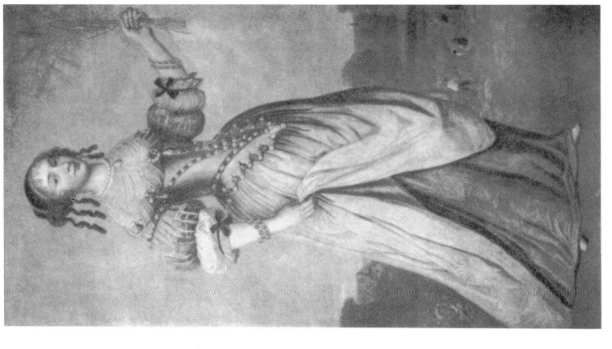

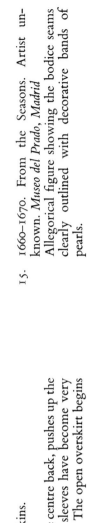

15. 1660–1670. From the Seasons. Artist unknown. *Museo del Prado, Madrid*
Allegorical figure showing the bodice seams clearly outlined with decorative bands of pearls.

14. c. 1670. Monument, Sir Richard and Lady Atkins.
*St. Paul's Church, Clapham, London*
The straight-fronted bodice, tightly laced at the centre back, pushes up the breasts to the high horizontal neck line. The sleeves have become very short and reveal the soft sleeves of the chemise. The open overskirt begins to be draped towards the back.

16. *c.* 1670. Katerina Agatha von Rappolstein. By T. Roos. *By courtesy of the Earl of Southesk*
Detail of a portrait showing the richness of the lace collar and chemise flounces

17.  1670–1680. Lady in town dress. I. D. de St. Jean
Back draping of the trained skirt. As the sleeve shortens, long gloves are worn

# Construction of
# Seventeenth-century Dresses

No farthingales, bodices for formal wear or skirts from the first quarter of the seventeenth century have been preserved either in England or in France. From contemporary records, bills, etc., however, we can see that the bodice was lined with some stout material and was possibly whaleboned. It was worn over an under-bodice stiffened by quilting, paste or glue and also by whalebones. As the bodice had only two side seams the bones were set straight round the front of it and there was also a slot centre front to hold the 'busk', that is, a separate piece of heavier whalebone, wood, horn, etc. The large sleeves would be mounted on an inner sleeve of fustian or linen extended by cane, wire or whalebone. The early epaulettes were often tabbed, that is made from strips of material caught together. The informal embroidered jackets might be lined or unlined. In later jackets the seams were sewn together and the gussets inserted before the embroidery was worked. The stitching is so beautifully fine that the seams are barely visible from the outside. Occasionally, in early specimens, the back seams, gussets and sleeve seams are outlined with a heavy embroidery stitch. These bodices would be pinned in position centre front.

The 1630's was a transition period. Sometimes the short-waisted bodice was lined with canvas only and was worn over a separate 'boned body'; sometimes the lining of the bodice itself was boned. First the lining would be seamed and boned, then the covering material was seamed, and finally the two were sewn together round the neck, down the fronts and round the waist. The sleeve and sleeve lining were seamed separately and gathered together, the bottom into a band and the top gathering arranged on the shoulders and down the back of the armhole. A short strip of linen with lacing holes was usually sewn to the lining as far as the waist, each side of the front opening, when the bodice was laced across a separate stomacher piece that had been inserted either above or below the lacing. The epaulettes were stiffened with canvas and the outer edge was often sharpened by the insertion of a thin strip of whalebone.

The long bodice, c. 1645–1680, was always mounted on a lining of stiff linen that had been solidly whaleboned. The lining was cut high under the arm so that the armhole was smaller than the very large sleeve armhole. Whalebones were inserted straight at the centre front, centre

33

back and underarm, and in consequence followed the angle of the side, front, and back seams when these had been joined together. This gave a more rounded shape to the body than the early cut. The bones stopped at the sleeve armhole, and as the front neckline was now rather high they stopped an inch or two below this in order not to flatten the bust too much. There was a slot centre front for the busk; the centre back was open with lacing holes each side. The outer material, which had also been previously seamed, was then laid over the boned lining. Sometimes, however, the outer material was stretched over the lining and seamed from outside, a method which obviated wrinkling and could simplify seaming. The raw edges of bodice and lining were stitched or bound together round the neck and waist—waist tabs were always bound. The centre back was stitched about half an inch in on each side so that the lacing was hidden, and the epaulettes, now very narrow, were still stiffened and whaleboned. These bodices became so excessively rigid that they were almost pieces of sculpture. See plates 10, 11; Diagrams V, VI. For informal wear, bodices and sleeves were lined, but the boning was simplified or eliminated altogether. As a rule informal bodices and jackets opened centre front.

Skirts worn with the later bodices were set in very small regular pleats round the waist—leaving a few inches plain centre front—and the pleating was held in position by several rows of running threads inside, a stitch catching the edge of each pleat. If the material was very stiff the top was left raw, and when pleated was trimmed and bound; otherwise the top was pleated and then turned in a couple of inches and sewn to a waistband by whipping stitches. As far as can be ascertained the skirts were not lined though sometimes the hem was faced for several inches or bound with braid. See Diagram VI.

# Cutting Diagrams

For full explanation see Notes on the Cutting Diagrams, page 303

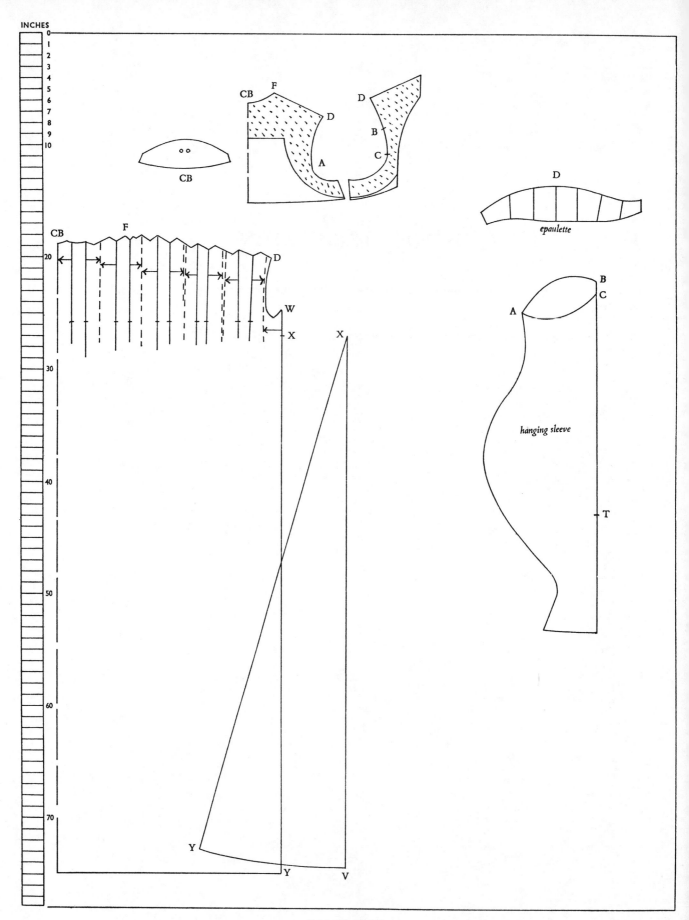

INCHES

DIAGRAM I

GOWN *c.* 1600 *Victoria and Albert Museum*

INCHES
0
1
2
3
4
5
6
7
8
9
10

20

30

40

50

60

70

DIAGRAM I

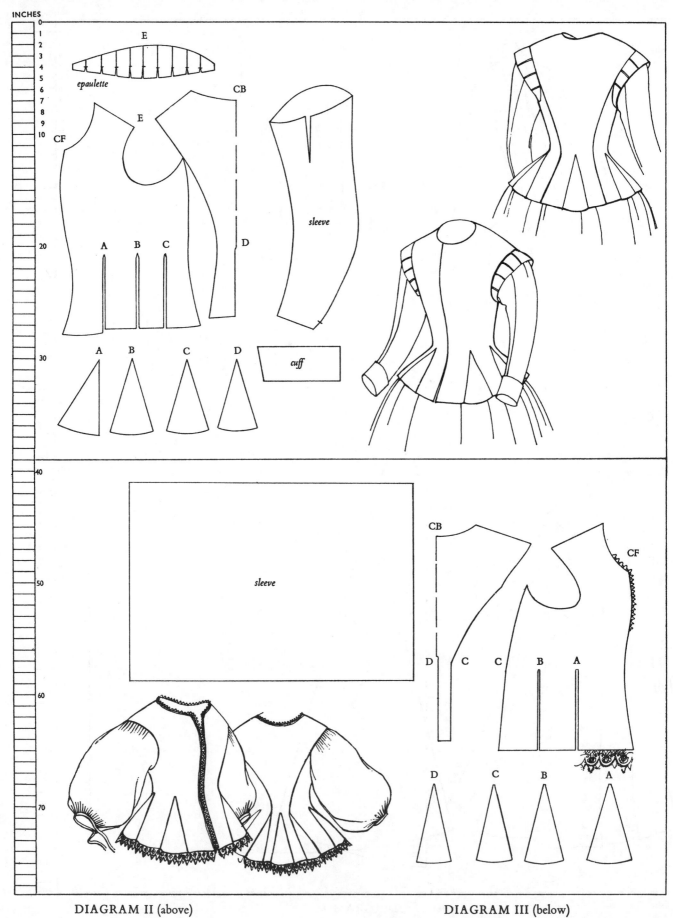

INCHES

0 1 2 3 4 5 6 7 8 9 10

20

30

40

50

60

70

E

epaulette

CB

E

CF

sleeve

A B C

D

A B C D

cuff

A B C D

sleeve

CB

CF

D C C B A

D C B A

**DIAGRAM II** (above)

EMBROIDERED JACKET *c.* 1610. *London Museum.*

**DIAGRAM III** (below)

EMBROIDERED JACKET 1625–30. *Victoria and Albert Museum*

INCHES

0
1
2
3
4
5
6
7
8
9
10

20

30

*lining*

CB

CB

CB

*epaulette*

*cuff*

40

50

60

70

CB D

C

A

B

CF

*boned lining*

A

*sleeve*

*sleeve*

CB D

C A

B

CF

C D

CF

A B

CB

CF

**DIAGRAM IV** (above)

BODICE *c.* 1635. *London Museum*

**DIAGRAM V** (below)

BODICE 1650–60. *London Museum*

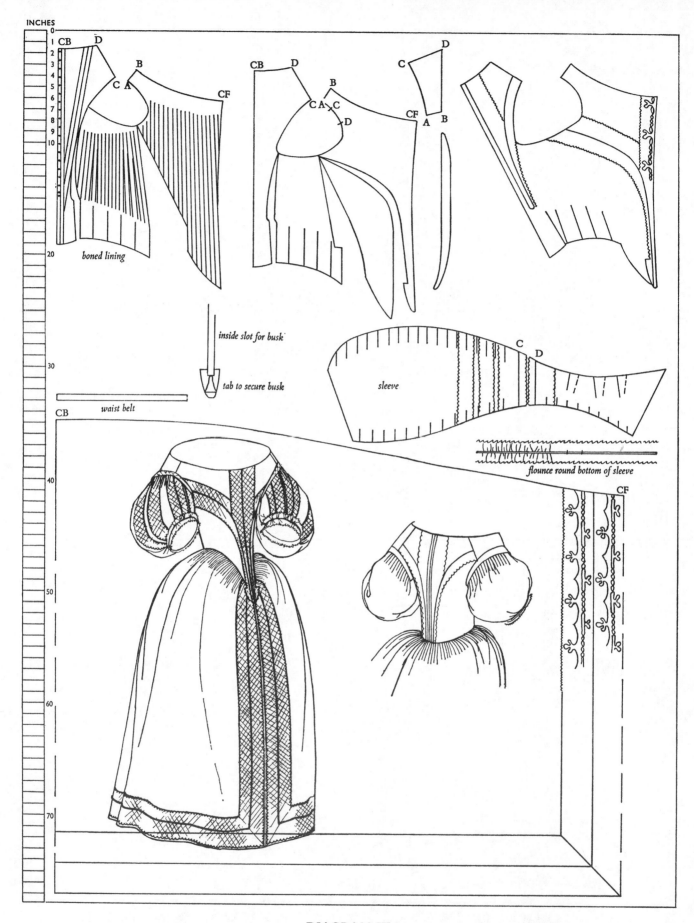

INCHES

CB D

B

C A

CF

boned lining

CB D

B

C A C

D

C

CF

A B

inside slot for busk

tab to secure busk

waist belt

CB

C D

sleeve

flounce round bottom of sleeve

CF

DIAGRAM VI

DRESS 1660's. *Museum of Costume, Bath*

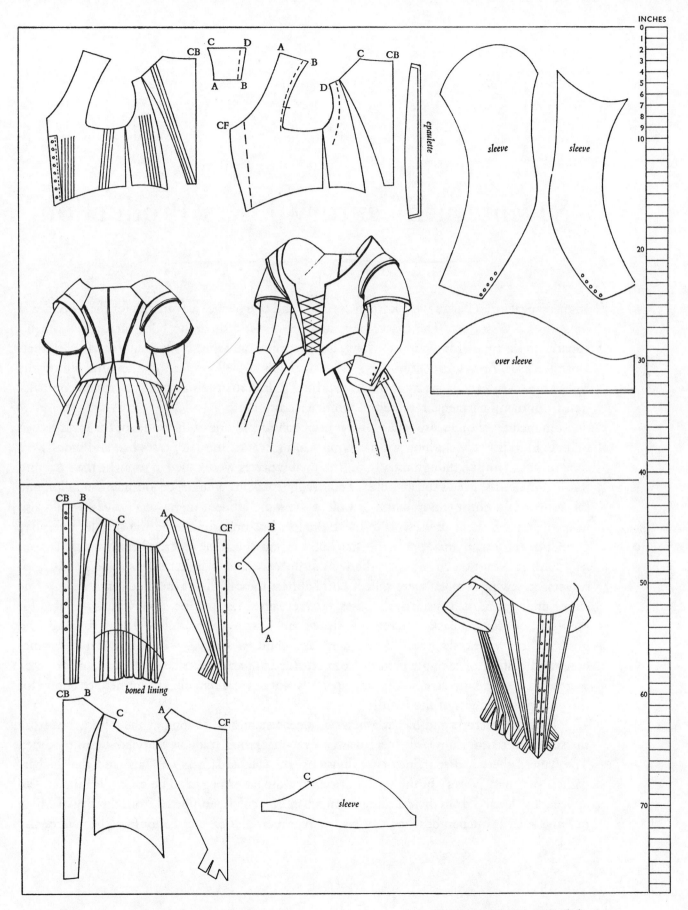

INCHES
0
1
2
3
4
5
6
7
8
9
10

20

30

40

50

60

70

CB  C  D  A  B  C  CB

CF  D

epaulette

sleeve        sleeve

over sleeve

CB  B
C  A  CF  B
C
CF
A

boned lining

CB  B
C  A  CF

C

sleeve

DIAGRAM VII (above)
BODICE 1650–60. *Victoria and Albert Museum*

DIAGRAM VIII (below)
BODICE 1670–80. *Privately owned*

# Seventeenth-century Dress Production

In mediaeval times tailors were known as *cissorii* and one of the early names for their guild was 'Fraternitate Cissorem'. The cissor, or tailor, cut out and made up both men and women's apparel. In the time of Edward I the king, queen, prince, and the king's daughter had each their separate cissor. As tailors continued to make women's as well as men's clothes until almost the end of the seventeenth century it is not surprising to find many similarities of cut and construction from men's garments repeated in women's costume.

From mediaeval times also it had always been considered one of the duties of the mistress of a household to provide clothing for her family and servants. In many cases flax and wool were spun on the premises, though usually professional weavers were called in to make the yarn into finished materials. Men's suits would, of course, be made by a tailor, or journeyman tailor, and the ladies of the court and nobility, as well as the more affluent merchants' wives, would also have their gowns and dresses made by the tailor, but underlinen and the simpler everyday garments were usually made at home. In a humble household the mistress herself would cut out and do the sewing; on large estates she would supervise and train her maids to be good semp-stresses – as sewing women were called. Until almost the middle of the nineteenth century the cut of underlinen, such as shirts, chemises, etc., remained fairly static. One width was used for the front, one for the back, one for each sleeve, and a strip was cut into collar, wristbands and gussets; there was no shaping. The women's and children's gowns would be cut by the time-honoured custom of taking a pattern from an existing garment. Silks, velvets, damasks, etc., were always very expensive, so dresses, especially skirts, were remade, retrimmed, or cut up for the younger members of the family.

Goldsmiths, mercers and haberdashers had been established as long as the tailors, but from the sixteenth century onwards there was an ever-increasing trade in household commodities. The haberdashers had split into two divisions – the 'Haberdashers of Hats' and the 'Haberdashers of Small Wares'. In the sixteenth century the latter began to be called 'Milliners': 'an appellation derived from their dealing in merchandize, chiefly imported from the city of Milan in Italy, such as ouches, broches, agglets, spurs, capes, glasses, etc. Amongst other wares also which constituted a part of the haberdashery of that period were pins. There were few of these Milliners' shops in the Reign of Edward VI, not more than a dozen in all London, but in 1580, every street in Westminster embraced the business of woollen drapers, cutlers, upholsterers, glass and earthenware men, perfumiers and various others dealing eastwards until the whole town became full of them.'

In the seventeenth century, although the milliners still sold a diversity of merchandise, they were beginning to specialize more and more in dress accessories–ribbons, laces, gloves, bands (collars), and 'pretty toies for Gentlewomen'.

Much lower down the scale were the Frippirers, or rag-men who dealt in second-hand clothes or who sold simple ready-made clothes for both men and women.

It was during the seventeenth century also that the sempstress attained professional status and set up her own establishment where she made and sold men's shirts, ruffs, cravats, etc., and the more negligée types of women's clothes and dress accessories: 'The Seamster or Seamstry work follows next in order to adorn the Head, Hands and Feet, as the other (taylor) is for the covering of the Body; nay, very often the Seamster occupieth the room and place of a Taylor in furnishing the Nobility and Gentry with such conveniences as serve the whole body, especially in the Summer Season. . . .'

Names of Things made by Seamsters

> SHIRT or SHIFT for a Man
> SMOCK or WOMAN'S SHIFT
> RUFFS, pleated Bands of two or three heights
> ROUND ROBINS, narrow Ruffs only about the Doublet Collar
> CRAVATS, CUFFS
> RUFFLES for the hands, both Plain and Laced
> SLEEVES, BOBS, BIGGINS
> HANDKERCHIEFS for Women's Necks, both round and square
> WHISKS to be worn with a Gown
> A ROMAN DRESS, the mantua cut square behind and round before
> WOMEN'S HEAD DRESSES
> WOMEN'S SLEEVES
>
> *Academy of Armory*, Randle Holme

There is practically no information about the cut and construction of women's clothes until the nineteenth century. The two early Spanish books on tailoring: *Libro de Geometrica Practica y Traca*, Madrid, 1589, Juaan de Alcega; and *Geometrica y Traca*, Madrid, 1618, La Rocha Burguen, give patterns for women's clothes but it must be remembered that these diagrams are given not for styles of cut but to show how to use different widths of material to the best advantage. The other seventeenth-century book on tailoring, *Le Tailleur Sincère*, Paris, 1671, le

Sieur Benist Boullay, is chiefly concerned with men's garments though he does give a lady's riding cloak.

The *Academy of Armory*, 1688, by Randle Holme, an early form of encyclopaedia, contains a good description of women's dress of the third quarter of the seventeenth century:

'In a WOMAN'S GOWN there are these several parts, as:

The STAYES, which is the body of the Gown before the Sleeves are put too, or covered with the outward stuff: which have these peeces in it, and terms used about it.

The FORE PART, or FORE BODY: which is the Breast part, which hath two peeces in it: as,

The RIGHT SIDE of the Fore-body.

The LEFT SIDE of the Fore-body.

The two SIDE PARTS, which are peeces under both Arms on the sides.

The BACK.

The SHOULDER HEADS, or SHOULDER STRAPS: are two peeces that come over the Shoulders and are fastened to the Fore-body: through which the Arms are put.

SCOREING, or STRIK LINES on the Canvice to sow straight.

STITCHING, is sowing all along the lines with close stitches to keep the Whale-bone each peece from other ... is the cleaving of the Whale-bone to what substance or thickness the workman pleaseth.

BONING THE STAYS, is to put the slit Bone into every one of the places made for it between each stitched line which makes Stayes or Bodies stiff and strong.

CORDY ROBE SKIRTS to the Staies are such stayes as are cut into Labells at the bottom, like long slender skirts.

LINING THE BODIES, or STAYES: is covering the inside of the Stayes with Fustian, Linnen, and such like.

BINDING THE NECK, is sowing Galloon at the edge of the Neck.

EYELET HOLES, or EIGLET HOLES, little round holes whip-stitched about, through which laces are drawn to hold one side close to the other.

The WAIST, is the depth of the Stayes from the Shoulders to the setting on of the skirts: now it is distinguished by the Back Waiste, and the fore body Waist, which is each side of the Stomacher.

SIDE-WAISTED, is long or deep in the Body.

SHORT-WAISTED, is short in the body.

The STOMACHER, is that peece as lieth under the lacings or binding on the Body of the Gown. Which said body is sometimes in fashion to be:

OPEN BEFORE, that is to be laced on the Breast.

OPEN BEHIND, laced on the Back, which fashion hath always a Maid or Woman to dress the wearer.

The PEAKE, is the bottom or point of the Stomacher, whether before or behind.

A BUSK, it is a strong peece of Wood, or Whalebone, thrust down the middle of the Stomacher to keep it streight and in compass, that the Breast nor Belly shall not swell too much out. These Buskes are usually made in length according to the necessity of the Persons wearing it: if to keep in the fullness of the Breasts, then it extends to the Navel; if to keep the Belly down, then it reacheth to the Honour.

A POINT

COVERING the Bodies or Stayes, is the laying the outside stuff upon it, which is sowed on the same after diverse fashions: as,

SMOOTH COVERED

PLEATED or WRINKLED in the covering.

The WINGS, are WELTS or peeces set over the place on the top of the Shoulders, where the Body and Sleeves are set together: now Wings are of diverse fashions, some narrow, others broad, some cut in slits, cordy Robe like, others Scalloped.

The SLEEVES, are those parts of the Gown, as covers the Arms: and in these there is as much variety of fashion as days in the Year: I shall only give the terms of the most remarkable.

The CLOSE, or NARROW SLEEVE, which reacheth from the Shoulder to the Wrist of the Arm, and is not much wider than for the Arm; which were of old turned up at the Hand, and faced or lined with some other sort of stuff.

The WIDE, or FULL SLEEVE, is such as are full and long, and stand swelling out: such are tied about the Elbows close to the Arm, with a Ribbon.

The OPEN SLEEVE, such are open the fore part of the Arm, that their bravery under may be seen whether it be a mock or cheat Waist-coat with Imbrauthery or the like; else their fine Linnens and Laces.

The SLASHT-SLEEVE, is when the Sleeve from Shoulder to the Sleeve hands are cut in long slices, or fillets; and are tied together at the Elbow with Ribbons, or such like.

The SLEEVE and HALF SLEEVE

The SLEEVES with HANGING SLEEVES, is a full Sleeve in any of the fashions aforesaid, with a long hanging Sleeve of a good breadth hanging from under the back part of the Wing down behind even to the ground; on the greater sorts of Gallants trailing a good length on the ground. . . .

The SKIRT, or GOWN SKIRT, is the lower part of the Gown, which extends from the body to the ground these are made several fashions, as

OPEN SKIRTS, is open before, that thereby rich and costly Peti-coat may be fully seen.

TURNED UP SKIRTS, are such as have a draught on the Ground a yard and more long, these in great Personages are called Trains, whose Honor it is to have them born up by Pages.

BEARERS, ROWLS, FARDINGALES; these are things made purposely to put under the skirts of Gowns at their setting on at the Bodies; which raise up the skirt at that place to what breadth the wearer pleaseth, and as the fashion is.

SKIRTS about the Waist, are either whole in one entire peece with Goares, or else cut into little laps or cordy robe skirts; Gowns with these skirts are called Waistcoat Gowns.

WASTCOAT, or WAISTCOAT; is the outside of a Gown without either stayes or bodies fastned to it; It is an Habit or Garment generally worn by the middle and lower sort of women, having Goared skirts, and some wear them with Stomachers.

GOARE, is a Cant or three cornered peece of cloth put into a skirt to make the bottom wider than the top. So are Goared Peti-coats.

PETI-COAT, is the skirt of a Gown without its body; but that is generally termed a Peti-coat, which is worn either under a Gown, or without it: in which Garment there are

PLEATING, that is gathering the top part into pleats or folding to make it of the same wideness as the waist or middle of the wearer.

LACEING, is setting a Lace of Silk, Silver or Gold about the bottom of it; which in a Peti-coat is called the Skirt.

BORDERING, is the lineing of the Peti-coat skirt or bottom in the inner side.

BINDING, is the sowing of some things (as Ribbon, Galloon or such like) on both sides the Edge of the skirt to keep it from ravelling; sometimes it is done by a Hem: the top part of the Peti-coat hath its Binding also; that is, it hath either Incle, Filleting, or Galloon, sowed about the Edges of it, when pleated; which keeps the Pleats in their Pleats, the ends helping to make it fast about the wearer's waist. . . .

The RIDING SUITE for Women.

The HOOD.

The CAP.

The MANTLE, it is cut round, which is cast over the Shoulders to preserve from rain or cold

The SAFEGARD, is put about the middle, and so doth secure the Feet from cold, and dirt.

The RIDING COAT, it is a long Coat buttoned down before like a Mans Jacket, with Pocket holes; and the sleeves turned up and buttons. . . .

PATTERNS Paper cut in fashions according as the work is to be made.

# Seventeenth-century Tailors' Patterns

PARA Cortar efte verdugado de feda, fera neceffario doblar la tela la mitad fobre la otra mitad, haziendo lomo por la vna parte, y del lado de nueftra mano izquierda fe cortara la delantera defte verdugado, y luego fe cortara la trafera, todo a feda doblada, y la feda que refta fe defdoblara a lo ancho, poniendo la mitad de las baras fobre la otra mitad, y cortarfe han los cuchillos pie a cabeça. Ha fe de aduertir, que los cuchillos delanteros han de yr hilo con hilo, y los cuchillos traferos han de yr fefgo con hilo, y afsi no aura en los coftados defte verdugado fefgo ninguno, ni dara de fi por ningun cabo. Y la delantera defte verdugado lleua mas ruedo que la trafera, y de la feda que fobra fe podra echar vn ruedo. Lleua de largo efte verdugado bara y media, y de ruedo poco mas de treze palmos, lo qual me parece que es baftante ruedo para efte verdugado: y fi le quifieren echar mas ruedo, fe puede echar por efta traça.

1. *Libro de Geometrica Practica y Traca* Juaan de Alcega. 1589
A Farthingale 'To cut this silk fathingale one half of the material must be folded over the other half making a fold on one side; from the left side the front and then the back of the fathingale are cut out in the double silk; the remainder of the silk should be spread out and doubled full width and then the gores cut with the widest part of the one alongside the narrowest part of the other. It should be noted that the front gores go straight to straight and the back gores a cross to straight, so that on the sides there will be no cross and it will not drop. The front will have more fullness than the back; with the silk left over a valance can be added. The length of the fathingale is a 'vara' and a half, and the width round the bottom slightly more than thirteen handspans, which in in my opinion is full enough for the fathingale, if more fullness is wanted it can be added to the pattern'

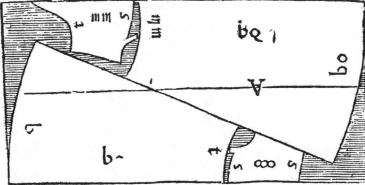

PAra cortar efta vafquiña, y cuerpo baxo de raxa, fera neceffario defdoblar la tela a lo ancho, y luego fe doblara de fuerte q por el vn cabo y por el otro aya lomo, y por medio del paño efté las ori llas de fuerte q por medio defte paño por donde efta vna raya, eftan las orillas del paño, y luego fe cortara la delantera defta vafquiña, y encima la cadera de la delantera, fale la efpalda del cuerpo baxo y de nfa mano derecha fe cortara la trafera, y encima el quarto delantero. Y lleua efta vafquiña fo los dos cuchillos, el vno en la delantera, y el otro en la trafera, y en los medios ay recado de ribete para efta vafquiña por efta traça: y fi le quifiere echar otros dos cuchillos, fe cortaran como los otros, y fe coferan. Y afsi tendra efta vafquiña quatro cuchillos. Lleua de largo efta vafquiña bara y quarta, y de ruedo lleua catorze palmos, como parece figurado.

2. *Libro de Geometrica Practica y Traca* Juaan de Alcega. 1589
A woman's dress, with a 'low body' made of 'raxa', a coarse type of cloth

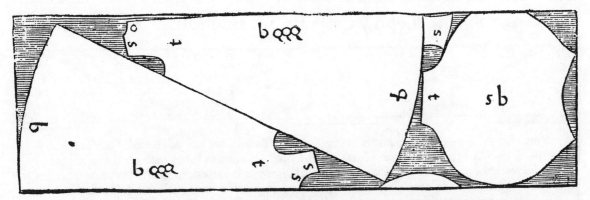

PARA Cortar esta ropa de paño, se ha de entender que el cuerpo de la ropa se ha de cortar pie a cabeça, cortádo por el lomo del paño la delantera de bara y tres quartas de largo, y diez y seys palmos de ruedõ, y de la parte de nuestra mano derecha se cortaran las mangas para esta ropa, y en los medios salen collares y tablas de mangas, y los demas recados.

3. *Libro de Geometrica Practica y Traca* Juaan de Alcega. 1589
A loose gown of cloth, with full sleeves

## Iubõ de tela.|bboiii|tt.|Iubõ de seda.|bboiii|tt|Iubõ de seda.|bboiii.|tt.

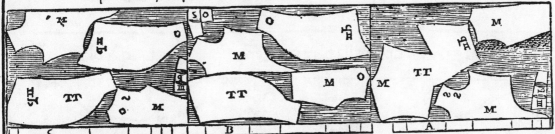

Para cortar este jubon se hã de trastrocar la tela a causa delas flores, si las tuuiere, y doblar la metad sobre la metad, y guiarse conforme la traça. Tiene de tela de bara de Castilla dos baras y ochauo y tres dedos: y de bara Valenciana dos baras: y de Aragon dos baras quarta y dos dedos. Y saldra de qualquiera de dichas baras por esta traça.

Para cortar este jubõ de tafetan, es menester guiarse por la traça conforme esta figurada. Tiene de seda de bara de Castilla dos baras ochauo y tres dedos: y de Valencia dos baras: y de Aragon dos baras quarta y dos dedos: y de cana de Cataluña la metad menos de las baras de Aragon. Y saldra de qualquiera de las dichas baras por esta traça.

Para cortar este jubon de muger con manga de armar es necessario trastrocar la seda por si tiene flores, y doblar la metad de la seda sobre la otra metad a lo ancho, y guiarse por la traça. Tiene de seda de bara de Castilla dos baras ochauo y tres dedos: y de Valencia dos baras: y de Aragon dos baras quarta y dos dedos. Y saldra de qualquiera de dichas baras por esta traça.

4. *Geometrica y Traca.* F. de La Rocha Burguen. 1618
Three high necked bodices with sleeves, note the pattern on the right shows a hanging sleeve

## Ropa, vaſquiña, jubon, y eſcapulario de eſtameña.    tVbbb | iiibb.

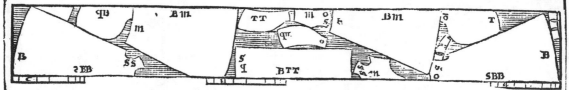

Para cortar eſta ropa, vaſquiña, jubon, y eſcapulario de eſtameña, que tenga de bara de Caſtilla ocho baras menos tercia, y de largo la ropa dos baras menos ſeſma, y la vaſquiña bara y media, y el eſcapulario bara y dos tercias, es neceſſario tender la eſtameña a lo largo, y de la parte de nueſtra mano yzquierda ſalen los quartos delanteros de la ropa, cuchillo traſero de la vaſquiña, y vna manga, traſera de la vaſquiña del lomo de la eſtameña, eſcapulario, mangas juſtas, eſpalda de jubon, delantera de vaſquiña, quartos delanteros de jubon, quartos traſeros de ropa, cuello de jubon, la otra manga de ropa, y cuello de ropa, y de los medios ſale eſtameña para riuetes, y recaudos para dicho veſtido de muger. Lleua de eſtameña de bara de Valécia ſiete baras: y de bara de Aragon ocho baras: y de Cataluña la metad menos de las baras de Aragon. Y ſaldra de qualquiera de las dichas baras por eſta miſma traça.

5. *Geometrica y Traca.* F. de La Rocha Burguen. 1618
A dress with a fitted bodice, and a gored skirt, also a loose gown with full sleeves

## Saya grande de lanilla para muger.   ✽   qXbbb. | b.

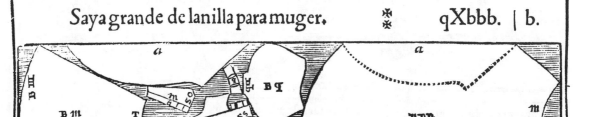

Para cortar eſta ſaya grande de lanilla, que tenga de bara Caſtellana treze baras menos quarta, es neceſſario doblar la mitad de las baras encima la otra mitad, y de la parte de nueſtra mano yzquierda ſalen los quartos delanteros, y encima ſalen los cuchillos traſeros, eſpalda, y delanteros de euera, cuello, y mangas, y encima ſale la halda traſera, y de los medios recaudo de riuetes para dicha ſaya. Lleua de lanilla de bara de Valencia doze baras: y de bara de Aragon catorze baras menos dozauo: y de Cataluña la metad menos de las baras de Aragon. Y ſaldra de qualquiera de las dichas baras por eſta traça.

6. *Geometrica y Traca.* F. de La Rocha Burguen. 1618
A dress with a fitted bodice, a gored skirt with a train, and full sleeves

## Galerilla de raxa para muger.   bbbt. | btt.

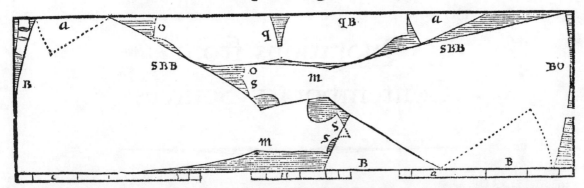

Para cortar esta galerilla de raxa, que tenga de bara de Castilla tres baras, y de largo dos baras menos sesma, es necessario tender la raxa a lo largo, y de las orillas a la parte de nuestra mano yzquierda salen los quartos delanteros, y encima los quartos delanteros salen los cuchillos traseros, y del otro cabo de la raxa de la parte de nuestra mano drecha salen los quartos traseros, y del lomo de la raxa arrimados a los quartos traseros salen las mangas, y cuchillos delanteros, y de la despuntadura delantera sale el cuello, y de los medios recaudos de raxa para dicha galerilla. Lleua de raxa de bara de Valencia tres baras y dos dedos menos quarta: y de bara de Aragon tres baras y sesma: y de Cataluña la metad menos de las baras de Aragon. Y saldra de qualquiera de las dichas baras por esta traça.

7. *Geometrica y Traça.* F. de La Rocha Burguen. 1618
A fitted gown, cut without a waist seam

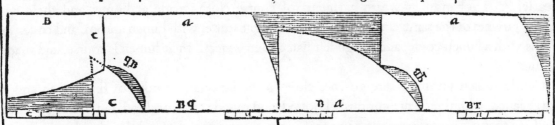

| ## Manteo, o faldellin de grana. | ## Manteo, o faldellin de grana para |
| qbbb. | bb. | muger.   qbbb. | bb. |
|---|---|

Para cortar este manteo de grana, que tenga de bara de Castilla tres baras menos quarta, y de largo bara y tercia, es necessario tender la grana a lo largo, y de la parte de nuestra mano drecha sale el arbol, encima del arbol salen las camas y pieças de camas. Tiene de grana de bara de Valencia dos baras y media: y de bara de Aragon tres baras menos dozauo: y de Cataluña la metad menos de las baras de Aragon. Y saldra de qualquiera de las dichas baras por esta misma traça.

Para cortar este manteo, o faldellin de grana, q̃ tenga de bara de Castilla tres baras menos quarta, y de largo bara y tercia, es necessario tender la grana a lo largo, y de la parte de nuestra mano yzquierda salen las camas, y debaxo sale el arbol del lomo de la grana, y recaudo de riuete para dicho manteo si a caso le quierē de grana. Lleua de bara de Valencia dos baras y media: y de Aragon tres baras menos dozauo: y de Cataluña la metad menos de las baras de Aragon. Y saldra de qualquiera de dichas baras por esta traça.

8. *Geometrica Practica y Traça* La Rocha Burguen 1618.
Two full length cloaks, to be made from fine red cloth. The left-hand pattern is for a man, and the right-hand pattern for a woman

# Quotations from Contemporary Sources

1592

England—Besides the famous Broad cloth, it yields for clothing many Stuffes, whereof great quantitie is also imported. And I will not omit, that howsoever it hath silke from forraigne parts, yet the English silke stockings are much to be preferred before those of Italy, Spaine, or any part in the World.

The wives of Merchants, though little yielding to others in pride or expence, yet have long used, and still retaine a decent attire, with little or no inconstancy in the fashion. They weare a gowne of some light stuffe or silke, gathered in the backe, and girded to the body with a girdle, and decked with many gardes at the skirt, with which they weare an apron before them, as some silke or stuffe, or fine linnen. They weare upon their heads a coyfe of fine linnen, with their haire raised a little at the forehead, and a cap of silke, or a little hat of beaver, yet without fit difference of estate or condition, and some weare light French chaines and necklaces of pearle. . . . Husbandmen weare garments of course cloth, made at home, and their wives weare gownes of the same cloth, kirtles of some light stuffe, with linnen aprons, and cover their heads with a linnen coyfe, and a high felt hat, and in generall their linnen is course, and made at home.

Gentlewomen virgins weare gownes close to the body and aprons of fine linnen and goe bareheaded, with their haire curiously knotted, and raised at the forehead, but, many against the cold (as they say) weare caps of haire that is not their owne, decking their heads with buttons of gold, pearles, and flowers of silke, or knots of ribbon. They weare fine linnen, and commonly falling bands, and often ruffles, both starched, and chaines of pearle about the necke, with their breasts naked. The graver sort of married women used to cover their head with a French hood of Velvet, set with a border of gold buttons and pearles: but this fashion is now left, and they most commonly weare a coyfe of linnen, and a little hat of beaver or felt, with their haire somewhat raised at the forehead. Young married women sometime goe bare headed, as virgins, decking their haire with Jewels, and silke ribbens, and more commonly they use the foresaid linnen coyfe and hats. All in generall weare gownes hanging loose at the backe, with a

52

kirtle and close upperbody of silke or light stuffe, but have lately left the French sleeves borne out with hoopes of whalebone, and the young married Gentlewomen, no lesse than the Virgins shew their breasts naked.

France–Frenchwomen weare very light gownes, commonly blacke, and hanging loose at the backe, and under it an upper-body close at the breast, with a kirtle of a mixed or light colour, and of some light stuffe, laid with many gardes, in which sort the women are generally attired. They weare sleeves to their gownes borne out with whalebones, and of a differing colour from the gowne, which besides hath other loose hanging sleeves cast backward, and aswel the upper-bodies, as the kirtles, differ from the gowne in colour and stuffe. And they say, that the sleeves borne up with whale-bones, were first invented, to avoid mens familiar touching of their armes. . . . In France as well men as women, use richly to be adorned with Jewels. . . . The Ladies weare their Jewels commonly at the breast, or upon the left arme, and many other waies, for who can contain the mutable French in one and the same fashion.

FYNES MORYSON, An Itinerary 1617.

1596

*Pleasant Quippes for Upstart New-Fangled Gentlewomen*

> These privie coates, by art made strong
>  with bones, with past, with such like ware,
> Whereby their backe and sides grow long,
>  and now they harnest gallants are;
>  Were they for use against the foe,
>  Our dames for Amazons might goe.
>
> But seeing they doe only stay
>  the course that nature doth intend,
> And mothers often by them slay
>  their daughters yoong, and worke their end,
>  What are they els but armours stout,
>  Wherein like gyants Jove they flout.
>
> These hoopes, that hippes and haunch do hide,
>  and heave aloft the gay hoist traine.
> As they are now in use for pride,
>  so did they first beginne of paine:
>  When whores in stewes had gotton poxe
>  This French devise kept coats from smocks.

STEPHEN GOSSON

1600

Inventory of Queen Elizabeth's wardrobe, exclusive of Coronation, Mourning, Parliament, and Garter robes:

| | | | |
|---|---|---|---|
| Robes | 99 | Cloaks and safeguards | 31 |
| French gowns | 102 | Safeguards | 13 |
| Round gowns | 67 | Safeguards and jupes | 43 |
| Loose gowns | 100 | Doublets | 85 |
| Kirtles | 126 | Lapmantles | 18 |
| Foreparts | 136 | Pantofles | 9 |
| Petticoats | 125 | Fans | 27 |
| Cloaks | 96 | | |

F. W. FAIRHOLT, *Costume in England*

1602

*The Poetaster*

Chloe: Alas, man, there was not a gentleman come to your house in your t'other wife's time, I hope. Nor a lady, nor music, nor masques. Nor you nor your house were so much as spoken of, before I disbased myself from my hood and my fartingal, to these bum-rowls and your whale-bone bodice.

But, sweet lady and say: am I well enough attired for the court, in sadness?

Cyth.: Well enough! excellently well, sweet mistress Chloe; this strait-bodiced city attire, I can tell you will stir a courtier's blood, more than the finest loose sacks the ladies use to be put in: and then you are as well jewell'd as any of them; your ruff and linen about you is much more pure than theirs.

BEN JONSON

1602–3

Queen Elizabeth – The Queen wore a dress of silver and white 'tabi', edged with bullion, and rather open in front, so as to display her throat, enriched with pearls and rubies mid-way down the breast, the swell of her gown was much greater than is the fashion in France, and descended lower; her head-dress being of false hair, such as nature could not have produced; on her forehead were large pear-shaped pearls, and frontlets resembling an imperial crown or cap; she made a great display of jewels and pearls, her person even below the bodice being well nigh covered with jewelled golden girdles, and with detached precious stones, such as carbuncles, balass, rubies and diamonds; and on her wrists in lieu of bracelets were double rows of pearls above the middle size, and although seventy years of age, she bears them well, from nature's bounty to her, rather than through the aid of art.

*Venetian Calendar*

1604

*Looke to it, for I'll stabbe ye*

*You whom the Devill (Pride's father) doth perswade*
*To paint your face, and mende the worke God made,*
*You with the Hood, the Falling bande, and ruffe*
*    The Moncky-waste, the breeching like a Beare;*
*The Perriwig, the Maske, the Fanne, the Muffe,*
*    The Bodkin and the Bussard in your haire;*
*You Velvet-cambricke-silken-feather'd toy,*
*That with your pride do all the world annoy,*
*        I'll stabbe ye.*

F. W. FAIRHOLT, *Satirical Songs and Poems on Costume*

1605

Goe fetch my cloathes: bring my petty-coate bodyes: I meane my damask quilt bodyes with whale bones. What lace doe you give me heere? this lace is too shorte, the tagges are broken, I cannot lace my selfe with it, take it away, I will have that of greene silke: when shall I have my under coate? give me my peticoate of wrought crimson velvet with a silver fringe. . . . Give me my whood, for me thinketh it is some-what colde. . . . Set up my French whood and my Border of Rubies, give me another head attyre: take the key of my closet and goe fetch my long boxe where I set mine Jewels that I used to weare on my head, what is become of my wyer: where is the haire cap, have you any ribans to make knots? where be the laces for to binde my haires? . . . Call my Taylor to bring my gowne, not the close one but my open gowne of white Sattin layd on with buttons of Pearle. Shall I not have no vardingale. . . . You doe playe the foole, doe you not see that I want my buske? what is become of the buske-point. . . . Let me see that ruffe. How is it that the supporter is so soyled? I knowe not for what you are fit, that you cannot so much as to keep my cloathes cleane, take it away: give me my Rebato of cut-worke edged, is not the wyer after the same sorte as the other? . . . Is there no small pinnes for my Cuffes? Looke in the pinne-cushion. Pinne that with a blacke pinne; give me my girdle and see that all the furniture be at it. . . . Have I a cleane handkercher? I will have no Muffe for it is not colde, but shall I have no gloves? Bring my maske and my fanne. Help me to put on my Chayne of pearles.

Mercer: Of which would you Madame? plaine Velvet, Rased velvet, pinkt, unwrought velvet, or tufte-taffata, and of what colour would you have?

Lady: I would see some of blacke, of white, of gray, of ash colour, of greene, of red, of yellowe, of crimson, of purple, of tawny, of blewe, of celestial colour, migrene colour, russet colour, Peache colour, strawe colour.

Mercer: Have you no need of any cloath of gold or silver?

Lady: Yes I must have some. What shall I pay you for your cloath of golde, doe not holde it too deere, and I will take some tenne yardes of it.

Mercer: You shall pay foure pounds a yarde.

Lady: It is too much, you are too deere, I will give you fiftie shillings for it.

Mercer: I cannot sell it at that price, it cost me more than you offer me. Take it for three pounds and tenne shillings, and you may say that you have not ill bestowed your money.

PIERRE ERONDELLE, The French Garden

1612–3

John Chamberlain to Mrs. Carleton

One thing I had almost forgotten, that all this time there was a course taken, and so notified, that no lady or gentleman should be admitted to any of these sights with a vardingale, which was to gain the more room, and I hope may serve to make them quite left off in time.

BIRCH, The Court and Times of James the First

1616–1617

1616 September. Upon the 29th I bought of Mr. Clebom who came to see me a clock (cloak) and a saveguard of cloth laced with black lace to keep me warm on my journey.

1617 April. The 12th I began to dress my head with a roll without a wire. The 25th my Lord St. John's tailor came to me hither to take measure of me and to make me a new gown.

June. The 13th I sayed on my sea water green satin gown and my damask embroidered with gold, both of which gowns the Tailor which was sent from London made fit for me to wear with open ruffs after the French fashion.

November. All the time I was at the Court I wore my green damask gown embroidered without a farthingale. The same day I sent the Queen by my Lady Ruthven the skirts of a white satin gown all pearled and embroidered with colours which cost me fourscore pounds without the satin.

December. The 28th I went to Church in my rich night gown and petticoat, both my women waiting upon me in their liveries.

LADY ANNE CLIFFORD, Diary

1617

Queen Anne–Her Majesty's costume was pink and gold with so expansive a farthingale that I do not exaggerate when I say it was four feet wide in the hips. Her bosom was bare down to the pit of the stomach, forming as it were an oval. Her head dress, besides very valuable diamonds and other jewels, consisted of such a quantity of false hair dressed in rays that she looked exactly like a sun flower.

Venetian Calendar

1627–1629

1627 May 18 *For Claude de Lorraine*

Robe of the new fashion, in black Tours taffeta trimmed with silk braid round the edges; also round the edges a Milanese lace braid twisted with gold thread; with 720 buttons of fine gold Milanese lace; lining of black Lyons taffeta for the body and of Florence black satin for the collar, sleeves and half-sleeves; black Tours silk ribbon, tied round the gown; a piece of canvas, and a piece of black Constance linen.

16½ aunes Tours taffeta, 1 ounce braid, 48 aunes lace braid, 1 aune Lyons taffeta, 1¼ aune satin, 2 aunes black silk ribbon, 5 aunes woollen ribbon, 2 aunes canvas, 1½ linen, 2 ounces sewing silk.

1628 May 1 *For Claude de Lorraine*

Bodice with balloon-slashed sleeves, pale carnation Florence satin; lined with Lyons satin; trimmed with Tours silk braid round the edges, with 6 buttons of the same braid to each sleeve; pale carnation silk ribbon tied in front; a piece of canvas, and 4 *côtes* of whalebone. 1¾ aunes satin, 1½ aunes taffeta, 1 ounce braid, 3 aunes ribbon, 1½ canvas, ½ ounce sewing silk.

1628 July 16 *For Claude de Lorraine*

Robe de chambre of flowered Genoa damask, pale crimson; trimmed with fine silver braid round the edges, the collar, the slits, and the sleeves; with 84 buttons of silver braid; lining of Florence scarcenet taffeta, pale crimson; under the lining a piece of black Constance linen. 9½ aunes damask, 7½ ounces braid, 5 aunes taffeta, 2 aunes linen, 2 ounces sewing silk.

1629 February 16 *For the Duchesse Nicole*

Bodice and petticoat with balloon-slashed sleeves in crimson Florence satin; a fine silver braid and also lace with silver round the edges and sleeves; four rows of the same round the bottom (of the skirt); 6 buttons of fine silver lace on each sleeve; lining of beige taffeta; woollen braid round the hem; a piece of canvas, and 6 *côtes* of whalebone.

9 aunes satin, 4½ ounces braid, 40 aunes lace weighing 8½ ounces, 50 aunes trimming weighing 18½ ounces, 8 aunes taffeta, 4 aunes ribbon, 1½ aunes canvas, 3 ounces sewing silk.

1629 March 25 *For Claude de Lorraine*

Cloak and safeguard in green Segovia serge, the edges trimmed with fine silver braid; with 48 large buttons of fine silver Florence lace, silver cord on the buttonholes; lining of green Florence scarcenet; ribbon ties of green silk.

5 aunes serge, 8 ounces braid, 4 ounces cord, 5½ aunes scarcenet, 6 aunes ribbon, 1½ ounces sewing silk.

Farthingale-roll, filled with horsehair and strengthened with wire, either of Florence flowered damask or Florence taffeta, with a black Tours silk ribbon to tie round, as a belt.

1 taffeta, 1 ounce braid, 2 aunes ribbon, 1½ black linen, ½ ounce sewing silk.

False sleeves—about 3 pieces of heavy cane, each of 7 aunes, ¾ white taffeta for the covering and 1½ white satin for the puffing.

[Aune de Paris—118 centimetres—46½ inches. Braids with gold or silver metal in them were sold by weight.

Whalebone was sold by the piece, *côte*, and then had to be cut into strips.]

HIPPOLYTE ROY, *La Vie, la Mode et le Costume au XVII Siècle*

1631

### Rhodon and Iris

*But, in her tyres, so new fangl'd is she,*
*That which doth with her humour now agree,*
*To-morrow she dislikes; now doth she sweare,*
*That a loose body is the neatest weare;*
*But, ere an houre be gone, she will protest,*
*A strait gowne graces her proportions best;*
*Now calls she for a boistrous fardingall;*
*Then to her hips she'll have her garments fall;*
*Now doth she praise a sleeve, that's long and wide,*
*Yet, by-and-by that fashion doth deride.*

STRUTT, *Complete view of the Dress and Habits of the People of England*

1631–1635

1631. I have sent you some patterns of stuff such as is worne by many, but not much laes upon those wrought stuffs; but the newest fashion is plaine satine, of what collor one will imbroydered all over with alcomedes, but it is not like to hould past summer. They weare sattine wascots, plaine, rased, printed, and some imbroydered with laes, more than any one thing and whit holland ones much.

1635. Madame, ye tailor saieth, for gownes, either a wrought silke grogorine or a tuffe taffety in graine, ye collor greene or tawny, which your Ladyp. pleaseth; he requireth fourteen yardes for ye gowne, besides the facings, of half a yarde broade.

LADY JANE CORNWALLIS, *Private Correspondence*

1650

The upstart impudence and innovation of naked breasts, and cutting or hallowing downe the neck of womens garments below their shoulders, an exorbitant and shamefull enormity and habit, much worn by our semi-Adamits, is another meere peice of refined Barbarisme. . . .

Another foolish affection there is in young Virgins, though grown big enough to be wiser, but that they are led blind-fold by custome to a fashion pernitious beyond imagination; who thinking a Slender-Waste a great beauty, strive all that they possibly can by streight-lacing themselves, to attain unto a wand-like smalnesse of Waste, never thinking themselves fine enough untill they can span their Waste.

JOHN BULWER, *Artificial Changeling*

1655

*Musarum Deliciae*

*Your faces trick'd and painted bee,*
  *Your breasts all open bare;*
*So farr that a man may almost see*
  *Unto your lady ware:*
*And in the church, to tell you true,*
  *Men cannot serve God for looking on you.*
    *O women, monstrous women,*
    *What do you mean to do?*

*Doublets, like men, they weare,*
  *As if they meant to flout us,*
*Trust round with poynts, and ribbons fayre,*
  *But, I pray, lett's look about us;*
*For since the doublett so well doth fitt'um,*
*They will have the breeches, and if they can get'um.*
    *O women, monstrous women,*
    *What do you mean to do?*

1658

*Wit Restored*

*Heer patches are of every art,*
  *For pimples, and for scars;*
*Heer's all the wandring plannett signes,*
  *And some o'th'fixed starrs,*

*Already gumm'd, to make them stick,*
  *They need no other sky,*
*Nor starrs, for Lilly for to view,*
  *To tell your fortunes by.*
    *Come lads and lasses, what do you lack?*
*Here are perriwiggs will fit all hayres,*
  *False beards for a disguise;*
*I can help lasses which are bare*
  *In all parts, as their thighs.*

F. W. FAIRHOLT, *Satirical Songs and Poems on Costume*

1662

### BILL FROM THE VERNEY PAPERS

For Sir Ralph's sister Elizabeth—John Wade, June.
For the honal Mis Varney a haire Collor Ferrentene gown and sattene petticote.

| | |
|---|---|
| For stayes and stiffnings | 00:04:00 |
| For silke | 00:02:06 |
| For callicoe to lay under ye outside | 00:01:10 |
| For buckrum to tacke ye sleeves | 00:00:08 |
| For ribbin, bordering and gallone | 00:03:10 |
| For lineing For bodies and sleeves | 00:03:00 |
| For sasnet to bind the hands and the borders and for a silke pockett | 00:01:08 |
| For making the gowne lacd 2 in a place with scollops under cutting and siseing ye scallops | 00:15:06 |
| For a large box | 00:01:02 |
| For makeinge for sattin petticote | 00:02:00 |
| For ribbon and bordering | 00:02:06 |
| For silke and a pocket | 00:01:00 |

1659–1668

1659–1660. Aug. 30th. This the first day that ever I saw my wife wear black patches since we were married.

1660–1661. March 24th. Comes La Belle Pierce to see my wife, and to bring her a pair of perruques of hair as the fashion now is for ladies to wear; which are pretty, and are of my wife's own hair, or else I should not endure them.

April 15th. With my wife, by coach, to the New Exchange, to buy her some things; where we sawe some new-fashion petty-coats of sarcenett, with a broad lace printed round the bottom and before, very handsome, and my wife had a mind to one of them.

June 2nd. This day, my wife put on her slashed wastecoate, which is very pretty.

June 29th (Lord's day). To church with my wife, who this day put on her green petticoate of flowered satten, with fine white and black gimp lace on her own putting on, which is very pretty.

June 25th. She by my Lady's advice desires a new petticoat of the new silk striped stuff very pretty. So I went to Pater Noster Row presently, and bought her a very fine rich one—the best I did see there, and much better than she desires or expects.

1663-1664. April 10th (Lord's day). She had put on her new best gown, which indeed is very fine now with the lace; and this morning her taylor brought home her other new-laced silk gown with a smaller lace, and new petticoat I bought the other day: both very pretty.

1665-1666. April 28th. She was also to look after a necklace of pearl, which she is mighty busy about, I being contented to lay out £80 in one for her.

April 30th. My wife comes home by and by, and hath pitched upon a necklace with three rows, which is a very good one, and £80 is the price.

June 11th. Walking in the galleries at White Hall, I find the Ladies of Honour dressed in their riding garbs, with coats and doublets with deep skirts, just, for all the world, like mine; and buttoned their doublets up the breast, with perriwigs under their hats; so that, only for a long petticoat dragging under their men's coats, nobody could take them for women in any point whatever; which was an odde sight, and a sight did not please me.

1666-1667. March 22nd. My wife having dressed herself in a silly dress of a blue petticoat uppermost, and a white satin waistcoat and white hood, though I think she did it because her gown is gone to the tailor's, did, together with my being hungry, which always makes me peevish, make me angry.

1667-1668. December 25th. So home, and to dinner alone with my wife, who, poor wretch! sat undressed all day till ten at night altering and lacing of a noble petticoat.

1668-1669. March 2nd. My wife this day put on first her French gown, called a Sac, which becomes her very well, brought over by W. Batelier.

April 12th. Home, and, after sitting a while, thrumming upon my viall, and singing, I to bed, and left my wife to do something to a waistcoat and a petticoat she is to wear to-morrow.

SAMUEL PEPYS, *Diary*

1665

A strange effeminate age when men strive to imitate women in their apparell. . . . On the other side, women would strive to be like men, viz., when they rode on horsback or in coaches weare plush caps like monteros, either full of ribbons or feathers, long periwigs which men used to weare, and riding coate of a red colour all bedaubed with lace which they call vests, and this habit was chiefly used by the ladies and maids of honor belonging to the Queen, brought in fashion about anno 1663, which they weare at this time at their being in Oxon.

*The Life and Times of* ANTHONY WOOD

1671–1676

1671. March 18th. Madame the Duchess de Nevers came in with her hair dressed in the most ludicrous fashion, though you know that as a rule I like uncommon styles. La Martin had had the fancy to create a new coiffure and had cropped her! Her hair had been cut and rolled on paper curlers which had made her suffer death and agony a whole night long. Her head was like a little round cabbage – nothing at the sides. My dear, it is the most ridiculous sight you can imagine.

April 1st. The *hurluberlu* coiffures are amusing me very much.

April 4th. I told you the other day about Mme de Nevers' new coiffure, now La Martin is spreading the fashion . . . I saw yesterday the Duchess de Sully and the Countess de Guiche; their heads are charming, I give in; this hair style is just what will suit you, you will look like an angel and it is quickly done. . . . Now just imagine the hair parted peasant fashion to within two inches of the back roll; the hair each side is cut in layers and made into round loose curls which hang about an inch below the ear; it looks very young and pretty – two bouquets of hair on each side. Don't cut your hair too short because the curls require a lot of hair as several ladies have found out and are an example to others. Ribbons are arranged in the usual fashion and a large curl on top which sometimes falls down the neck. I don't know if I have explained it very well. I shall have a doll dressed with this hair style and send it to you.

1676. November 6th. Mme de Coulanges has been telling me about transparencies: have you heard about them? They are dresses made from the most exquisite gold and sky-blue brocade, and over this transparent material, either beautiful English lace, or chenille on black gauze, like the winter laces which you have seen: this is a transparency, they can be all black, or all gold and silver, or any colour one wishes; it is the latest fashion. This was the dress worn at the ball on St. Hubert's day. M. le Prince has told the ladies that their transparencies would be a thousand times more beautiful if they would wear them next their skin.

MME DE SÉVIGNÉ, *Lettres*

1670

You could make a robe de chambre of the grey gown I have sent you: they are worn closed in front and widening on the shoulders: if one wishes they can be trimmed with lace; I myself wear them plain; sometimes if one wants to go to the expense beautiful under sleeves are worn but many people don't have these. I have forgotten the ribbons but you shall have them soon. Your black lace will do very well for a winter gown.

MME DE MAINTENON, *Lettres*

PART TWO

Eighteenth Century
*c.*1680–*c.*1795

Femme de qualité en deshabillé d'esté

se vend à Paris sur le quai des grands augustins aux deux globes.    auec pri. du Roy 1683

# 1680-1720

The change in style in women's dress that took place towards the end of the seventeenth century was similar and just as revolutionary as that taking place in men's clothes. As the stiff doublet was being replaced by the coat so the heavily-boned bodice was making way for the looser gown. The distinctive style of dress design which evolved from the loose gown was achieved not by cutting, but by draping the material into pleats which moulded the figure and then fell in graceful folds into the skirt. This method allowed full advantage to be taken of the beauty of the new stiff silks with their large rich patterns which would have been spoilt if broken into by seaming. In England the new gown was called a 'mantua', probably because early examples were made from Italian silk from Mantua. In France it was also called a *mantua*, or *manteau*, but in its early phase it was usually referred to as a *robe de chambre*.

This change of style in women's clothes did not receive the publicity that royal patronage gave to the man's coat, but Randle Holme in the *Academy of Armory*, 1688, does mention it though the clothes he describes are those worn in the third quarter of the seventeenth century. 'There is', he says, 'a kind of loose Garment without, and stiffe Bodies under them, and was a great fashion for women about the Year 1676. Some called them Mantuas.'

## MANTUA

The heavily-boned bodice of the 1670's must have been so extremely uncomfortable that it is not surprising ladies began to discard it whenever possible wearing instead their loose gowns. This gown, which was originally cut in two pieces—back and front—was kimono-shaped; that is, the sleeves were in one piece with the garment. At first worn loose, or held in at the waist by a sash only, it was gradually given more style. The superfluous material was pleated on each shoulder into several folds, usually held together with a cord or narrow strap, the folds being held in position again round the waist, back and front, by a sash or belt. See plate 19. Later, the pleats were reduced to one or two on each side of the front, which began to be worn open, and two pleats only each side of the centre back. Although the shoulder was now seamed, the

65

original style was maintained by the joining of the outside pleats on each side to form an un-broken line over the top of the body, the head of the sleeves–which were now also cut sepa-rately–being covered by this. The sleeves continued to be cut from the horizontal grain of the material, as in the original loose gown. They were still fairly wide and about elbow length, at which point they turned back to form a cuff, often caught at the bend of the arm by cords. The pleats of the bodice were stitched into position back and front to a level just below the waist, and then fell into folds in the skirt, which itself followed the earlier arrangement, the front skirts being draped round the hips and caught up to the centre back while the back fell into a long train.

The body of the mantua was never boned, but when it lost its negligée appearance it was worn over 'stays'. These were derived from the boned lining of the earlier bodice and so called because they stayed or supported it. The front of the stays was visible but decorated or, more usually, covered with a separate piece of material, the stomacher. The sides of the bodice were pinned to the stays, or were sometimes tied across with ribbons, such ribbon ties forming a series of bows which came to be known as an *echelle*. In the late 1680's the line of the mantua, which at first had been slender and rather dull, began to widen, and inverted pleats were added to the skirt at the side seams from the waist. Sometimes the bodice may have been cut separately at the waist of the front and side panels, but the centre back was still cut in one. The fullness of the front pleats was sometimes reduced by a dart taken from under the pleats into the shoulder or armhole. The front pleat was often simulated; that is, it was a separate piece of material ending at the waist. (See plates 20, 22). Once established this type of construction was evident in bodices until the 1770's. The arrangement of the skirt, however, was to be influenced by the introduction of the hooped petticoat.

## OTHER TYPES OF DRESS

The jacket, or waistcoat, with short basques, was too useful a garment to be discarded and continued to be worn for negligée wear and especially by working women. There were also simple bodices, laced up centre back or perhaps crossing in front or caught together centre front with bows. These were for more casual wear and were habitual for children and young girls. The riding coat was a replica of the man's coat, and was always worn with cravat and cocked hat. It was frequently used for travelling. An informal version of the mantua, but with undraped skirts, was called the *andrienne*.

## COURT DRESS

Etiquette as regards dress was much stricter at the French Court than it was in England. Louis XIV did not approve of the mantua, so in the presence of royalty, the ladies of France continued to wear the rigid boned bodice. This developed into a distinctive style of Court dress, *le grand habit* or *habit de cour*, which was worn until the French Revolution. The bodice was always mounted on a heavily-boned foundation with an off-the-shoulder neck line, the small sleeve being almost hidden with lace flounces. A long train was worn over the petticoat. The petticoat and trimmings, however, always followed the contemporary fashions.

## MATERIALS, DECORATIONS, ETC.

Although the cut of the mantua remained fairly static, fashion in materials, trimmings and accessories changed much more rapidly. French silks, satins, damasks, brocades, etc., were now superior to the Italian ones, and the formal Italian designs were replaced by large floral patterns. Stripes were very popular. In the early days when the line was still slender the gown was often untrimmed and the petticoat either of the same material or in a contrasting one and having a simple border of lace, fringe, etc. In the 1690's the petticoat increased in width in order to support the modish baroque style of ornament, carried out in laces, braids, fringes, tassels, etc. The petticoat was heavily ornamented and the gown often trimmed down the open fronts of the bodice and skirt. Stiff under-petticoats, *criardes*, with hip pads and bustles were essential. Early in the eighteenth century trimmings became lighter, and flounces and ruchings, furbelows and *falbalas*, replaced the heavier braids. Embroidery, often in gold and silver, was much used, especially for Court dress. Jewellery now consisted chiefly of diamond-set pieces. With the discovery of the brilliant form of diamond cutting at the end of the seventeenth century the diamond had become the most valuable and fashionable of all the precious stones. In Court dress the cords and ties for day wear were replaced by jewelled clasps, and buckles and gem-set stomacher pieces were designed specially for the fronts of Court bodices.

The chemise was still visible at the neck and below the sleeve. With more elaborate dress the chemise frills were of lace and were often separate pieces; the neck frill was called the 'tucker' and sleeve frills were ruffles, or *engageantes*. Neckerchiefs were still worn informally and by the working classes, and in the 1690's the ladies for a time wore the man's cravat–the 'steinkirck'. Laces, *point de Venise*, *point de France*, *point d'Angleterre*, *Mechlin*, etc., were thickly patterned but lighter in texture than those previously worn. Knee-length aprons with little bibs were very fashionable. Long scarves cut to form a cape round the shoulders were worn for warmth, as were also fur tippets or *palatines*.

# 1720–1770

With the introduction of the hoop petticoat or *panier* (*c.* 1711 in England and a little later in France), the fashionable silhouette once again exchanged length for breadth. The hoop petticoat came in a variety of shapes, at first round and dome-shaped (see plate 23), but in the 1730's it flattened front and back and extended on either side. In England the type was somewhat rectangular, while in France a kidney-shape was preferred. The hoop petticoat was at its widest in the 1740's, after which it became smaller or was discarded altogether. It was always worn with formal and Court dress. Small pocket hoops appeared *c.* 1760, but by the late 1770's were replaced by hip pads and bustles (false bums, cork rumps, *cul de Paris*).

## SACK

With the passing of Louis XIV in 1715, the rigid discipline of the French Court was relaxed. The new king was only a child, so there were very few ceremonial occasions when the ladies had to appear before him attired in full Court dress. The mantua itself had become so formalized that it too was discarded, and in the easygoing atmosphere of Regency France the ladies once again adopted a looser and more comfortable dress. The new robe was given many names, *robe battante, robe volante, innocente, sacque*, etc. In England it was usually called a sack or sacque. Its shape was probably influenced by the mantua, for it was similar in cut, but as it was at first intended rather for negligée wear the pleats, front and back, hung unconfined from shoulder to the ground, the back pleats being fuller and deeper than those of the mantua. Sometimes it was worn open in front; sometimes the front was seamed from just below the waist, or was closed by ties or buttons. The sleeves now had a separate cuff pleated to fit the bend of the arm. At first the back pleats, wide across the shoulders, would sometimes vary in arrangement, but eventually they became more formalized and were always set in two double box pleats. This garment was usually worn over a hoop petticoat, with or without stays. A shorter version, cut to knee level, was called a *casaquin*. See plate 23; Diagrams X, XI.

With the coming to maturity of Louis XV all the rules governing Court life for etiquette

68

and dress returned. The sack lost its negligée appearance, though the long loose back flowing into a train was retained. It was always worn with stays. At first the front fullness was fitted to the body by side darts to the waist, but soon the front bodice was cut separately and seamed to the skirt. The sleeves now fitted the arm and from *c.* 1740 the cuff was replaced by flounces; first by one, then by two or three. They were cut to hang very short inside the bend of the arm and long over the elbow. The rounded sides of the panier were accommodated by a fan of radiating pleats. If the panier was small they began at the waist from the side seam, but over a large panier the front and back skirts extended horizontally from the waist, being joined on top and then ending in the fan-shaped pleats. This top seam was very often open part of the way to form a pocket. The sack was worn open in front to show the stomacher and petticoat, which were usually of matching material. Probably the most typical of all eighteenth-century dresses, the sack was as much worn in England (from *c.* 1740) as in France and indeed all over the continent. See plates 29, 30, 31; Diagrams XV, XVIII.

## MANTUA

In its early loose form the *robe battante* was not very popular with Englishwomen, who always preferred something more fitted. They continued to wear the mantua. This preference led to the French later in the century distinguishing the two styles by calling the sack a *robe à la Française* and the mantua a *robe à l'Anglaise*. The cut of the mantua remained as hitherto, the pleating stitched back and front to fit the body. The sleeves were still fairly full but the cuff, as in the sack, was now separate, and pleated to fit round the bend of the arm. The earlier style of skirt drapery was, however, no longer possible owing to the hoop-petticoat's ever increasing volume. In the late 1720's and 30's, before drapery was finally discarded, there was a transition period. The front skirts were pleated to lie over the top of the hoop and held by a cord, while the long train was looped up and caught underneath, or looped up on the outside and arranged centre back (plates 23b, 24; Diagram XII). During the 1740's the skirt was cut separate from the bodice in front and folded round to the centre back. Finally, the side pieces were removed and the back panel only was cut in one with the bodice, and the skirt was now worn ground length. Short basques were added to the bodice at the sides to hide the gap between it and the petticoat (see Diagram XVII). This style seems to have become the prototype for English Court dress, when the back panel was elongated into a train. Usually there was then a seam just below waist level, so that a wider piece could be added for the train. The heavily-boned French Court bodice was worn in England only by Royalty on ceremonial occasions, and was known as a 'stiff-bodied' gown.

Another version of the mantua which appeared in the 1730's was particularly English. The bodice was cut as before, but the front was separated from the skirt round the waist as far as the back pleats. The centre back was still cut in one long piece from the shoulders to the ground and was then extended either side at waist level and pleated to the bodice round to the front. This type of gown was also worn open in front but occasionally the skirt was continued all round (the closed gown). It was worn without, or over, a small hoop and usually had no train. (See plates 25, 26; Diagram XIV).

English nomenclature during the eighteenth century is somewhat confusing. The name *Mantua* for a gown was more often used up to the middle of the century; after that it was called a 'night gown', which name was applied to a dress worn in the evening or for a fashionable occasion such as a wedding. Another usage was the French word *robe* for a 'sack'.

## PETTICOAT

The underskirt of a gown was still known as a petticoat. It was always cut straight without any gores. If worn over a small hoop, the fullness was pleated into the waist. When worn over a large hoop, the front at the waist was left plain and tied on either side to the back, the fullness on the sides being gathered separately onto a tape. In England in the 1740's another variation was worn with the mantua over a very large oblong hoop. The front and back were cut with long side seams shaped to fit over the hoop, and the extra fullness was either pleated or gathered into these side seams.

## OTHER TYPES OF DRESS

The riding coat continued to be based on the man's coat, but in the 1740's, in order to allow for the riding hoop, the front was cut separately and a basque was added. The back was still cut in one, and was open from the waist, and there were often pleats from the side seams. The *casaquin* was now called a *pet en l'air*, and there were other jackets for informal wear, some cut like the riding coat but with low neck and short sleeves. There were also wrapping gowns, some with loose fronts and fitted back like the mantua. The bed-gown or countrywoman's three-quarter length gown was what is now usually called a dressing-gown. Long circular capes with hoods were for going out in the evening or for travelling in bad weather. See Diagrams XXX, XXXI.

## MATERIALS, DECORATIONS, ETC.

Gowns from the 1720's to the 1740's were usually worn untrimmed (except for court). The silks of this period were especially beautiful, very heavy but crisp, and they fell into such lovely sculptural folds that no other decorations were required. Figured damasks in white, pale blue, pink, and bright clear yellow were very popular. There were also brocades and figured silks with large floral designs, and also with wide stripes. Quilted petticoats were often worn with the mantua. By the middle of the century silks, though still firm and crisp, were lighter in texture. As well as flowers there were ribbon, shell and lace patterns, also a fur motif designed as a compliment to the French Queen who was of Polish origin; *c.* 1760, stripes with floral sprays were popular. The scale of the patterns was not so large as on the earlier silks. *C.* 1750 the front pleats, known as 'robings' began to be decorated, some with embroidery or lace, but more usually by trimmings made from strips of the same material as the dress. This was gathered into puffs or pleats and edged with a narrow braid. They were set all round the open edge of the sack and arranged in patterns either side of the skirt and also on the petticoat. The *echelle*, now separated into individual bows, might decorate the stomacher, matching bows being placed on the sleeves. Laces – Brussels, Mechlin, Valenciennes, etc. – were also getting lighter in texture. Lace sleeve ruffles were shaped like those of the gown sleeves, while these latter were sometimes carried out in very fine lawn, either plain or delicately embroidered. Neckerchiefs were still worn with informal dress, the long ends being caught in front by the stomacher ties. Long aprons of fine lawn or of gauze were worn. For Court dress, gold and silver laces or embroidery in coloured silks and gold and silver were always heavily applied, and as much jewellery worn as one possessed or could borrow. Matching pieces of jewellery – necklace, *girandole* ear-rings, bracelets, stomacher pieces, sometimes also an aigrette for the hair – were known as a *parure*. In the second half of the century more jewellery was worn, and the glitter of diamonds was imitated in paste, marcasite, cut steel, etc.

*EXTREME ONCTION.*

# 1770-1795

## SACK, OR ROBE À LA FRANÇAISE

The sack was worn into the 1780's, but *c.* 1760 fashion was again returning to a more slender line and the back pleats gradually narrowed. By the end of the 1770's the bodice was usually separated side back and the skirt was pleated on to the bodice round to the side front. By this time the open front and the stomacher piece were being discarded, and bodices were made with a closed centre front. This was cut from two pieces of material with a centre front opening (which met) shaped in to the waist. The neck line was low, and the waist in front long and rounded. When the hoop began to decrease the full skirts of the sack were sometimes draped through the side pockets, this leading to the back drapery so characteristic of the later half of the eighteenth century. As the back of the sack was always cut long the later versions of it usually have tapes inside so that it could be looped up if required. By the 1780's the sack was only worn on very formal occasions. See plates 31, 32, 33; Diagram XX.

## MANTUA, OR ROBE À L'ANGLAISE

The mantua, or night gown, with its fitted body, had never gone out of fashion in England. In the late 1770's this too was given the new closed front bodice, and the back pleats moved so far to the centre back and became so reduced in depth that it is not surprising to find them replaced eventually by seams, and the skirt often being cut separate all round. There was a centre back, one or two side back seams and underarm seams. The back seams were subtly shaped to fit into the small of the back and then sloped down to a point centre back a few inches below waist level. The sleeves were very tight and came over the elbow, and later down to the wrist. The longer sleeves were cut from the vertical of the material. The full skirt, set in very small pleats to the bodice, had a train and was worn open in front to show the petticoat, which might be of the same material or of a lighter one. In addition this skirt often had tapes attached inside so that it also could be looped up. It was never worn with hoops, but with hip pads and bustle. See plates 35–38a; Diagram XXII, XVI.

72

## POLONAISE

The last quarter of the eighteenth century produced an amazing variety of fashions. As well as the sack, the *robe à l'Anglaise* and the Court dress, there were a number of lighter and more informal types. One of these was the Polonaise. Though this term is often applied to any eighteenth-century dress with back drapery it belongs, strictly speaking, to an over dress that appeared *c.* 1775. This was cut like the man's coat of the same period, with centre back and two far-back side seams all terminating in inverted pleats, the front being in one piece with an underarm dart. It was caught to the top of the bodice centre front, and fell back into slight folds shewing a tight-fitting bodice, or *corsage*, and the petticoat. The side seams of the skirts had tapes, or rings through which tapes could be threaded, to loop the material into puffs. See plate 33; Diagrams XXI, XXIII.

## OTHER TYPES

Variations of the Polonaise, *robe à l'Anglaise* and sack, were *robe à la circassienne*, *à la turque*, *levite*, etc. It is difficult to differentiate between them except by details such as sleeve styles, decorations, etc., though the *levite* and *robe à la turque* seem to have been worn undraped and trailing on the ground. Various styles of short jackets were still worn and became fashionable morning wear in the 1780's. They also had a variety of names–*caraco*, *juste*, *pet en l'air*, *pierrot*, etc. They were worn open with the corsage, or closed, and with a matching petticoat, or one of a lighter material. This applies to all informal styles and in general these petticoats were worn much shorter, well off the ground.

The riding coat with separate basque continued to be worn. In the 1770's there appeared another version which was strictly speaking a driving or carriage coat since it was copied from the man's great coat. It was made in cloth, ground length, the back being in one but having separate skirts front and sides with a pleat where the skirt joined the back. It had revers, collar, capes, and was closed with buttons down the front, or worn open over a waistcoat. The Englishwoman wore this as her day dress when living in the country, but by the 1780's it had become town wear as well. The French version carried out in silk, was cut like the *robe à l'Anglaise* but with the additional capes, revers, waistcoat, etc. which transformed it into the *redingote*. See plates 38c, 38d; Diagram XXIV.

## CHEMISE DE LA REINE

The dress, however, which was to have the most influence on future styles was the famous *chemise de la reine*, called by this name after a portrait by Vigée le Brun of Marie Antoinette in such a dress had been exhibited at the Paris Salon in 1783. The origin of this style was the *robe à la creole* brought to Paris by Frenchwomen from the West Indies. (They also, incidentally, introduced the practice of washing this garment with a blue rinse.) The robe, of very fine soft Indian muslin, was cut very full and loose, almost like a chemise, the body fullness being held into the waist by a deep sash and the full sleeves to the arms by ribbon ties. See plates 38c, 39; Diagram XXV.

## COURT DRESS

In France until the Revolution full Court dress, *le grand habit*, was obligatory when a lady was presented to the King, Queen and Royal family, and at ceremonial balls, *bals parés*. In the 1780's it was replaced on other formal occasions by the *robe à la Française*, or sack. In England also the sack was worn for formal Court dress. The full Court dress worn at the Drawing-Rooms had now a contemporary style bodice but very large hoop and separate train.

## MATERIALS, DECORATIONS, ETC.

As the eighteenth century progressed, materials, trimmings, laces, etc. became ever lighter and more delicate. By the 1780's silks were of paper weight, and their patterns were reduced to finely-drawn floral designs, tiny spot motifs and narrow stripes. Puffed robings were replaced by flat pleatings and by ruchings with pinked edges, and these in their turn gave way to trimmings of contrasting materials–transparent gauzes, nets, laces, ribbons and flowers. There was still a superabundance of trimmings in the 1770's and early 1780's. During the 1780's, however, the cult of simplicity, developed in France by Rousseau and other writers, and in England by the addiction of the nobility to country life and pursuits, was beginning to leave an imprint on taste and fashion. At first the fashionable *robe à l'Anglaise* was decorated with pleatings and ruchings, and the sleeve had a ruched cuff shaped to take the bend of the arm. Later, except for an occasional narrow fringe or braid edging, it was worn untrimmed but with its severity relieved by accessories such as fichus, scarves, sashes, etc. With the cotton as well as silk dresses, long aprons of fine gauze or of linen, sometimes with bibs, were another interpretation of country-life styles.

Printed cottons and fine muslins had become the fashionable dress materials. They were first brought from the Indies in the seventeenth century, and by their novelty and rarity had set a new fashion in dress materials. The silk weavers protested, and many laws were passed forbidding their import and wear. However, by the last half of the eighteenth century Europe had learnt to print on material and the cotton industry had been so much developed that the earlier laws against its use were finally abolished.

# Construction of
# Eighteenth-century Dresses

Although the arrangement of the pleating in eighteenth-century dresses was always very skilfully done the internal finish was rather rough by modern standards. These dresses are mounted
on a tight-fitting body lining of firm unbleached linen, the edges of which around armhole, waist,
etc. have usually been left raw. The lining is cut from four pieces of linen—two for the side
fronts and two for the back. The centre back seam is slightly sloped in to the waist, but in
sack-back dresses is frequently left open to within about two inches at the top, and there are
tapes or lacing holes on either side so that the fit could be adjusted. Sometimes a narrow strip
with lacing holes is attached to each side of the front lining so that the dress could be laced
across. Until the 1770's, practically all eighteenth-century dresses open in front over a stomacher
piece. At first this was not attached to the dress; later it is more likely to be sewn to the lining
and may open centre front with buttons for fastening. It was then called a *compère*. The lining of
the dress would be first seamed centre back, shoulders and sides, and the pleating of the dress
material then arranged over it. The back pleats of a sack dress are set in two double box pleats.
These vary in depth from dress to dress but the outside pleats are always very deep, being folded
to the centre back (where there is often an extra small pleat). This allows the group of box pleats
to hang out from the shoulders, and the side back of the dress under them to fit in to the body.
Such back pleats are held in position for about three inches from the top by a row of herring-
bone stitching done from the inside. The arrangement of the front pleats varies, but if there are
two on each side the top one is usually simulated; that is, it is a separate piece. When the front
pleating has been arranged it is lightly stitched in position to the lining. If the side seams of the
bodice to the waist have not already been seamed together they are sewn from the outside by
top-stitching. Each side of the front skirt is top-stitched to the waist of the bodice. The side
skirts are joined to the back and the fullness at the top set in radiating pleats at the side waist if
there is no panier, or only a very small one. Otherwise, the two sides are joined horizontally for
a distance of from three to nine inches according to the size of the panier and the radiating
pleats are then formed. Alternatively, and in later dresses, the front pleating is arranged on the
front lining and the back pleating on the back lining. The raw edges of the side bodice seams are

75

turned in together and joined by whipping stitching. The sleeves, cut always from the horizontal weave until the 1780's, are lined, and sewn to the dress from the inside as far as the head of the sleeve, which, left raw, is arranged in small pleats on to the outside of the lining on top of the shoulders. This is then covered by sewing the outside front pleat, or the front pleat if there is only one, to the outside back pleat. The back neckline is neatened by a narrow strip of material placed across the pleating and mitred each end. This awkward piece of sewing preserves the unbroken line of pleating over the shoulders so characteristic of eighteenth-century dresses. It was retained until the 1770's, when the back pleating became so narrow that this method was no longer feasible. The sleeve was then sewn in all round from the inside. Later versions of the sack sometimes also have the lining lightly boned.

In the mantua the pleating, back as well as front, is lightly stitched to the lining for about a quarter of an inch in, down to the waist. The sleeves are sewn in like those of the sack, with the unbroken shoulder line.

The width of eighteenth-century silks varies from about 19 to 21 inches. As a general rule the sack-back gown without a panier and the mantua gown are cut from six widths of silk. The sack with large panier requires seven widths, and the petticoat usually has six widths.

When the back pleating of the mantua, or *robe à l'Anglaise*, was replaced by seams the standard of workmanship became very much higher. Each piece of the bodice is mounted separately onto a similarly cut lining piece, the raw edges being turned in together and the pieces seamed with very fine whipping stitching. Sometimes a fine piece of whalebone or cane is inserted on either side of the centre back and side seams. The two front pieces are shaped into the waist centre front and sides and a dart or separate shoulder piece is also necessary, to fit the top of the body. Sometimes the front of this bodice is cut with a diagonal line from the neck centre front to the waist at the side, and a separate front piece inserted – a style more usually found in French dresses. The Polonaise is also lined as far as the waist.

Skirts of dresses and petticoats are unlined. When the dress skirt opens in front, the front sides are cut with an extra four to six inches of material which is then turned under to make a facing. Hems are sometimes faced a few inches up with very thin silk. Where the skirt is pleated the pleats are made and then the raw edge on the top is turned in one or two inches and whipped on to the bodice. The pleats of the earlier dresses, when the silks were very stiff, are spaced about one inch apart. They are set on either side of the waist facing inwards to the side seam, where they make an inverted pleat on each hip. The light silks of the 1780's are set in very narrow, closely packed pleats.

Flounces are pleated, not gathered, on. The edges of flounces made from the early stiff silks have a narrow hem and are edged with braid; later silks have these edges pinked.

Eighteenth-century gowns are always worn over stays. These, whether fully boned or half boned, are very straight, and in front have the same neckline as the dress. The rigid shape resulting makes fitting easier, and it seems probable that stays were used as a pattern from which to cut the bodice. When an open front gown was put on, the stomacher would first have been pinned to the stays and the gown pulled tightly into position and secured by pins (when there are no lacing holes). When the *robe à l'Anglaise* had a boned back the stays used had a heavily boned front, but the back had only the two bones at the centre where it was laced. The centre front of this dress would have been fitted tightly over the stays and pinned into position. Hooks and eyes were not used in the eighteenth century. From the late 1770's onwards a much lighter version of the stays was being worn with informal dress. It was cut like the others but had hardly any bones; the French called it a *corset*. The tight-fitting bodice worn with a petticoat under the Polonaise and also some other late eighteenth-century styles, was called a *corsage*, or *corset*.

Boucher: Les Precieuses ridicules. Molière-Udg. 1734.

# Cutting Diagrams

---

For full explanation see Notes on the Cutting Diagrams, page 303

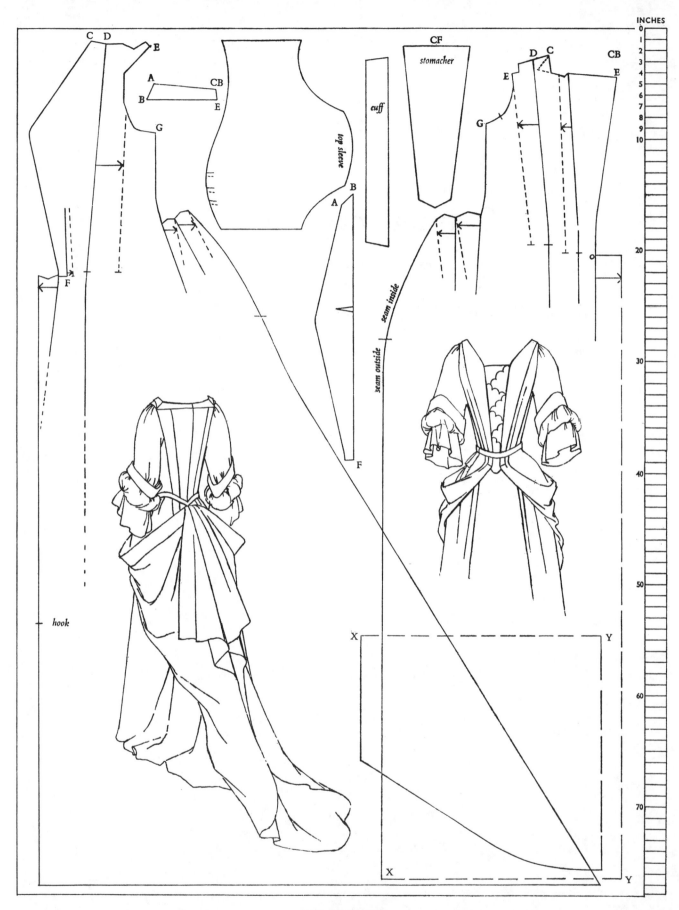

INCHES
0
1
2
3
4
5
6
7
8
9
10

20

30

40

50

60

70

C D E
A CB
B E
G
F

CF
stomacher
cuff
top sleeve
A B
seam outside
seam inside
F

D C CB
E E
G

hook

X Y
X Y

DIAGRAM IX

MANTUA *c.* 1700. *Metropolitan Museum, New York*

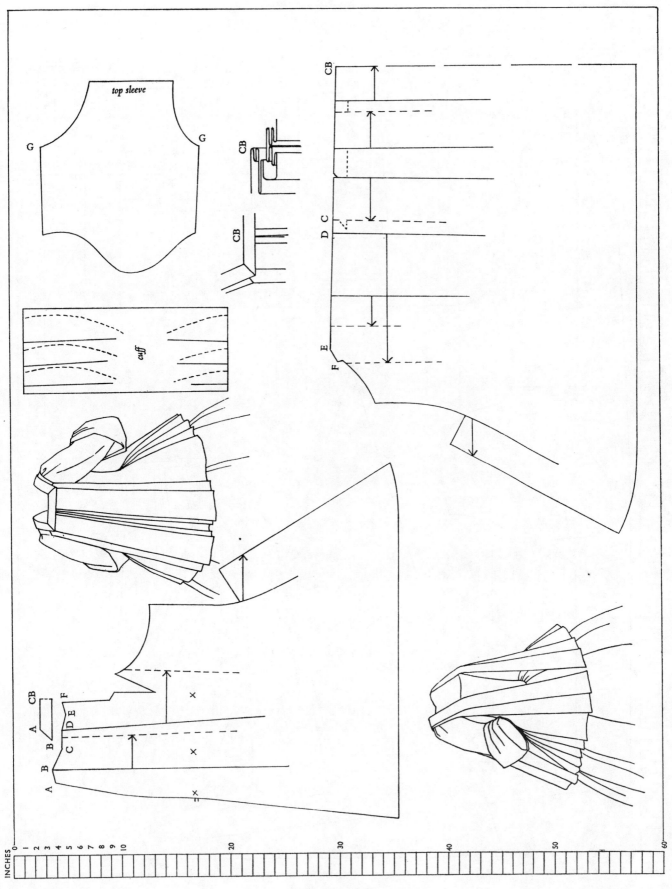

top sleeve

G          G

CB

CB

cuff

CB

D C

E

F

CB

A   CB

A   B   F

B   C D E F

×

×

×

INCHES
0 1 2 3 4 5 6 7 8 9 10        20        30        40        50        60

DIAGRAM X

CASAQUE 1730's. *London Museum*

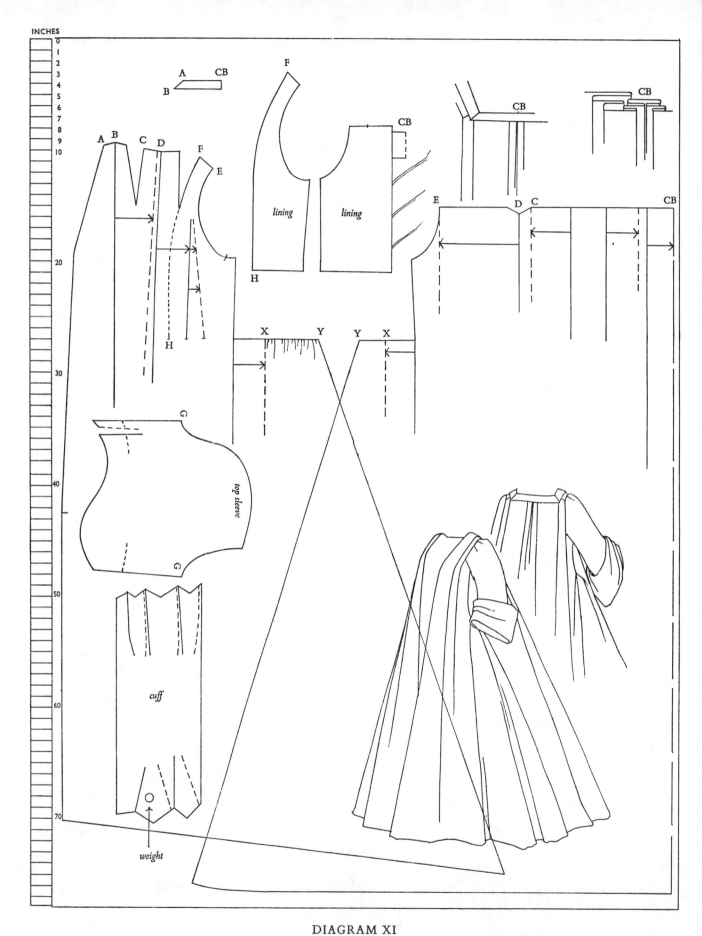

INCHES
0 1 2 3 4 5 6 7 8 9 10
20
30
40
50
60
70

A  CB
B

F  CB

A B  C D  F  E

lining   lining

CB

CB

E  D C  CB

H  H

H

X  Y  Y  X

G

*top sleeve*

G

*cuff*

*weight*

DIAGRAM XI

ROBE BATTANTE (SACK) 1725–35. *Centre de Documentation du Costume, Paris*

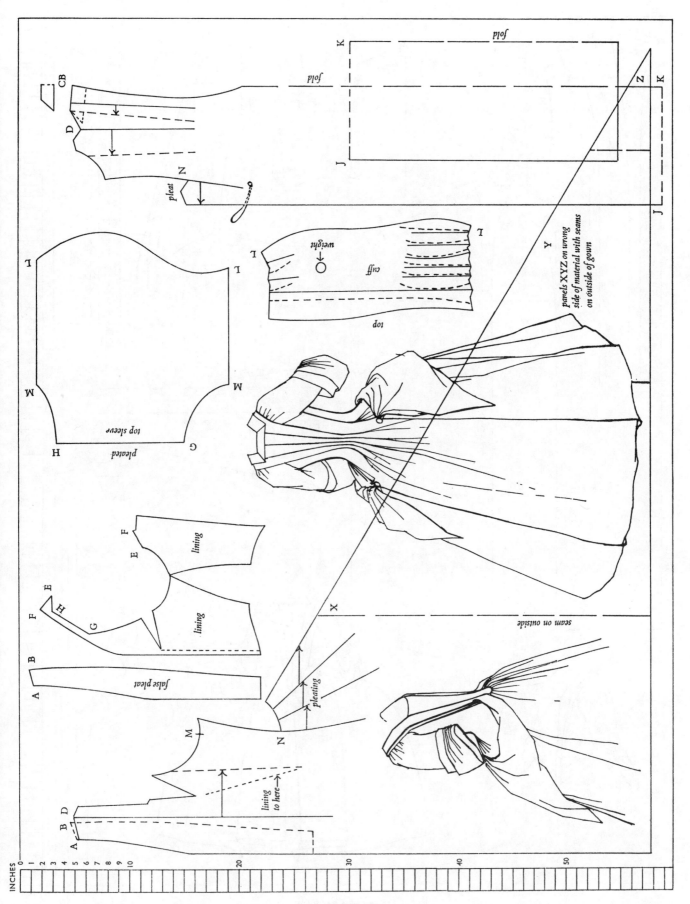

panels XYZ on wrong
side of material with seams
on outside of gown

seam on outside

pleat

weight

cuff

top

top sleeve
pleated

lining

lining

false pleat

pleating

lining
to here

DIAGRAM XII

MANTUA 1735–40. *London Museum*

INCHES

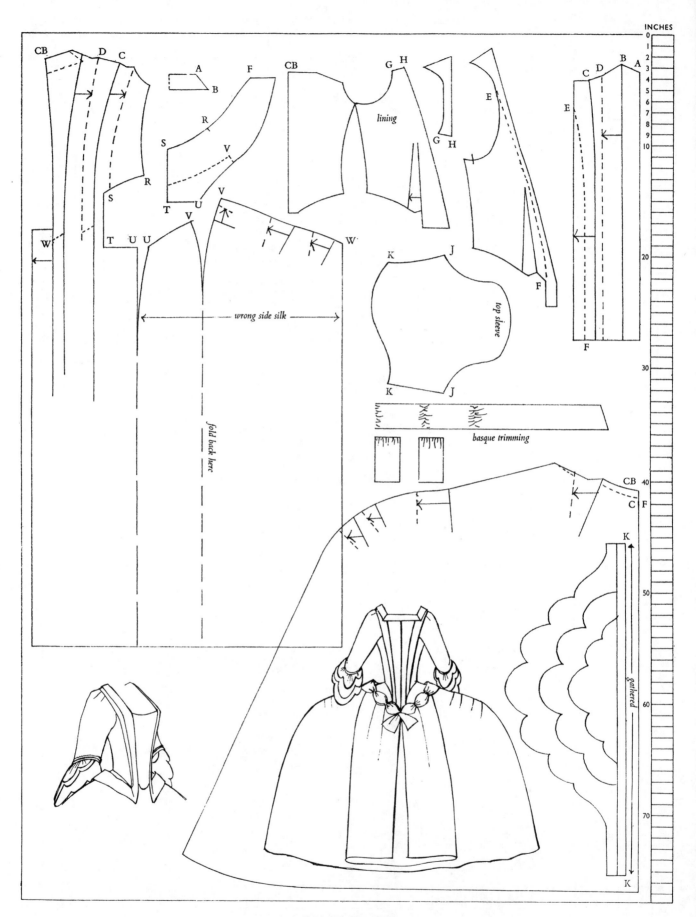

INCHES

CB D C

A
B F CB G H

lining

E
G H

R
S V

R
S E

T U V

T U U V W C D B A

C

E

wrong side silk

K J

top sleeve

F

fold back here

K J

basque trimming

CB
C F

K

gathered

K

DIAGRAM XIII

MANTUA (LARGE PANIER) 1740's. *Victoria and Albert Museum*

INCHES

A  C
B
D  E

lining

top sleeve

G

G

A    CB
B

E  C  D  CB

X

pleated towards centre from  X  to  Y  meeting in inverted pleat

Y

X

cuff

DIAGRAM XIV

MANTUA 1740-50. *Victoria and Albert Museum*

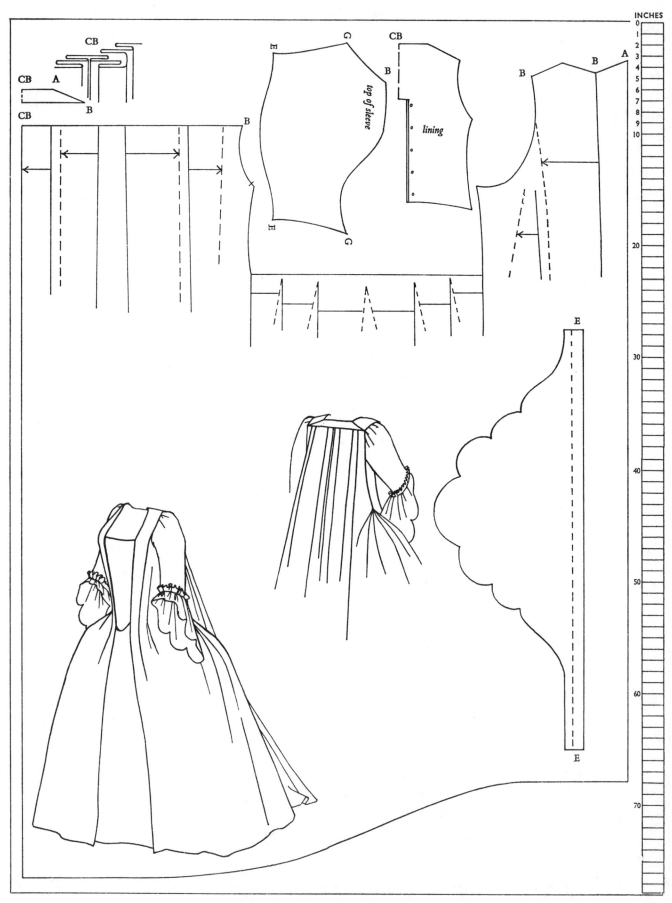

CB

CB    A

B

CB

B

G

E

B

top of sleeve

CB

B

lining

B

B    A

E

E

G

E

E

INCHES

DIAGRAM XV

SACK DRESS 1740–50. *London Museum*

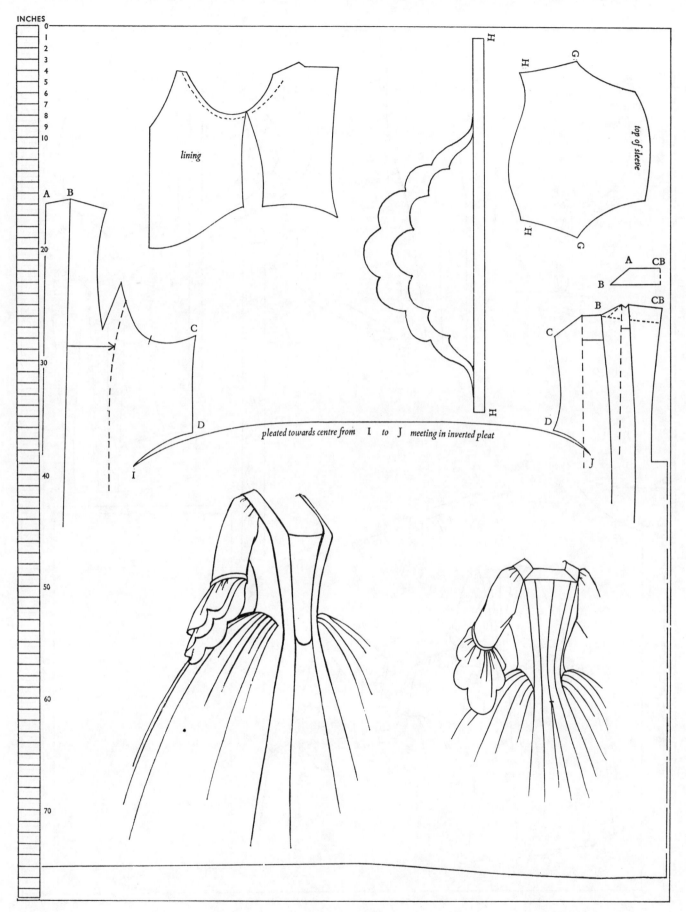

INCHES

0 1 2 3 4 5 6 7 8 9 10

20

30

40

50

60

70

*lining*

*top of sleeve*

A B

C

D

I

H

H

H

G

H

G

A CB

B

B CB

C

D

J

*pleated towards centre from* I *to* J *meeting in inverted pleat*

DIAGRAM XVI

MANTUA 1740–50. *Leeds City Art Galleries*

INCHES

*lining*

A  B     A  B         L

K                    *top sleeve*

E   G
E     J   I         CB
F   H              CB

J                    B  A   CB

I
C
J C

H  G

Y

Y                    X
X

*gathered to 10"*              *gathered*

CB

CF

DIAGRAM XVII

MANTUA (LARGE PANIER) 1750's. *London Museum*

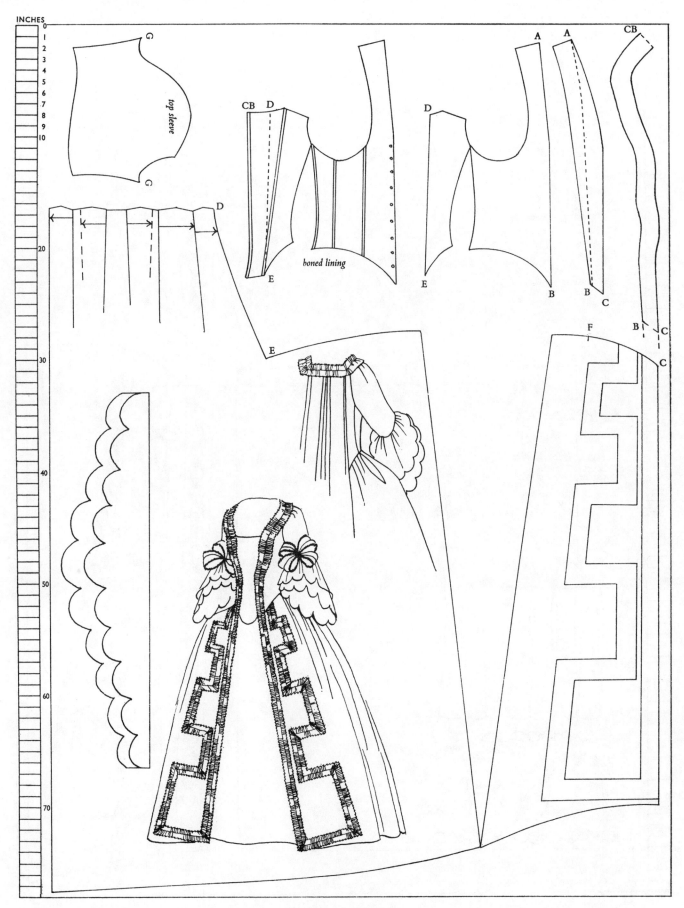

INCHES
0
1
2
3
4
5
6
7
8
9
10

20

30

40

50

60

70

top sleeve

G

G

CB D

boned lining

E

D

E

A A CB

D

B B C

B C

C

F

E

DIAGRAM XVIII

SACK DRESS 1755–60. *Leeds City Art Galleries*

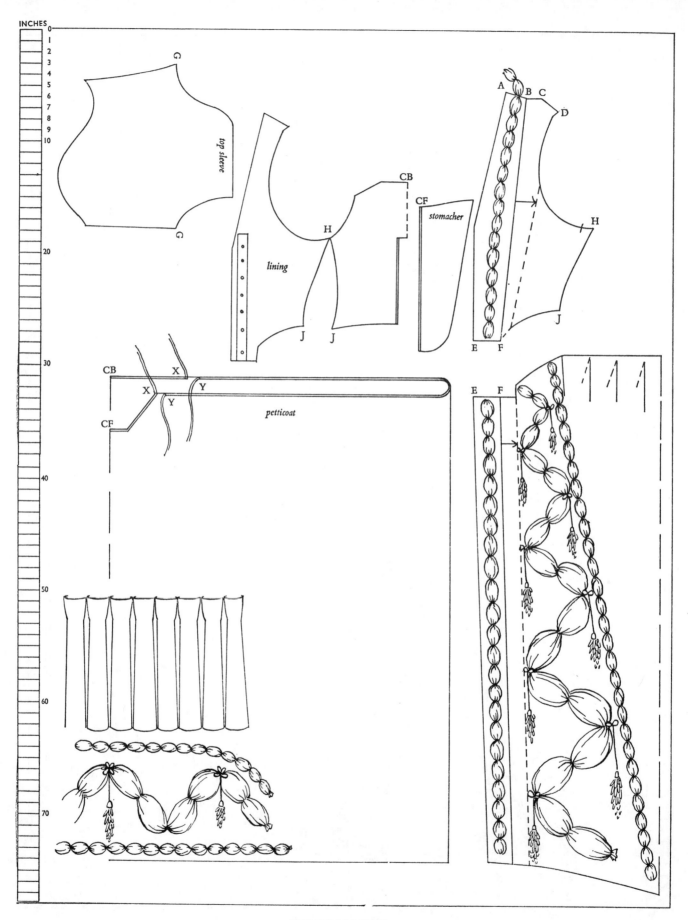

INCHES

0
1
2
3
4
5
6
7
8
9
10

20

30

40

50

60

70

*top sleeve*

G

G

*lining*

CB

H

J      J

CF

*stomacher*

A   B   C

D

H

E   F   J

CB

X

X

Y

Y

CF

*petticoat*

E   F

DIAGRAM XIX

SACK DRESS 1770's. *London Museum*

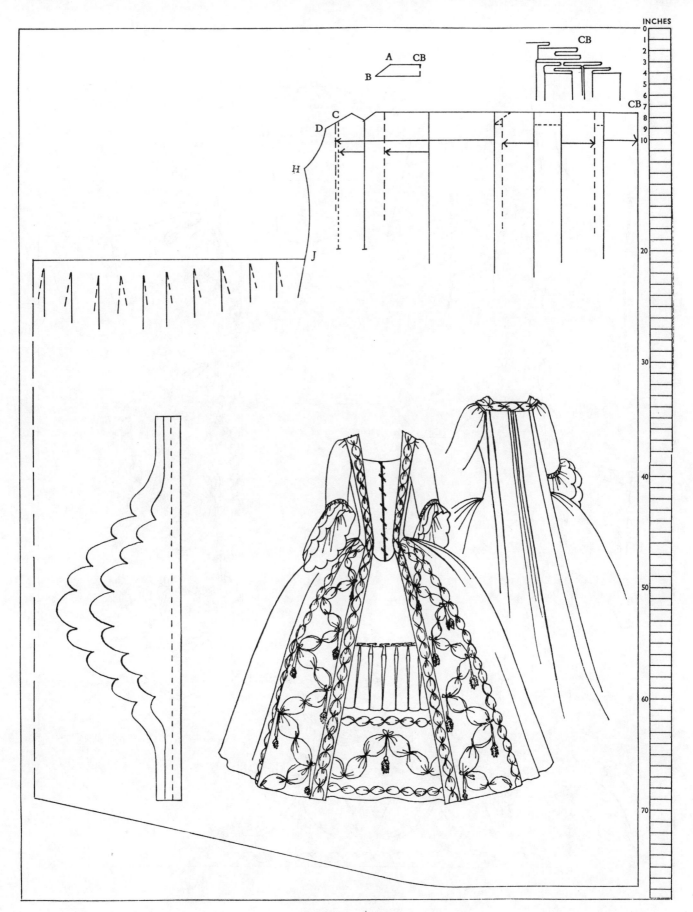

DIAGRAM XIX

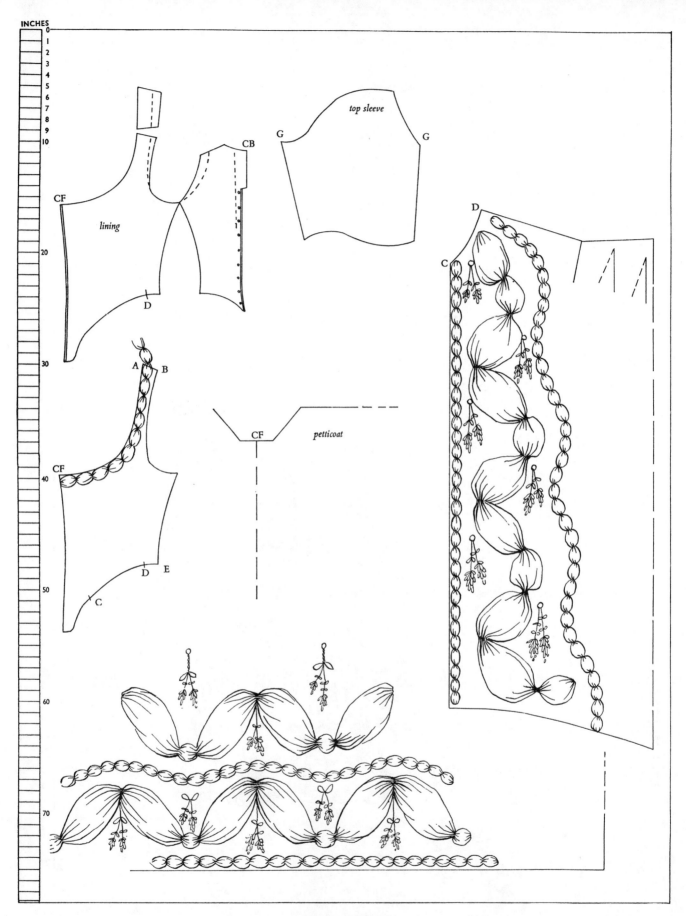

INCHES
0
1
2
3
4
5
6
7
8
9
10

20

30

40

50

60

70

top sleeve

G                    G

lining

CF

CB

D

D

C

A    B

CF

CF                    petticoat

D    E

C

DIAGRAM XX

SACK DRESS (LARGE PANIER) late 1770's. *Victoria and Albert Museum*

INCHES
0
1
2
3
4
5
6
7
8
9
10

20

30

40

50

60

70

A
B
CB

D E
E

X

X
o

Y

Y

DIAGRAM XX

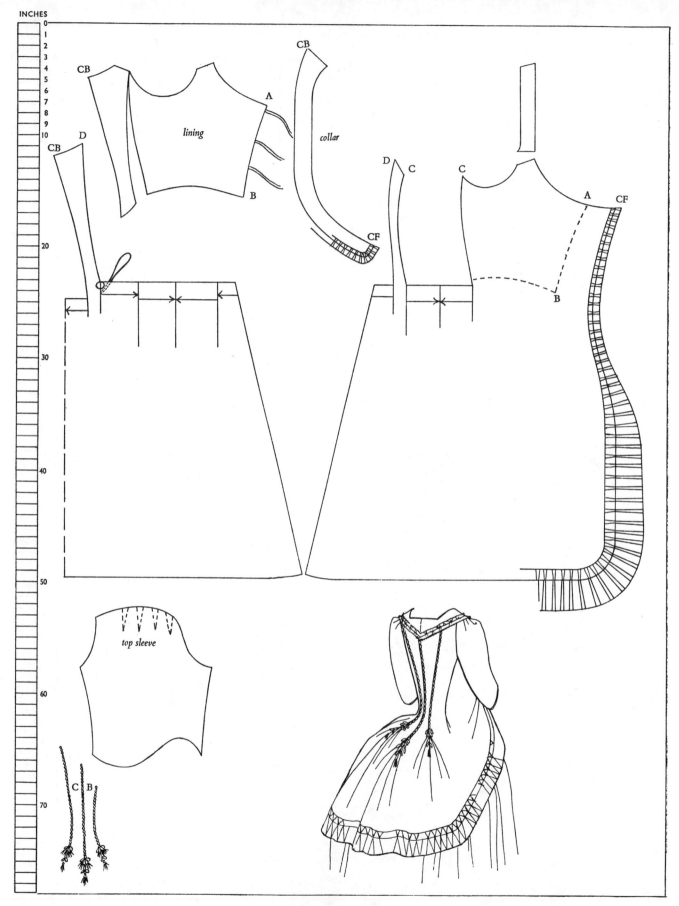

INCHES

0
1
2
3
4
5
6
7
8
9
10

20

30

40

50

60

70

CB

CB

A

CB

*lining*

*collar*

D

CF

CB

D

C

C

A

CF

B

B

O

*top sleeve*

C B

DIAGRAM XXI

POLONAISE, late 1770's. *Victoria and Albert Museum*

INCHES
0
1
2
3
4
5
6
7
8
9
10

20

30

40

50

60

70

shoulder strap

CF
B

top sleeve
B          B

CB

A
X

X tape to tie with
tape X inside skirt

A

CB

DIAGRAM XXII

ROBE A L'ANGLAISE 1775–80. *Leeds City Art Galleries*

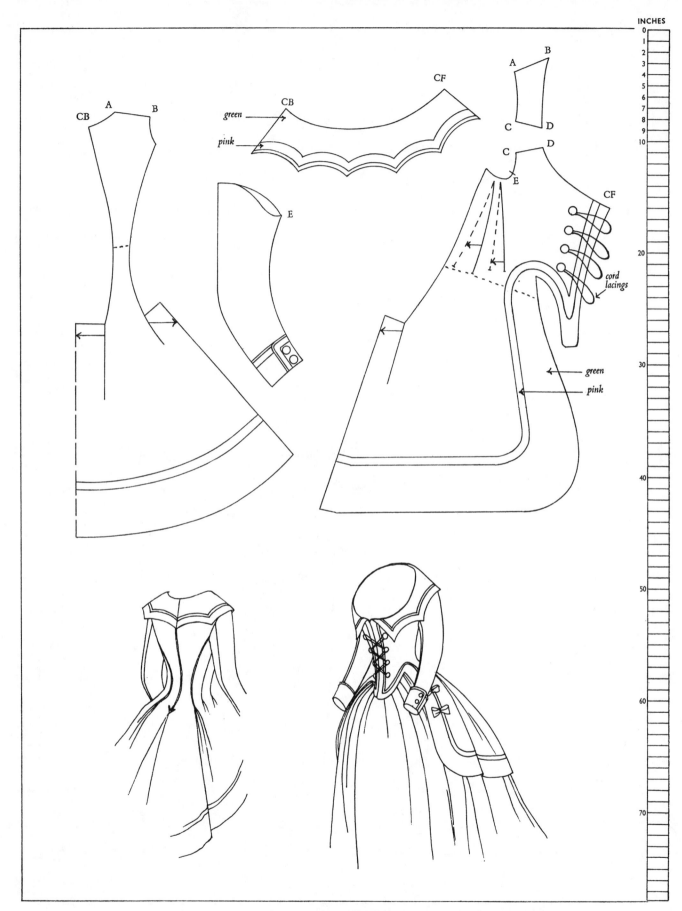

INCHES

green
pink

CB    A      B

CF

A      B

C      D

C      D

E

E

CF

cord
lacings

green

pink

DIAGRAM XXIII

POLONAISE STYLE JACKET, early 1780's. *Leeds City Art Galleries*

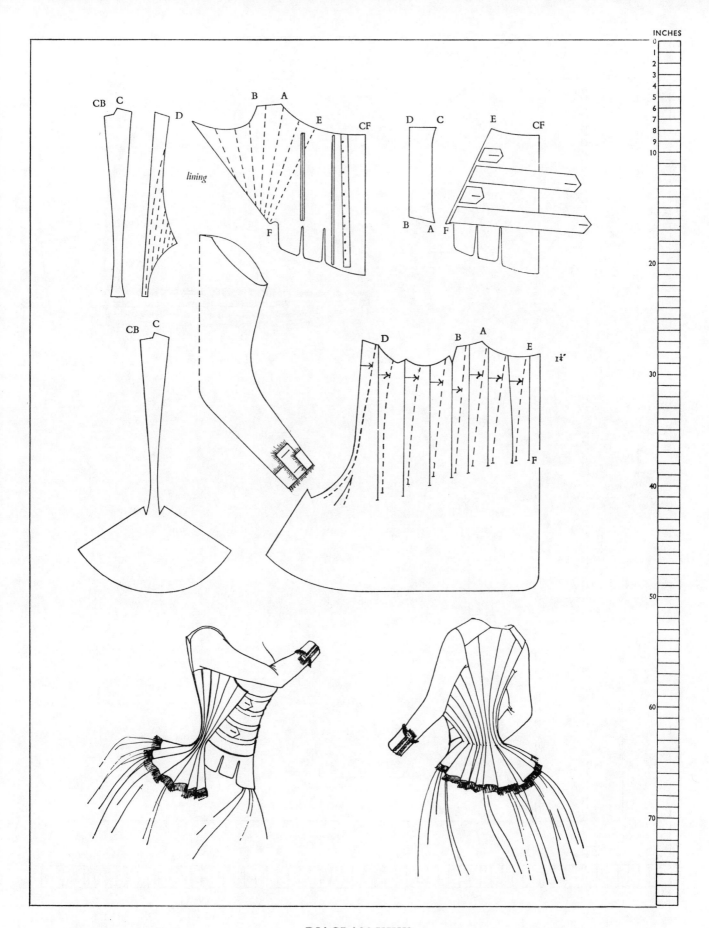

INCHES

**DIAGRAM XXIV**

PIERROT JACKET, late 1780's. *London Museum*

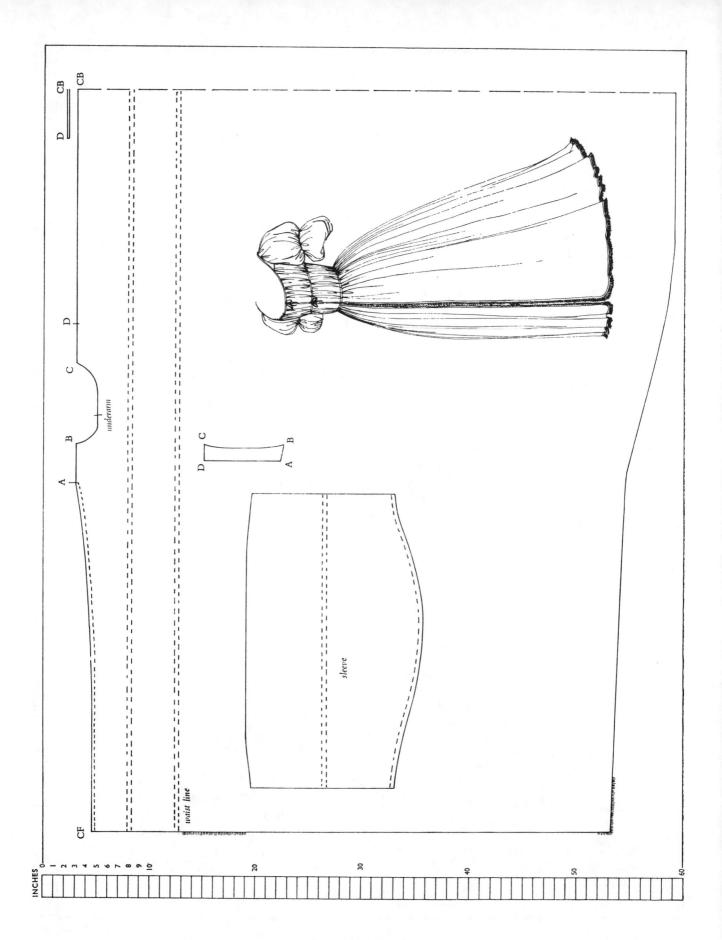

INCHES

0 1 2 3 4 5 6 7 8 9 10 20 30 40 50 60

CB
CB
D

D
C

A
B
underarm

C
D
A
B

CF

waist line

sleeve

DIAGRAM XXV

CHEMISE DRESS *c.* 1785. *Gallery of English Costume, Manchester*

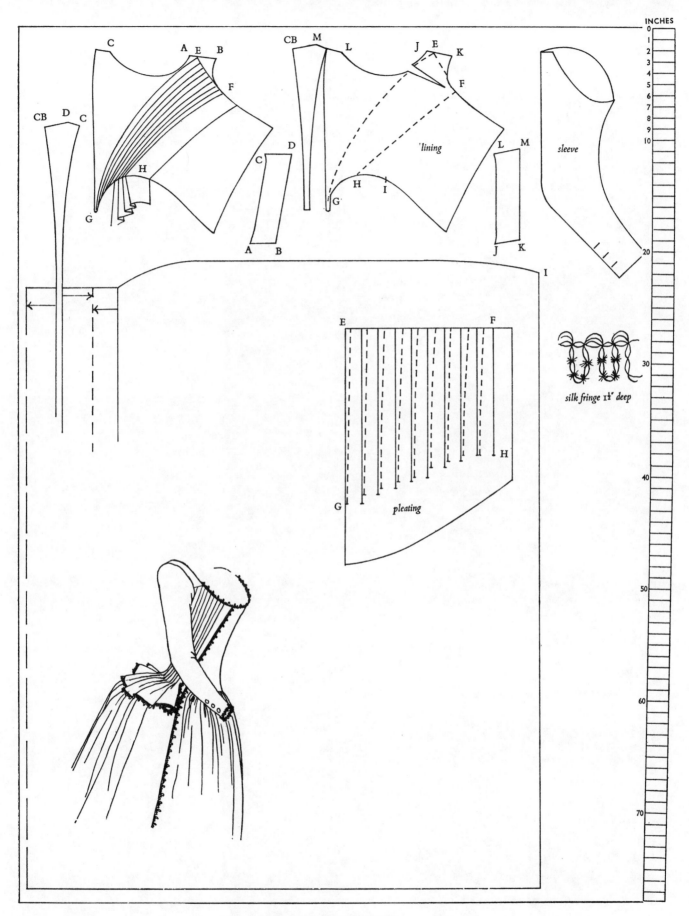

INCHES
0
1
2
3
4
5
6
7
8
9
10

20

30

40

50

60

70

CB D C

C

A E B

F

H

G

CB M

L

J E K

F

'lining

H I

G

L M

D

C

A B

L M

sleeve

J K

I

silk fringe 1½″ deep

E F

H

G

pleating

DIAGRAM XXVI

ROBE À L'ANGLAISE, early 1790's. *London Museum*

# Eighteenth-century Dress Production

When the loose gown (the mantua) became fashionable wear at the end of the seventeenth century, the seamstress, who had been making these gowns for some time, came into her own and adopted the more dignified name of 'mantua-maker'. From this time onwards, though there are occasional references to 'men-mantua-makers', all women's clothes were usually made by women. Dressmakers were called mantua-makers until almost the middle of the nineteenth century, long after the gown had ceased to be called a mantua. The stays which entailed heavier workmanship were still made by men. Tailors also continued to make the women's riding coats.

As the eighteenth century progressed, the increasing importance given to dress and all the accessories required to complete the fine appearance of the man or woman *à la mode* led to the development of a number of luxury trades. A diversity of shops and establishments appeared, each with its own speciality: shoes, gloves, fans, feathers, artificial flowers, perfumes, powder and paint. The status of the milliner rose, for now she too was making all the frivolous accessories which lightened and gave variety to the conventionally cut gown produced by the mantua-maker: caps, fichus, sashes, sleeve ruffles, capes, aprons and finally the ornate head-dresses and hats of the time.

If the mistress of the house was a lady of fashion, she no longer did any dress-making herself, but a maid who could sew and adjust the milliner's wares was a necessary and valuable asset. Many ladies who were not of the highest rank, however, still continued to make their own dresses, or, as silk materials were still very expensive, refurbished and remade their old ones. Patterns would be taken from gowns, often borrowed from a more fashionable acquaintance, and there was a great interchange of patterns between family and friends.

Extracts from *A General Description of all Trades, digested in Alphabetical Order*, London, 1747:

'*Mantua-Maker*. This Trade belongs entirely to the Women, both as to the work and the Wear, and a very extensive one it is, as well in the Country as in the City. It is reckoned a genteel as well as profitable Employ, many of them living well and saving Money. They take

Girls and young Women Apprentices . . . to make a Mistress, there is little else wanting than a clever Knack of cutting out and fitting, handsome Carriage, and a good set of Acquaintance.

*Stay-Makers.* Stays, notwithstanding they are Women's wear, are principally made by Men though both Women and Men work on them, and the Work may very well be called a Branch of Tayloring, and as nice and profitable as any one, but not the easiest. They take Apprentices (who are but rarely Girls).

*Milliners.* This is a considerable Trade, in the Shop-Keeping Way, carried on by Women, who buy all Sorts of fine Linens and Laces in whole Pieces, which they cut out into various Necessaries, and having them ready made up, both for Men and Women's wear, but chiefly for the latter; it is a most genteel Business for young Maidens that are good Proficients at their Needle especially if they be naturally neat, and of a courteous Behaviour.

*Hoop-Petticoat-Makers.* Though this Business seems to be only a Part of Stay-making, by Reason of the much Whale-bone used in them, yet the wear of these extending Attires has so much increased, as well as their Sizes, that of late it is become a separate Trade from that; these Goods being a great Part of the stock of divers Shops, where many Things chiefly for Women's Use are sold. Girls are those who principally learn this Sort of Work. . . . but there are several men-dealers in this Way likewise.'

The laws governing the trade guilds were much stricter in France than in England. Until 1675 only master tailors had the right to make women's dresses. France also had its sempstresses, *couturières*, and during the seventeenth century, they, like their English counterparts, were supplying women with the more negligée type of garment–petticoats, *robes-de-chambre*, etc., so it is interesting to note that it was at the same time as the English sempstresses became mantua-makers that the *couturières* petitioned Louis XIV for the right to have their own guild and be recognized as women's dress-makers, with the rider that 'as also it was more seemly and becoming to women's modesty to allow them to be dressed by their own sex'. Their petition was granted in 1675 when they became *Maîtresses Cougufières*. Their statutes allowed them to make *robes-de-chambre*, petticoats (*jupes*), jackets (*justaucorps*, or *justes*), bed-jackets (*camisoles*) and bodices and petticoats for young girls and children of both sexes up to the age of eight. Tailors reserved for themselves the right to make stays (*corps à baleine*) and the Court dress, that is, the boned bodice of the Court dress and the train.

After 1776 the *couturières* were allowed to make stays, corsets, paniers, dominos, etc. (The corset was a lighter version of the stays, cut like them, but with only a couple of bones centre front and the same centre back, it was replacing the heavily-boned stays.) In 1789 all restrictions on *couturières* were removed.

In France the equivalent of the milliner was the *marchande des modes*: 'whose skill, consists principally in arranging and decorating head-dresses, dresses, petticoats, etc., that is to say, making up and sewing on all the fashionable decorations which she and her client are continually devising. These decorations are usually made from gauzes, ribbons, nets, pieces of material, fur, etc. They also make some articles of dress such as the cape (*mantelet*), the pelisse (*plisse*) and the Court mantilla (*mantille du Cour*).' *Description des Arts et Métiers*, 'L'Art du Tailleur', F. A. Garsault.

N.B. If the trimmings or robings, and the stomacher (*compère*) were of the same material as the dress they were considered the work of the *couturière*; otherwise, it was the *marchande des modes* who did all the decorations. Rose Bertin and Madame Éloffe, who worked for Marie Antoinette, were *Marchandes des Modes*, and not *couturières*.

The first technical description of dress-making for the eighteenth century is the section on tailoring by M. Garsault in the encyclopaedia *Description des Arts et Métiers*, Paris, 1769. The section is called *L'Art du Tailleur—contenant Le Tailleur d'Habits d'Hommes. Les Culottes de Peau; le Tailleur de Corps de Femmes et Enfants; l'Art de la Couturière et la Marchande des Modes.*

As none of the eighteenth-century French Court dresses seem to have survived, the following description, by M. Garsault, is of interest: 'The Court dress (*grand habit de Cour*) consists of a closed bodice heavily whaleboned, and a train: the bodice is covered with material; the train and also the petticoat are of the same material. The Tailor makes the bodice and the train, the *couturière* the petticoat; and the *Marchande des Modes* adds all the ornaments (*pompons*) and trimmings (*agréments*).

'The day the Lady is presented to the King and Queen, etc., the bodice, train and petticoat must be black: but all the trimmings are of lace, net, etc. The upper arm, except at the top close to the shoulder where the black sleeve of the bodice is seen, is covered with two flounces of white lace, one below the other, to the elbow. Under the lower flounce there is a decorated band (*bracelet noir, forme de pompons*). There is also a border of white lace round the neck-line and under that a narrow black tippet (*palatine*), also decorated from neck to waist: the petticoat and bodice are decorated with puffs, all of which are made from net, lace, etc., also gold.

'When the day of presentation has passed, everything that was black is replaced by coloured or gold material. This style of dress has long been worn and has remained unchanged until the present day for ceremonial wear.

'If the Lady to be presented is not able to endure the heavily-boned bodice then she is allowed to wear a lighter one, covered with a mantilla, with the court train and petticoat. As the mantilla covers the upper arm the top lace flounce, which would not be seen, is omitted. The mantilla is made from any light material such as gauze, net, lace, etc.'

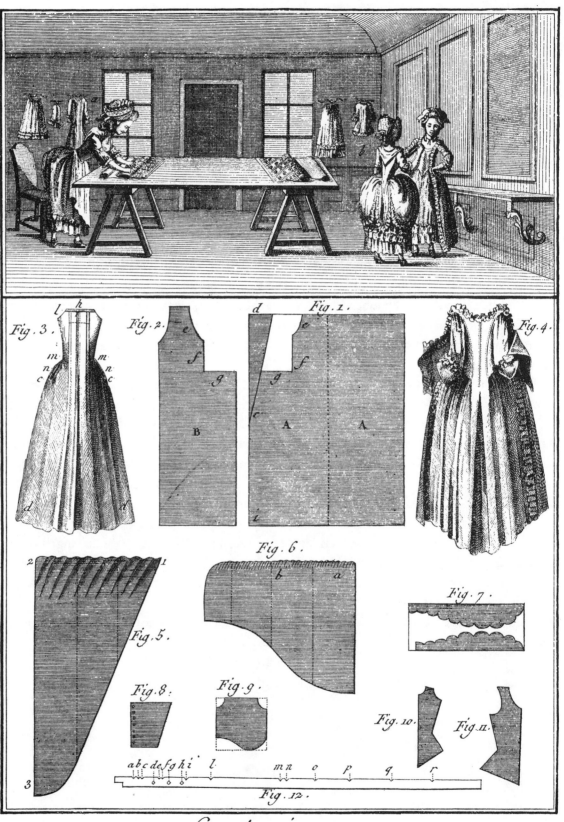

*Couturiere.*

# Eighteenth-century Tailors' and Dressmakers' Patterns

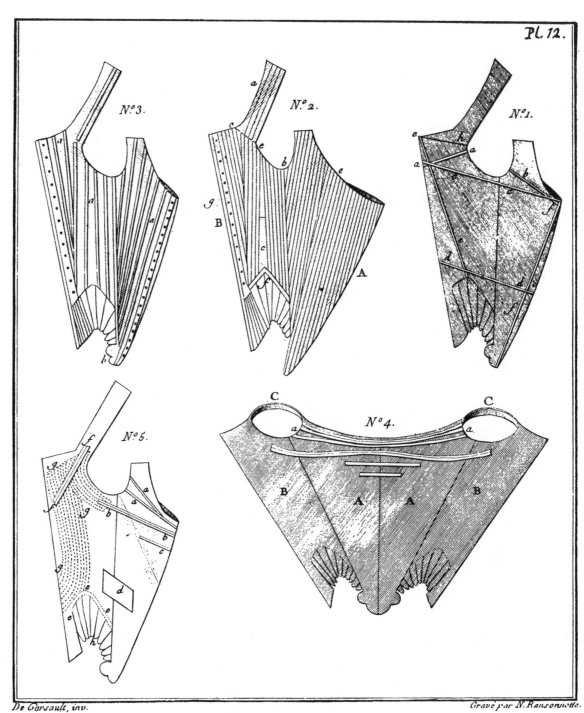

*Description des Arts et Métiers*, Paris, 1769, M. GARSAULT

9. THE STAY-MAKER (*Le Tailleur de Corps*)

Fig. 1. The lines indicate where measurements should be taken.
Fig. 2. Fully-boned stays (*entièrement baleine*).
Fig. 3. Half-boned stays (*demi-baleine*).
Fig. 4. Inside of stays, the lines indicate extra whalebones.
Fig. 5. Inside showing extra strengthening and whalebones.

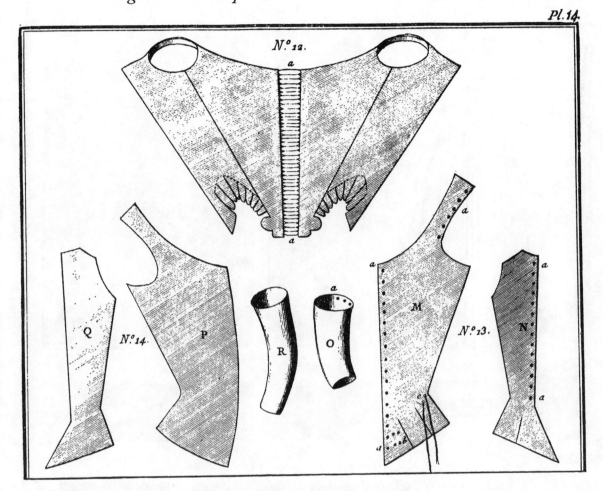

10. THE STAY-MAKER

Fig. 12. English stays (*corps à l'anglaise*). These lace in front.
Fig. 13. White corset (*corset blanc*). This is usually made in white linen and
lined; it is only boned each side of the centre front. The centre back
can be sewn together, or open and laced. The fronts can be laced,
buttoned, or tied with ribbon ties. The sleeve O may either be sewn
in, or just laced on top of the shoulder.
Fig. 14. Bed jacket (*camisole*). This is less fitting than a corset and usually ties
in front with ribbons. R is the sleeve.

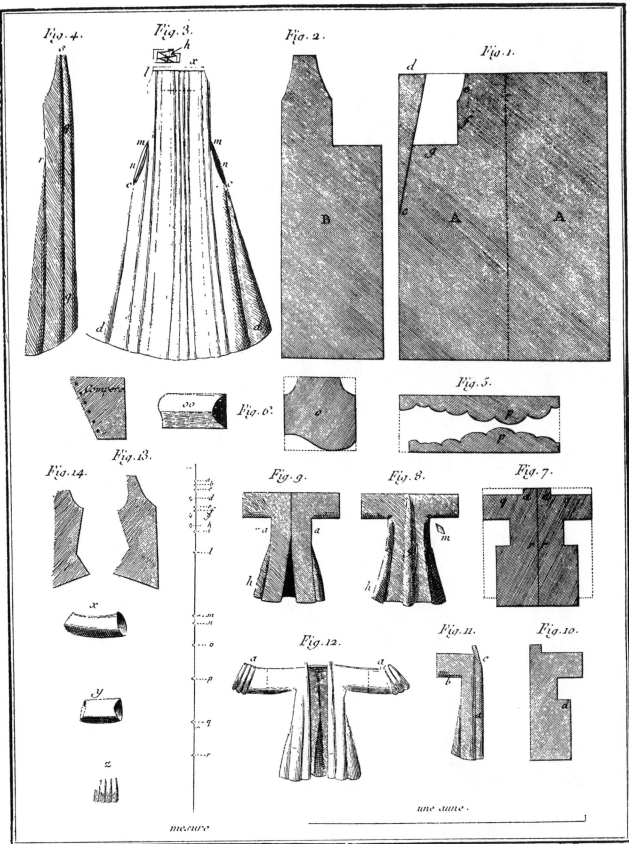

Pl. 15.

Fig. 4.    Fig. 3.    Fig. 2.    Fig. 1.

Fig. 5.

Fig. 6.

Fig. 14.    Fig. 13.    Fig. 9.    Fig. 8.    Fig. 7.

Fig. 11.    Fig. 10.

Fig. 12.

une aune.

mesure

De Garsault, inv.                                   Gravé par N. Ransonnette.

*Description des Arts et Métiers*, Paris, 1769, M. GARSAULT

## 11. THE MANTUA-MAKER (*L'Art de la Couturière*)

Figs. 1, 2, 3, 4, 5, 6. The gown (*robe*). This requires six widths of narrow material, about half an aune wide. Fig. 2, the back has a triangle *c, d,* cut out which is then added to the bottom to form a gore. The top is set in double box pleats, *h,* which are stitched together from inside, along the dotted line, Fig. 3. Fig. 2, the front is arranged to form a pleat on the shoulder. The sides of the backs and fronts are set in pleats, *m,* Fig. 3; *m, c,* are the side pockets; the back pleats are neatened at the top by a band, *x,* about one inch deep. Fig. 6 is the sleeve, and Fig. 5 the sleeve flounces. The *compère* replaces the earlier stomacher piece and is sewn each side of the front bodice and buttons centre front. The petticoat (*jupon*) is made from five widths of material, sewn together; sometimes the opening is at one of the side pocket slits, sometimes at centre back. The top is pleated to fit the waist, and tapes sewn either side of the opening.

Figs. 7, 8, 9, 10, 11, 12. The bed-gown (*manteau-de-lit*). This is cut from two or four lengths of material according to the width. The sleeves are cut *en chemise,* that is, in one with the body; the squares cut from the sides of the gown are added to the sleeves to give extra length. Figs. 8, 9, the back, is cut straight across the top and has an inverted pleat centre back. The front, Figs. 7, 10, 11, has an extra piece on top, *a,* which is formed into a pleat and folded to fit the neck, *c,* Fig. 11. An inverted pleat is set each side the waist, *d,* Fig. 10.

Figs. 13, 14. The jacket (*juste*). This is usually worn by countrywomen. The sides are sewn down to the waist only, and then are left open to form basques. The sleeves are either plain to the elbow, *x,* or shorter, *y,* in which case a pleated frill, *z,* is added. The jacket is lined and the edges bound with ribbon; it fastens in front with ribbon ties.

aune—118 centimetres, or about 46½ English inches.

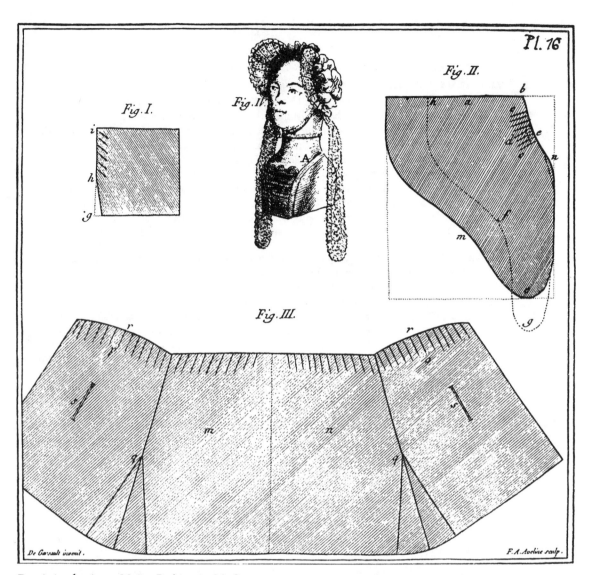

*Description des Arts et Metiers*, Paris, 1769, M. GARSAULT

12. THE MILLINER (*La Marchande de Modes*)

Figs. I, II. The cape with hood (*manteau et son coqueluchon*). This is for outdoor wear and is made from taffeta or satin, and lined with the same material and edged with black lace; they are also sometimes made from fine lawn. The cape, Fig. II, is cut from one and a half aunes of material (two-thirds or half an aune wide). This is folded double lengthways; the neckline *b*, *n*, is shaped and then the curve, *m*, to go over the arms; the neck is pleated, *o*, *o*. The hood, Fig. I, is cut from two-thirds of material folded double lengthways; two small triangles, *h*, *g*, about four or five inches high, are cut each side the back, and the rest of the back is arranged in circular pleats which are caught together at *h*, this fits the middle of the back of the head. The hood is then joined to the neck of the cape, and inside a ribbon is sewn over the join to form a slot through which a cord is threaded to draw up as desired.

Fig. III. The pelisse (*plisse*). This is also a type of cape but more ample, and has the hood. It is made from taffeta or satin and lined with the same material, or in winter with fur. It requires three and a half aunes of material. This is cut into four equal lengths. The centre back is joined on the straight; at the top of each side of the back and two fronts a triangle is cut which is then added to the bottom at *q*, to form a gore; the sides are sewn together and the corners rounded off; the fronts are also rounded at *r*, centre front. About the middle of each front a slot is cut for the arms to go through. The hood is made as for the cape, Fig. I, and joined to the top of the pelisse which is arranged in pleats.

Fig. II. The Court cape (*mantille de cour*). This is worn with Court dress and has no hood. It requires one and a half aunes and is made from some light material such as gauze, net, or lace. The cut is the dotted line in Fig. II, which is shorter at the back and longer in front than the cape. The neck is arranged with a few pleats on the shoulders.

Fig. IV. The cap (*bonnet en papillon*). This design is to show how the bonnet is kept in position on the head by ribbons pinned to it over each ear; the ribbons cross under the chin and tie behind.

# Quotations from Contemporary Sources

END OF THE 1670's

Mme de Fontange—let us follow our young beauty as she goes hunting with her prince. That day she was wearing an expensively embroidered riding habit and a hat covered with the most beautiful plumes procurable. She looked so elegant in this costume none other could have suited her better. As they were returning in the evening, a little breeze blew up which obliged Mme de Fontange to remove her hat. She tied up her hair with a ribbon which just fell over her forehead and the king liked this so much that he asked her to wear her hair dressed in this fashion in the evening. The next day all the Court ladies appeared with the same coiffure. That is the origin of the high head-dresses that are still worn and which from France have spread throughout all the Courts of Europe.

CARDINAL DUBOIS, Mémoires

1680–1684

1680. Articles stolen: A black serge gown, stiff bodied; two large black flowered silk skirts; a white silk petticoat laced; a mantua, lined with pink-coloured silk; a white mohair petticoat, laced; a yellow silk net petticoat, with bone lace.

1682. A large portmantle full of women's clothes lost or stolen:

A mantua and petticoat of grey silk and silver stuff, with broad silver lace; another mantua and petticoat, flowered with liver-coloured and some flesh-coloured spots; a quilted petticoat of lead-coloured satin; a gold-coloured tabby toilet and pin-cushion, with silver lace; two point coifs, two pair of *point d'Espagne* ruffles; a laced night rail and waistcoat; one pair of *point de Venise* ruffles; a black laced scarf; three black satin caps, and some little bands and cuffs.

Another parcel:

A striped silk mantua; a light-coloured gown, striped with yellow and white; a blue flowered silk petticoat; a pair of blue striped stays; a black fresener hood, and a yellow-spotted hood.

1684. Lost between Hackney and London:

A petticoat of musk-coloured silk, shot with silver on the right side, the flowers trail silver, and the wrong side the ground silver, the flowers musk-coloured, with a deep white thread bone lace; a white fringe at the bottom, and a gold one over it; six breadths, lined with Persian silk of the same colour.

J. P. MALCOLM, Manners and Customs of London

1687

It is not surprising that you are wearing fontanges because everybody here does from little girls seven years old to old women in their eighties, the only difference is that young people wear them in all colours, whereas their elders have only black or dark-coloured ones.

MADAME, DUCHESSE D'ORLÉANS, Correspondence

1689

The rest of the day I was cutting out linen for my children's garments and arranged for them to be made up. Then I gave Cordredonne my old skirts to make clothes for my son.

COMTESSE DE ROCHEFORT, Journal

1694

Apparel, or the Ladies Dressing-Room

A *Commode*, is a frame of Wire, two or three Stories high, fitted for the Head, or cover'd with Tiffany, or other thin Silks; being now compleated into the whole Head-dress.

An *Echelles*, is a Stomacher lac'd or ribbon'd in the form of the Steps of a Ladder, lately very much in request.

*Engageants* are double Ruffles that fall over the wrists.

A *Font-Ange*, is a modish Top-knot first worn by Mademoiselle de Fontange, one of the French King's Misses, from whom it takes its name.

A *Palatine*, is that which used to be called a Sable-Tippet, but that name is changed to one that is supposed to be finer, because newer.

A *Mont la Haut*, is a certain Wier that raises the Head-Dress by degrees or stories.

A *Spagnolet*, is a Gown with narrow Sleeves and Lead in them, to keep them down *À la Spagnole*.

A *Sultane*, is one of these new fashioned Gowns trimmed with Buttons and Loops.

A *Tour*, is an Artificial dress of Hair, first invented by some Ladies that had lost their own Hair.

JOHN DUNTON, The Ladies Dictionary

1695–1702

1695. I don't know why people have so many different styles of dress; I only wear Court dress (*le grand habit*) and a riding habit; no others; I have never worn a robe de chambre nor a mantua, and have only one robe de nuit for getting up in the morning and going to bed at night.

22. *c.* 1690. Madame la Duchess Electoral de Bauierre. H. Bonnart
The petticoat is now heavily decorated. The fontange is high and narrow

23a, b, c
1727. Taken from the set.
Collection of divers
Fashions of the day.
Hérisset

Les Paniers
The voluminous robe battante,
similar in cut to the pattern
given in Cutting Diagram II.
The cuff is now cut separately
from the sleeve

Les Manteaux
The train of the mantua is
folded away behind (for
explanation see Cutting
Diagram XII), and the
petticoat spread over a bell
shaped improver. Later this
rounded shape became
flattened front and back and so
developed into the full
eighteenth-century paniers

Les Casaquins
The short informal jacket worn
over a petticoat. See Cutting
Diagram X

24.   *c.* 1730. Lady wearing a mantua with black draping. Gravelot.
      See Cutting Diagram XII

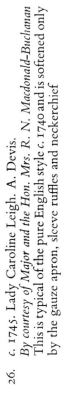

26. *c.* 1745. Lady Caroline Leigh. A. Devis.
*By courtesy of Major and the Hon. Mrs. R. N. Macdonald-Buchanan*
This is typical of the pure English style *c.* 1740 and is softened only
by the gauze apron, sleeve ruffles and neckerchief

25. *c.* 1740. Lady wearing a quilted petticoat. A Devis.
*By courtesy of M. Bernard*
An open robe or mantua, very simple in style and probably
identical to Cutting Diagram XIV. The pleats at the side fronts
are cut in one with the bodice and not yet applied separately

27a. 1751. Coronation robes of Queen Louisa Urica of Sweden. *Royal Armoury, Stockholm*
Court robes still retain the close bodice with its low oval neckline as worn during the third quarter of the
seventeenth century, although the petticoat is worn over a full eighteenth-century panier

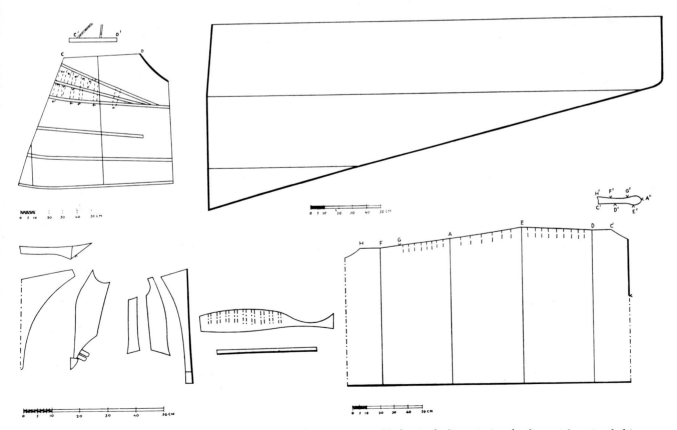

27b. Pattern of Coronation robes, *Kungl, Livrustkammaren, Stockholm*, including panier, bodice with trained skirt
and matching petticoat

29. 1755. Madame Pompadour. F. Boucher. *Wallace Collection*
This gown and petticoat made from the crisp light silks of mid-eighteen century is tied across the bodice with an echelle of ribbons, and has matching bows on the sleeves,

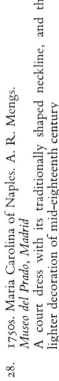

28. 1750s. Maria Carolina of Naples. A. R. Mengs. *Museo del Prado, Madrid*
A court dress with its traditionally shaped neckline, and the lighter decoration of mid-eighteenth century

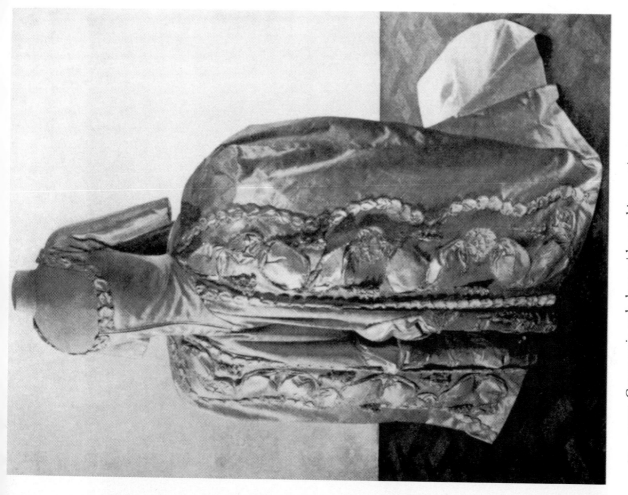

31. 1770s. Cream satin sack dress with matching petticoat.
*Victoria and Albert Museum*
A more elaborate trained dress, the skirt fronts and the petticoat being decorated with puffings and ruchings of the same silk. See Cutting Diagram XIX

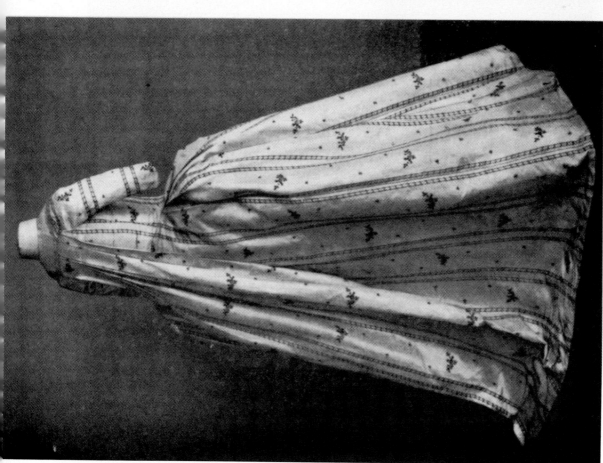

30. 1760–1770. Sack Dress. *Victoria and Albert Museum*
A typical sack dress of delicately patterned brocade. The sleeves are fitted well into the back of the bodice and are still cut with the warp threads running horizontally round the arm. The sleeve flounces are missing

32. Late 1770s. Mrs Cadoux. British School. *Tate Gallery*
This sack dress can be compared with Cutting Diagram XIX. The wide panier has
noticeably diminished by this date

33.  Late 1770s. La Sortie de L'Opera. G. Malbeste after Moreau
Both these principal dresses show even more ruching and elaborations of light decoration. The figure on the extreme right shows a sack dress being worn without a panier and the side skirts pulled through the pocket slits on either side, while in the adjacent back view we can see the curving back seams and drawn-up skirt of the polonaise.

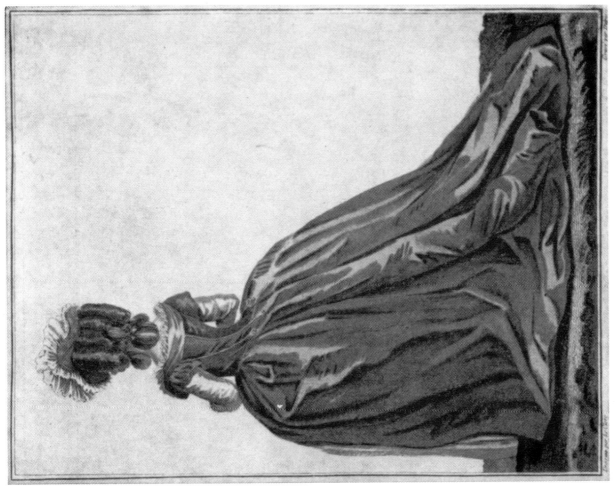

35.　1780. La Gallerie des Modes
In this type of robe the two centre back panels often continue in an unbroken line down to the hem. The curved back seams of the bodice are
usually outlined with braid and terminate in inverted pleats below the
waist

34.　1779. La Gallerie des Modes
A court dress still being worn with the now outmoded panier

36.  *c.* 1780. Madame de Mongirand. J. L. David. *By Courtesy of Mrs P. Denman*
   By this date the bodice of the robe a l'anglaise is often cut quite separately from the skirt, it
   being no longer practical to cut the back panels without a join at the waist because of the close
   proximity of the curving back seams. See Cutting Diagram XXII

37.  *c.* 1790. Jeune Femme avec des fleurs bleues. Louis-Leopold Boilly. *Private Collection*
The narrow striped silk of the robe a l'anglaise shows the long tight sleeve now being cut
vertically. The soft gauze petticoat and fichu herald the new interest in transparent muslin
for fashionable clothes.

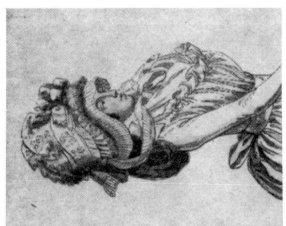

Chemise dress.
See Cutting Diagram XXV

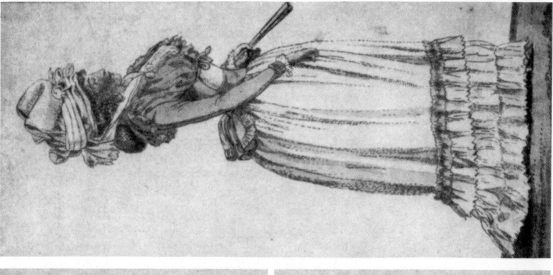

Pierrot jacket.
See Cutting Diagram XXIV

38. 1791–1793. FASHION PLATES

A Riding Jacket

(*left and top right*) Robe a l'anglaise.
See Cutting Diagram XXVI

39. *c.* 1790. Antoine Laurent Lavoisier and his wife. J. L. David.
*By courtesy of The Rockefeller University, New York*
The Chemise dress. A completely softened line, simple and free of decoration. See Cutting Diagram XXV

1702. At Versailles which is considered the royal residence, everyone who comes into the King's presence or into ours, must be in full Court dress, but at Marly, Meudon, and Saint-Cloud, mantuas are worn, as also for travelling. I find Court dress much more convenient than mantuas which I can't endure.

MADAME, DUCHESSE D'ORLÉANS, *Correspondence*

1702

The Duchess de Bourgogne lay down on her bed exhausted by the weight of the gown she wore yesterday at the Comedy because it had been overloaded with too many jewels.

DANGEAU, *Journal*

1706

*Mantoe*, or *Mantua*–Gown, a loose upper Garment now generally worn by Women, instead of a straight-body'd Gown.

PHILLIPS (ed. Kersey), *Dictionary*

1709–1710

1709. I have not thoroughly examined their new-fashioned Petticoats, but shall set aside one Day in the next week for that Purpose.

1710. Advertisement–Whereas Bridget Howd'ee, late Servant to the Lady Fardingale ... withdrew her self on Wednesday last from her ladyship's Dwelling-House, and, with the Help of her Consorts, carried off the following Goods of her said Lady, viz: A thick wadded Callico Wrapper, a Musk-coloured Velvet Mantle lined with Squirrel-Skins, Eight Night-Shifts, Four Pair of Silk Stockings curiously derned, Six Pairs of Laced Shoes, new and old, with the Heels of Half Two Inches higher than their Fellows, a Quilted Petticoat of the largest Size, and one of Canvas with Whalebone Hoops; Three Pair of Stays, boulstered below the Left Shoulder, Two Pair of Hips, of the newest Fashion. Six round-about Aprons with Pockets, and Four striped Muslin Night-Rails very little frayed.

*The Tatler*

1710

The King went again in the evening to see the Duchess de Bourgogne whom he found resting on a couch wearing an *andrienne* (this was a robe de chambre undraped and with a long train; it was named after a dress of this style worn by an actress in the Comedy *Andrienne*).

MARQUIS DE SOURCES, *Mémoires sur La règne de Louis XIV*

1711

There is not so variable a thing in Nature as a Lady's Head-dress: within my own Memory I have known it rise and fall above Thirty Degrees. About ten Years ago it shot up to a very great

Height, insomuch that the Female Part of our Species were much taller than the Men. The Women were of such an enormous Stature, that we appeared as Grass-hoppers before them: At present the whole Sex is in a Manner dwarfed and shrunk into a Race of Beauties that seems almost another Species . . . they are at present like Trees new lopped and pruned, that will certainly sprout up and flourish with greater Heads than before.

*The Spectator*

### 1712

There is a certain female ornament by some called a tucker, and others the neck-piece, being a slip of fine linen or muslin that used to run in a small kind of ruffle round the uppermost verge of the women's stays, and by that means covered a great part of the shoulders and bosom. Having thus given a definition, or rather description of the tucker, I must take notice that our ladies have of late thrown aside this fig-leaf, and exposed in its primitive nakedness that gentle swelling of the breast which it was used to conceal.

*The Guardian*

### 1713

The Duke and Duchess of Shrewsbury arrived here a little while ago. She, a large woman who once was beautiful, wore a very low-necked bodice, her hair behind the ears, lots of rouge and patches. She thought our ladies' headdress ridiculous, which indeed it was. It was a structure of wire, ribbons, hair and geegaws more than two feet high which placed the head in the middle of the body. It shook with every movement and was extremely uncomfortable. The King, in everything else an absolute dictator, could not endure them; they had been worn for more than ten years and no matter what he said or did, could not get rid of them. What the King could not achieve was accomplished with surprising rapidity by a silly old foreigner. After being so extremely high they then fell extremely low. These simpler easier hair styles, which are much more becoming, are still worn.

SAINT-SIMON, *Mémoires*

### 1714

Among the several female extravagancies I have already taken notice of, there is one which still keeps its ground. I mean that of the ladies who dress themselves in a hat and feather, a riding coat and a perriwig, or at least tie up their hair in a bag of ribbon, in imitation of the smart part of the opposite sex.

*The Spectator*

### 1718–1721

1718. It was Mme de Montespan who designed the *robes battantes* to conceal her pregnancies because this style of dress hid her figure. But when she appeared in them it was precisely as if she had publicly announced that which she affected to conceal, for everybody at Court would say: 'Mme de Montespan has put on her *robe battante* so she must be pregnant'.

1721. I only follow the fashions from afar and there are some which I will have nothing to do with, like paniers which I won't wear and *robes battantes* which I detest. I find them indecent and will not allow them in my presence. They look as if one was just going to bed. There are no regulations about fashion; tailors, all those who make dresses, and hair-dressers invent them to please themselves.

MADAME, DUCHESSE D'ORLÉANS, *Correspondence*

### 1720–1723

1720. At present all the ladies are cutting their hair and only keep a few short bits at the back which they curl and call a *tignon: le corps en sac*, which they call a sack and wear everywhere, even in church, is a long gown undraped and buttoning in front–*le cul en panier*, which has been worn for the last two years, is a sort of farthingale which they put under their skirts to make them fuller and wider round the bottom. They have taken this fashion from Englishwomen and call it a panier.

1721. Indian cottons–A law was passed on 8 July 1721 giving the penalties against those who sell or wear cottons. Life imprisonment for those who bring them into the country and also for those who trade in and stock them. Banishment for the tailors, rag-men, mantua-makers. For a second offence the galleys for the men and perpetual banishment for the women. A fine of 3,000 liv. for those who wear them, etc.

1723. All the ladies are again wearing robes of Indian cotton although this has been so often prohibited; another law was passed on the 5 July which will be again ignored in three months time.

MATHIEU MARAIS, *Journal et Mémoires*

### 1733–1738

1733. Royal Wedding–the Princess of Orange's dress was the prettiest thing that ever was seen–a *corps de robe*, that is, in plain English, a stiff-bodied gown.

1738. Court dress–the Duchess of Bedford's clothes were the most remarkably fine, though finery was so common it was hardly distinguished, and my little pretension to it, you may imagine, was easily eclipsed by such spurious brightness. The Duchess of Bedford's petticoat was green paduasoy, embroidered very richly with gold and silver and a few colours; the pattern was festoons of shells, coral, corn, corn-flowers and sea-weeds; everything in different works of gold and silver except the flowers and coral, the body of the gown white satin, with a mosaic pattern of gold; facings, robings and train the same as the petticoat; there was an abundance of embroidery, and many people in gowns and petticoats of different colours.

MRS. DELANY, *Autobiography and Correspondence*

1740

Royal Wedding–Mrs Purcell sent to me yesterday, to ask if I would see the princess Mary's clothes and laces. . . . There are four night-gowns (three trimmed), and one blue tabby embroidered with silver; four sacks or robes, all trimmed–that for the wedding-night is silver tissue, faced and doubled to the bottom before with pink-coloured satin, and trimmed with a silver *point d'Espagne*. The stiff-bodied gown she is to be married in is very nearly the same as the princess royal's was. . . . There are four more fine gowns besides these; four fine laced Brussels heads–two looped and two grounded; and two extremely fine point ones, with ruffles and tippets; six French caps and ruffles; handkerchiefs, etc. without number.

COUNTESS HART-POMFRET, *Correspondence*

1751–1754

1751. You ask me whether sacks are generally worn; I am so partial to 'em that I have nothing else–a sack and apron, with a very small hoop, when I am undressed, the whole ones when I set out.

1754. One thing is new, which is, there is not such a thing as a decent old woman left, everybody curls their hair, shews their necks, and wears pink, but your humble servant. People who have covered their heads for fifty years now leave off caps and think it becomes them, in short we try to out-do our patterns, the French in every ridiculous vanity.

LADY JANE COLE, *Letters*

## MIDDLE OF THE EIGHTEENTH CENTURY

Most English women are fair and have pink and white complexions, soft though expressive eyes, and slim, pretty figures, of which they are very proud and take great care, for in the morning, as soon as they rise they don a sort of bodice which encircles their waists tightly. They are fond of ornaments, and old and young alike, wear four or five patches, and always two large ones on the forehead. Few women curl their hair, and they seldom wear ribbons, feathers, or flowers, but little head-dresses of cambric or of magnificent lace on their pretty, well-kept hair. They pride themselves on their neatly shod feet, on their fine linen, and on their gowns which are made according to the season either of rich silk or cotton from the Indies. Very few women wear woollen gowns. Even servant-maids wear silks on Sundays and holidays, when they are almost as well dressed as their mistresses. Gowns have enormous hoops, short and very wide sleeves, and it is the fashion to wear little mantles of scarlet or of black velvet, and small hats of straw that are vastly becoming. Ladies even of the highest rank are thus attired when they go walking or to make a simple visit.

CÉSAR DE SAUSSURE, *A Foreign View of England in the Reigns of George I and George II*

1754

The hoop has been known to expand and contract itself from the size of a butter churn to the circumference of three hogsheads. . . . At present it is nearly of an oval form, and scarce measures from end to end above twice the length of the wearer. The hoop has indeed, lost much of its credit in the female world, and has suffered much from the innovation of short sacks and negligées; which, it must be confessed, are equally becoming to the lady of pleasure and the lady of quality.

*The Connoisseur*

1754

Two or three days before the Court leaves for Fontainebleau or Compiègne ladies are permitted to wear a robe de chambre. Those who are not travelling or who do not go in the carriages of the Queen, Madame la Dauphine or Mesdames, must always wear full Court dress.

DUC DE LUYNES, *Mémoires de la Cour de Louis XV*

1757–1760

BILLS FROM THE RUSSELL PAPERS

1757 August 4. Hoop Maker S. BROWN

The Right Honourable the Lady Caroline Russell

| | £ | s. | d. |
|---|---|---|---|
| To a blue hoop | 1. | 8. | 0. |
| Paid for eleven yards of lutestring at 6s. per yard | 3. | 6. | 0. |
| Paid for pinking the flounce | | 14. | 0. |
| For flouncing a hoop | | 14. | 0. |
| Paid for a hoop box | | 4. | 0. |

1758 Habit Maker WILLIAM THOMPSON

Riding Habit for the Right Honourable Lady Caroline Russell

| | | | |
|---|---|---|---|
| 12 yards fine white jean at 3s. 6d. per yard | 2. | 2. | 0. |
| 3¾ yards superfine blue cloth at 18s. per yard | 3. | 7. | 6. |
| 4½ yards white silk serge at 5s. per yard | 1. | 4. | 9. |
| Gold and silver buttons | 1. | 11. | 2. |
| Making the habit, with linings, pockets, etc. | 2. | 14. | 0. |

1758 October 15                                    Sack Maker F. METIVIER (man)

The Honourable Lady Caroline Russell Debtor to Francis Metivier

| | | | |
|---|---|---|---|
| To making a black silk sack and Petticoat | 1. | 1. | 0. |
| To pinking | | 4. | 0. |
| To lining, binding and buttons | | 5. | 6. |

1759 January 27

| | | | |
|---|---|---|---|
| To making a bombazine sack | 1. | 6. | 0. |
| To lining and binding | | 5. | 0. |

1760 June 2                                    Mantua Makers, E. & J. MUNDAY

The Right Honourable Lady Caroline Russell Debtor to Elizabeth and Jane Munday

| | | | |
|---|---|---|---|
| Making a pink and silver gown and coat | | 14. | 0. |
| Body lining | | 2. | 6. |
| Full trimming the gown and coat | 1. | 10. | 0. |
| Making a striped lady's gown and apron | | 8. | 0. |
| Body, sleeve linings and ferret | | 4. | 6. |
| Pinking, trimming, and stomacher | | 6. | 0. |
| October 9 Making a crepe gown | | 8. | 0. |
| Body and sleeve linings | | 4. | 0. |
| Pinking the ruffles | | 2. | 0. |
| Making a bombazine gown and coat | | 14. | 0. |
| Body and sleeve linings | | 4. | 0. |
| Ferret and buttons | | 2. | 6. |

GLADYS SCOTT THOMSON, *The Russells in Bloomsbury*

1761

I then went to Lady Bute's where I saw (except those for her Head) all the Queen's Jewells. There are an amazing number of Pearls of a most beautiful Colour and prodigious Size. There are Diamonds for the facings and Robings of her Gown, set in sprigs of Flowers; her Ear Rings are three drops, the Diamonds of an immense Size and fine Water, they are all well set and very light. The Necklace consists of large Brilliants set round; there is a string of the same to hold a Cross. The Stomacher, which is valued at £60,000 is the finest piece of Magnificence and Workmanship I ever saw. The Fond is a Network as fine as Cat Gut of Small Diamonds and the rest is a large pattern of Natural Flowers, composed of very large Diamonds, one of which is 18, another 16 and a third 10 Thousand Pounds apiece. The middle Drop of the Ear Rings cost £12,000.

DUCHESS OF NORTHUMBERLAND, *Diaries of a Duchess*

1761–1766

1761. If anything should put you off coming (which I hope it won't), pray send a pair of stays for a measure, as the embroidery is to be measured upon them, and that is the longest piece of work.

1766. To be perfectly genteel you must be dress'd thus. Your hair need not be cut off, for 'tis too pretty, but it must be powdered, curled in very small curls, and altogether be in the style of Ly Tavistock's, neat, but it must be high before and give your head the look of a sugar loaf a little. The roots of the hair must be drawn up straight, and not frized at all for half an inch above the root; you must wear no cap, and only 'little little' flowers dab'd in on the left side; the only feather permitted is a black or white sultane perched up on the left side, and your diamond feather against it. A broad, puffed ribbon collier with a tippet ruff, or only a little handkerchief very narrow over the shoulders; your stays very high and pretty tight at bottom; your gown trimmed with the same straight down the robings, and a narrow flounce at bottom, to button with a *compere*, and to be loose at the fore part of your robing. The sleeves long and loose, the waist very long, the flounces and ruffles of a decent length not too long nor so hideously short as they now wear them. No trimming on the sleeves but a ribbon knot tied to hang on the ruffles.

LADY SARAH LENNOX, *Life and Letters*

1768

False locks to supply deficiency of native hair, pomatum in profusion, greasy wool to bolster up the adopted hair, and grey powder to conceal the dust—A hairdresser is described as asking a lady how long it was since her head had been opened and repaired; she answered, not above nine weeks; to which he replied that that was as long as a head could well go in summer; and that therefore it was proper to deliver it now, as it began to be a little *hazardé*.

*London Magazine*

1770

Paris—Vast bouquets are quite the fashion here! the Ladys suit their Colours to that of their clothes. The little Madame had one last night at the Opera of Roses only very near as big as herself which is saying a great deal.

DUCHESS OF NORTHUMBERLAND, *Diaries of a Duchess*

1771

Very few English women with their own natural complexions look well in powder; it requires that quantity of rouge the French women constantly wear to give it a sufficient relief.

Notice is hereby given, that, at the installation at Windsor, on Thursday the 25 instant, ladies are expected to appear in the chapel or hall there, full dressed with hoops; but ladies who propose to dance, and such as shall sit in the front rows at the ball in the evening, are expected to come full dressed, as to the Court at St James.

*Lady's Magazine*

1775

Marie Antoinette – The Queen sent the Empress her mother her portrait shewing her new style of dress, that is to say, her head ornamented with many very high feathers. It is said that this august sovereign returned it to her saying that there must have been some mistake as she had received a portrait, not of the Queen of France, but of an actress.

BACHAUMONT, *Mémoires Secrets*

1775

I hear nothing but balls and high heads – so enormous that nobody can sit upright in their coaches, but stoop forward as if they had got the children's collick.

MRS. DELANY, *Autobiography and Correspondence*

1776–1777

1776. The true art of dress is, in my opinion, and in the opinion of many others – (however singular it may seem) – to wear every thing which is suitable to the complexion, size, etc. – yet is this art so little understood, or so inconsiderately neglected, that we frequently see very large women in short sacks and petticoats; crooked women in jackets; and others, who have long backs and thin shapes in scanty night-gowns, which look as if they were glewed to their side.

1777       *The Ladies Head-Dresss*

*Give Chloe a bushel of horse-hair and wool,*
 *Of paste and pomatum a pound,*
*Ten yards of gay ribbon to deck her sweet skull*
 *And Gauze to encompass it round.*

*Of all the bright colours the rainbow displays*
 *Be those ribbons which hang on her head,*
*Be her flounces adapted to make the folks gaze,*
 *And about the whole work be they spread.*

*Let her flaps fly behind, for a yard at the least,*
 *Let her curls meet just under her chin,*
*Let those curls be supported, to keep up the jest,*
 *With an hundred, instead of one pin.*

> *Let her gown be tuck'd up to the hip on each side,*
> *Shoes too high for to walk or to jump;*
> *And, to deck the sweet creature complete for a bride,*
> *Let the cork-cutter make her a rump.*
>
> *Thus finish'd in taste, while on Chloe you gaze,*
> *You may take the dear charmer for life;*
> *But never undress her–for, out of her stays*
> *You'll find you have lost half your wife.*
>
> *Lady's Magazine*

## 1778

She has a very pretty little figure, with a face not handsome, but well enough, and her dress in the afternoon is a polonaise trimmed with gauze; upon recollection, I am telling you wrong, for it is a *Circassian*, all over loops and tassels (like the one Mrs Stuart brought from Paris last year), and a little black *Henri Quatre* hat upon her head, with her hair dressed up to it behind. In a morning she wears an orange-coloured habit embroidered, or rather embossed, with gold, and a great rich gold stuff waistcoat, with broad laced ruffles, and a little white beaver hat with a bunch of white feathers upon the top, and a black stock, so that she looks the finest French figure you ever saw. Everything seems to go on in a great state here. The Duchess appears in a sack and hoop and diamonds in an afternoon.

LADY LOUISA STUART, *Gleanings from an Old Portfolio*

## 1778

I have been at as great a loss to get you a few yards of the Indian dimity. Your neighbour, Manchester, has brought that manufacture to so great a perfection, that it is difficult to know which is right. However, I cut the matter short by sending you four yards, ell-wide, that I had by me, of finer than I can meet with, and I am sure it is Indian, tho' not now as white as Manchester, but will wash of a very good colour.

MRS. DELANY, *Autobiography and Correspondence*

## 1779

The Duchess told me that a habit-maker returned from Ampthill is gone stark in love the Lady Ossory, on fitting her with the new dress. I think they call it a *Levite*, and says he never saw so glorious a figure–I know that; and so would you be in a hop-sack, Madam–but where the deuce is the grace in a man's nightgown bound round with a belt.

HORACE WALPOLE, *Letters*

1782–1783

Ladies are better dressed today than they have ever been before in a style which combines lightness, freshness, elegance and decency. Dresses of light materials can be renewed more often than those resplendent with gold and silver; they take their colours from the flowers, changing with each season. Only the hands of the *marchande de modes* can give such variety to gauze, lawn and ribbon. . . . Colbert said that fashion was to France what the mines of Peru were to Spain. The imagination of the *marchandes de modes* who invent new models is inexhaustible: a special journal gives details of all the many designs which differ, not only for Court, town, and country, but also for the salon, the boudoir, and the *chaises longues*. The *marchandes de modes* are artists who are as much superior to bonnet-makers as Voltaire is to Maisonneuve. The sempstresses who cut and sew the dresses and the tailors who make the stays and corsets are the masons of the edifice and the *marchand de modes* who creates the accessories that give the final graceful touches, is the architect and decorator.

LOUIS-SÉBASTIEN MERCIER, *Tableau de Paris*

1783

Marie Antoinette–It is understandable that I preferred to paint the Queen in simple dresses instead of full Court Dress and the large panier. These portraits were given to her friends, sometimes to ambassadors. One of them showed her wearing a straw hat and in a white muslin dress with the sleeves gathered close to the arm; when this was exhibited at the Salon some malicious tongues said the Queen was wearing a chemise. For this was 1783 and already people were slandering her.

MME VIGÉE-LEBRUN, *Souvenirs*

1783

The Salon–Mme le Brun has exhibited three portraits of the royal family–the Queen, Monsieur and Madame. The two princesses are wearing chemises, a dress recently devised by the ladies. Some have thought it improper to expose to public view these august persons in dresses which should be reserved for their private apartments, so it is to be presumed that the painter received permission as she would not otherwise have taken such a liberty.

BACHAUMONT, *Mémoires Secrets*

1783–1785

1783. The Duchesse de Bourbon had introduced at the Court of Montbéliard, a fashion that we all hastened to adopt; it was that of *cadogans*, hitherto worn only by gentlemen. Nothing could be prettier or more gallant-looking when one wears it with the little hat and plume.

1785. It had been the fashion for some years to wear two watches. The watch-chains were loaded with ornaments called *breloques*–trifles which were often very expensive.

BARONESS D'OBERKIRCH, *Mémoires*

## 1783–1784

1783. My wife, though she has as peacable a man for her husband, as any in the three kingdoms, whips on her habit, as soon as she gets out of bed, sets down to breakfast in her beaver, and goes to market in her boots: she appears, indeed in no other dress till toward evening; then all close covering is thrown off, and she sallies forth in a large bell-hoop, low stays, and so transparent a piece of drapery is thrown over the bosom, that it discovers, what it attempts, apparently, to conceal. Now I cannot, by any means, approve of this method of dressing: she is so inclosed from head to foot all day, when she is with me, that I cannot see a single charm lower than her chin; at seven, or eight, in the evening, she is quite undressed for company, and every man who falls in her way, has an opportunity to gaze on those beauties which are exhibited for the observation of all men.

1784. When down dances my rib in white, but so bepukered and plaited, I could not tell what to make of her: so turning about, I cried, 'Hey, Sally, my dear, what new frolic is this? It is like none of the gowns you used to wear.' 'No, my dear,' crieth she, 'it is no gown, it is the *chemise de la reine*'. 'My dear,' replied I, hurt at this gibberish, which I was half ashamed to own I did not understand; 'What is it? You know I am not like you, master of French; let us have the name of your new dress in downright English.' 'Why then,' said she, 'if you must have it, it is the queen's shift.' Mercy on me, thought I, what will the world come to, when an oilman's wife comes down to serve in the shop, not only in her own shift, but in that of a queen.

*Lady's Magazine*

## 1784

I went to the concert in one of the muslin chemises with fine lace that the Queen of France gave me. . . . In the Evening I went to the Ball. I had an English night gown of muslin with small silver sprigs and all white.

Georgina, Duchess of Devonshire, *Extracts from Correspondence*

## 1785

Mrs Freeman went to thank their Majesties for their visit the next Court-day. Mrs Freeman thought it would be a sad worry to her, as she had not been at court since Mr Freeman's death, and was fearful no suit she had would do; but luckily on her going to the mantua-maker's she found no alteration in the fashion for court dress for years, whereas common ones change every month. Flounces and trimmings, tho' quite out elsewhere, trebled cuffs and long dangling ruffles as formerly.

*Passages from the Diary of* Mrs. Philip Lybbe Powys

1785

Marie Antoinette—Her Majesty sent for Mlle Bertin and told her that in November she would be thirty years of age: that she wanted her dresses now to be made without all those frivolous additions which were more suitable to younger women; that she would no longer wear feathers or flowers. The etiquette for dress also has been changed so that the Queen will no longer wear *Pierrots, Chemises, Redingotes, Polonaises, Levites, Robes à la Turque, Circassiennes;* that the more imposing gowns with pleats will again be worn; that for visits of ceremony the Princesses have been asked to forbid any other styles, and that ladies who arrive so dressed will not be admitted without special permission.

BACHAUMONT, *Mémoires Secrets*

1782–1788

1782. I was soon busily employed to get my first satin gown made. It was of a puce colour, trimmed with white satin, and a petticoat of the same colour to match the trimming.

1784. Abbey Concerts—evening dress with the exception of feathers, which were forbidden. The Queen wore the same character of dress as that in which she appeared at the ancient concerts—a *sacque*, which had a bodice to fit, which met to the lower point, where it branched off, and was trimmed down each side the petticoat, underneath being trimmed to correspond, and the stomacher, being covered with jewels. The part of the gown that denoted the sacque was the fulness required for the back breadth which was laid in deep double plaits between the shoulders, and only once confined about an inch below the original tacks, and hung loose from there. The Queen's train was about three yards in length, and was held up by a page of honour; those of the Court attendants were two yards long and could be looped up elegantly. The sleeve was close to the arm, with rows of lace from the top, terminating in three deep ruffles at the elbow. The material was gold or silver tissue for the dress in summer, and for the winter the tissue in satin. The headdress was a cap with Court lappets, and jewels, but not in profusion. . . . The ladies all wore hoops, but that of the Queen was much smaller than the Court hoop.

1785. It was a brilliant Court. The dresses were showy, as steel embroidery was introduced this season, and very generally worn. My puce satin, for this fourth year, I had trimmed with a row of flat steel down each front, the white being taken off, cap and petticoat being trimmed to match, and steel buckles on black satin shoes.

Fashion was not then *exigeant* in the matter of continual change. A silk gown would go on for years, a little furbished up with new trimmings.

1786. My puce satin was once more done up, with a white gauze handkerchief trimmed with narrow blonde, and with the same on the sleeves and cap, and looked very neat and smart.

1788. My dress was the puce satin, with the trimmed sleeves and gauze handkerchief as before, the ends of it being fastened in front by three white satin broad straps buckled with steel buckles. The last addition was a gauze apron as long as the gown, which met behind at the waist and was finished off with two equal bows and ends lying upon the bustle, and a large nosegay of artificial flowers, given to me by the Princess Elizabeth, and tied by her for the occasion.

MRS. PAPENDIEK, *Private Life in the Time of Queen Charlotte*

## 1785

The intolerable stiffness, added to the great confinement which stays occasion to a lady, make her unfit for the society of either men or women. . . . A well-made woman, requires nothing to amend her shape. The French ladies, who have such an easy carriage, and are in general finely made, never wear any thing more than a quilted waistcoat, which is called *un corset*, without any kind of stiffening. Indeed married women in the summer generally wear less, having even no quilted waistcoat.

The hoop has never totally been laid aside. . . . It has always been considered as a most essential part of the full dress, and indeed, at different periods, looked upon as greatly ornamental in an undress, provided the size be kept within certain bounds; the forms have been also varied, particularly in those of the undress, which, when most contracted, were not only the most becoming, but the most convenient for the purpose. The magnitude of the full dress hoop, carries with it a most noble-majestic appearance, and I hope will never be given up.

*Lady's Magazine*

## c. 1785

Ladies, old and young, at this period, wore preposterous pads behind; and, as if this fashion wanted a counterbalance, enormous false bosoms were contrived of puffed gauze, so that they might be compared to pouter pigeons.

HENRY ANGELO, *Reminiscences*

## 1786

It is already common knowledge that the goddess of fashion suffers from quotidion fever, which, it has often been noticed, at a certain degree of heat runs to madness; as the get-up of four ladies attested, who entered a box during the third play, with such wonderfully fantastic caps and hats perched on their heads, that they were received by the entire audience with loud derision. Their neckerchiefs were puffed up so high that their noses were scarce visible, and their nosegays were like huge shrubs, large enough to conceal a person.

SOPHIE DE LA ROCHE, *Sophie in London*

## 1785–1789

1785. Tunbridge Wells.–Now for Article of fashions. I like your habit very much. I hope you wear no powder, all who have fine hair go without and if you have not quite enough 'tis but buying a few curls. . . . My Habit is what they call Pitch colour–a sort of blackist green not beautiful but the most stilish now worn. Dark blues are very general—indeed all dark colours are fashionable. Cambric frills and white waistcoat. Rather large yellow buttons.

Washing gowns of all kinds are the ton. . . . As a Dress gown I have brought down a Robe à la Turque—violet colour—the peticoat and vest white-Tiffany, gauze and pale yellow ribbons—with that a sash and buckle under the Robe. Gauze gowns and clear muslin gowns are very much worn in full dress. . . . Miss Belsay has taken a particular fancy to every article of dress she has seen me wear and frequently applys for patterns, this I most readily comply with.

1786. London—However you may tell her as a friend gradually to reduce her Stuffing as Rumps are quite out in France and are decreasing here but can not be quite given up till the weather grows warmer. The handkerchiefs are not so much puff'd out . . . the hair loose—curls without pins and the toupée as if it was curled and a comb run thro' it. Aprons very general, chiefly tucked. Most fashionable collours dark green, pale straw collour, and a very bright purple.

1788. Hats are also worn, like riding hats. The Hair universally dress'd very loose in small curls. . . . As to gowns—all kinds—Chemises, Round gowns, with flounce or not. Great coats made very open before to shew the peticoat. . . . I must add to my chapter of Fashions that fur Muffs (very large) and Tippets are universal.

1789. Wednesday they all sup here and there is to be quite a crowd so I make up a new dyed sattin Gown for the occasion. We are to have the Prince, Duke of York, Mrs Fitzherbert, all the fine people. . . . We are all busy making our gowns and aprons for tomorrow Evening so I must leave off.

BETSY SHERIDAN, *Letters from Sheridan's Sister to her Sister in Dublin*

1787–1790

*Livre-Journal of Madame Éloffe, Marchande de Modes To Marie Antoinette*

1787. 20 March. FOR THE QUEEN—30 aunes of striped muslin with embroidered scalloped border to trim a pierrot and skirt, round the skirt and cuffs, at 7s.=10f. 10s. (at seven franks per aune, and twenty sous to the frank, the total for thirty aunes is ten franks ten sous); making and applying the trimmings to the pierrot and skirt, 9f.; 30 aunes muslin with embroidered scalloped border for a second pierrot and skirt, at 7s.=10f. 10s.; making, 9f.

1 November. FOR THE QUEEN—2 aunes ¼ blonde lace to go round a corset of clear red velvet with gold sequins, at 4f.=9f.; 1 aune ½ bordered tulle, for ruffling on the sleeves of the corset, at 3f.=4f. 10s; ⅔ fine silver braid for the sleeves, at 3f.=2f.; making the trimming for the corset, 1f. 4s.

1788. 26 May. FOR THE QUEEN—3 aunes ⅝ of very beautiful lawn batiste for 3 very large fichus at 26f.=94f. 5s; making the 3 fichus, at 8s.=1f. 4s.; repairing a robe of lawn 1f. 4s.; lengthening 3 lawn skirts, 3f.; repairing a second robe of lawn, 1f. 4s.; lengthening 2 skirts, 2f.; remaking the waistbelt of 2 gauze skirts, 1f. 16s.

19th November. FOR THE QUEEN–2 aunes $\frac{3}{4}$ black taffeta, for the outside of a wadded cape, at 5f.=3f. 15s.; 2 aunes $\frac{3}{4}$ black taffeta for the lining, at 4f. 10s.=12f. 8s.; 12 aunes $\frac{1}{4}$ black lace *d'Angleterre*, for trimming, at 19f.=232f. 15s.; 1 aune $\frac{3}{4}$ English ribbon to go through the slot at 22s.=1f. 19s.; wadding and making, 5f.

1790. 29 January. FOR THE QUEEN–Making the trimming for a Court dress of cerise velvet trimmed with 3 bands of martin fur on the skirt, and one at the bottom of the robe, 15f.; retrimming a short cape of blond lace and martin, 4f.; 1 aune $\frac{3}{4}$ English ribbon to tie the cape, at 22s.=1f. 19s.

COMTE DE REISET, Modes et Usages au Temps de Marie Antoinette

## 1789

All the sex now–from fifteen to fifty and upwards (I should rather say downwards) appear in their white muslin frocks, with broad sashes, with their hair curled over their foreheads, and hanging down behind, to the bottom of their backs–and all without caps.

There have always been some few amongst us who seem to have changed sexes; and of late, I think, women appear, in their great coats, neckcloths, and half-boots, with so masculine an air, that if their features are not very feminine indeed, they may easily be mistaken for young fellows; especially when a watch is suspended on each side of a petticoat. While men, making the same appearance to the waist at least, with the addition of a large muff and shawl, it may be certainly difficult at first, to know in what manner to address so equivocal a figure; and whether sir or madam would be the most proper appellation.

Lady's Magazine

## 1798

I believe I shall make my new gown like my robe, but the back of the latter is all in a piece with the tail, and will 7 yards enable me to copy it in that respect?

JANE AUSTEN, Letters

## END OF THE EIGHTEENTH CENTURY

Old ladies were once a species apart, they were sexless and had no pretensions to gallantry or fashion. Now the poor old ladies distress me when I see their flowered caps, *fichus menteurs* and their juvenile paraphernalia; involuntarily one compares them with their grandchildren, and the result is indeed frightful. I believe that the ridiculous get-up of old women is largely responsible for the lack of respect, or rather the insolence, shewn them by young people nowadays.

LA MARQUISE DE CRÉQUY, Souvenirs

1792

Drawing-room for the King's Birthday.–Her Majesty, upon this occasion, was dressed with more magnificence than we remember to have ever seen her before.

The petticoat was of green silk, entirely covered with Brussels point, thrown very fully over it, with a loose drapery of lilac silk, covered with lace, and drawn up in festoons with large bouquets of diamonds, each bouquet consisting of one large rosette, from which rise bending sprigs in imitation of snow-drops. From each rosette fall two large diamond chains and tassels, and upon each festoon of the drapery, is a chain of large diamonds.

At the bottom, a flounce of fine lace, headed with rows of large diamonds.

The robe and train white and silver silk, trimmed round with a border of lilac silk covered with lace. The cap blonde, with bandaus, and girdle of diamonds.

Each bouquet of the petticoat has a central stone in the rosette valued at 2,000 pounds; the rosette, including the stone is valued at 3,000; and the bouquets, of which there are six, at 8,000 each. Adding to the amount of these that of the other diamonds upon the petticoat, and those upon the head-dress and stomacher, the dress worn by her majesty could not be worth less than an hundred thousand pounds; and the taste displayed in the arrangement of the whole was well suited to such an expenditure.

*The Lady's Magazine*

PART THREE

Nineteenth Century
1795-1890

# 1795-1810

In the last quarter of the eighteenth century many contributory factors had been preparing the way to another complete change in dress design. The 1790's were years of transition, when the popularity of cotton and muslin influenced cutting, and the classical styles of the new French Republic finally decided the course the new line would follow and hastened its acceptance.

The draped folds of the large fichu billowing above the low neck of the *robe à l'Anglaise*, and the softly gathered bodice of the *chemise de la reine* with its deep waist sash were styles admirably suited to fine muslin–a material that requires soft folds and little shaping. By 1790 the eye too had grown accustomed to the new fullness at the top of the body, and the waistline began to rise. After years of constriction the natural roundness of a woman's body was creating a new fashion line. See plate 40; Diagrams XXXII, XXXIII, XXXIV.

## ROUND ROBE

This dress was a combination of the *chemise de la reine* and the *robe à l'Anglaise*. Sometimes it was cut without a waist seam, but as a rule the bodice and skirt were cut separately and joined at the waist. By 1795 the robe had become very high-waisted but was still very full. The back at first retained the numerous seams of the long 1780's bodice but as the waist rose they were gradually eliminated until only the two back seams remained. These were narrow on the shoulders and almost met at the waist. The shoulder seam was still set far to the back, starting from the very short back neckline and running down into the armhole, where it usually met the back side seam. This gave a very small back which was further emphasized by the sleeve being still set far in. The cut is similar to that of the 1630's bodice, and helps to mitigate the bulk of a high-waisted dress with full skirt. There were many variations for the front bodice. It was gathered at neck and waist, or fitted and worn with a fichu, or the fichu was incorporated in the bodice which gave a V or cross-over front. The skirt was cut from several widths of material, usually unshaped, and the fullness was gathered in front, but the back generally arranged in small box pleats over a pad. The sleeve was fitted but varied in length, being either short, to the elbow, or down to the wrists.

131

By the end of the eighteenth century the Greek influence was reflected in the robe *à l'athénienne* which was the round robe divested of its fullness and cut from the most diaphanous materials. The bodice had the same variations of style as before but with the front fullness considerably reduced. From early in the nineteenth century this bodice often fitted very closely round the breasts and was cut very low, with short sleeves. The front of the skirt had no fullness, but required a little gathering at the sides to allow for the discrepancy in width between rib cage and hips; sometimes the front was gored on the side seams, which eliminated the gathers at the waist and threw the skirt out at the back. Extra fullness gathered into the centre back allowed for movement, though sometimes, if the skirt was very narrow, it was slit up the side seam. Sometimes there might be a tunic overskirt, suggesting the Greek *peplos*. The robes of this period always had very long trains which by being held out on the ground, or caught up and wrapped over the arm, drew the muslin close to the body to outline the limbs. They usually fastened centre back, but, from 1800 to *c.* 1810, there was another construction which was very common – the bib, or apron front. The bodice back and side fronts were mounted on a lining which had front flaps that pinned round the breasts to act as a kind of brassière. The skirt was attached to the bodice across the back, and then slit on either side. The front of the robe bodice was sewn to the front of the skirt, tapes being attached either side at the waist. When the apron front had been placed in position it was pinned on each shoulder and the tapes tied at the back, either outside or under the skirt. By *c.* 1806 day dresses no longer had a train.

For day wear, the bodice could be high to the neck or have the low front filled in by a habit shirt or chemisette. Sleeves, long or short, were becoming fuller and an over-sleeve was very general. Sometimes the sleeves were cut on the cross, and the bodice also. Men's pantaloons and breeches had been cut from the cross way of the material from the end of the eighteenth century so it is not surprising to find this method now being applied to women's clothes. The cross grain is more elastic than the straight weave; it clings closer to the body and requires less seaming. This use of the cross grain to fit the front of the body was to become the characteristic cut which gave the nineteenth-century woman her well-rounded bust. See plates 40–43; Diagrams XXXII, XXXIV, XXXV.

## OPEN GOWN

This dress, worn with the closed robe or a petticoat, was also derived from the *robe à l'Anglaise* and was worn during the 1790's. The cut was the same as that of the closed robe. Sometimes the centre back was cut in one to the ground, while inverted pleats starting from the high waist centre back and back side seams gave the necessary fullness to the skirt. Occasionally the fronts also were cut in one, but as a rule there was a waist seam. The front bodice had the same variations of style as the front of the round robe but was always more fitted. There was a train at the back, and the skirts were open in front, or met, or crossed over, or were set far to the sides of the bodice. The sleeves were usually long and fitting. When the day dresses lost their trains an over dress which opened down the front, the 'pelisse', began to be worn. It was cut like the round robe, sometimes in cotton, but more usually in warmer materials that could be lined with fur. See plates 40, 42a, 42c; Diagram XXXIV.

## COURT DRESS

In England the hoop petticoat was obligatory Court wear until 1820. It was worn with a train, drapes, and the high feather head-dress, the bodice following contemporary fashion.

When France became an Empire Napoleon ordered ceremonial dress to be worn at the French Court. The woman's dress was cut like her fashionable robe but with a separate train from the high waist, attached to the centre back with large hooks and to the sides by smaller ones. The short puffed sleeves had also long detachable sleeves for very official occasions. The neck was very low in front, dipping to a V at the centre back. A standing collar of lace, the *cherusque*, followed the neckline round the back and over the shoulders.

## OTHER TYPES

The riding habit was cut like the robe, but had, of course, longer skirts. The bodice, with short basques sides and front, had long sleeves, collar, cuffs, and was double-breasted, or open to show the habit shirt. Bodice and skirt were joined, or were attached at the back only with an apron front skirt, or were sometimes two separate pieces. This habit was made in cloth as a rule, but sometimes carried out in heavy cotton (nankeen) for summer. It was still worn for travelling.

The spencer was a short jacket, cut like the bodice, with high collar and long sleeves. It was usually made of dark velvet and worn open in front. There were also various capes and mantles.

## MATERIALS, DECORATIONS, ETC.

The texture of materials in the late 1780's and at the beginning of the nineteenth century was extremely light and soft, especially the Indian muslins. Other dress materials were cambric, lawn, printed cotton, cashmere, silk, satin, velvet, etc. The open robe of the late 1790's was usually of very thin, light, crisp silk with narrow stripes or small spot patterns. No applied trimmings destroyed the hang of the materials, but the cottons and muslin dresses, which were invariably white, were delicately embroidered with floral and Greek patterns used as borders, as all-over spot motifs, or in vertical lines. This embroidery was usually white as well, but for evening wear gold and silver thread and tiny sequins were used. French Court dress was always heavily decorated in gold and silver, with gold fringes, tassels, etc.

A ruff of fine lawn or lace, the 'betsie', was worn round the neck of high-necked dresses, or a neckerchief round the shoulders crossed in front and tied round the waist at the back. Long aprons almost covering the skirt were also worn. The classical line was preserved by the wearing of shawls and long scarves for warmth, especially by the fashionable, who wore their dresses very low and their sleeves very short. A great deal of practice and dexterity were essential requisites for the well 'draped' woman. The cashmere shawl, fine, soft and warm, lent itself admirably to this purpose. The first kashmir shawls were sent from Egypt by Napoleon to Joséphine. They were very expensive, but were soon being imitated by manufacturers in France and Scotland. There were also long narrow tippets of fur or swansdown, and large flat muffs, also of swansdown or maribou. Jewellery was influenced by the recent excavations at Pompeii, so that designs for it were Roman rather than Greek. The *parure* for Court wear was still set with precious stones, but now there were also matching ear-rings, necklaces, brooches, hair-combs, etc., carried out in gold with cameos and semi-precious stones, coral, cornelian, garnets, etc. Gold substitutes, such as pinchbeck, imitated the early Roman techniques.

The Marchioness of Townshend in full Court dress

# 1810–1828

Although there was little change in cut, the flowing classical line of the early years of the nineteenth century was beginning to straighten and grow more angular as the soft, untrimmed muslins were replaced by firmer materials and the dress was stiffened by applied decoration.

## DRESS

From *c.* 1810, the cut of the bodice began to settle, with very little variation, into two main types which were worn until the 1840's. If the front had no fullness, it was cut on the cross and fitted by two darts running from the point of each breast in towards the centre front. If gathered, it was cut from the straight of the material and the fullness was evenly distributed round the neck, but at the waist the gathers were drawn in towards the centre front. The back was always cut on the straight with two pieces each side of the centre back opening, the side seams from the armholes slightly curving in towards the centre back at the waist. The shoulder seam was still towards the back, and with a low cut front there were usually separate shoulder pieces, cut from narrow strips of material on the straight. The back also might be gathered like the front, in which case it was usually cut from two pieces only. The armhole had now moved back to its normal position. Sleeves varied between a short puff cut on the cross, or a short puff worn over a long sleeve, or a long sleeve which might be caught in puffs down the arm, etc. From *c.* 1820 the top of the sleeve began to expand. Flounced epaulettes soon became the ornate 'mancherons' which were much worn, especially in the 1820's with the larger sleeve. In the 1820's also, a long transparent sleeve was worn over the short puffed one for evening dress.

The line of the skirt in 1810 was still straight, but by 1825 it had gradually widened at the base to become very triangular. There were no trains, except for Court wear. The skirt, which cleared the ground, was always gored, the angle of the gores becoming more acute as the skirt widened. At first, and for simple dresses, the skirt was cut from two pieces and the front gored each side. Later, and more usually, an extra gore was added each side. Occasionally, in the 1820's, there were two gores each side, but the centre back was always straight. The seams were

135

set gore to straight so that the skirt hung close to the body in front and was thrown out at the
back, the fullness which was gathered across the back being more concentrated at the centre
back, and sometimes at the centre back only. In very soft silks the side seams are sometimes gore
to gore, for soft materials pucker when sewn cross to straight. When the bottom of the skirt
widened the hem was often padded to hold it out. Small bustle pads were sometimes worn.

The bodice was always very high-waisted though it varied slightly and some years was very
high indeed. From 1820 it lengthened and was set into a waist band, and by 1825 it had reached
the normal waist. The centre front was sometimes slightly pointed, or worn with a Swiss belt
which is pointed above and below the waist centre front.

The pelisse, or carriage dress, was cut like the dress but open down the front, as it could be
worn over another dress. It was high to the neck with a collar and often with one or more
capes. The centre back was sometimes cut in one with the skirt, without a waist seam, and was
then pleated at the waist instead of gathered. The spencer was still worn, but now it fastened
up the front and was made from various materials. See plates 44, 45; Diagrams XXVII,
etc.

## MATERIALS, DECORATIONS, ETC.

Cottons became firmer and there were many variations of woven stripes and spot patterns;
many all white, but some with colours. More silks, foulards, satins, etc. were being worn, and
for evening crape, net, fine muslin, etc. were worn over silk or satin slips. Embroidered white
muslins were still worn but now the embroidery was sometimes in colours, and the embroidery
was heavier and coarser. There were many applied trimmings, at first light but later heavier—
round the bottom of the skirt, on the bodice and sleeves. Tucks, flounces, vandyked frills and
ruching appeared round the bottom of the skirts; for evening it would be gauze caught with
narrow rouleaux of satin or silk, leaf and vandyke trimmings bound with narrow piping, or
bindings of satin or silk, artificial flowers, etc., or embroidered with gold, silver, and spangles.
Shawls were still worn, as were also tippets, but muffs became smaller. There was less jewellery,
and this consisted mainly of brooches, lockets, and crosses on chains round the neck.

# 1828-1840

◦◦◦◦◦◦◦◦

From the beginning of the century a new form of stays or corset began to develop. It was a long, fitted under-bodice shaped to the body by the insertion of gussets at the top which gave roundness to the breasts, and gussets at the bottom to allow for the hips. It had a centre front busk, and bones for lacing centre back. Later, when the bodice fitted down to the waist, more seams were added and more bones, with sometimes a basque for the hips instead of gussets. This was the basic cut of corsets during most of the nineteenth century, until the late 1880's.

The angular line which had been developing for some time reached its peak in the 1830's, when the extension at the top of the dress and the extension at the base formed two triangles, the apexes meeting at the waist. In the late 1830's, when the sleeve collapsed, the silhouette became more rounded.

## DRESS

Bodices were cut as before but were now invariably lined. Instead of being trimmed with applied decoration the outer material was often draped. Pleated folds from the shoulders met centre front, or crossed over, or were draped to form a bertha round the top of the bodice. This drapery was cut on the cross and then arranged on to the tight-fitting lining front and then back and seamed together on the shoulders and underarm. The shoulder seams were low at the back and the back side seams curved from the armhole in to the centre back. The neckline widened and the top of the armhole moved out on to the shoulder. By the end of the 1820's the sleeve had become so extended that it required extra support underneath – down-filled pads, stiffened interlining, whalebones, etc. They were known as 'gigot', or 'leg of mutton' sleeves. Their triangular shape, very full at the top and fitting at the wrist, was achieved by cutting the sleeve on the cross with a large circular head. For evening the sleeves were wide and short, and still often worn with a tansparent over-sleeve. Mancherons and wide collars gave further emphasis to the shoulder width. Then, in 1836, having reached its ultimate fullness, the sleeve rather suddenly began to collapse. At first the excessive material at the top was gathered or

137

pleated to fit round the top of the arm, but as the eye became accustomed to the new line the sleeve became close-fitting.

By 1828 the skirt was shorter—ankle length—and no longer gored but cut from several widths of unshaped material. The fullness was at first arranged in pleats radiating from the centre front and round the sides and gathered at the centre back. By the end of the 1830's it was gathered all round. The bustle (a padded roll), or extra flounces, held the dress out at the back.

With the large sleeves the pelisse was no longer practical as an over-garment, but it continued to exist as the pelisse-dress. The pelisse proper was replaced by capes, sometimes with wide hanging sleeves. See plates 46, 47; Diagrams XLI, XLII.

## MATERIALS, DECORATIONS, ETC.

At first the dresses were still trimmed with applied decoration, which now was placed on the skirts at knee level. Later, with the large sleeves, draped bodice and fuller skirt, there was less applied decoration and more of patterned materials—printed cotton, chintz, patterned challis (a mixture of silk and wool), cashmere, merino, etc. For evening, silks and coloured gauzes were used. With less trimming, there were now more accessories: wide collars spreading over the shoulders; fichu-pelerines, that is, wide collars with long fichu ends that hung down in front or were caught in to the belt; canezous, that is, chemisettes that came down to the waist front and back and were worn over the bodice. All these were made in fine white lawn or muslin, embroidered or trimmed with frills, lace, etc. The fichu-pelerine was also made in silk. There were short aprons, and tippets. More jewellery was worn, gold with semi-precious stones—turquoise, topaz, amethyst, etc., and there were brooches, ear-rings and bracelets to match. Bracelets especially were much worn from the mid twenties. There were jewelled combs and the *ferronière, c.* 1825, this latter was a small jewel or ornament which lay on the middle of the forehead hanging from a chain or ribbon placed round the top of the head.

# 1840-1869 The Crinoline

For the next twenty years women's dress was to be dominated by the crinoline. When sleeves decreased, skirts increased, and their growing volume required artificial means of extension. Petticoats of horsehair, *crin*, appeared in the late 1830's and were worn during the 1840's. In the 1850's, whalebone, steel and cane were inserted to extend the base. *C.* 1856 an improved processing of steel, making it light and flexible, produced the cage crinoline, which consisted of many rows of steel held in position by vertical tapes. When the circular form became too large to be comfortable, *c.* 1860, the crinoline flattened in front and swelled out behind. Crinolines were also made in cotton with inserted steels, but the cage variety was lighter.

## 1840-1850

In the early 1840's the bodice became very long and pointed centre front, and by 1845 the centre front was being cut again on the straight of the material. As the front of the bodice was only fitted by means of the waist darts this brought the cross grain on either side of the body. Sometimes there would be one, sometimes two, and occasionally (in the 1850's) three darts each side. These darts, very subtly shaped, began from the point of the breast, curved in and ran down to the waist, almost meeting at the centre front. This cut gave to the nineteenth-century woman the characteristic ogee-shaped body–very different from the rectangular line of the seventeenth and eighteenth centuries. It was used for the foundation fitting of the front bodice right into the early years of the twentieth century, though the line of later corsets modified the curves. In the 1840's the darts were sometimes replaced by seams which continued the dart line up into the shoulder seams, in which case the side pieces were cut separately from the cross grain. From the late 1840's this version was retained for evening bodices only, where it was useful in fitting the low neckline.

Bodices were still cut with extra front fullness. In the 1840's such fullness was usually arranged into pleats which were then stitched into position from bust down to waist. The bodice of the evening dress had a horizontal neckline and a deep falling collar, or the draped bertha of the

139

1830's. The latter, however, was now a separate piece attached to the fitted bodice and made from cross-way strips of material mounted on a bertha-shaped lining. From the late 1840's the full body might be similarly arranged – the fullness being a piece of material separate from the fitted body. The back was cut as before, though some of the 1840 bodices have no back side seams. The shoulder seam was towards the back, and the armhole line very low off the shoulders. C. 1846, the bodice began to be cut with a basque. The sleeves were now tight-fitting and cut on the cross. C. 1844, they began to widen below the elbow. There was often a very short over-sleeve, the 'jockey'. Evening sleeves were very short and fitting.

Skirts were cut from several widths of material, unshaped. From 1841–1850 the waist full-ness was gauged, the gauging pleats being deeper in the centre back where there was more material. This, together with the horsehair petticoat, gave a dome-shaped silhouette. Skirts were now longer, just clearing the ground. Flounces, which at first were just round the bottom, increased in number and began to move higher up the skirt. Bodices and skirts were attached, and fastened at the centre back. See plate 48; Diagrams XLIV, XLV, XLVI.

## 1850–1860

Bodices were back to waist level. For day wear the jacket bodice with its basque was fashionable. This was worn buttoning up the centre front and was now separate from the skirt. When worn over a flounced skirt this basque became, so to speak, the top flounce. The sleeve widened to become the 'pagoda' sleeve. When it became very full it was pleated on top and the pleats were stitched down a couple of inches, or the pleats were mounted on to a very short lining sleeve which was hidden by the jockey. It was usually cut in one piece, and the seam, set rather forward, either sewn or left open. A little later, *c.* 1856, came the 'bishop' sleeve, which was a full two-piece sleeve gathered or pleated top and bottom round the wrist. The neckline of the evening bodice, wide off the shoulders, dipped centre front and was trimmed with flounces or with the draped bertha. The centre back as well as the centre front waistline was usually pointed; the sleeve a short puff.

Skirts continued to increase in width and were unshaped. Thin materials were gathered at the waist, but heavier ones were pleated front and sides and gathered at the centre back. The flounced skirt was more typical. The flounces, which gave added width, were gathered onto the foundation skirt, starting just below waist level. There were many variations of them – two or three deep ones, or a number of shorter ones, or a deep top flounce with shorter ones below, etc. The silhouette was still dome-shaped but the top was flatter and the base wider. See plate 49; Diagram XLVII.

## 1860–1869

With the change of silhouettes – now flat in front, and out behind – the bodice basque was short in front and longer at the back, with inverted pleats from the back side seams and centre back. The waist rose, and by 1863 was quite high. The waistline was straight all round and was worn with a belt, very often a Swiss belt. For informal wear blouses and skirts were introduced. Blouse-bodices, of fine white muslin, often pleated or tucked, might be worn with a bolero, or a Swiss belt, or a Swiss belt with shoulder braces. The bolero was also worn with day dresses though sometimes it was suggested by the trimming. In the early 1860's the pagoda sleeve was being replaced by the bishop sleeve, which in its turn gave way to the two-piece 'coat' sleeve, semi-fitting and three-quarter length, with a cuff. At first the evening bodice might be pointed centre front and centre back; later the pleated back basque, tabs, or a sash were more usual.

In order to hang well over the new-shaped crinoline and to add ever-increasing width round the base, skirts were gored from 1860–the gores being sewn straight to cross in order to throw the skirt out behind. The number of gores varied, the centre back being either on the straight or also gored. The fullness round the waist was set into pleats–inverted pleats centre front which became four double box pleats sides and back. In simpler skirts the back fullness might still be gathered. When the silhouette became more angular, *c.* 1865, the gores became more acute and the front was kept plain, with or without the addition of small side pleats, and with the back fullness set in pleats. As all skirts were now long and trained, from the middle 1860's walking dresses began to be looped up round the bottom. Evening dresses frequently had double skirts. From 1863 onwards dresses began to be cut without a waist seam, *en princesse*, a style named after Princess Alexandra of Wales. The bodice seams fitted into the waist and then swung out to shape the skirt. Skirts were sometimes made with two bodices, one for day, the other for evening. As a rule, bodice and skirt were now separate; day bodices buttoned up centre front and evening bodices either back or front according to style. See plate 50; Diagrams XLVIII XLIX.

## MATERIALS, DECORATIONS, ETC.

To assist the revival of the silk trade, which had suffered with the popularity of cottons, more silks were being used for both day and evening dresses: plain silks, watered silks, gros grains, satins, etc., heavier for day and lighter in weight for evening. Other dress materials were cashmere, merino, and other lightweight woollens, with cottons, piqués, etc. for summer. Flounced summer dresses were made from patterned muslins; for evening wear gauze, tulle, tarlatan, etc. were used.

The demure line of the 1840's was repeated in the simplicity of trimmings, or in the absence of trimming. The ogee-line was emphasized by a band of pleating or ruching which circled the top of the dress behind, and from the shoulders curved in to the centre front and then out again and down the front of the skirt. Sometimes there were tucks or flounces round the bottom of the skirt, or the front only was decorated, *en tablier*. The flounces of the 1850 dresses were often *à disposition*, that is, with the pattern woven in position–deep borders with floral, striped,

Scottish plaid designs, etc. Strips of the patterned piece were also used for bodice and sleeve decoration. The edges of the flounces might be scalloped or be trimmed with fringe. By the middle of the 1860's dresses, especially for evening, were much more trimmed. The style of decoration changed to suit the new gored skirts. Flounces were now only round the bottom of the skirt, or on the under section of a double evening skirt. In the late 1860's flounces began to be pleated. For day wear bands of cross-way material, braid, Hungarian cord (black or white), fringes, beaded braids and fringes, etc., were arranged as motifs to go round the base of the skirt, or *en tablier*, or down the seams. Belts, or sashes with bows and long ends, accentuated the back fullness. In evening bodices, the lines of the bolero and Swiss belt were suggested by using different materials, or by trimming. Evening trimmings were kept very light so that the thin silk and gauze skirts should float out unhampered by their multitudinous but fragile ornamentation of lace flounces, gauze kiltings, pleatings of paper-thin ribbons, flowers, etc.

Small turn-down collars were worn with high-necked bodices, and a chemisette filled in the V-shaped or square (1863) neckline. Full under-sleeves of fine lawn, often embroidered, were worn with the pagoda sleeve. From the 1850's the low neck of the evening bodice was edged with a frill of lace or net drawn up on a narrow black velvet ribbon. More lace was being used – Chantilly, blond, Maltese, etc., in both black and white.

Except for a brooch at the throat little jewellery was worn in the 1840's and 50's. The brooches were usually of gold set with semi-precious stones, or cameos, or mosaic work, etc. Much more jewellery was worn in the 1860's. The elaborate evening dresses worn at the receptions and balls given by the French Imperial Court brought back the *parure*, and with it the coronet, or tiara. The Empress Eugénie's love of pearls made them fashionable again; long drop pearl ear-rings, and necklaces of one or more rows of pearls with a diamond clasp. A row of single stones, precious or semi-precious, called a *rivière*, was a favourite form of necklace for both day and evening.

Shawls were still worn. For outdoor wear there was a great variety of capes or mantles, loose or semi-fitting, with as great a variety of names – shawl-mantle, pelisse-mantle, burnouse, sortie-de-bal, etc. From *c.* 1850 tailors were making coats and jackets for day wear in addition to the riding habits which, of course, they had always made.

# 1869-1890 The Bustle

When the crinoline of the 1860's had reached the limit of backward expansion it began to subside, and, as had happened a hundred years earlier, the surplus material was draped. To support the drapery a smaller crinoline was provided with an additional steel frame which was attached to the back at the waist. Or a separate bustle, or *tournure*, made from several layers of pleated horsehair flounces, was worn over a small crinoline. In the early 1870's the crinoline was discarded altogether and the bustle, now elongated, took its place. When, in 1875, the fashion line became slender round the hips, the bustle was, so to speak, in the drapery of the dress itself and as a rule no bustle was worn, but only a trained petticoat to hold out the long train. In the early 1880's hip drapery and a wider skirt brought back the bustle, now called the 'crinolette' – a kind of half crinoline, with steels which continued up the back to end in a melon-shape throwing the skirt out almost horizontally from waist level behind. Throughout the whole of this period bustles were either separate steel frames which tied round the waist, or petticoats with inserted steels behind. The basic principle of cut for the bustle dress was always the gored skirt with the back fullness at the waist gathered or pleated into three or four inches and the front width gored each side, but the number of side gores and the amount used for back fullness varied according to the width of the material and the fashionable silhouette.

## 1869–1875

At first there was little change in bodice styles, but with the decreasing volume of skirts, by *c.* 1873 the bodice was down to the normal waistline, and by 1874 it was continued over the hips, fitting tightly like a corset. This was called the 'cuirasse' bodice. As the long waist and swelling hips required more fitting, the back was given an extra seam each side which sometimes ran into the shoulder seam, or more usually into the armhole; these back seams sloped into the waist and then out again to take the shape of the hips. The front of the bodice was still fitted by darts, but as the sides were on the cross grain a horizontal waistline dart, taken from the bust dart to the side seam, lifted the material back to the straight to give a good fit round the hips.

143

In the early 1870's there was a return of the pagoda sleeve. This was now a two-piece sleeve widening below the elbow. But the straight two-piece sleeve with cuff was more usual.

The first bustle skirt was the double skirt of the late 1860's – both gored, but with less fullness and fewer gores. By the early 1870's these skirts were cut to fit the hips round the waist, the only fullness at the centre back. The overskirt was at first just caught up on the seams, and at the back tapes were sewn inside and at the waist which, when tied together, pulled the material into puffs. Later, in order to give more fullness to the puffs, the sloped side of the gores – which were joined to the straight back length – were cut longer than the back and the extra fullness was gathered or pleated into the seams. The front of the overskirt might be open, apron front, a separate piece *en tablier*, or bodice and skirt *en princesse*. *C.* 1873, when there was less fullness round the hips, the overskirt, or 'pannier' as it was called, became drapery incorporated in the skirt. It was usually the centre back length which was now cut longer, and pleated or gathered to the side gore, tapes underneath from seam to seam keeping the fullness in position at the back. The front skirts became draperies pleated into these seams – *en tablier*, *en princesse*, or Polonaise, etc. The Polonaise suggested an overdress, the bodice front worn open or closed to the waist, and the skirts draped round the hips and arranged into the back seams. Bodices usually buttoned centre front and were separate from the skirt but were often attached to the pannier. See plate 51; Diagrams LI, LII.

## 1875–1882

By 1875 the dress was fitting the figure very closely down to the hips and all down the front, while well below hip level the fullness centre back draped up, and then fanned out into a very long train. Tapes down the side seams tied centre back drew the dress close to the figure in front so that this style was popularly known as the 'tie-back' dress, though the fashionable name was the 'fourreau'. The cuts were the cuirasse body, or the princess, or a mixture of the two – cuirasse back and princess front, or cuirasse front and princess back. The princess style was fitted down to the hips, the front with the waistline dart like the cuirasse bodice; skirt fullness was given by deep inverted pleats at the back seam starting from the widest part of the hips. Sometimes there were additional pleats from the side seams nearest the centre back one. This dress was often undraped in cutting but with additional long scarf draperies, or with the lines of the cuirasse bodice, apron front or Polonaise, indicated by flat trimming. The back fullness of the skirt worn with the cuirasse styles was usually draped and might be mounted on a lining to which the long full train was attached. These are the basic principles, but there was infinite variety and invention in the cutting and draping of all bustle skirts and particularly in this period. The sleeves were three-quarter length and fitting; for dinner or evening dress they came to the elbow, while for ball dress there was hardly any sleeve. The neckline was high with a narrow frill, square or a small V; for full evening dress it was very low, in various styles. A

40.  1794. Fashion plate. N. Heideloff
Ladies wearing round robes of muslin with high waists (the left-hand figure wears also an open gown of silk).
These dresses still retain a soft bulkiness before being reduced to the sheath-like garments of *c.* 1800.
See Cutting Diagrams XXXIII and XXXIV

41. *c.* 1803. From *Le Bon Genre*

Dresses designed to outline the limbs, and made from the softest muslins. Generally white in colour and reflecting a strong classical influence. Although the turban head-dress is still popular it is now being worn without the extremely high feathers seen in the previous illustration. See Cutting Diagram XXXV

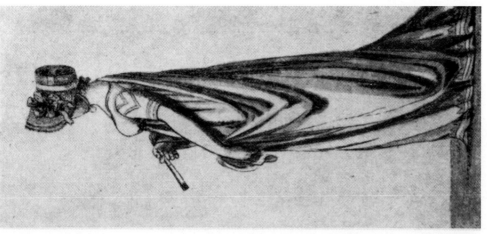
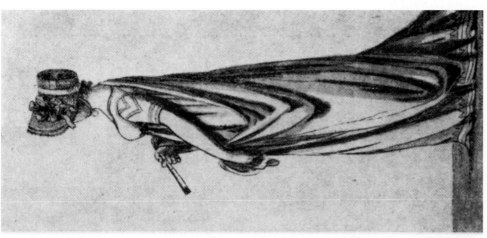

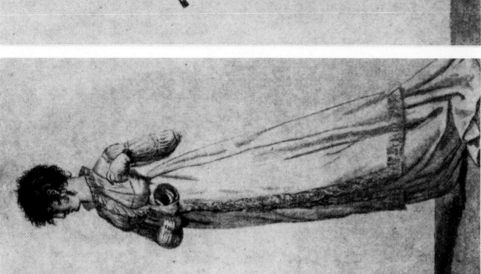

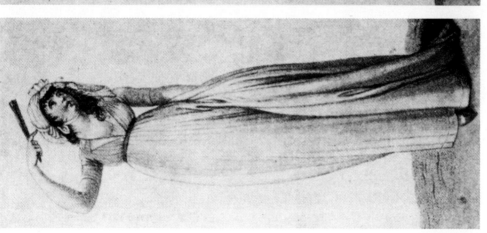
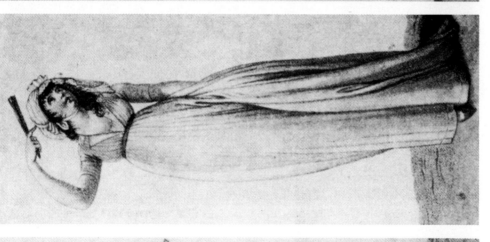

a. Open robe

b. Round robe

c. Round robe, worn with a shorter transparent open robe. The latter soon develops
into the pelisse

d. Long scarf draped in the classical
manner, worn with an early poke
bonnet

42.  1799–1809. FASHION PLATES

43.  *1803–1805*. Muslin dress. *The Gallery of English Costume, Manchester*
A bib-fronted dress or round robe, showing the bodice construction. Note the little pad
sewn inside at centre back to prevent the skirt from falling into the hollow of the back

a. Pelisse. 1815

b. Walking dress. 1819

c. Evening dress. 1823

44. 1815–23. FASHION PLATES
Costume Parisien

The waistline gradually descends, whilst the decorative emphasis, which is now very three dimensional, is placed on the lower part of the skirt and the tops of the sleeves. See Cutting Diagrams, XXXVI, XXXVII, XXXVIII, XXIX

45.  1827. Day dresses. Costume Parisien

46.  1830. Day Dress. Costume Parisien

The wide-brimmed hats help to balance the width across the shoulders produced by the full sleeves, extended collars and epaulettes. By 1830 the skirt is gathered all round the waist. See Cutting Diagrams XL and XLI

47.  1836. Morning and Evening Dresses
The full sleeves shown on the previous plate have now been restricted at the top with tuckings and ruchings
and so create the drooping shoulder line. The wide-brimmed hat also seems to be forced into the same
downward curve. See Cutting Diagrams XLII and XLIII

48. *c.* 1840 Morning Dress, Evening Dress and Evening Bodices.
Both dresses are typical of this date with their simple untrimmed skirts, any decoration
coming from the pattern on the fabric. See Cutting Diagrams XLIV and XLV

49.  1855. Day Dresses
The tiered skirts now show an increasing volume, and the basqued bodice curves well out over the hips often forming the first flounce. See Cutting diagrams XLVI and XLVII

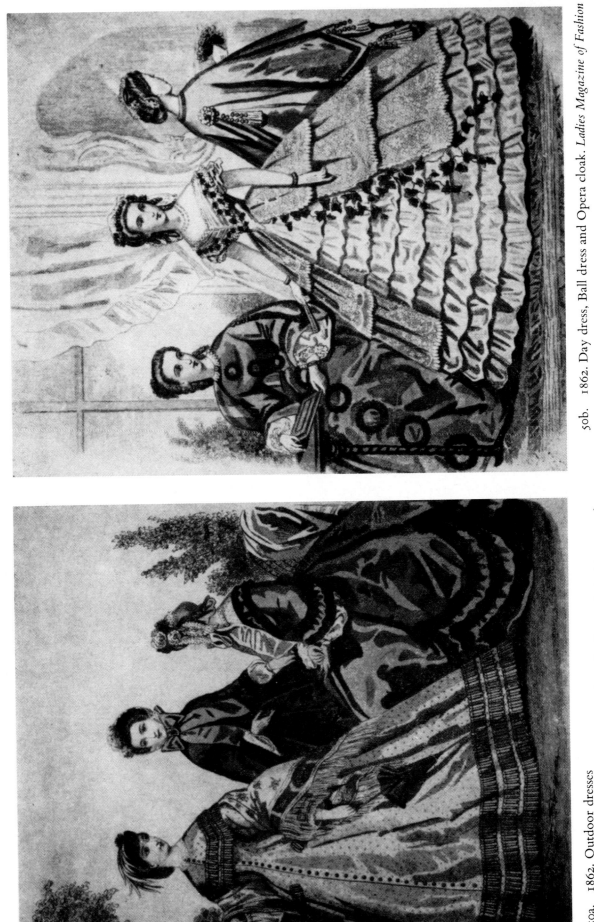

50b.  1862. Day dress, Ball dress and Opera cloak. *Ladies Magazine of Fashion*

50a.  1862. Outdoor dresses

Both standing figures show a more triangular line to their skirts now that these are cut straight to gore.  The dress on the extreme left is cut "*en princesse*"

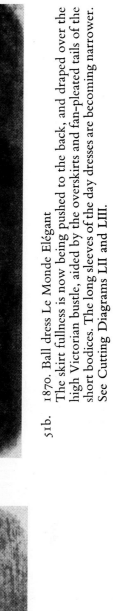

51b.  1870. Ball dress Le Monde Elégant
The skirt fullness is now being pushed to the back, and draped over the high Victorian bustle, aided by the overskirts and fan-pleated tails of the short bodices. The long sleeves of the day dresses are becoming narrower. See Cutting Diagrams LII and LIII.

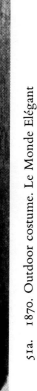

51a.  1870. Outdoor costume. Le Monde Elégant

52. *c.* 1876. Outdoor Costume. *The English Woman's Domestic Magazine*
The high bustle, having been temporarily removed, leaves the back drapery of the skirt collapsing to the floor. See Cutting Diagram LIV

53.  1876. Fashion Plate. *The Gentleman's Magazine of Fashion*
Ladies double breasted Alexandra Pelisse. See Nineteenth-Century Tailors' Patterns, page 200.

54. 1881. Outdoor and Indoor Dress
The cuirasse bodice and tightly-draped skirt was difficult to wear and did not remain fashionable for very long. The revival of the bustle can already be detected from the figure on the right. See Cutting Diagram LV

56. 1885. Outdoor costume
Collars and neckbands are high, and a new fullness is just perceptible at the sleeve headings. Bustles are squared out at right angles to the small of the back, and day dresses are being worn without trains. See Cutting Diagram LVI

55. 1883. Outdoor costume. *The World of Fashion*

57a, b  1890. Walking costumes. The simple practical skirts which were necessary for the more active woman left the jacket and bodice to be freely applied with more feminine decoration.

pleated flounce all round the bottom of the skirt and placed inside another, the *balayeuse*, which was a stiff muslin pleated frill trimmed with lace, kept the skirt out at the back. Day dresses lost their trains *c.* 1878.

Dresses buttoned centre front or centre back, and many of the silk dresses laced centre back. The fashionable dress for a few years from 1875 was the princess, often worn untrimmed. Its style depended on expert cutting and fitting, and sometimes additional scarf drapery very skilfully done. Few dressmakers could achieve this elegant line, so at the end of the 1870's drapes swathed round the hips and a multitude of trimmings disguised poor workmanship, and incidentally poor figures too. The sheath dress developed too rapidly and was too drastic a change for women who for years had concentrated on a small waist to the detriment of the hips. See plates 52–4; Diagrams LIV, LV.

## THE TEA-GOWN

In the late 1870's the fashionable dress had become so uncomfortable that when ladies changed their afternoon dresses before putting on their evening toilettes they relaxed in their dressing-gowns to drink tea. Afternoon tea became a social function with gentlemen present, so the dressing-gown became an elaborate affair of silk, satin, lace, etc.–the tea-gown.

## 1882–1890

Tailor-made jackets with matching skirts became fashionable wear in the early 1880's. They were cut like the fitted bodice but with revers and collars, and their severity of style was also repeated in day dresses. The cuirasse body was now cut higher on the hips to allow for the return of drapery–the front long and pointed and the back extending in a long tail to lie over the new protruding bustle. By the end of the 1880's the bodice came just below waist level, and was pointed centre back and centre front. The tailor-made habit jacket, worn over blouse or waistcoat, was copied by giving dress bodices revers, and false fronts. This front, the 'plastron' was either plain waistcoat style, or gathered and ruched to suggest a blouse. As skirts became simpler bodices became more elaborate and by the end of the 1880's cross draperies were also being added. The foundation bodice itself still fitted like a corset under all the additional decoration. A narrow collar was added to the bodice and by 1885 had become the high 'officer' collar. The long tight sleeve was now set high on the shoulder, and from 1885 the head of the sleeve began to rise and be cut fuller. Evening bodices, usually untrimmed until the mid 1880's when they also were draped, were glove-fitting, and for ball dresses no sleeves were worn, instead, there was a shoulder strap, or ribbon ties. The habit-shirt worn with the tailored jacket developed into the loose unlined blouse which began to be worn from the late 1880's.

Whereas in previous styles the drapery had been produced largely by the cut of the skirt itself, in the 1880's the draperies and decorations were all separate pieces arranged on to a foundation skirt. This simplified dressmaking but was an artificial device and led to the gradual elimination of drapery and a return to the plain skirt. With added draperies and a wider skirt the 1880's acquired a new distinctive silhouette. As the front of the skirt was still kept straight all the extra width circled from the sides round the back, held out horizontally from centre back at the waist by the new bustle from which the skirt, being clear of the ground, hung almost vertically. The foundation skirt which was the basis of this new line was still the gored skirt, straight in front and fitted closely round the hips with hip darts, the back fullness being gathered or pleated. This was worn over the bustle. From the middle of the 1880's the bustle was often incorporated in the foundation skirt itself. Three or four rows of steel were inserted in the back length and tied underneath to bulge as desired, a pad of horsehair being attached inside to the waist centre back. Rows of pleating and ruching were sewn round this skirt and the draperies arranged and sewn to it.

With the tailored style of bodice, skirt drapery gradually became simplified. The back drape became an overskirt. Still draped centre back at waist level to emphasize the horizontal line but in later undraped versions it might be pleated. Gradually this overskirt moved round to the front, open centre front or on the side, hanging straight or draped one side. The trimming round the lower skirt also became simpler, usually just deep pleats in various styles. By the end of the 1880's the overskirt had become a complete skirt. This might be pleated or, as the fullness subsided, cut like the foundation skirt, still with back fullness but with its severity in front relieved with apron drapery. The princess cut continued throughout the 1880's when, open in front and with the skirts draped to the sides, it was called a Polonaise. In full evening dress the back overdress became a long train. Ball dresses were still profusely draped. Evening dresses generally laced centre back; day dresses fastened with buttons or hooks and eyes centre front.

Capes, Ulsters, Inverness capes, dolmans, shooting jackets, yachting jackets, etc., were made by tailors and based on the men's styles of the period. See plates 55, 56; Diagram LVI.

## MATERIALS, DECORATIONS, ETC.

Cashmere, merino, silk, velvet, and the new foulard, surah silk, etc., produced the flowing lines of the dresses of the 1870's. In the 1880's materials became heavier, and the draping stiffer and more sculptural in consequence. Cloth, serge, Ottoman silk, Duchesse satin, velvet, broché velvet, plush, etc., were used, and their cheaper imitations—sateen, velveteen, etc. For ball dresses from the mid 1870's and during the 1880's tight-fitting bodices, usually untrimmed and of silk or satin (later velvet or plush) were worn with skirts of multiple transparent draperies over a silk or satin foundation. Tulle, net and tarlatan, which in the 1880's were spotted with sequins, and transparent dewdrops, were used for the overskirts. The most interesting draping effects were obtained by unsymmetrical arrangements of the material. In the early 1870's two shades of one colour were popular. The dress would be in the paler tone, the cuirasse bodice having its centre front and centre back panel of the darker one, which was also repeated in the trimmings for cross-way bands and pleatings on the skirt. Two or more contrasting materials of the same colour – and in the 1880's of different colours – were almost always used in a dress; silk and velvet, wool and velvet, velvet, silk and brocade, etc. *C.* 1876 cream was the fashionable and impractical colour for the long-trained princess dresses, which in some cases were also trimmed with bands of dark velvet, black, garnet, olive green, etc.

From the late 1860's and during the 1870's pleated frills provided the main type of decoration, the pleats being arranged in an infinite variety of designs, with several variations in one dress. In the 1880's the pleatings were simpler, being knife, kilt or box type; there was also ruching. Other trimmings were braid, passementerie, ball fringe, chenille fringe, etc. For ball dresses, lace, ribbon, flowers, and in the 1880's also ostrich feather fringes, fruit, birds, butterflies, etc. were used. A military note was introduced in the mid 1880's by decorating jackets with Hussar froggings and braidings; braided designs were also used on day dresses. Fur muffs and trimmings, beaver, astrakhan, softened the hard line of the tailor-mades. The first fur garments – sealskin and beaver jackets – appeared in the late 1870's.

More jewellery was worn. In the 1860's a locket or cross on a velvet ribbon, tied round the throat, softened the naked look of the lower necklines in day dresses, while pendant ear-rings were hung from ears now exposed by the new hair styles. Brooches were larger, and there were also gold and silver necklaces. More silver was used as well as gold or pinchbeck for day wear. Garnets, peridots and opals were favourite semi-precious stones.

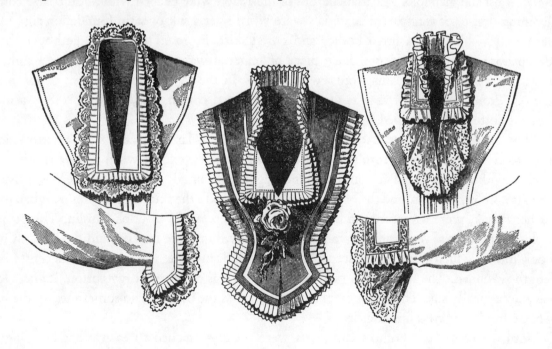

# Construction of
# Nineteenth-century Dresses

The bodice, and also the sleeves, of the very soft muslin dresses of the late 1790's and early nineteenth century were lined with fine cotton, the lining being stitched first and the muslin placed and sewn over it. The skirt was unlined. Later, and until the end of the 1820's white muslin dresses, both bodice and skirt, were unlined and always beautifully made. The skirts were attached to the body by whipping stitching and the fullness was gauged. Early nineteenth-century bodices fastened centre back with buttons, later with hooks and eyes. The neckline until the early 1820's was generally hemmed, and a narrow gathering cord or thin ribbon inserted, later the neckline was piped. Bodices of silk dresses, and the pelisse, were usually lined with soft muslin, bodice and lining being made up separately and joined together round neck, waist and armhole. The mancherons of the 1820's were backed with a stiff coarse cotton. Evening dresses of transparent materials were worn over a silk or satin foundation slip, made separately, which had a fitted bodice and gored skirt. From *c.* 1830 all bodices were lined, except for some muslin dresses. Each piece of material was now mounted on to a similarly cut lining piece and all seams were sewn together. In the 1830's the lining was of soft white cotton. From the 1840's this was usually a fine glazed cotton, and from the 1880's a much heavier cotton, often striped, was used.

From *c.* 1818–1828 skirts had a padded hem which was later replaced with a cotton facing four to five inches deep. From the 1840's the whole skirt, except when of fine muslin, was backed with a firm glazed cotton lining and edged with braid. A little later there was usually an extra, stiffer, facing round the bottom. During the 1860's the skirts of day dresses, when made of heavy silk, were sometimes unlined but had a deep facing of book muslin. The princess styles of the 1870's were lined down to the hips only, but were faced round the bottom with book muslin which went much deeper up the train. Sometimes the whole of the centre back length was lined. The foundation skirt of the 1880's was of linen, heavy cotton, Italian cloth, very occasionally silk. There was extra stiffening round the bottom and sometimes up the back —book muslin or crinoline muslin.

Until the late 1840's bodices and skirts were usually attached to each other by gauging.

Gauging is the method used when a large amount of fullness has to be drawn to a small space. The top of the skirt is cut straight and turned in (to a curve centre front if the bodice is pointed); a series of running stitches are made, large stitches being taken on the wrong side and very small ones on the right; each stitch in succeeding rows lies directly under the one above, as in smocking. The threads are then drawn up to the requisite size. When the bodice is to be attached, the skirt is whipped on by taking a small stitch into the outside of each fold. When, in the late 1820's, skirts became fuller, firm materials were set in radiating pleats front and sides and gauged centre back. From the late 1830's, during the 1840's and occasionally in the 1850's, most skirts were gauged, the pleats being always deeper in the centre back. This method was also applied for gathered bodices and for the top of very large sleeves. Gauging is an excellent way of giving even fullness, but needs to be done by hand. The flounces of the 1850's skirts are gathered. The gored skirts from *c.* 1860 have the waist fullness set in pleats, with the back sometimes gauged, set in four double box pleats, or other variations of pleating.

Bodices began to be boned *c.* 1835, at first up the centre front only. By the late 1830's darts and side seams were boned, and from the 1870's, with the cuirasse bodice and princess styles all seams–the length of the bones on the back seams being about the same as the underarm one, which stopped about an inch below the armhole. From *c.* 1815 piping was being inserted round the armhole and neck; from the late 1820's, and during the 1830's, piping usually featured on all seams except the underarm one; in the 1840's there was piping on the neck, armhole, waist and bottom of the sleeves. After that, piping was little used. Until the early 1870's, when the bodice began to be made with more and straighter seams, the very curved back side seams had to be top-stitched to the centre back piece; otherwise there was an awkward piece of sewing. Small crescent-shaped pads of cotton wool or horsehair were usually set in the front of the bodice at the armhole between the lining and the dress material to fill in the hollow between the shoulder and the rise of the bust. The bust itself was sometimes padded. With the very small waist, from the 1850's onwards the centre front of the bodice was usually cut slightly curved. Day bodices buttoned or hooked in front; evening bodices varied.

The amount of material required to make a skirt was worked out according to the width of the material, which varied considerably, silks being from 19 to 24 inches, woollens double that width. The following quantities are taken either from dresses or magazines:
'Plain unshaped skirts–late 1820's, 90 inches wide; 1830's, 94 inches wide; 1840's, 126 inches wide; 1850's, 170 inches wide; 1850's, with flounces, 107 inches wide for foundation skirt, 129 inches for top flounces, 150 for the lower one.'

The amount in gored skirts varied considerably; those given below are for silks 24 inches wide:
'1860, day dress, one width centre front, 4 widths (8 side gores), one width centre back.
'1867, evening dress, 3–5 widths centre front, 3 widths (6 side gores), 2 widths centre back (gored centre back).

'1869, one width centre front, one width (2 side gores), 2 widths centre back.

'1870, one width centre front, 2 widths (2 side gores), 2 widths centre back.

'1876, one width centre front, 2 widths (4 side gores), 2 widths centre back.

'One width centre front, 4 widths (8 side gores), 2 widths centre back.

'One width centre front, one width (2 side gores), 3 widths centre back.'

Construction of 1880's foundation skirts with built-in bustle:

'1883. "For making the skirts stand out insert three steels the lowest 27 inches from the hem and 22 inches long, above it one of 18 inches, and above that one of 13 inches. These are kept out by a small mattress 8 inches long by 5 inches wide, or else by a small crinolette tied by strings on either side of the skirt so that they do not shake about independently."

'1889. "The skirt foundation has a front breadth of 9 inches above, 29 inches below; one gore at each side, 16 above, 24 below; back breadth 37 and quite straight; a small pad bustle may be used with one steel, 12 inches long, placed about 10 inches below the waist." '

These foundation skirts were also darted round the waist to fit smoothly over the hips.

Nineteenth-century dresses were as a rule beautifully made and were all hand-stitched until the invention of the sewing machine: chain-stitching from 1854, then lock-stitching. Dresses from the 60's onwards were usually machine-stitched.

(For technical construction of dresses from the middle of the nineteenth century see contemporary instructions pages 183–190).

# Cutting Diagrams

———·⚹·———

For full explanation see Notes on the Cutting Diagrams, page 303

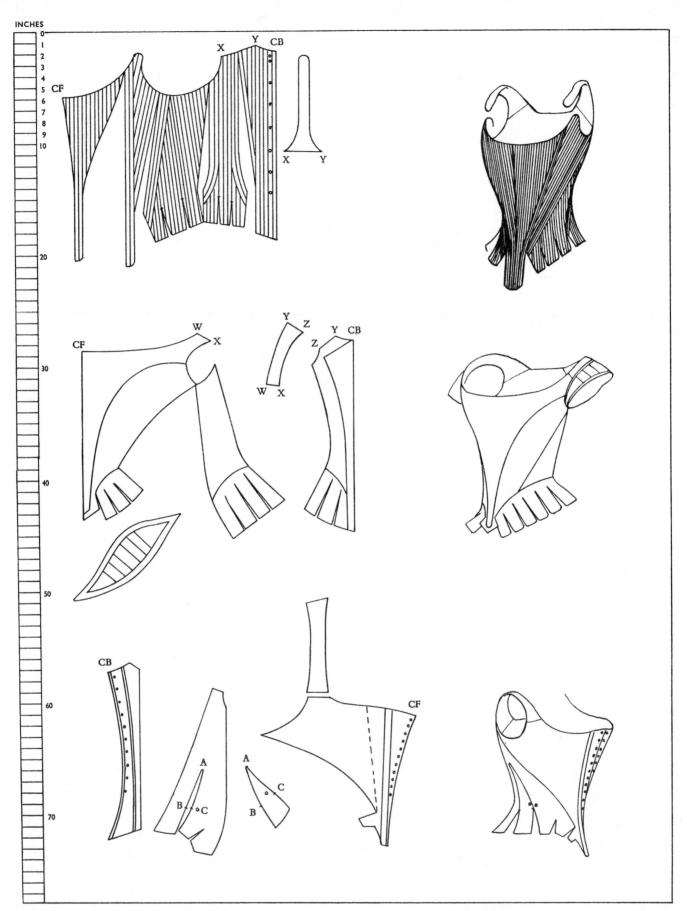

INCHES
0
1
2
3
4
5
6
7
8
9
10

20

30

40

50

60

70

**DIAGRAM XXVII** (above)
STAYS, mid-eighteenth century, after Leloir

**DIAGRAM XXVIII** (centre)
CORSAGE OF MARIE ANTOINETTE 1780'S. M. PARQUEZ

**DIAGRAM XXIX** (below)
CORSET OF LADY HAMILTON 1790'S. *Victoria and Albert Museum*

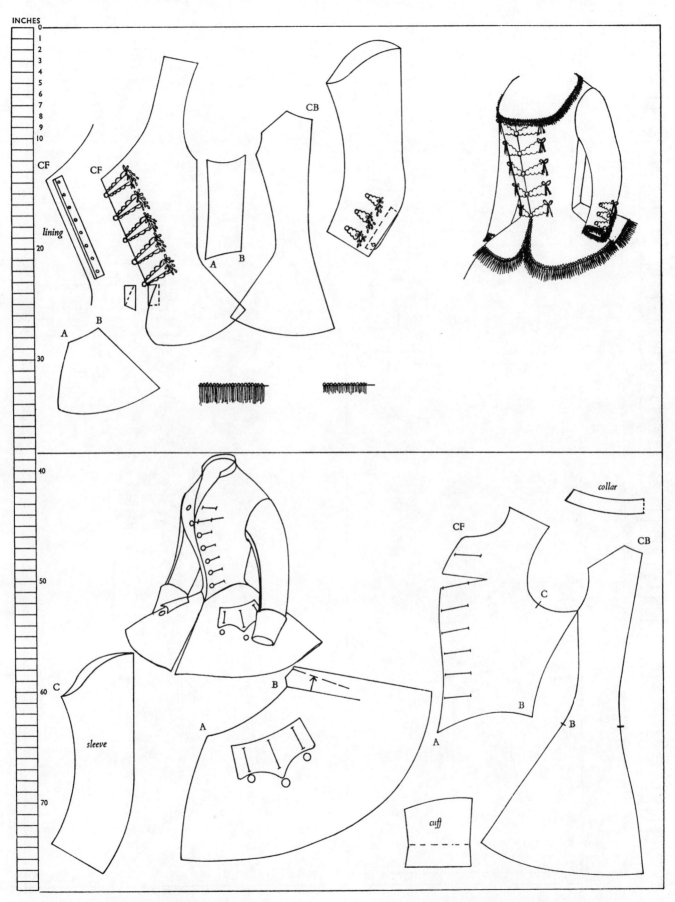

INCHES
0
1
2
3
4
5
6
7
8
9
10

CF

CF

*lining*

20

30

CB

A
B

A
B

A
B

40

*collar*

CF

C

CB

50

B

60

C

*sleeve*

B

A

A

B

B

70

*cuff*

DIAGRAM XXX (above)

JACKET 1760–70. *Gallery of English Costume, Manchester*

DIAGRAM XXXI (below)

RIDING COAT 1750–70. *Victoria and Albert Museum*

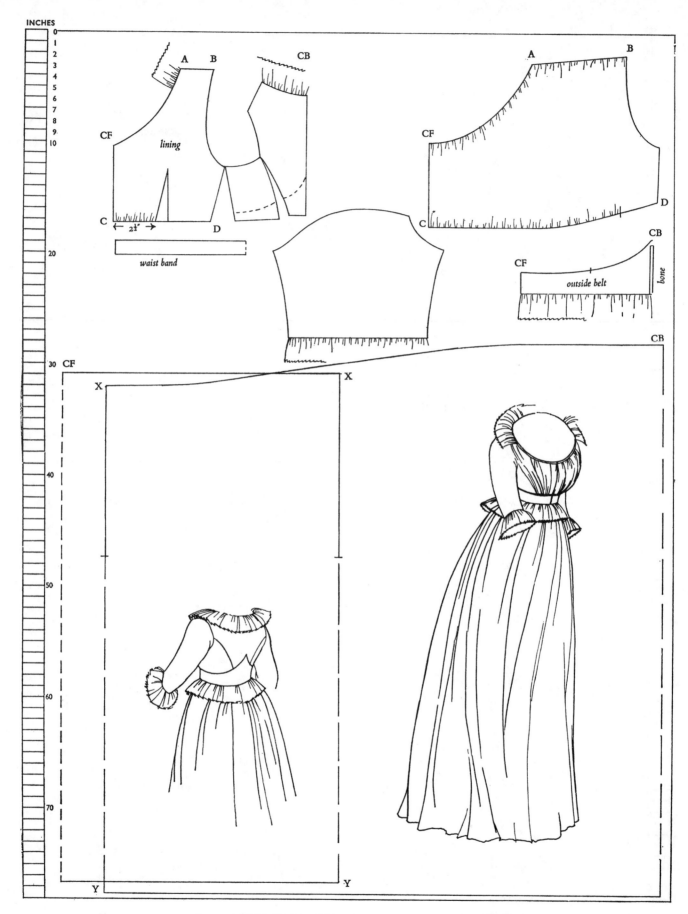

INCHES
0
1
2
3
4
5
6
7
8
9
10

20

30

40

50

60

70

A B CB

CF

*lining*

CF

A B

CB

C ← 2¼" → D

*waist band*

CF

C D

CF

C D

*outside belt* *bone*

CB

CF

X X

Y Y

DIAGRAM XXXII

ROUND ROBE *c.* 1795. *London Museum*

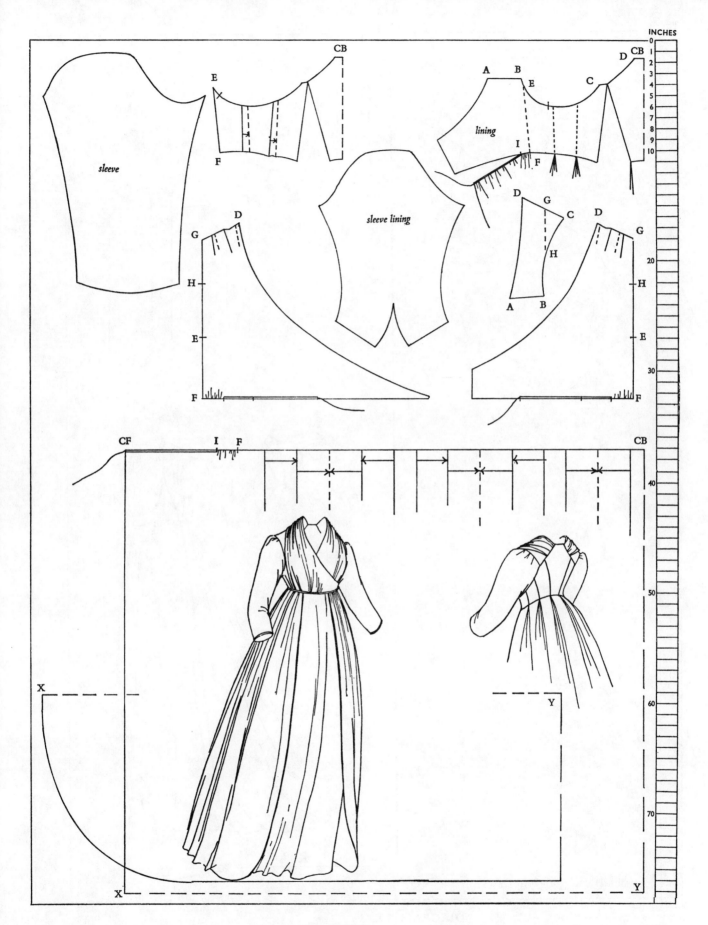

INCHES

sleeve

CB

E

F

lining

A  B

E

C

D  CB

I

F

D  G

C

H

D

G

H

A  B

sleeve lining

D

G

H

E

F

G

H

E

F

CF          I  F                                    CB

X                                                    Y

X                                                    Y

DIAGRAM XXXIII

OPEN ROBE *c. 1797. Museum of Costume, Bath*

INCHES

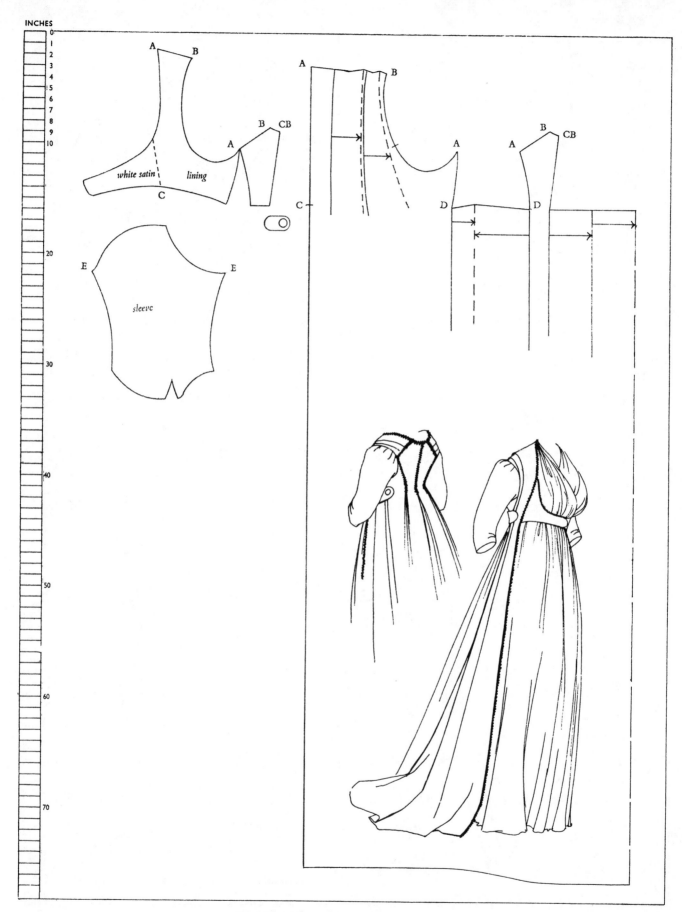

white satin    lining

C

sleeve

A    B

A    B    CB

E    E

A    B

A    B    CB

A    A

B    CB

C

D    D

DIAGRAM XXXIV

OPEN GOWN *c.* 1795. *Victoria and Albert Museum*

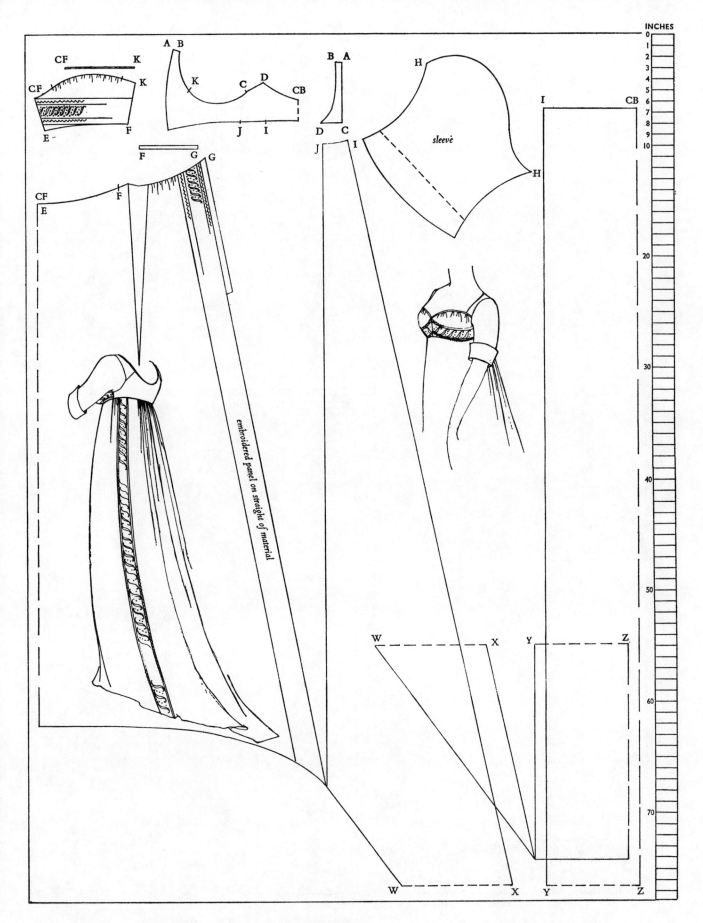

INCHES

CF K
CF K
E F

A B
K
C D
CB
J I

B A
D C

H
sleeve
I CB
H

CF F
E

F G G

J I

embroidered panel on straight of material

W X Y Z

W X Y Z

DIAGRAM XXXV

ROBE WITH 'BIB' FRONT *c.* 1803. *Cheltenham Museum*

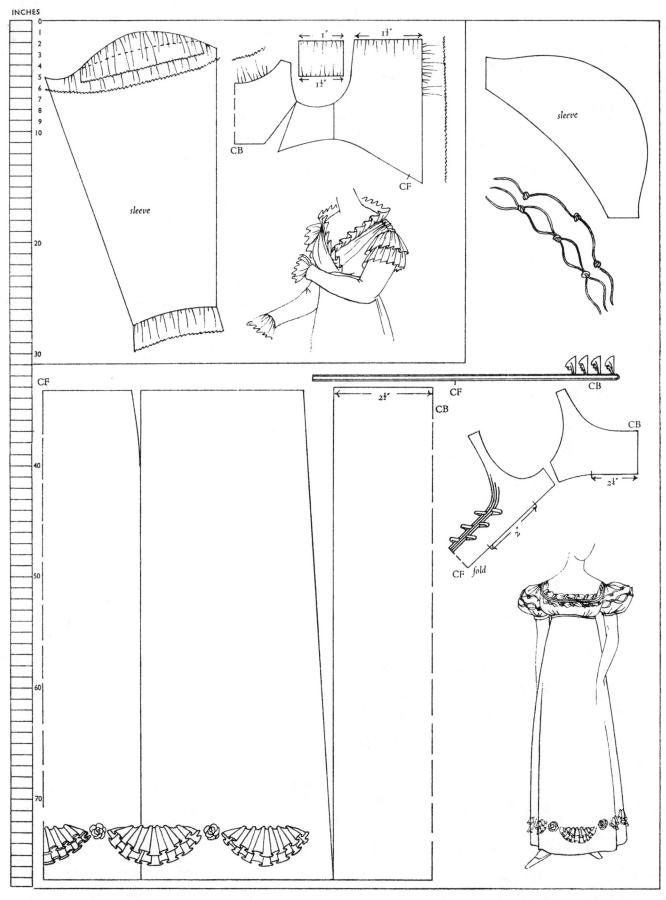

INCHES

CB

CF

sleeve

1″    1½″

1½″

CB

CF

sleeve

2¼″

CF

CB

CB

2¼″

2″

CF    fold

CF

40

50

60

70

20

30

0 1 2 3 4 5 6 7 8 9 10

**DIAGRAM XXXVI** (above)

BODICE OF DRESS *c.* 1810. *London Museum*

**DIAGRAM XXXVII** (below)

EVENING DRESS 1816–19. *Gallery of English Costume, Manchester*

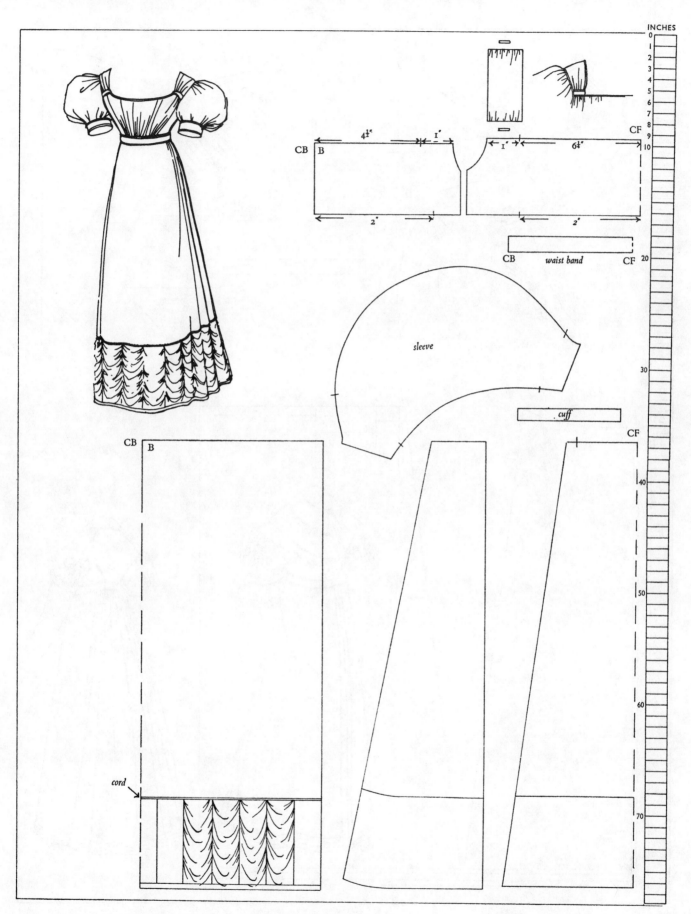

INCHES

4½" 1" 1" 6½"
CB B CF
2" 2"

CB waist band CF

sleeve

cuff

CB B CF

cord

## DIAGRAM XXXVIII

DAY DRESS 1816–19. *Privately owned*

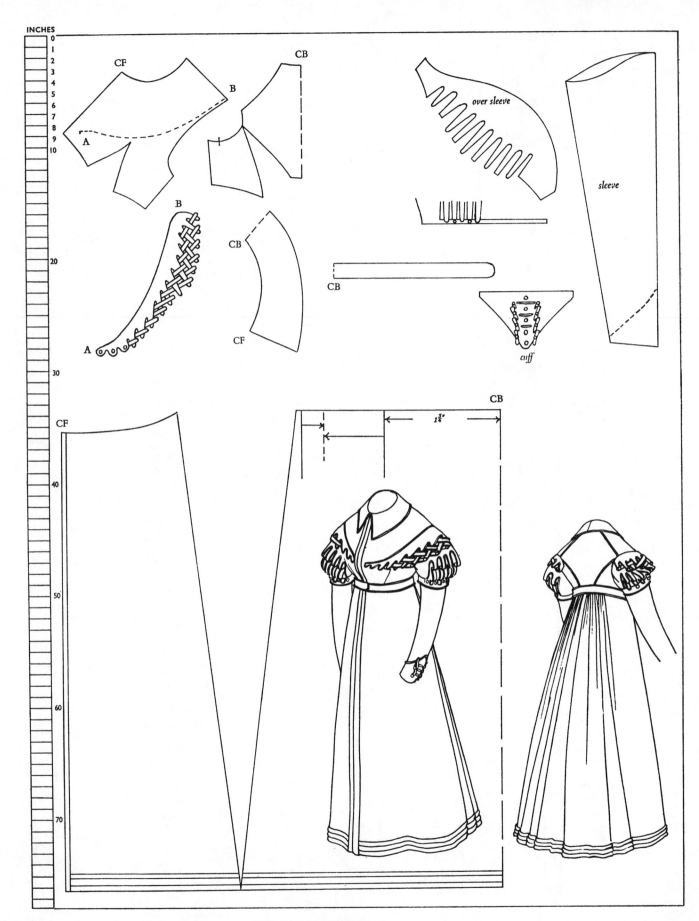

**INCHES**

CF

CB

B

A

over sleeve

sleeve

B

CB

A

CB

CF

CB

cuff

CB

$1\frac{3}{4}''$

CF

DIAGRAM XXXIX

PELISSE *c.* 1820. *Central School of Art and Design, London*

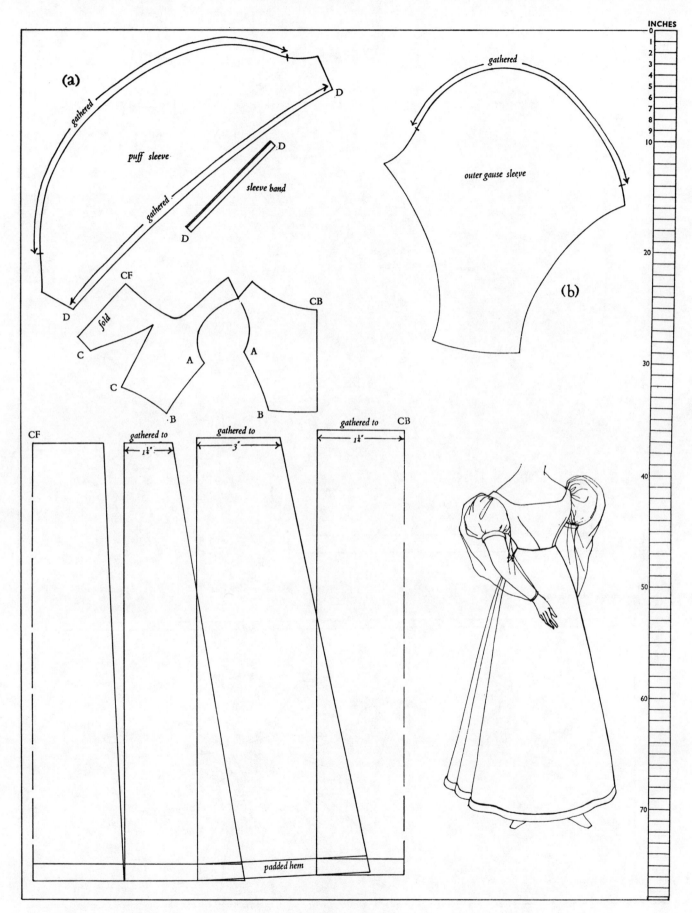

INCHES
0
1
2
3
4
5
6
7
8
9
10

20

30

40

50

60

70

(a)

gathered

gathered

puff sleeve

D

D

gathered

sleeve band

D

D

(b)

gathered

outer gause sleeve

CF

fold

CB

C

C

A

A

C

B

B

CF

gathered to

1¼"

gathered to

3"

gathered to

1¼"

CB

padded hem

DIAGRAM XL

EVENING DRESS c. 1825. Gallery of English Costume, Manchester

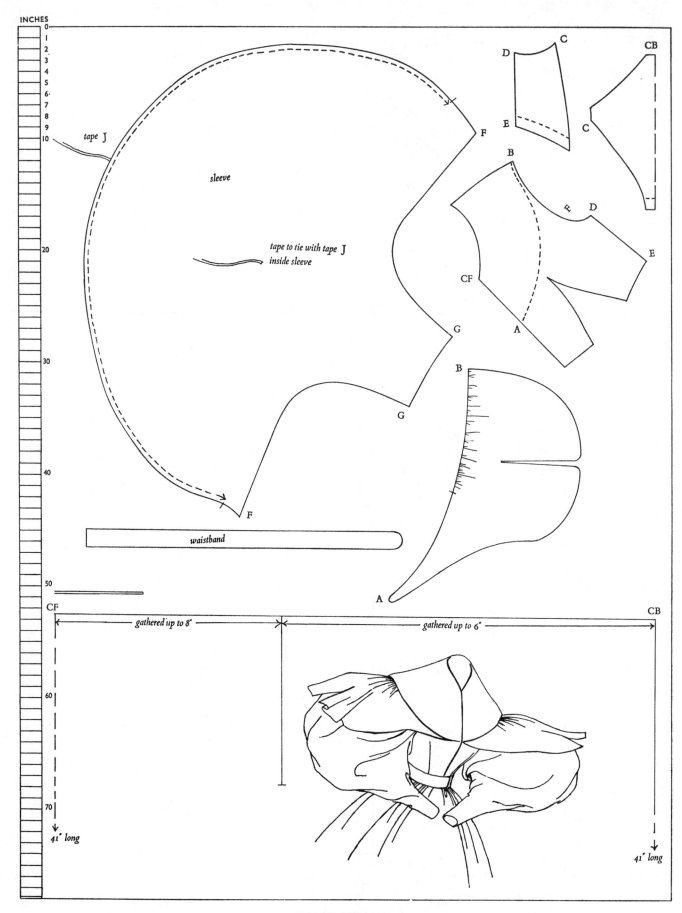

INCHES

tape J

sleeve

tape to tie with tape J
inside sleeve

D        C        CB
E
C

F

B

CF        E    D

E

G

A

B

G

waistband

A

CF                                                                CB

gathered up to 8″                    gathered up to 6″

41″ long

41″ long

DIAGRAM XLI

DAY DRESS c. 1834. *Privately owned*

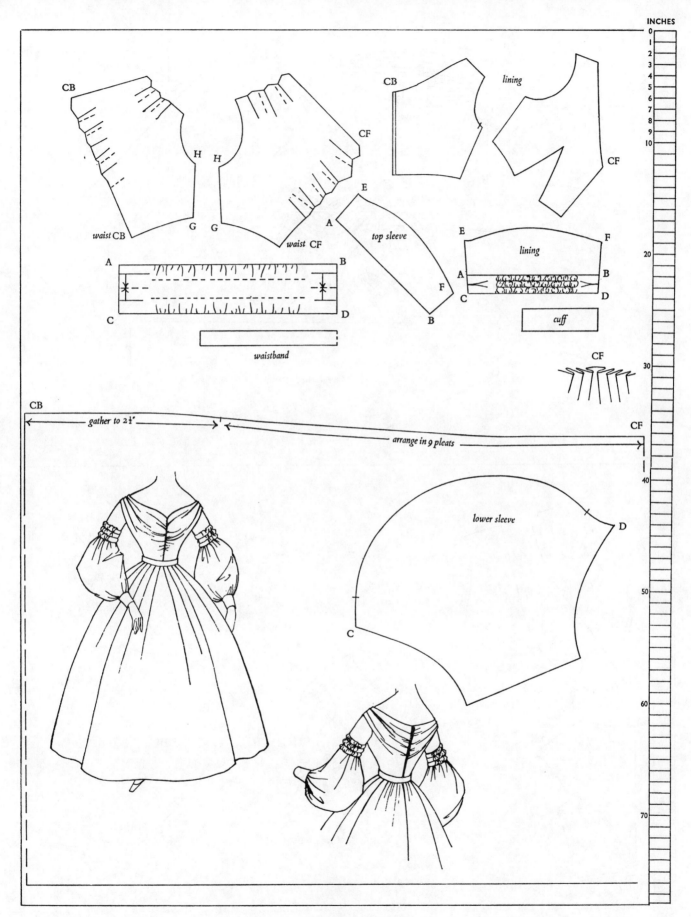

INCHES
0
1
2
3
4
5
6
7
8
9
10
20
30
40
50
60
70

CB

*lining*

CF

H    H

G    G

*waist* CB          *waist* CF

E

*top sleeve*

A

F

B

E                                    F

*lining*

A                                    B

C                                    D

*cuff*

CF

A                                    B

C                                    D

*waistband*

CB                                                                   CF

← *gather to* 2½″ →                    ← *arrange in 9 pleats* →

*lower sleeve*

D

C

DIAGRAM XLII

DAY DRESS *c.* 1837. *Museum of Costume, Bath*

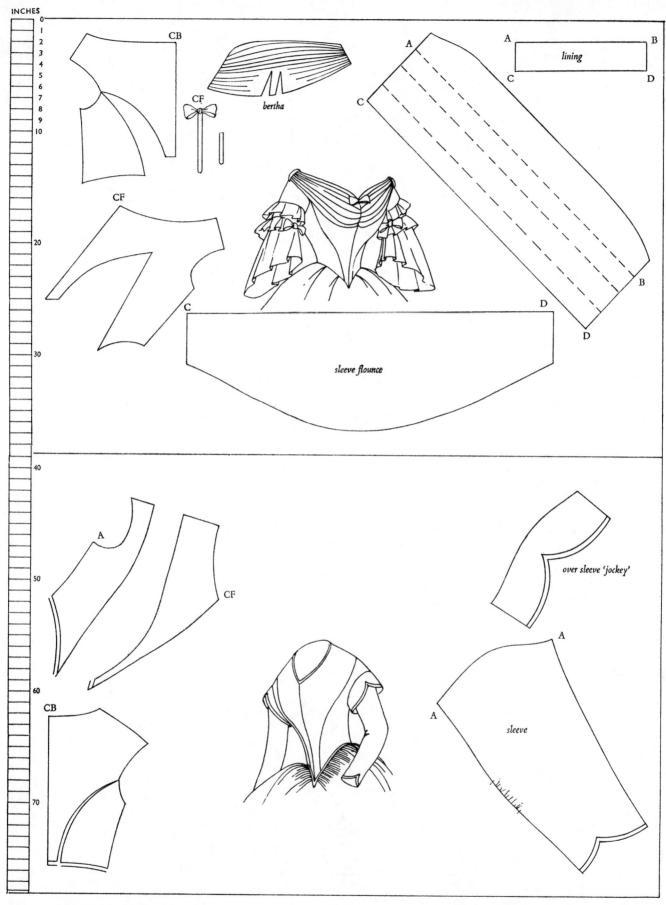

INCHES
0
1
2
3
4
5
6
7
8
9
10

20

30

40

50

60

70

CB

CF

bertha

CF

C

D

sleeve flounce

A          A          B
lining
C          D

C

B

B

D

D

A

CF

CB

over sleeve 'jockey'

A

A

A

sleeve

DIAGRAM XLIII (above)

BODICE c. 1839. *Central School of Art and Design, London*

DIAGRAM XLIV (below)

BODICE, early 1840's. *Central School of Art and Design, London*

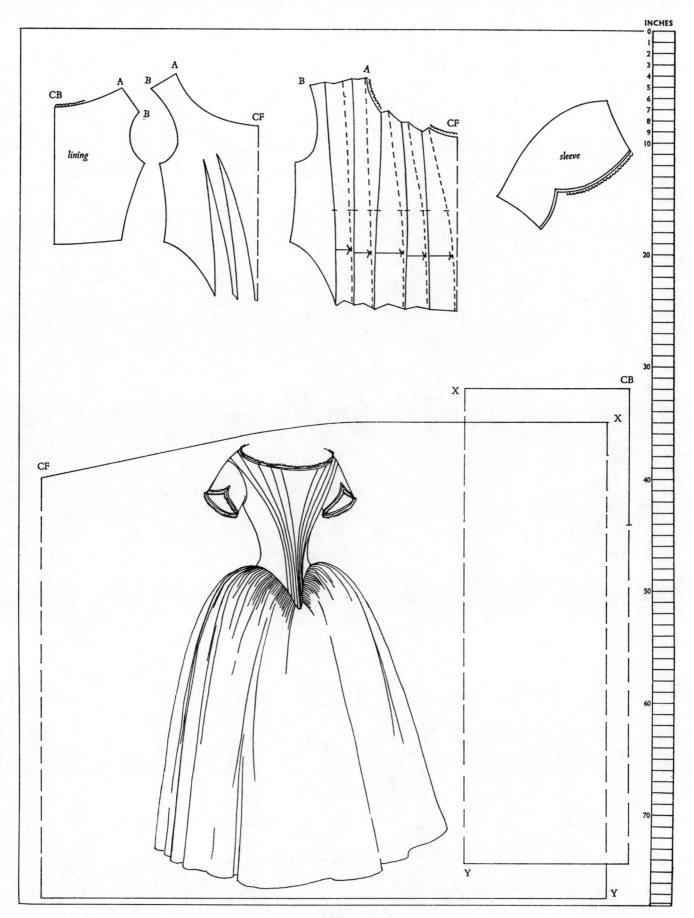

CB · A · A · B · A · CF · B · A · CF

*lining*

*sleeve*

CB

X

X

CF

Y

Y

DIAGRAM XLV

EVENING DRESS, early 1840's *Privatly owned*

INCHES

INCHES

0 1 2 3 4 5 6 7 8 9 10

20

30

40

50

60

70

A    B

CF

A

CF

B

CB

C    top sleeve    C

sleeve

sleeve lining

X    CB

X

CF

Y    Y

DIAGRAM XLVI

SUMMER DRESS, early 1850's. *Central School of Art and Design, London*

INCHES

CB

CF

A       B

C       D

*sleeve*

A       B
C       D
*lining sleeve*

CB

CF

DIAGRAM XLVII

CARRIAGE DRESS, late 1850's. *London Museum*

INCHES
0
1
2
3
4
5
6
7
8
9
10

20

30

40

50

60

70

CB

CF

A

B

CF

A

B

CB

CF

CB

DIAGRAM XLVIII

EVENING DRESS, early 1860's. *Central School of Art and Design, London*

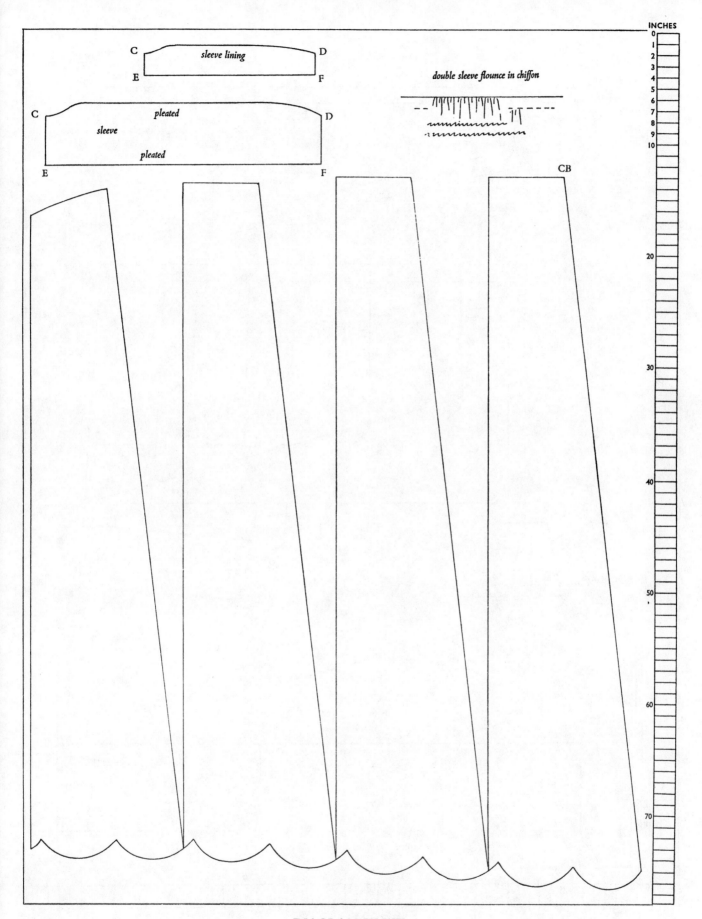

C    sleeve lining    D
E                     F

double sleeve flounce in chiffon

C                pleated        D
sleeve
     pleated
E                             F                    CB

INCHES
0
1
2
3
4
5
6
7
8
9
10

20

30

40

50

60

70

DIAGRAM XLVIII

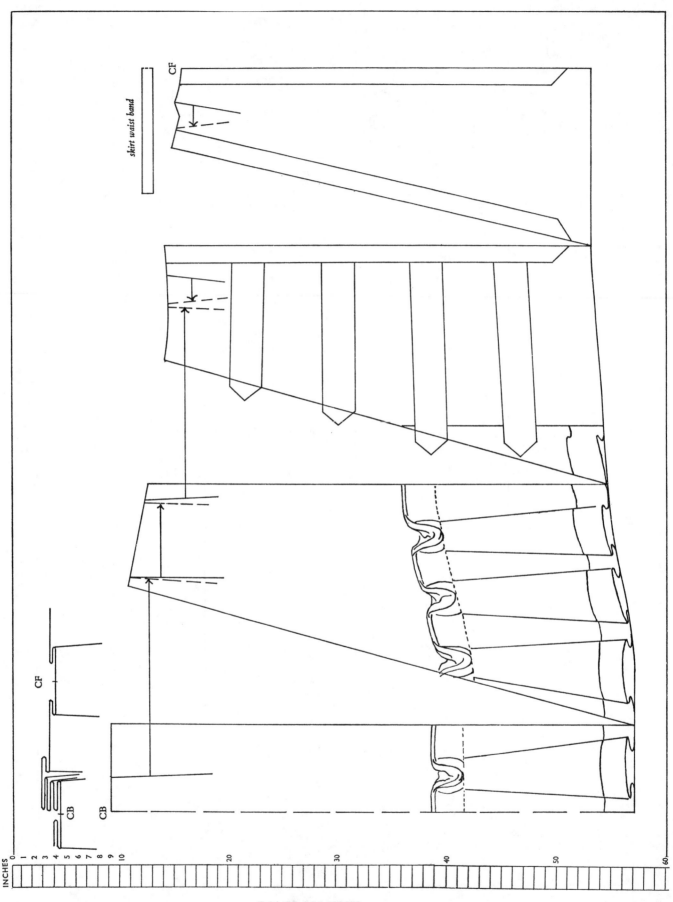

skirt waist band

CF

CF

CB

CB

INCHES

0 1 2 3 4 5 6 7 8 9 10      20      30      40      50      60

DIAGRAM XLIX

**AFTERNOON DRESS** *c.* 1868–9. *Privately owned*

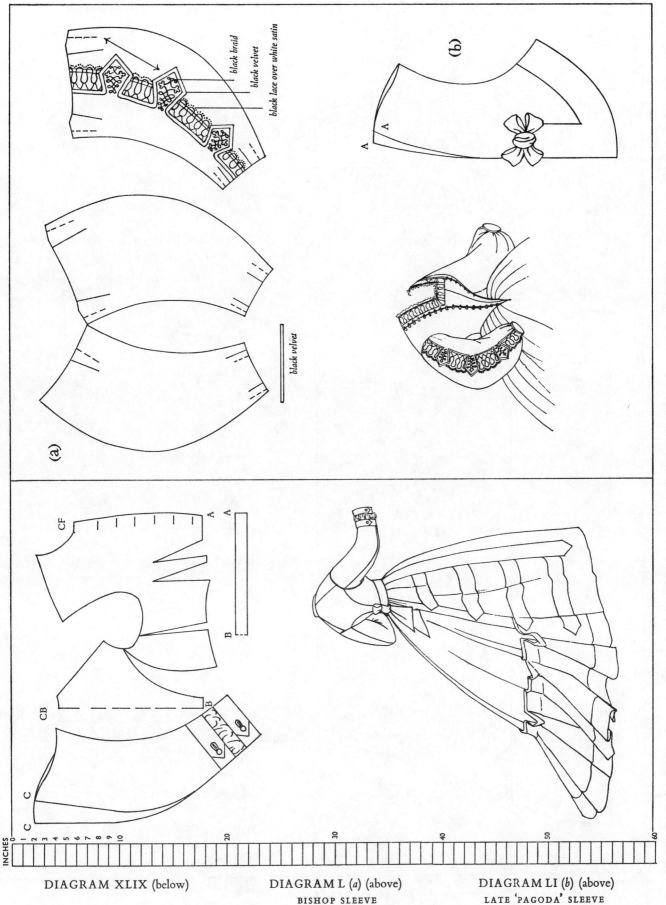

black braid
black velvet
black lace over white satin

black velvet

(a)

(b)

black velvet

CF
A
A

B

B
CB
B

C
C
C

INCHES
0 1 2 3 4 5 6 7 8 9 10                  20                  30                  40                  50                  60

DIAGRAM XLIX (below)          DIAGRAM L (a) (above)          DIAGRAM LI (b) (above)
                                    BISHOP SLEEVE              LATE 'PAGODA' SLEEVE

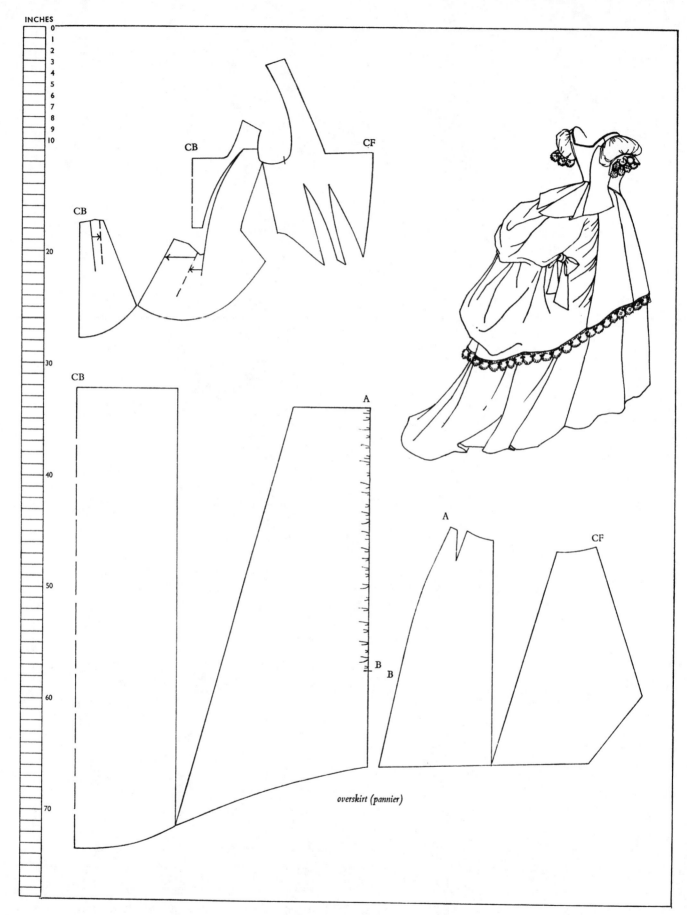

INCHES

0
1
2
3
4
5
6
7
8
9
10

20

30

40

50

60

70

CB

CB

CF

CB

CB

A

A

CF

B

B

*overskirt (pannier)*

## DIAGRAM LII
EVENING DRESS (BUSTLE) *c. 1870. Central School of Art and Design, London*

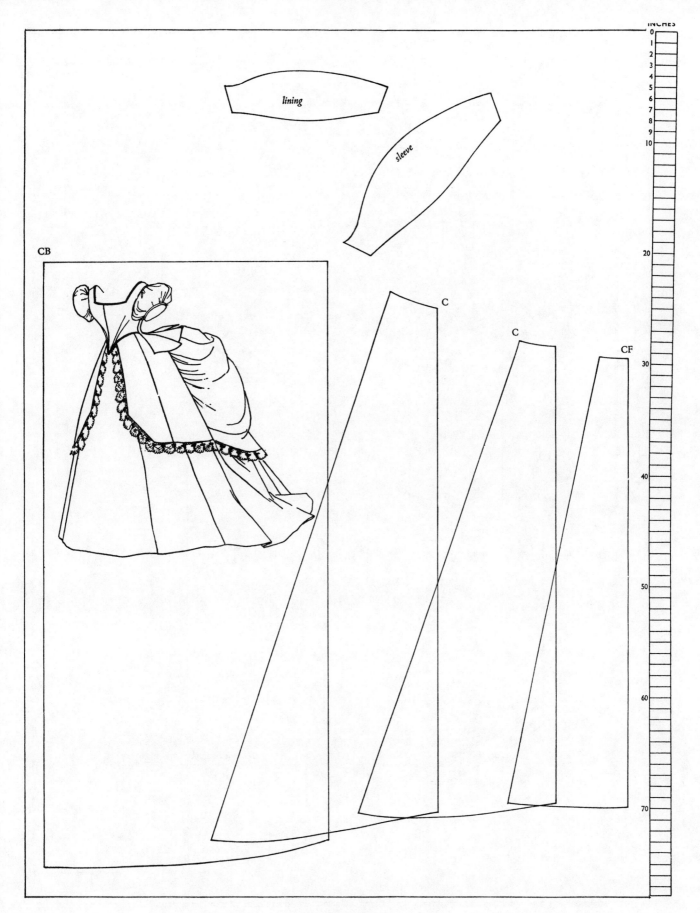

*lining*

*sleeve*

CB

C

C

CF

0
1
2
3
4
5
6
7
8
9
10

20

30

40

50

60

70

DIAGRAM LII

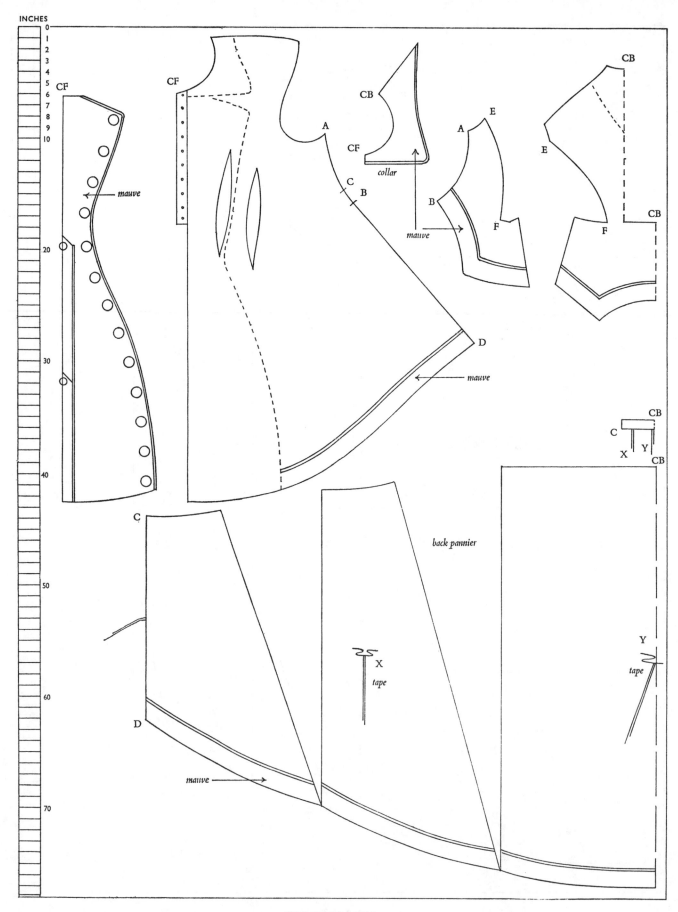

INCHES

0
1
2
3
4
5
6
7
8
9
10

20

30

40

50

60

70

CF

CF

CF

CB

CB

A

CB

A

E

E

CF

C

B

*collar*

B

F

F

CB

*mauve*

*mauve*

*mauve*

D

*mauve*

C

CB

X  Y

CB

*back pannier*

C

X

*tape*

Y

*tape*

D

*mauve*

DIAGRAM LIII

**DAY DRESS (BUSTLE)** 1873. *Cheltenham Museum*

INCHES
0
1
2
3
4
5
6
7
8
9
10

20

30

40

50

60

70

*sleeve*

CB

CB

CF

DIAGRAM LIII

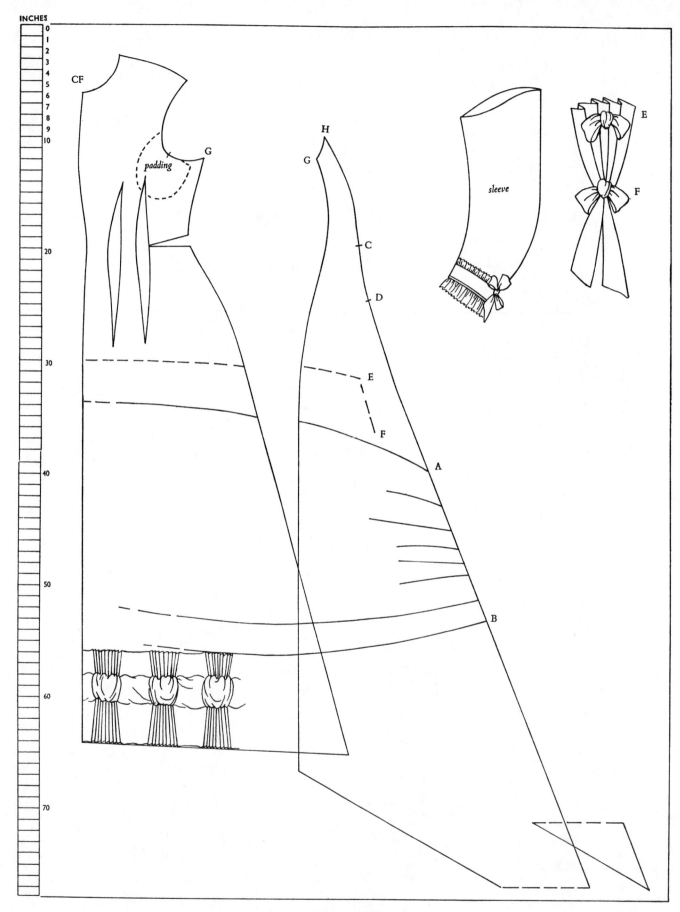

INCHES
0
1
2
3
4
5
6
7
8
9
10

20

30

40

50

60

70

CF

G

*padding*

H

G

C

D

E

F

A

B

*sleeve*

E

F

DIAGRAM LIV

AFTERNOON DRESS (BUSTLE) 1878. *Central School of Art and Design, London*

INCHES
0
1
2
3
4
5
6
7
8
9
10

20

30

40

50

60

70

CB

H

C

D

CB

CB

X

Y

X

Y

DIAGRAM LIV

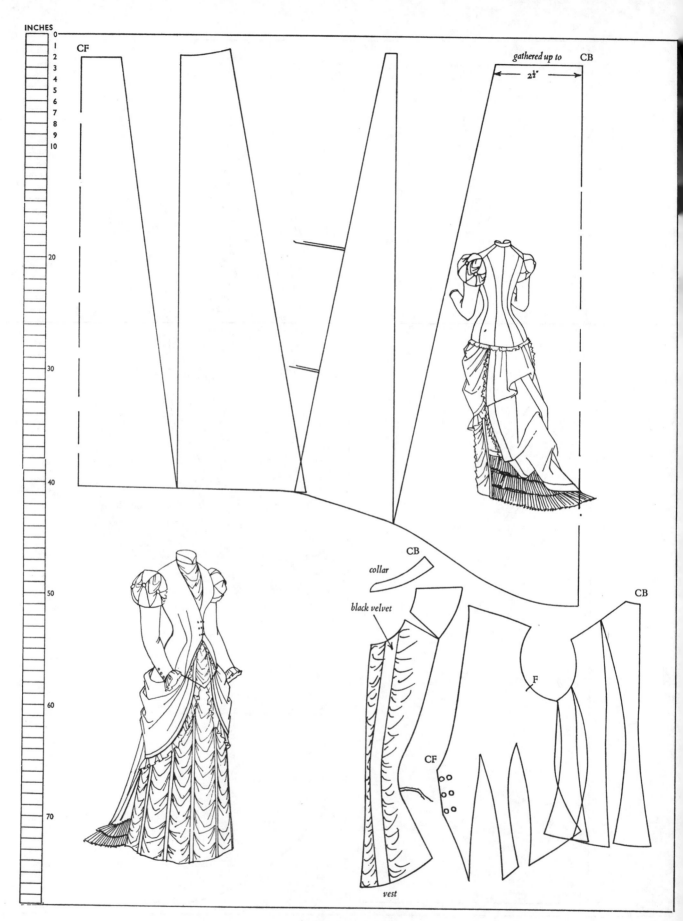

INCHES
0
1
2
3
4
5
6
7
8
9
10
20
30
40
50
60
70

CF

*gathered up to*

CB

2¼"

CB

*collar*

*black velvet*

CB

F

CF

*vest*

DIAGRAM LV

AFTERNOON DRESS (BUSTLE) *c.* 1883. *Gallery of English Costume, Manchester*

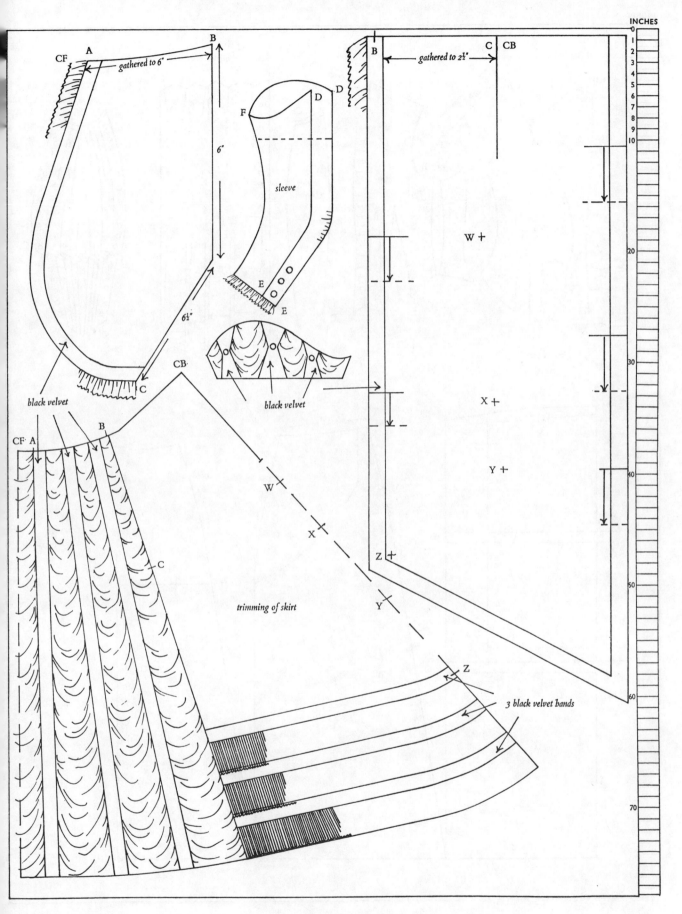

CF   A      *gathered to 6"*      B

B     *gathered to 2½"*     C   CB

D   D

F

6"

*sleeve*

6½"

E

E

CB

C

*black velvet*

*black velvet*

CF   A

B

C

W +

X +

Y +

Z +

*trimming of skirt*

W

X

Z

Y

Z

*3 black velvet bands*

INCHES

0
1
2
3
4
5
6
7
8
9
10

20

30

40

50

60

70

DIAGRAM LV

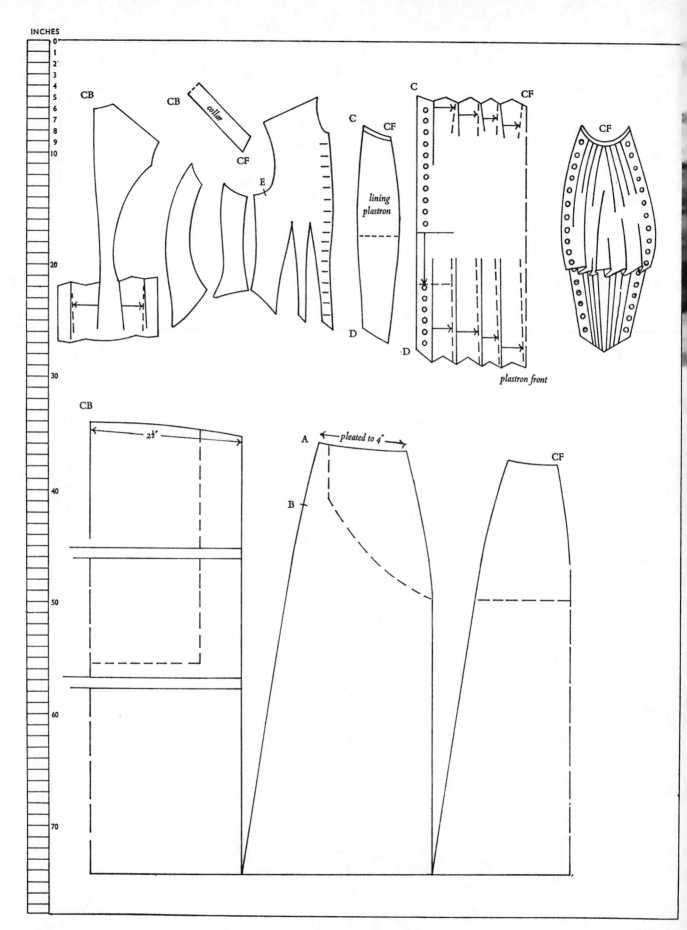

INCHES

CB  CB  collar  CF  E  C  CF  lining plastron  D  D  C  CF  C  CF  plastron front  CF

CB  2¼"  A  pleated to 4"  B  CF

DIAGRAM LVI

DAY DRESS (BUSTLE) *c.* 1888. *Victoria and Albert Museum*

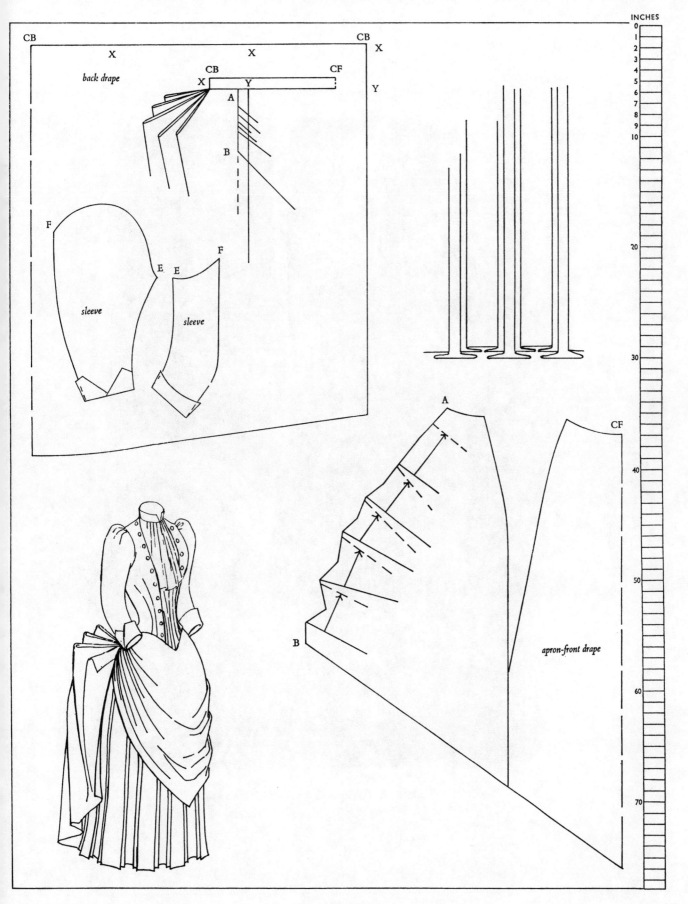

back drape

sleeve

sleeve

CB          X          X          CB      X
X          CB      CF
back drape          X          Y          Y
A
B

F          F
E          E

A          CF

B          apron-front drape

INCHES
0
1
2
3
4
5
6
7
8
9
10

20

30

40

50

60

70

DIAGRAM LVI

Toilette de Réception ou de Théatre 1874.

# Nineteenth-century Dress Production

At the beginning of the nineteenth century dresses were made by the mantua maker or at home, the materials and accessories, as in the eighteenth century, being supplied by individual shop-keepers, each dealing in one particular type of merchandise–gloves, shawls, silks, linens, ribbons, lace, etc. By the middle of the nineteenth century the growing prosperity of the middle classes, and the ever-increasing number of women who wished to be well and fashionably dressed, was having its repercussions. Already in England in the 1840's there were shops selling a diversity of goods; these were the forerunners of the department stores. The number of women's journals whose main concern was dress started to snowball, paper patterns were being sold, and finally there was M. Worth, who began Haute Couture.

Dressmakers during the first half of the nineteenth century were women, with one distinguished exception, Leroy, who dressed Joséphine and other ladies of the Napoleonic Court. Leroy began his career as hairdresser to Marie Antoinette. Later he became a *marchand des modes*, and eventually a *couturier*. Although he created no new styles, his transformation of the simple lines of the muslin dress into a sumptuous Court robe of heavily embroidered satins and velvets evinced all the elegance of the eighteenth century that was so sadly missing in the ostentatious men's Court suits of this period.

With the passing of the gay society of Regency London and the Napoleonic Court, there was no Duchess of Devonshire or Joséphine to inspire the dressmaker. The milliner began to concentrate on hats and caps, and the dressmaker to make dresses. These were made up from material already purchased by the customer, and in styles chosen from the fashion magazines. Sometimes a dressmaker with more imagination would invent a trimming or vary a sleeve style, but the basic line remained unchanged for many years and became in the 1840's even more simplified to suit the decorous taste of the new middle class customers. Worth's career began at an auspicious moment; the Great Exhibitions of the early 1850's in England and Paris had broadened the outlook of the bourgeoisie, and Paris once more had an Imperial Court. Worth, like his predecessor Leroy, again transformed a simple dress into an elegant gown worthy to grace an Imperial Court and extravagant enough to display newly-acquired riches.

183

The story of the emergence of Worth as a dress designer is romantic. For some years he had been working for one of the most important shops in Paris, the Maison Gagelin, which sold materials, shawls, cloaks, etc., and in 1848 he married one of the shop assistants, a very attractive young girl. Inspired by her beauty and by the lovely materials surrounding him he began to design dresses for her and supervise their execution. By choosing a particular material, using it as the texture suggested and modelling it on a human body, Worth revitalized dressmaking, or rather elevated it into dress designing. Worth's dresses were a success, and the Maison Gagelin allowed him to make models some of which were displayed at the Great Exhibitions, and orders poured in for his firm. Worth began to visualize dressmaking on a large scale basis but the Maison Gagelin were too well established on their own lines to co-operate, so eventually, in 1858, Worth founded his own business. He filled his workrooms with materials, lace, trimmings, etc. bought direct from the manufacturers, and from this store he created dresses not only to suit individual customers but model gowns which were bought by the large shops and high-class dressmakers to be copied in workrooms all over the world. Very soon, houses run on similar lines were opened in Paris. It was the beginning of Haute Couture.

Ready-made garments which required no fitting, such as underclothes, capes, mantles, etc., had been on sale from the eighteenth century, but it was not until the beginning of the nineteenth century, when the simple muslin dresses were being worn, that one hears of ready-made dresses and these were only partly made. 'Sewed muslin' dresses are mentioned in 1845. These probably had the full front bodice which could be easily adjusted. As long as the body of the fashionable dress fitted tightly, the production of ready-made dresses was limited, but in the 1850's the problem was partly solved by selling made-up skirts together with a length of material sufficient to make the bodice and sleeves–a custom which was continued until 1908.

In the second half of the nineteenth century more shops selling an ever-widening variety of goods were being opened all over the world. They had large dress departments. They established workrooms where an efficient staff copied model gowns bought from the Paris houses, they made dresses for individual customers, and they designed and executed their own models of ready-mades and partly ready-mades. But the service supplied by the shops was only just beginning; there were still a great number of private dressmakers ranging from the high-class Court dressmaker with her own workroom down to the little village dressmaker coping by herself. Dresses had become too complicated to be made at home, though with the aid of the visiting sewing woman they were altered, re-trimmed or cut up and remade. Labour was cheap, and hundreds of women toiled until the early hours of the morning for a mere pittance.

The new mathematical approach to tailoring which was being developed during the nineteenth century was also used by tailors when making women's riding habits, and later–from the 1850's–jackets, coats, Ulsters, etc. Many of the tailor's cutting books from the beginning of the century include instructions and diagrams for riding habits; from the 1850's occasionally for coats and jackets, and by the 1880's for a variety of women's outdoor garments. This new approach to cutting was not used by the dressmaker, who found it difficult enough to draft out a pattern from the scaled diagrams supplied by the women's journals and dressmaking manuals.

Embroidery designs for borders, caps, etc. were given in ladies' magazines from the beginning of the nineteenth century, but scaled diagrams were rare before the 1840's. These invariably had the same bodice pattern with only slight variations of sleeves, collars, etc. In England after 1850 *The World of Fashion* was publishing full scale patterns for bodices, mantles, underwear, etc. These were all drawn out on a single sheet of paper, which folded into the magazine. The separate pieces of the pattern were distinguishable from each other by the line–unbroken, dots, dashes, etc.–so that 'the models may be traced with ease'. Other magazines followed suit. The many magazines of the second half of the century often ran a paper pattern service, and their contents included dressmaking notes and correspondence columns devoted to advice on the making and remaking of dresses.

There was a very good German magazine–*Bekleidungskunst für Damen–Allgemeine Muster-Zeitung* (Dressmaking for Ladies–Universal Pattern Journal), Dresden, 1844. As well as the usual magazine material, stories, correspondence, fashion notes, etc., it also gives a simple system of cutting from measurements, by H. Klemm. The folded-paper diagram sheets include full scale patterns for bodices and sleeves, and also scaled diagrams, with variations of sleeves, mantles, bodice trimmings, illustrated by engravings. (Pages 195–198.)

Paper patterns were sold from the first quarter of the century onwards by firms specializing in 'models made up in paper'. These were designed for the professional dressmaker rather than for home use. Advertisement: 'February Fashions for 1834. Madame and Mrs. Follet, in returning thanks for the extensive patronage they continue to receive, beg to announce to ladies in business, that their indefatigable exertions to produce the earliest arrivals of Fashions will be unremitting, a comparison of their extensive assortment of coloured French paper Models in every description of Millinery and Dress, will be convincing evidence of their great superiority–Sold in sets at 10s. (comprising four articles) packed for any part of the United Kingdom at 3s. extra.' Production of paper patterns on a large and wider scale came later–Buttericks from 1863, Weldons from 1879.

Two early books on dressmaking–*Instructions for Cutting out Apparel for the Poor*, 1789, and the *Workman's Guide*, 1838, were, as their titles suggest, intended for the assistance of ladies engaged in charity work. The patterns are very simple and the instructions good. Three of the best early dressmaking manuals are: *The Ladies' Handbook of Millinery, Dressmaking and Tatting*, 1843 (good instructions); *The Handbook of Dressmaking*, Mrs. M. J. Howell, 1845 (good diagrams and instructions); and *A New and Complete Method of Dressmaking*, Mrs. T. Whiteley, 1855, who also published later on, *The Complete Dressmaker for the Million*, in 1875. As Mrs. Whiteley's instructions are the least complicated, here are her instructions for making a bodice and skirt:

1855. 'For an ordinary sized person, to make a plain skirt, full body, and trimmed sleeves:

14 yards of silk, or 9 yards of double width (such as Merino), 10 yards of Print; for Flounces or Tucks allow about 6 yards, according to the width of the material; 6 yards of double width lining for Skirt; one yard of Holland, or one and a quarter of Calico for the Body; one and a quarter of ditto for Sleeves; Hooks and Eyes, Sewing Silk, Cotton Cord, Whalebone, and Braid for the bottom of the Skirt. Trimmings must be according to taste or fashion.

*Bodice.* The shoulder should be in a straight line just behind the rise of the shoulder, the seam under the arm in the centre of the waist from the armpit to the top of the hip, the bosom plaits (darts) about half the length of the body from the breast to the waist, the back the same.

*To make a plain body.* Take the holland pattern, lay it smoothly on the wrong side of the material, tack in all the pin marks and seams, cut it to the pattern, allowing for turnings, baste it together by the marks, every seam to match, hem the backs, sew on the hooks and eyes, then try it on to see that it fits, before stitching the seams together; the most inexperienced could discover and correct any little fault while it is on the figure. When stitched together make a casing for whalebone in the bosom plaits (darts) and down the front, also under the arms; cut a piece of piping on the cross, enclose a cord, sew it round the neck and waist, and baste it round the armholes; great care must be taken, in sewing the piping round the waist not to contract the size and spoil the fitting. Trim with buttons, lace or fringe, or anything that may suit the material or wearer.

*Construction of sleeves.* Measure length; armhole to wrist, back of arm with it bent, inside arm from armpit to wrist, round the thick part of the arm, above the elbow, between elbow and wrist, and wrist. By measuring the arm as before directed, and transferring the size on a piece of paper folded double on the cross, you may at all times make a plain tight sleeve. . . . In putting in the sleeves in the armhole place the seam about an inch to the front of the seam under the arm, this will prevent the sleeve twisting and feeling uncomfortable.

*Skirt. Directions for making up.* Cut off as many breadths as required, allowing a finger length beyond the making-up measure, this will be half for top and bottom turnings; cut the lining the same length, then lay a breadth of lining on the table, baste a breadth of the material smoothly on it, join another breadth to that with the lining, spread it open, baste it the same as first, join again, and so on till all the breadths are together; then turn up a hem at the bottom, half a finger length, turn the two edges of lining and material together at the top; run them, to prevent the material from ravelling, this will also give a neat appearance; make the slit for the pocket-hole a quarter of a yard in length, hem the right side broad–the left narrow; run the braid at the bottom. Your skirt is then ready for plaiting or gathering. If tucks are required proper allowance must be made when cutting off the lengths of skirt, cut a piece of paper or card the depth of the tuck, lay it on the skirt and baste it round before running the tuck, then run one, having done so, mark the skirt the same for the second as first, and so on until all are run. You can measure and mark the skirt in the same manner for flounces by measuring the depth of flounce. Almost any material looks well cut on the cross, and the flounces hang much prettier than straight ones, especially a stiff material. In cutting flounces, allow one extra width of skirt, if cut straight, for fulness, beyond the width of skirt; if on the cross, the same number of widths as skirt, this will always be sufficient, as they do not look well when put on too full. Turn down the skirt to the length of measure and slope it according to the length of waist-point, confining the slope to one third of the width, so that whether gathered or plaited, the slope is not carried beyond the seam under the arm; the remaining portion to go to the back. This will cause the skirt to hang free and gracefully on the figure; if plaited, they should be formed before turning down the slope. Double plaits are at present very fashionable. These must be laid both ways to meet even in the centre. As belts are also much worn, double plaits all round look extremely pretty, and are quicker to make. The skirt is now ready to sew on the waist, you must, therefore, lay it carefully aside and finish the body.

1875. *Directions for making gored skirts.* For a walking length measure from the waist to the instep, cut one length for the front breadth according to measure allowing sufficient for hem at the bottom, fold the breadth double down the centre, then slope off the form of a gore, commencing from the point of width at the bottom, gradually narrowing to the top (this is for the front width only); then cut two more lengths measuring by the slope side, lay the two widths face to face in cutting them, so that you will have them right for each side; gore these both together, then cut two more half an inch longer; gore these, then cut one straight width for the back an inch longer, lay the front width open on the table, then pin one width on each side, commencing from the top, put the straight side to the cross side–that is, one selvage one cross together; the same with the other two widths, one on each side, same with the back width. When your skirt is pinned together, see that each gore is in its right place before you begin to run it up, in order to avoid mistakes; in running the seams of skirts, be careful not to pucker the cross side, as it would spoil the appearance and fit. When your seams are finished, double the skirt, lay it on the table, and pare off any little corners at the end of the seams, so as to make the bottom of the skirt a pretty round shape (the bottom of an ordinary sized skirt should measure about 100 inches), turn down the hem to depth allowed; in doing so, you will find a small plait come between the seams, these you must be careful in placing right, to prevent the hem twisting; if you baste the hem at the edge before sewing it, you will then see where the little plaits will fall easily before finishing it. In putting on the braid, hold it easily in the hand, so as not to stretch it, insert a pocket in the first front seam at the right hand about five inches from the top, leave the opposite side open about ten inches, hem the top of the skirt to give it a neat and finished appearance. It is now ready for any trimming you may think proper to put on, either flounces, cross-tucks, ruchings, panniers, or any trimming to suit the material and please the taste, their being such a diversity of styles and freaks of fashion, it would be impossible to give a specific rule for trimmings. Paper patterns of all styles of panniers can be readily obtained from the designers. The above make of skirt can be altered in width or length according to the material used or size of person it is intended for. By cutting the back width longer, you can form a trained skirt; in cutting the gown you must use your own judgment according to the width of material, as the wide width, such as French merino, would cut four gores or two side ones and one front, or two from one width, whereas silks, bareges, lamas–in fact, there are many materials so narrow in width that will only cut one gore; you must therefore exercise discretion accordingly. . . . The skirt can be sewn on a band or to the waist; the former would be more useful according to the present styles as the second skirts, or panniers, look better sewn on to the body. . . . In putting the gored skirt on the waist, allow a plain piece in the front about 8 or 9 inches according to the size of the waist and gather the back width into the space of about four inches.'

It is obvious from the contemporary references that in spite of the new systems the dressmaker still clung to the age-old methods when it came to cutting out a bodice. She either made a pattern by fitting her customer directly, in paper or holland, or, more often and more easily she took her pattern from an old bodice. Here are the two methods:

*The Ladies Handbook of Millinery, Dressmaking and Tatting*, 1843. 'Take the proper measures for the front and back of the body by fitting a paper pattern to the shape of the person for whom the dress is intended. The paper should be thin and you commence by folding down the corner the length of the front, and pinning it to the middle of the stay bone. Then let the paper be spread as smoothly as possible along the bosom to the shoulder, and fold it in a plait (dart) so as to fit the shape exactly, and bring the paper under the arm, making it retain its position by a pin. From this point you cut it off downward under the arm, and along the waist; the paper is then to be rounded for the armhole and the shoulder, and you must recollect to leave it large enough to admit of the turnings. In the same manner you proceed to form the back, pinning the paper straight down, and leaving sufficient for the hem, you fit it to the shoulder and under the arm, so as to meet the front. You will thus have an exact pattern of half the body. The linings are to be cut by the pattern and the silk by the linings. You must take care to cut the front on the cross way of the silk and in two separate pieces, which are afterwards joined in the middle. If the plait made in the pattern be very large, it must be cut out on the silk, or the body will not fit well to the shape; if small, it may be left, but we think that in all cases to cut it out is the preferable method. It is not generally advisable to cut out the half of the back all in one piece, as it fits better with pieces joined at the sides; these are called side bodies; and this method should always be adopted, unless the lady had a very flat back; in that case it is best to cut the half all in one piece. The backs must be cut straight and it is best to tack the material to the lining before cutting it.' N.B. By the end of the 1840's the front of the bodice is always cut on the straight, not the cross; and the back is always cut with side bodies.

*The Ladies Treasury*, 1876. 'It is almost impossible to learn dressmaking without taking lessons, while few are competent to teach; they almost invariably omit to describe minor details upon which completeness depends. *In a bodice*, the shoulder seam of the front should be rounded–that is, first cut straight, then the two ends rounded. The shoulder seam of the back, should, on the contrary, be cut diagonally. The armhole be rounded and cut in deep, next the bust, and at the side seam be cut up in a point. This is to prevent dragging when the arm is lifted. The back seam of the sleeve be placed mid-way between the shoulder seam and the side-piece at the back. *To cut out and fit a bodice.* Take an old bodice, lay the back flat on a table, upon this pin a piece of stout paper–pin it nearly close to the seams, then turn it on the right side, and with a very large needle prick it through the seams to the paper beneath. On taking off the paper cut an inch beyond these pin-holes. The side-piece is done in the same way. The front is more difficult. Take a large piece of paper, and pin it straight across the bust above the darts or gores; let the straight edge of the paper be about an inch beyond the places of the hooks or eyes in the front. Now pucker the paper up into one or more folds, which will form the darts, and cut the paper to within an inch of the armhole, and press the paper into the space under the arm to the side seam. Then tack the paper at the upper part of the bodice to the shoulder seam. Now prick through as before, and cut one inch beyond the pin-holes. This is a rough cast of the pattern, but it serves. Now take a piece of old calico or print and cut it the size of the paper pattern marking with coloured threads on the calico where the pinholes are on the paper. Tack the pattern together and try it on. Pin a piece of tape round the neck; put on the pattern with the seam edges outside. Pin it first at the neck then at the waist, then at the back, now fit it under the arms, then at the neck, and lastly, the darts. Measure the waist with a tape measure, and see that the bodice fits to this, of course allowing for the overlap for hooks and eyes or other fastenings. A little practice will enable you to cut a bodice as well as any dressmaker. One thing remember, to sew the sleeve into the armhole with the sleeve towards you. This gives the requisite fulness to the set of the sleeve, so that the roundness of the arm is complete and not strained by the sleeve; and in fitting the sleeve be sure there is no curb or tightness under the side seam.'

Even tailors advocated this method, as can be seen from the following extracts from *The Cutters' Practical Guide, Patterns–Taking Patterns from Old Garments*, Vincent, *c.* 1889: 'This is essentially the dressmakers' method. The dressmaker takes her pattern garment and pins paper on each part, and by placing it over her knees, she is enabled to get the exact shape, and then by allowing seams on all sides, she can thus produce a facsimilie garment; and it would be idle for us to say the method is not successful, as we have seen some first-class results produced in this way. Some of them go to the trouble of ripping one side of the old garment, and tracing with a wheel through exactly where the seam was sewn; and having done so to remake the garment.

'In contrast to this, however, we will show the *Tailors' Method*. As adopted by a well-known West End tailor, as follows: Whenever a garment was ordered which he was unable to measure the lady for, he would send the old garment to a firm of bust makers to have a dummy made to fit the Bodice, by which means he would be able to successfully cater for the wants of that particular customer, without a try on, even if she were in the Antipodes; as he would, for all practical purposes, have her duplicate to try on as many times as he would wish. This method, of course, entails an extra cost (about 10s. we are informed) on the first order; but the after result certainly justifies the outlay, and as the bust would be always ready for use any time, the first cost would be the only one, and would be of use for every kind of garment. Having once obtained this, it only remains to follow his usual method; but all tailors cannot follow this plan on account of the expense, so they usually fit the old Bodice on a dummy of figures as near the same size and shape as possible and pad it up to the Bodice wherever the figure is lacking.'

The 'dummy' method was not confined to tailors, it was also used by the best dressmakers though not always to the extent of ordering special dummies for each customer. Most dress-making establishments had at least one dummy and became expert in padding it up to the requisite size. Tailors used the dummy for fitting garments already cut out by drafting. Dress-makers not only used it for fitting but they began to cut direct on the dummy and it was this system that in the next century became known as the *Dressmakers' Method*. Skirts were always draped on a dummy, those of the 1880's were mounted on wire dress stands shaped to the fashionable bustle silhouette.

Instructions for making a skirt from *The Cutters' Practical Guide*, Vincent, c. 1889: '*Foundation Skirt*–the materials most used for foundations are linen, Italian cloth, silk, etc. The best of these is linen, as it combines all the advantages of silk, while it wears better and it is far less expensive. The foundation is seamed up with the seams to come outside, and a facing is put all round the bottom some 5 or 6 inches deep, so that the bottom is bound with this facing; on the top of this is a narrow kilt put also about 4 or 5 inches deep; this is done more with the view of keeping the skirt out round the bottom than for it to show, though as we write there is a decided tendency for them to be seen, and in some cases are put on the top of the drapery. It will be readily understood that foundations are, for the present, seldom used; all skirts are now being made up lined throughout, a facing put round the bottom some 5 or 6 inches deep, and in many cases braid is added just on the edge. They are invariably trimmed with cross-way bands, braid or flounces. *Draping*. The best ladies' tailors keep dummies made up for all their best customers. Take the foundation, and having put it into the waistband, etc., arrange your folds of drapery on this till the desired effect is produced. There is no golden rule for this; nothing but practice and experiment can teach you how to drape artistically for all your customers . . . materials vary considerably in the way they form folds, or, in other words, drape; so that what might be a good rule for one material or one figure, would not apply at all for another.'

Foundation skirts could be bought ready made: 1889. 'Patent Shapely Dress Association– This association supplies at a small cost, the foundation skirt complete, with steel, pocket, horsehair pad, and waistband, giving the basis of a well hung fashionable skirt.' This must have been a boon to the hardly pressed dressmakers.

# Nineteenth-century
# Tailors' and Dressmakers' Patterns

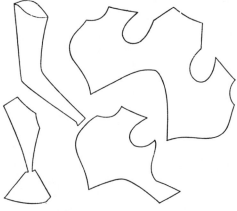

(above)

13. 1796. *The Taylor's Complete Guide, or A Comprehensive Analysis of Beauty and Elegance in Dress.*
'Containing rules for cutting out garments of every kind. To which is added a description of how to cut out and make the patent elestic Habits and Cloaks, without the usual seams, now in the highest estimation with the Nobility and Gentry, according to a patent granted by his Majesty.'

A diagram showing a bodice without the usual seams. This cut is possible with a very short bodice.

(right)

14. 1822. *The Tailor's Friendly Instructor.* J. Wyatt.
Fig. 1. Back of Pelisse.
Fig. 2. Front of Pelisse.
Fig. 3. Sleeve.
Fig. 4. Habit.
Fig. 5. Spencer. Garments of this description generally have a running string to draw them to the size of the waist. The bottom part is marked a little rounded to provide for this drawing in.
Fig. 6. A Collar, that will stand away from the neck and part fall down.
Fig. 7. A Collar to stand up and not fit close to the neck.
Fig. 8. Represents a habit skirt whole.
Fig. 9. Forepart of habit skirt to pleat up with side edge.

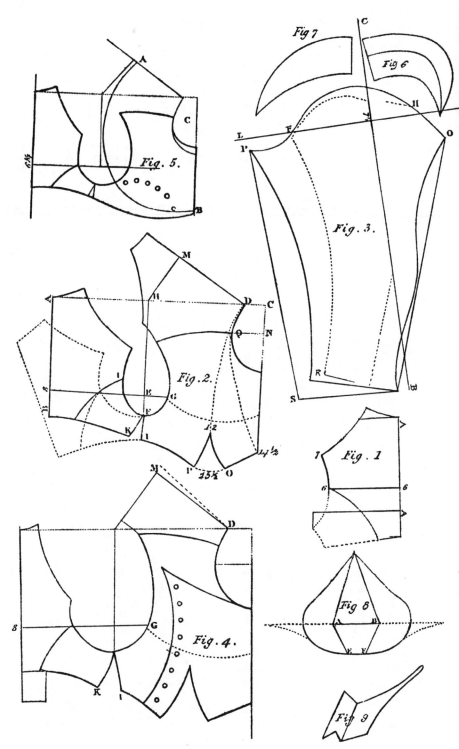

## Patterns of Dresses, Corsets, &c.

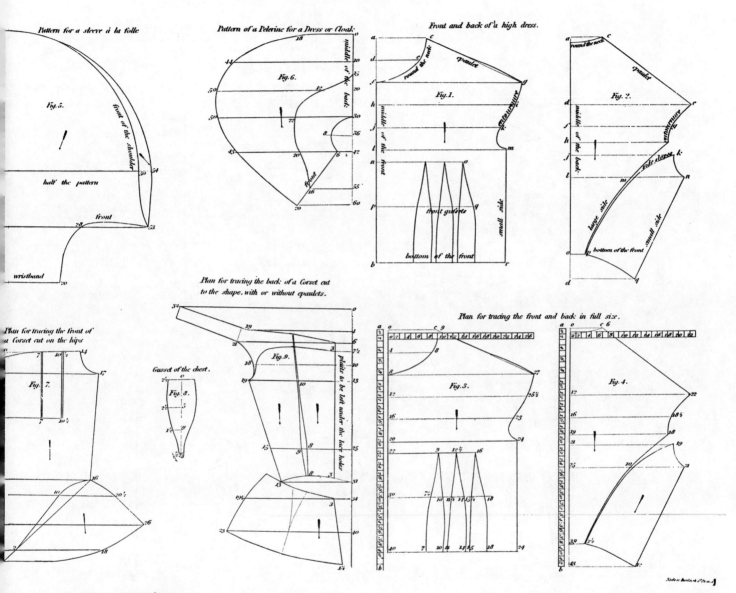

Pattern for a sleeve à la folle

Fig. 5.

front of the shoulder

half the pattern

front

wristband

Pattern of a Pelerine for a Dress or Cloak:

Fig. 6.

middle of the back

front

Front and back of a high dress.

round the neck

epaulet

Fig. 1.

middle of the front

small side

front gusset

bottom of the front

round the neck

epaulet

Fig. 2.

middle of the back

ouverture

side sleeve

large side

small side

bottom of the front

Plan for tracing the front of a Corset cut on the hips

Fig. 7.

Gusset of the chest.

Fig. 8.

Plan for tracing the back of a Corset cut
to the shape, with or without epaulets.

Fig. 9.

plaits to be left under the lace holes

Plan for tracing the front and back in full size.

Fig. 3.

Fig. 4.

15. 1834. *Petit Courier des Dames.*
Bodice, Sleeve, Cape and Corset.

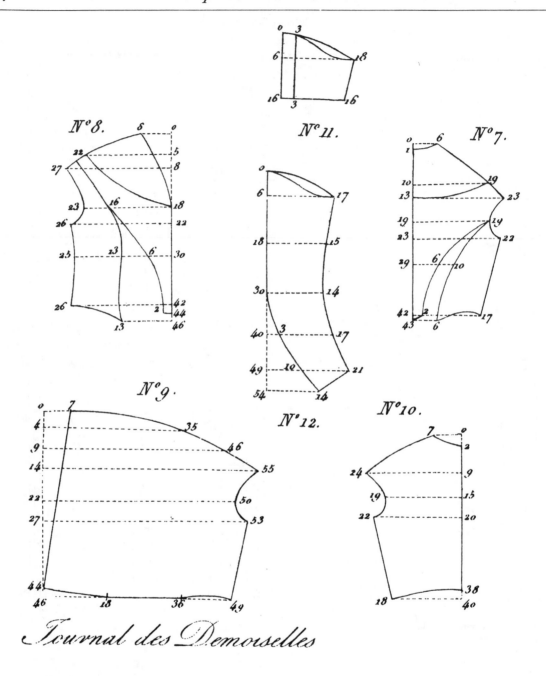

*Journal des Demoiselles*

16. 1843. *Journal des Demoiselles.*
    Composite Bodice pattern, showing tightly fitting bodice
    with a high or low neck.
    No. 7. Back.
    No. 8. Front.
    No. 9. and No. 10 show a draft for a bodice to be gathered or
       pleated from shoulder line and again at the waist, and
       often mounted on to a tightly fitting lining.
    No. 11. Short sleeve or over sleeve.
    No. 12. Long tight sleeve.

17. 1844. *Lehrbuch der Modernen Bekleidungskunst für Damen.*
    Bodices for Day and Evening wear. Note the extra under arm piece,
    not usual in England or France but very useful for fitting large figures.

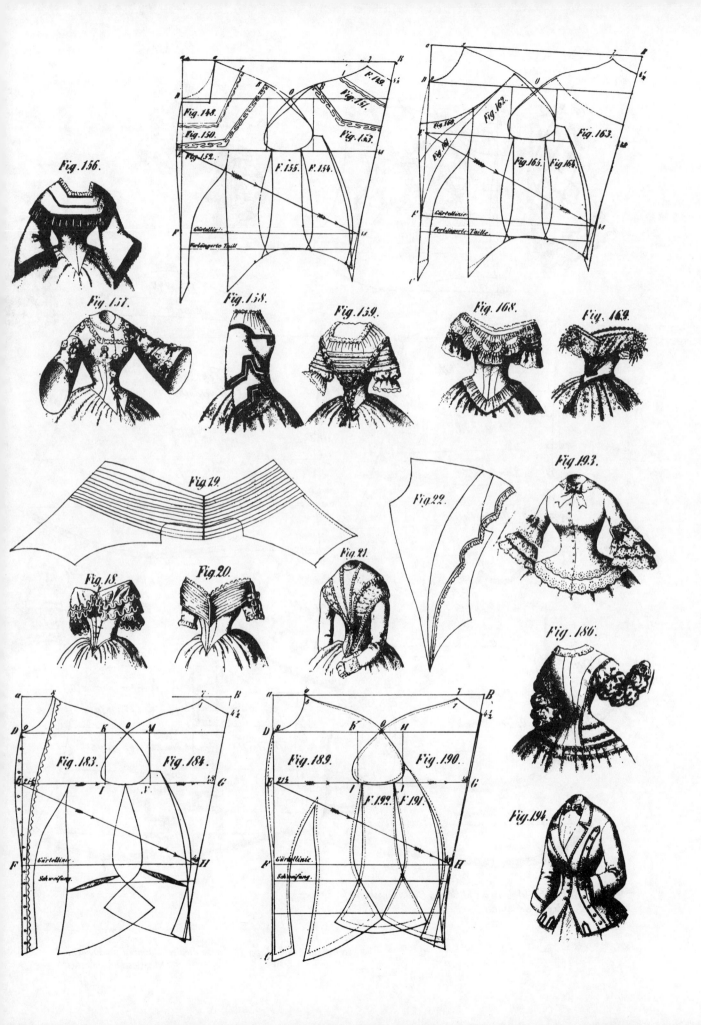

Fig. 156.

Fig. 148. Fig. 150. Fig. 152. Fig. 149. Fig. 151. Fig. 153. F. 155. F. 154.
Gürtellinie. Verlängerte Taill.

Fig. 162. Fig. 163. Fig. 165. Fig. 164.
Gürtellinie. Verlängerte Taille.

Fig. 157. Fig. 158. Fig. 159. Fig. 168. Fig. 169.

Fig. 19.

Fig. 22. Fig. 193.

Fig. 18. Fig. 20. Fig. 21.

Fig. 186.

Fig. 183. Fig. 184.
Gürtellinie.
Schweifung.

Fig. 189. Fig. 190. F. 192. F. 191.
Gürtellinie.
Schweifung.

Fig. 194.

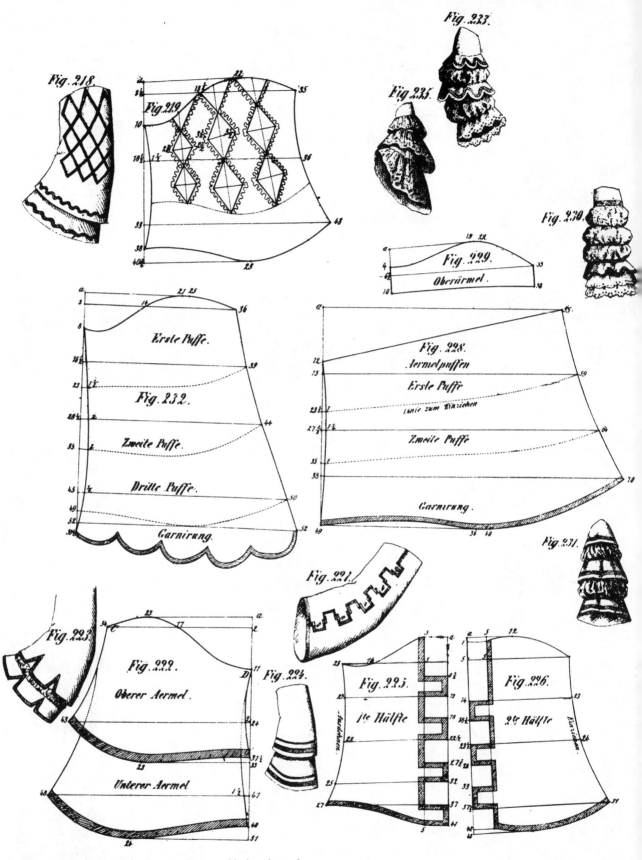

Fig. 218. Fig. 219. Fig. 227. Fig. 235. Fig. 230.

Fig. 229. Oberärmel.

Erste Puffe. Fig. 228. Aermelpuffen

Fig. 232. Erste Puffe

Zweite Puffe. Zweite Puffe

Dritte Puffe. Garnirung.

Garnirung. Fig. 231.

Fig. 221.

Fig. 233. Fig. 222. Fig. 224. Fig. 225. Fig. 226.

Oberer Aermel. 1te Hälfte 2te Hälfte

Unterer Aermel

18. 1844. *Lehrbuch der Modernen Bekleidungskunst fur Damen.*
   Sleeve variations.

19. 1844. *Lehrbuch der Modernen Bekleidungskunst fur Damen.*
   Mantles and Paletots.

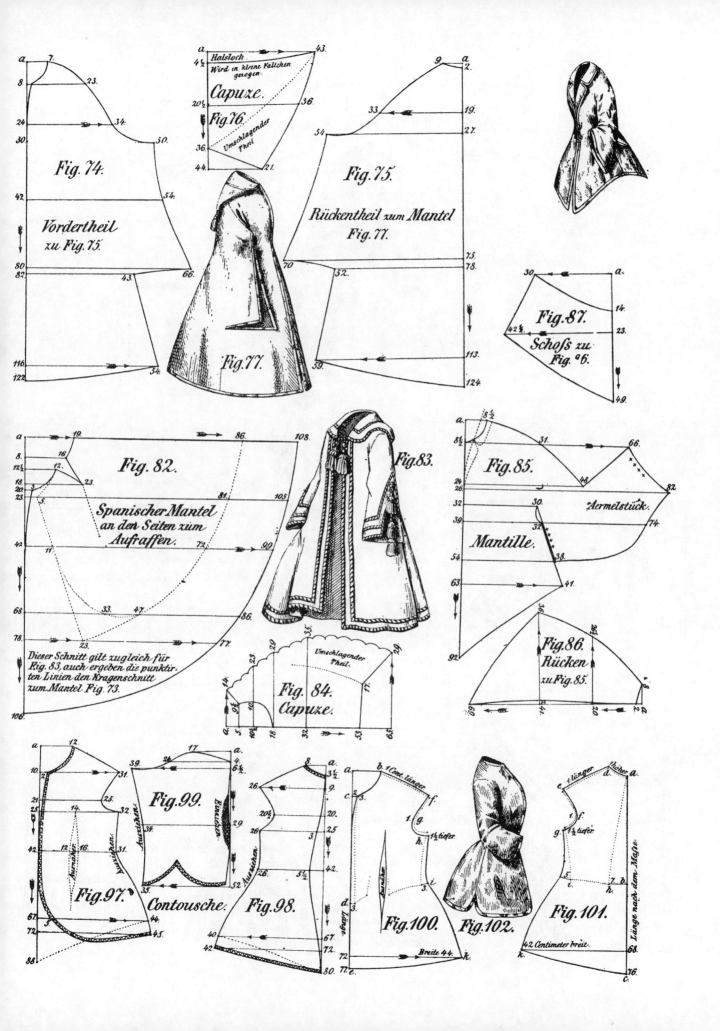

**Fig. 74.**

*a* 7.

8

23.

24 34.

30 50.

42 54.

**Vordertheil
zu Fig. 75.**

80

82 43. 66.

116 54.

122

**Fig. 76.**

*a* 43.

4½ *Halsloch
Wird in kleine Fältchen
gezogen*

**Capuze.**

20½ 36.

**Fig. 76.**

36 *Umschlagender
Theil.*

44 21.

**Fig. 75.**

9 *a* 2.

33 19.

54 27.

**Rückentheil zum Mantel
Fig. 77.**

75.

70 52. 78.

113.

59. 124.

**Fig. 77.**

**Fig. 87.**

30 *a.*

14.

**Fig. 87.**
**Schoſs zu
Fig. 86.**

42½ 23.

49.

**Fig. 82.**

*a* 19. 86. 108.

8. 16.

12½ 12.

18 23.

20 3

23 5.

81. 105.

42

11

72. 99.

68 33. 47.

78 23. 77. 86.

*Dieser Schnitt gilt zugleich für
Fig. 83, auch ergeben die punktir-
ten Linien den Kragenschnitt
zum Mantel Fig. 73.*

106

**Spanischer Mantel
an den Seiten zum
Aufraffen.**

**Fig. 83.**

**Fig. 84.
Capuze.**

35.
29.
23.
*Umschlagender
Theil.*
14.
9½
10.
17.
9
5. 10½ 18. 32. 53. 65.

**Fig. 85.**

8½
*a*
8½ 31. 66.

24 48.
26

32 30.

39 37. 74.

54 38.

63 41.

**Mantille.**

*Aermelstück.*

92 36.

**Fig. 86.
Rücken
zu Fig. 85.**

**Fig. 97.**

*a* 12.

10 31.

2

21 25.

25 14. 32.

34.

42 12. 16. 31.

*Aufziehen.*
*Aufziehen.*

67 5. 44.

72 45.

88

**Fig. 99.**

17. *a.*
39. 24. 4½

*Aufziehen.*

29.

35. 52.

*Aufziehen.*

**Contousche.**

**Fig. 98.**

8. *a.*
3½

26 9.

20½ 20.

26 25.

3.

42.

5½

40 67.

42 72.

80.

**Fig. 100.**

*a b.* 1 Cent. länger

*c.* 2 3.

*f.*

1. *g.*

*h.* 1½ tiefer

*Anziehen*

*d.* 3 3.

*Länge*

72 *Breite 44.* *k.*

*m.e.*

**Fig. 102.**

**Fig. 101.**

*e.* 1 länger 1 höher *a.*
*d.*

*f.*

1. *g.*

*g.* 1½ tiefer.

5. 7. *b.*
*i.* *h.*

42 Centimeter breit

*k.* 68.

*k.* 16.

*c.*

*Länge nach dem Maße.*

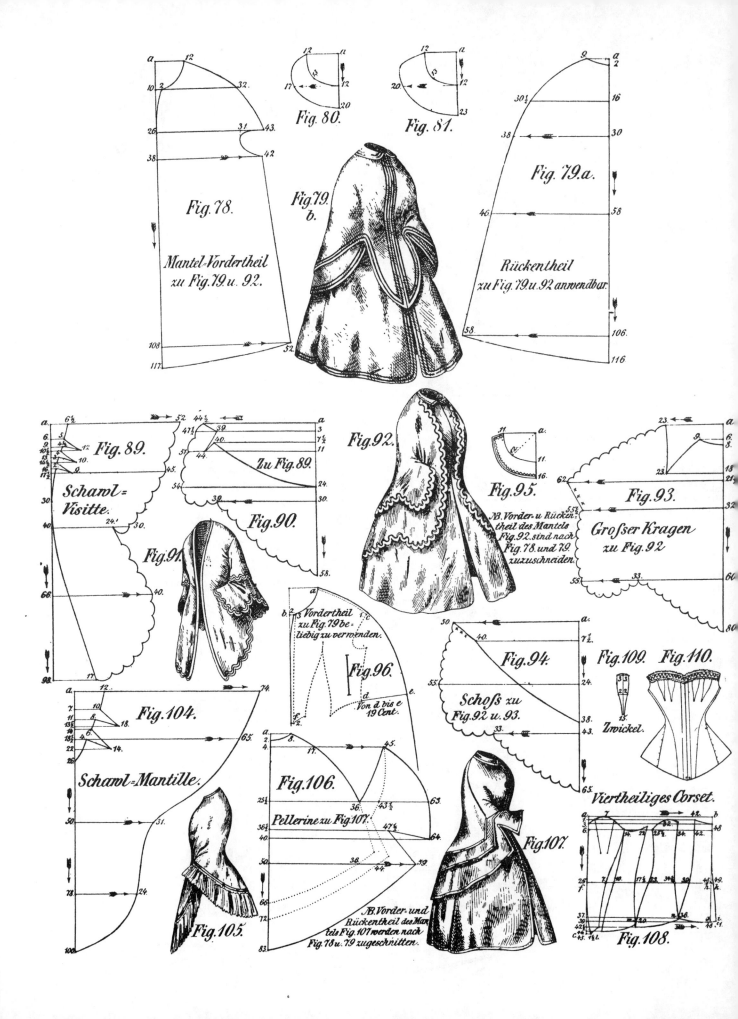

*Fig. 78.*

*Mantel-Vordertheil zu Fig. 79 u. 92.*

*Fig. 80.*

*Fig. 81.*

*Fig. 79. b.*

*Fig. 79. a.*

*Rückentheil zu Fig. 79 u. 92 anwendbar.*

*Fig. 89.*

*Schawl=Visitte.*

*Zu Fig. 89.*

*Fig. 90.*

*Fig. 91.*

*Fig. 92.*

*Fig. 95.*

NB. Vorder- u. Rücken-theil des Mantels Fig. 92. sind nach Fig. 78. und 79. zuzuschneiden.

*Fig. 93.*

*Grofser Kragen zu Fig. 92*

*Fig. 96.*

Vordertheil zu Fig. 79 be-liebig zu verwenden.

Von d. bis e 19 Cent.

*Fig. 94.*

*Schofs zu Fig. 92 u. 93.*

*Fig. 109.* *Fig. 110.*

*Zwickel.*

*Fig. 104.*

*Schawl=Mantille.*

*Fig. 105.*

*Fig. 106.*

*Pellerine zu Fig. 107.*

NB. Vorder- und Rückentheil des Man-tels Fig. 107 werden nach Fig. 78 u. 79 zugeschnitten.

*Fig. 107.*

*Viertheiliges Corset.*

*Fig. 108.*

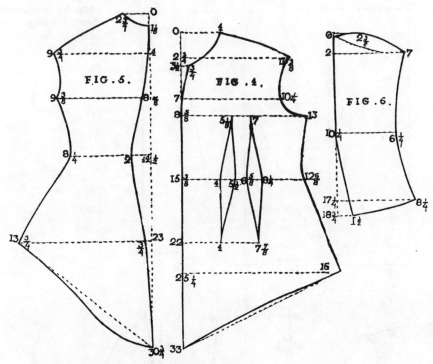

21. 1850. *The Gentleman's Magazine of Fashion.*
A Tailored Jacket.

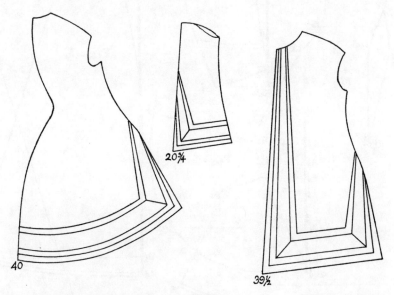

22. 1850. *The Gentleman's Magazine of Fashion.*
Ladies Paletot called the Victoria in honour of the patronage bestowed upon it by her Majesty. It has been made in cloth, merino and satin; the broad band in the centre is a trimming of velvet narrowing towards the top and has braid on either side. The side seam is open and laced half way with a silk cord ending in two tassels. For the Opera this Paletot is extremely elegant made in white cashmere, lined and trimmed with scarlet.

20. 1844. *Lehrbuch der Modernen Bekleidungskunst für Damen.*
Shawl, Mantles and Dolmans.

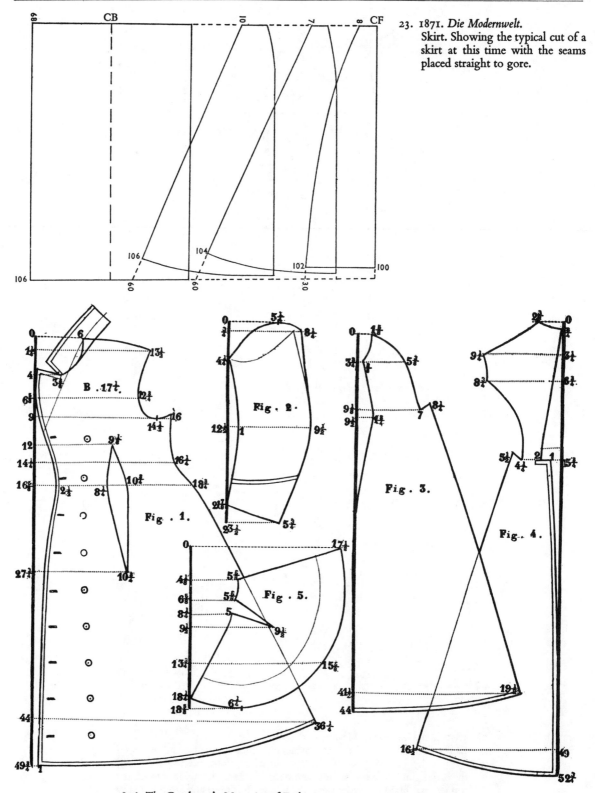

23. 1871. *Die Modernwelt.*
Skirt. Showing the typical cut of a skirt at this time with the seams placed straight to gore.

24. 1876. *The Gentleman's Magazine of Fashion.*
Double Breasted Alexandra Pelisse. To be made of light brown Homespun or Tweed. It is tightly fitting with a very long skirt, and can have the waist drawn in with a belt. The double row of buttons are always worn fastened. Fig. 5 is a Cape, which some ladies like, it may be made single or have several layers like a coachman's Box Coat.

25. 1878. *Myra's Journal of Dress and Fashion.*

Skirt. In cutting out this skirt it will be observed that no material, with the exception of cashmere, is of sufficient width to cut this side and back breadth. The material is therefore pinned together before cutting out this width, the pattern is then laid on it and cut out; the pleats are arranged with the folds towards the back. The hem should be lined, and the pleats fastened in place by a ribbon or tape sewn to each fold.

Two Plument Petticoats, for wearing under a trained skirt.

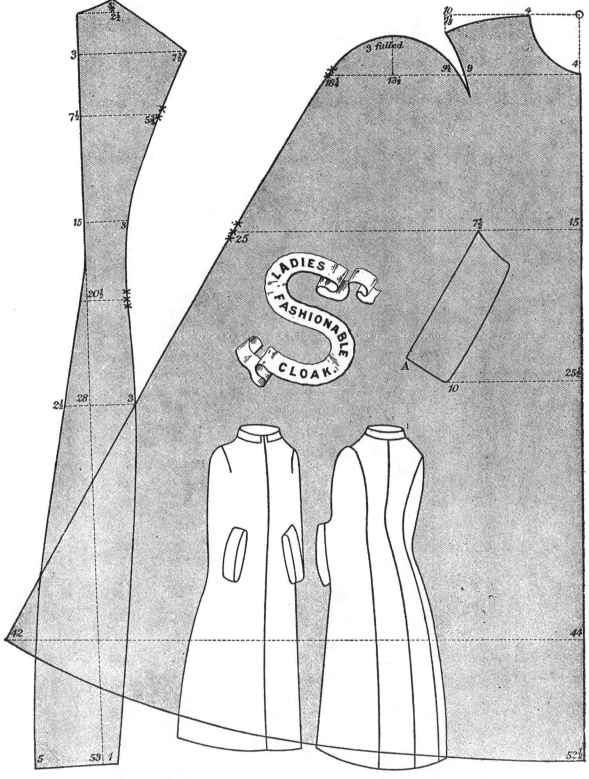

26. 1884. *The Ladies' Tailor.*
    A Ladies Fashionable Cloak. A simply cut morning Cloak, with only three long
    seams and two shoulder seams. The sleeve outlets or arm vents being a short straight
    slash, to be faced or bound. This garment can also be made from fancy silks, and is
    often seen with fur or feather trimming for evening or more elegant wear.

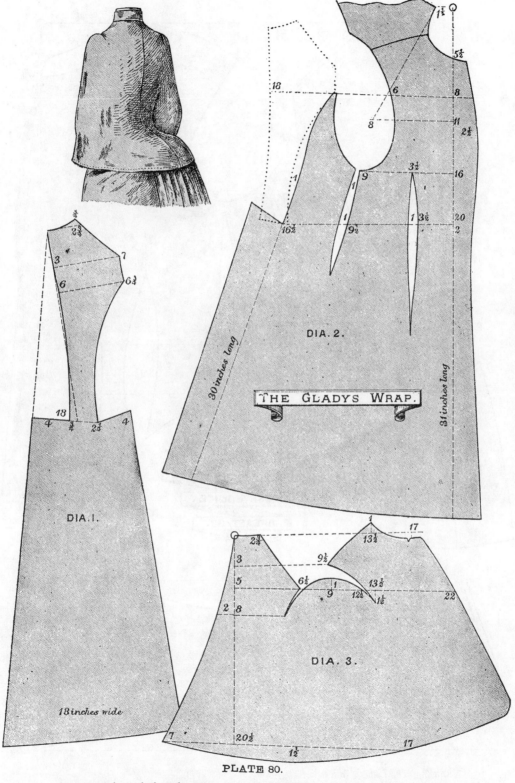

DIA. 1.

18 inches wide

DIA. 2.

30 inches long

31 inches long

THE GLADYS WRAP.

DIA. 3.

PLATE 80.

27. 1885. *The Ladies' Tailor.*

The Gladys Wrap. The back skirts of this garment can be made up with one box
pleat at the centre back seam, or with three box pleats; one at each seam. Or it can
be cut across, and the back skirt pleated on like a Battenberg. The armhole is so
arranged as to admit sleeves being worn if desired. The cape is usually sewn to the
neck of the wrap, and has a centre back seam, or may be left in the crease of the
material.

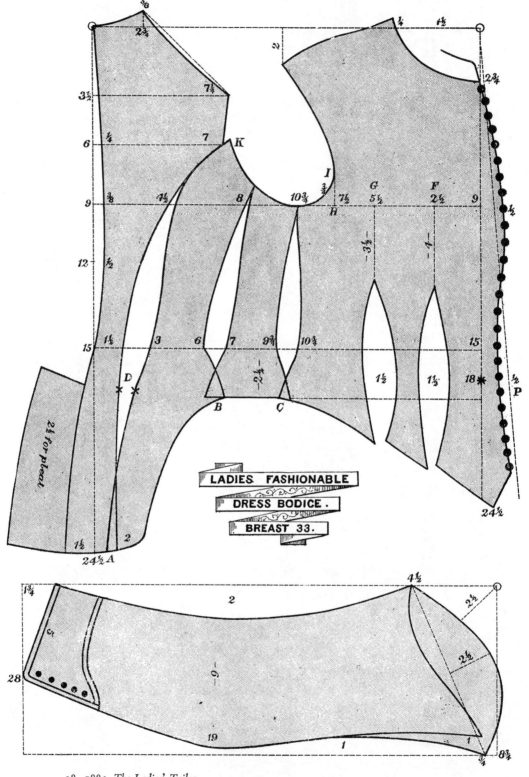

LADIES FASHIONABLE
DRESS BODICE.
BREAST 33.

28. 1885. *The Ladies' Tailor.*
    Ladies Fashionable Dress Bodice. Considered stylish and a first class fit. Suitable
for use when cutting costume bodices.

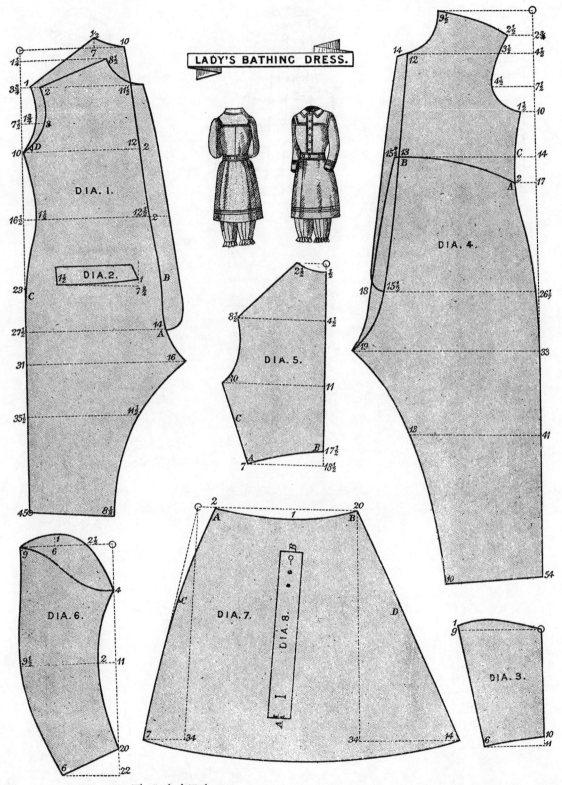

LADY'S BATHING DRESS.

DIA. 1.

DIA. 2.

DIA. 3.

DIA. 4.

DIA. 5.

DIA. 6.

DIA. 7.

DIA. 8.

29. 1885. *The Ladies' Tailor.*
    Bathing Dress. Combination dress, vest and drawers joined. This garment can be
    made from any of the many materials suited to the purpose, including linen and
    woollen fabrics. Blue serge being the one most usually used for bathing dresses.

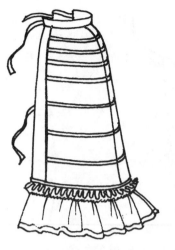

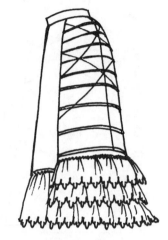

30. 1885. *Myra's Journal of Dress and Fashion.*

Half Crinolines. The half crinoline, or crinolette as it is sometimes called, continues the most popular form of this now indispensable article of attire. It is sometimes worn as a separate tournure, but is more convenient and less liable to get out of place, when it forms part of the skirt.

Foundation Skirt, with built in bustle. Tapes are tied across inside the skirt, from X to X to draw the steels into shape, and a small horsehair pad inserted centre back.

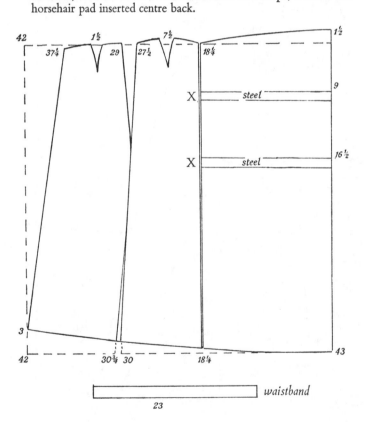

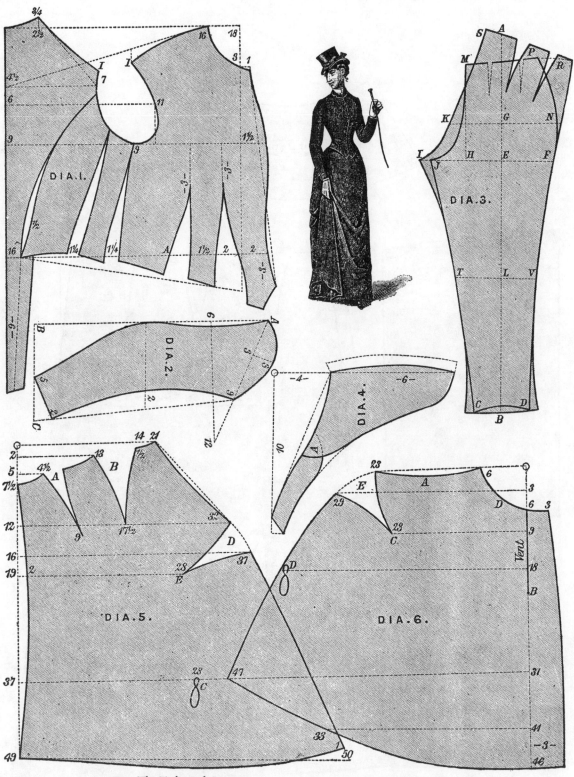

31. 1885. *The Tailor and Cutter*.

Ladies Riding Habit. Riding Habits change in style more slowly, being made to serve for more than one season. The bodice is seen to button well up to the neck, with a small lapel and a turn down collar. The waist is long and pointed in front, and sleeves are close fitting with only a slight fullness at the top. The train is made convenient for walking, in length, close fitting round the hips and with a range of 2 to 2½ yards around the hem. Trousers have the body part lined with chamois and a centre front fly like those of a gentlemans.

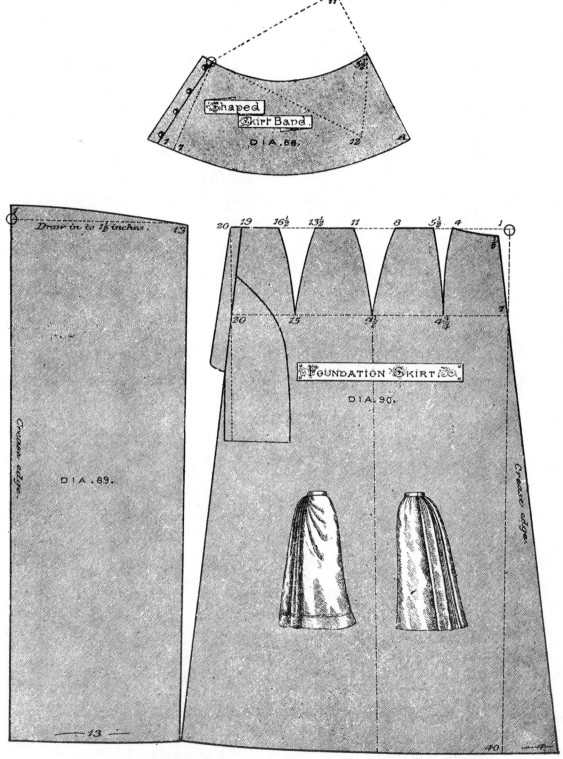

32. 1889. *The Cutters' Practical Guide.*
    Foundation Skirt, and Shaped skirt Band. The shaped skirt band can be used to
    form a smoother line over the hips, and can eliminate any darts or fullness at the
    waist by inserting the pleats or drapery of the skirt into a seam a few inches below
    the waist.

33. 1893. *The Cutters' Practical Guide.*
Measures and how to take them.

# Quotations from Contemporary Sources

—————•◦✦◦•—————

## LATE 1790's

Paris—I don't know whether these dancers were great admirers of Republican Greece but at any rate they had modelled their attire on that of Aspasia; naked arms, bared bosoms, sandals on their feet; hair twisted and plaited round their heads—the fashionable hairdressers take their styles from the antique busts. . . . For some time the chemise has been banished, it only disfigured the natural forms and moreover was a useless article of apparel. The corset of flesh-coloured silk tricot which clings to the body does not hide but rather discloses secret charms. . . . Just a little more daring on the part of the *Merveilleuses* and we shall see the ancient dances of Laconia—there is so little to remove that I don't think prudery will be offended by discarding transparent draperies. Flesh-coloured tights clinging closely to the skin stirs the imagination and reveals in all their beauty the most clandestine charms. These are the days that have followed the fall of Robespierre. . . . Wigs are with powder and some ladies change their wigs as often as their shoes and have as many as forty. . . . The pretty girls and goddesses sweep the muddy streets of the capital with the trains of their long transparent dresses. . . . On Sunday every *petite maîtresse* and every shop girl dons an *athénienne* robe and gathers it into folds over her arm to show off her figure *à l'antique* or at least to equal Venus with her attitudes.

LOUIS-SÉBASTIEN MERCIER, *Le Nouveau Paris*

## LATE 1790's

The ladies, having cut off those tresses which had done so much execution, exhibited heads rounded *à la victime* and *à la guillotine*; as if ready for the stroke of the axe. A drapery more suited to the climate of Greece or of Italy than to the temperature of an island situate in the fifty-first degree of latitude, classic, elegant, luxurious, and picturesque, but ill calculated to protect against damp, cold, and fogs, superseded the ancient female attire of Great Britain, finally levelling or obliterating almost all external distinction of costume between the highest and the lowest of the sex in the country.

SIR WILLIAM WRAXALL, *Historical and Posthumous Memoirs*

1798

The crowd itself was gay and pretty and those who had real beauty are wonderfully distinguished by the present dress. . . . and the transparent dresses that leave you certain there is no chemise beneath! the fault of the reigning fashion when carried to its extreme, even for the youngest and handsomest, is, to say the truth, *indecency*. Not that it shows so much more than people have done at many other times, but that it both shows and covers, in a certain way, very much answering certain descriptions our precious neighbours the French used to give in their instructive novels. The figures one meets walking in the street with footmen behind them are exactly what Crébillon would have painted lying on a sopha to receive a lover. And in a high wind! . . . Don't imagine me an old maid growling at the young people for some of the most remarkable statues in wet drapery are very fully my contemporaries at least.

LADY LOUISA STUART, *Gleanings from an Old Portfolio*

1799–1800

1799. The Duchess of Montmorenci is pleasing, lively . . . and excessively occupied with her toilette, but in so unaffected a way it rather diverts than fatigues you. The whole time of my visit she has employed herself in taking patterns of everything I possessed, and making up similar dresses with the ingenuity of a milliner or mantua-maker.

1800. Berlin—Just as I was going to dinner, Madame de Haugwitz, the wife of the chief Minister, who introduced herself to me last night by an encomium on my dress, sent her tailor for the pattern of my gown begging that this person, whom, in a note he showeth me, she calls *mon ami*, would engage me to put it on, that he might see what a good effect it had. I think this intolerably free and easy, considering I am a perfect stranger.

MRS. RICHARD TRENCH, *Selection from her Journals, Letters and Other Papers*

1799

Fancy is now racked for novelties of decoration, and dress is daily flying from *Greek simplicity* into *Eastern magnificence*. The embroidery of muslins has given a richness to the female robe which is truly captivating; and, what with the glittering effect of gold and silver, of high plumes, and of diamonds, the ball-room now presents a blaze of ornamental beauty, from which the sober and chaste elegance of last winter must shrink in dismay.

1800. White muslin is still the prevailing colour for robes. Indian muslins, plain or embroidered, are preferred to Florence and satins. The designs of embroidery for shawls are of infinite variety.

High ruffs promise to supplant the low-backed robe. They at least, look less naked during the winter season.

*Lady's Magazine*

1799–1800

1799. My gown is made very like my blue one, which you always told me sat very well, with only these variations: the sleeves are short, the wrap fuller, the apron comes over it, and a band of the same completes the whole.

1801. Mrs. Mussell has got my gown, and I will endeavour to explain what her intentions are. It is to be a round gown, with a jacket and a frock front, like Cath. Biggs', to open at the side. The jacket is all in one with the body, and comes as far as the pocket-holes–about half a quarter of a yard deep, I suppose, all the way round, cut off straight at the corners with a broad hem. No fulness appears either in the body or the flap; the back is quite plain in this form (almost a V), and the sides equally so. The front is sloped round to the bosom and drawn in, and there is to be a frill of the same to put on–occasionally when all one's handkerchiefs are dirty–which frill must fall back. She is to put two breadths and a half in the tail, and no gores–gores not being so much worn as they were. There is nothing new in the sleeves: they are to be plain, with a fulness of the same falling down and gathered up underneath just like some of Martha's, or perhaps a little longer. Low in the back behind, and a belt of the same. I can think of nothing more, though I am afraid of not being particular enough. . . . I find my straw bonnet looking very much like other people's. . . . Black gauze cloaks are worn as much as anything.

JANE AUSTEN, *Letters*

1800–1801

1800. I set off with my Father for Scotland. I can well remember how smart I thought we looked in our hats and feathers, habits with lapels, which when opened displayed waistcoats, frilled habit shirts, stand up collars and black silk handkerchiefs round our necks, so that to look at us through the windows of the carriage, if it were not for the feathers and curls, we might have been taken for two Youths.

1801. We went to a concert one evening, all the ladies wore, as they walked through the streets, Calashes over their large caps to save them from wind or rain, and an excellent protection it was. These Calashes were made of black silk and cane, the shape of a Calash over an open carriage. To prevent them from blowing back there was a long loop of ribbon hanging from the front, which the ladies held in their hands.

1802. I had a white 'curricle dress' . . . it was a short, open garment showing the petticoat in front, which was trimmed in the same way as the dress with short sleeves, the body open and low, showing an embroidered 'French habit shirt', now called a chemisette and a small white chip hat, gipsy shape, around which was a wreath of small pink roses.

The fashion then was to wear ruffs something like Queen Elizabeth's, only one frill fully quilled stood out round the neck, another much wider lay down on the shoulders.

SUSAN SIBBALD, *Memoirs*

1802

Lady Melbourne brought Madame Recamier, the celebrated Parisian beauty to Hoppners a few days ago. He does not think she is at all remarkable in that respect. Her dress was very bare both back and front, but she had a large veil on her head which she occasionally used as a screen –such is the latitude of female dressing.

*The Farington Diary by* JOSEPH FARINGTON, R. A.

1805

I abhor long tails–which cause the poor children and dogs more scoldings than they would have with short appendages to my apparel.

*Early married life of* MARIA JOSEPHA, LADY STANLEY

1806

Fashionable Anecdote. A Lady of ton going lately to attend a fashionable party, alighted from her carriage, and ascending the staircase, was ushered into the room where the guests were received. No sooner, however, had she advanced about half way across the floor, than a sudden jerk prevented her proceeding further. On some gentlemen present examining into the cause of this unexpected detention, it was discovered that the train of her Ladyship's gown had, by accident, been shut in the door of the carriage below.

*Lady's Monthly Museum*

1807

It was but yesterday I cheapened a pair of gloves with a little damsel, who, in point of nakedness, might have vied with any duchess in the land. It is whispered that the ladies *en bon point* will be quickly out of all repute; and the price of vinegar and salad is in consequence about to experience an extravagant rise.

*Lady's Magazine*

1808

I begin a new Science today–shoe-making. It is all the fashion. I had a master with me for two hours, and I think I shall be able to make very nice shoes. It amuses and occupies me, which at present is very useful to me.

HON. MRS. CALVERT, *Mes Souvenirs*

## EARLY NINETEENTH CENTURY

France–Joséphine–She had from three to four hundred shawls; she used them for dresses, for bed covers and for cushions for her dog. She always wore one in the morning which she draped over her shoulders more gracefully than anyone else that I have ever seen. Bonaparte who thought she was too much covered by these shawls, would pull them off and sometimes threw them into the fire. Joséphine then called for another.

When preparations were being made for the Coronation Joséphine surrounded by the best artists, dress-makers and shop-keepers together with them designed the new Court dress. There was no question of reviving the panier, but a separate long train was added to the fashionable robe, and a collar of blonde lace, the *chérusque*, which rose high behind the head and was caught on either shoulder *à la Catherine de Médici*. These collars are no longer worn with Court dress but the trains have been kept.

MME DE RÉMUSAT, *Mémoires*

## EARLY NINETEENTH CENTURY

Mme Tallien–She was the Capitoline Venus, more beautiful than the work of Phidas. She wore a simple dress of Indian muslin, shaped in the antique manner, caught at the shoulders with cameos. A gold belt, also adorned with cameos, encircled her waist, and a gold bracelet formed the sleeves fastening above the elbow. Her velvety black hair was cut short and curled– a style which in those days was called *à la Titus*. Round her beautiful white shoulders she had flung a red cashmere shawl, a highly original ornament. . . .

We wore at that time robes of black velvet, or velvets of other dark colours, especially with diamonds, so as to emphasise their brilliance. . . .

Court dress of the Empress Joséphine–The dress and the train were the same; both of tulle with exquisite fine embroidery of gold in a pattern of interlaced lozenges which gave the appearance of a golden net. The dress and the train were bordered with a short fringe. Round the neck, sleeves, and waist, were emeralds surrounded by diamonds. Her diadem, comb, and ear-rings were of emeralds. Another time she wore the same costume with pearls instead of emeralds. I don't know which I preferred. The Empress Joséphine had exquisite taste in dress.

DUCHESSE D'ABRANTÉS, *Mémoires*

### 1814

I am amused by the present style of female dress; the coloured petticoats with braces over the white Spencers and enormous Bonnets upon the full stretch, are quite entertaining. It seems to me a more marked *change* than one has seen–Long sleeves appear universal, even in *Dress*, the waist short, and as far as I have been able to judge, the Bosom covered–Petticoats short, and generally, tho' not always, flounced.

JANE AUSTEN, *Letters*

1814

Paris—The women's dress is affectedly simple—white muslin, very short waists, very full petticoats: but the ugliest part of their habiliments is the high chimneys on their hats, which chimneys are covered with feathers and flowers. When fashion is subject to taste, I like it, but when it is despotic and capricious, and subverts all taste, I cannot endure it. To my idea, the more nearly women's dress assimilates to the antique, the more beautiful.

LADY BARBARA CHARLTON, *Recollections of a Northumbrian Lady*

1819

Vienna—I must now give you an account of Lady Stewart's grand days of reception as Ambassadress of England. . . . She was dressed magnificently and beautifully, in a long trained round dress of patinet lace richly embroidered all over with gold—this was worn over white Satin. Her head was dress'd with the best of good taste, and all her ornaments were superb, Topazes and diamonds. The effect of the entire was great simplicity notwithstanding its richness.

Baden—Is worked muslin as much the rage in England as it was last year, or is it become vulgar? The excess of it here is past belief. My cook maid wears 7 flounces embroidered round her tail! and what I brought with me is not fit to decorate the tails of my kitchenmaid's smocks it is so inferior to what she wears.

Vienna—I have got back Mlle Henriette de la Pierre, our old governess. . . . She is an excellent ingredient in a family, gay, well-mannered, clever at her needle, makes stays, dresses, hats and caps, smartens up our decaying wardrobes to perfection and is capable of turning her hand to anything.

MARTHA WILMOT, *Impressions of Vienna*

1820

> *Long chains of gold about the neck,*
> *With Opera-glass depending;*
> *Bracelets the snowy arms to deck,*
> *And Jewels without ending.*
>
> *Bare ears on either side the head,*
> *Like wood-wild savage satyr!*
> *Tinted with deep vermilion red,*
> *To mock the flush of nature.*

> *Red elbows, thin gauze sleeves, that add*
>    *An icy covering merely:*
> *A wadded corset, Nelson pad;*
>    *Like Dutch women—or nearly.*
>
> *Such makes caprices! But, lovely kind,*
>    *Oh! let each mental feature*
> *Proclaim th'adorning of the mind,*
>    *And leave your charms to nature.*

*La Belle Assemblée*

### 1824

My dearest brother—I cannot thank you one half enough; it is the most beautiful, delightful present. The bracelet in itself is all this, and then the picture. . . . I go to a soirée tonight only because of my bracelet and having an insatiable wish to flaunt it to the Brussels world. The sleeve will not disgrace it. Gigot at top, *un seul pli*, and then innumerable little furrows and ridges between it and the paw. You are not perhaps aware that a magnificent bracelet now is as necessary to the existence of a woman as the air she breathes.

LADY HARRIET GRANVILLE, *Letters*

### 1831–1835

1831. We are certainly cleaner than our grandmothers, and much more comfortable, though it is not so long since my own head was dressed *à la giraffe*, in three bows over pins half a foot high, so that I could not sit upright in the carriage without knocking against the top of it. . . .

1835. The mere items of tight stays, tight garters, tight shoes, tight waistbands, tight arm-holes, and tight bodices—of which we are accustomed to think little or nothing, and under the bad effects of which, most young women's figures are suffered to attain their growth, both here and in Europe—must have a tendency to injure irreparably the compressed parts, to impede circulation and respiration, and in many ways which we are not aware of, as well as by the more obvious evils which they have been proved to produce, destroy the health of the system, affect disastrously all its functions, and must aggravate the pains and perils of childbearing.

FANNY KEMBLE, *Record of a Girlhood, Records of Later Life*

### 1832

Of all materials used for Dresses there has not been any in favour for so long a time as the Chaly (challis), it is adopted for morning wear, for the Theatres, for the most brilliant parties, and even for balls. . . . The draped Corsages are the most common. . . . Dresses which have ornaments all round, have them placed below the knee.

TOWNSEND'S *Parisian Costumes*

1837

I hope you who are so fashionable a person have already made all your sleeves quite tight to your arm – but the question is useless for I know you would not think of going out with such an old fashioned thing as a full sleeve at present, particularly when you hear that Lady Goodrich has asked for a pattern for one of these curtailed wings.

1842. Mourning – I think the best plan will be to have a black velvet made with a morning and evening waist, which will be sufficient for me, and I should like to have a good deal of black crepe sent, as it so soon gets shabby – perhaps thirteen yards.

*Cecilia, Life and Letters of* CECILIA RIDLEY

1846–1856

1846. Miss Dawson was at Paris, and has brought a lovely grey crape Herbault bonnet, not a Pamela, which she says are quite out; the gowns are still worn very full, that is seven breadths without, and six with flounces, and these last, and trimming of all sorts, are much worn very high up; evening gowns made with rows of fringe up to the waist . . . Buttons are the rage and sleeves are not worn open or short so much as they were. Bodies are made straight or cross as one likes . . . and collars are rather large.

1856. The Queen is rather in beauty, her face not at all red, and her petticoats much increased in circumference, which improves her excessively.

HON. ELEANOR STANLEY, *Twenty Years at Court*

1849

The Queen gave a State Ball last evening at Buckingham Palace. The invitations comprised the whole of the Diplomatic Corps, the Ladies and Gentlemen of the Royal Household, and the principal Nobility and Gentry, and numbered about 1900. The Queen wore a blue silk dress covered with blue tulle *en ruche*, and ornamented with bouquets with sweat peas and diamonds. Her Majesty's headdress was composed of sweat peas and diamonds to correspond to the dress.

*Evening Standard*

1858

But the crinoline, you say; the circular petticoats, the skirts with springs that have to be mended like watches by a watchmaker, isn't it hideous, abominable, vulgar, contrary to all art? We don't agree: women are right to wear the crinoline in spite of all the jokes, the caricatures, the songs and the insults. They are right to prefer these wide skirts, with their extravagant volume of material spreading over the ground, to the straight tubes which their mothers and grandmothers used to wear. From an abundance of pleats which flow out like the fustanelle of a derviche, the body rises slender and elegant; the shoulders are shown to full advantage and the whole effect is gracious. This mass of material forms as it were a pedestal for the bosom and head, the only important parts exposed when nudity is not allowed. Erudition and pleasantry apart, a young woman with a low-necked dress and bare arms, her hair beautifully arranged, her skirts billowing out behind in waves of antique moiré, satin, or silk, could never appear more beautiful nor be better attired, and we see no reason why art should disapprove.

THEOPHILE GAUTIER, *De la Mode*

1860

Paris—The following Wednesday—there was to be a great ball at the Tuileries—I wore the famous gown, and I can honestly say I have rarely seen one so lovely nor better made. It was in white tulle threaded with silver (a new material), sprinkled here and there with pink-centred daisies among wild grasses, which were veiled with white tulle. A white satin sash tied round the waist and I wore lots of diamonds. . . . Worth had his first success. The Empress immediately saw it was a *chef-d'oeuvre*. She came up to me and at once asked who had made this wonderfully pretty dress, so simple and yet so elegant. 'An Englishman, madame, a new star that has appeared in the world of fashion.' 'What is his name?' 'Worth.' 'Well!' replied the Empress, 'this star must have some satelites. Please tell him to come and see me tomorrow morning at 10 o'clock.' Worth was launched, I was lost, for from then on I knew there would be no more gowns for me at 300 francs.

PRINCESS PAULINE METTERNICH, *Souvenirs*

1860's

Female skill would indeed have had to be great in order to devise any advantage from such a peculiar fashion. To walk with so immense a paraphernalia around one was not very easy; and the narrow bust, placed in the centre of this volume of material, appeared to be detached from the rest of the body altogether. To be able to sit so as not to cause the rebellious springs to fly open, required a miracle of precision. To ascend a carriage without rumpling such light textures, at a time when the evening toilettes were made of tulle and lace, required a great deal of time, much quietness on the part of the horses, and much patience on the part of fathers and husbands, whose complaisance was put to an enormous test, compelled as they were to remain motionless in the midst of these 'nuages fragiles'.

This style tyrannized over a whole generation until at last the ladies found a deliverer in Worth. . . . We owe to the artistic taste of this great milliner, and to his intuition for aesthetic elegance, the revival of grace in dress. He modified the volume of skirts, he rendered the materials more flexible, and he always designed—roughly at first, it is true—for the body so as to allow it greater freedom; and, when in 1864 I arrived at the Court, scarcely any hoops were worn, whilst the round and narrow skirts permitted one to go out without causing any obstruction in the streets or catastrophés in the apartments.

MME CARETTE, My Mistress the Empress Eugènie

1860's

My mother wore a dreadful dress *à disposition*, that is to say, each flounce being woven with a border in a Greek key pattern in two colours. There were seven flounces over an enormous cage crinoline. It really was awful! Maria's dress was of plaid silk, red predominating, with a double skirt. Instead of a bodice she wore a Garibaldi shirt in red solferino foulard. Her beautiful chestnut hair was confined in a heavy net of red chenille which completely covered her back. Of all the hideous fashions of the Second Empire that of hair nets was the ugliest and most vulgar.

1863. It was just then that the Empress had begun to adopt short skirts. As they required less material and did not get dirty everyone was wearing them. Long dresses continued to be worn in the evening. Day dresses which were not of the new fashionable length had *tirettes*, that is to say, cords sewn underneath to the bottom of the skirt which came out at the waist and were caught together with a button. One pulled the button and the dress rose like a tent over the petticoat which was held out by a cage and was always very elegant—that is to say—elegant for that time. It was really hideous and the young girls who as a matter of course wore shorter skirts came off best.

GYP, Souvenirs d'une Petite Fille

1860's

Another of my mother's memoires of this period is of the delight on returning to the Legation (Rio de Janeiro), to receive from her sister Fanny, in a letter, a tissue-paper pattern of the new gored skirts, which had just arrived from Paris. Up till then skirts had been as many yards round the top as the bottom, and had been merely 'stroked' into a band at the waist and crinolines had replaced the masses of starched petticoats in 1854. The gored skirt was evidently an equally exciting innovation.

ELINOR GLYN, Romantic Adventure

1863

The most interesting part of the Princess Alexandra to me is not her present splendours, but her previous homely rather *poor* life, which makes such a curious contrast. . . . When she was visiting our Queen, after the engagement, she always came to breakfast in a jacket. 'My dear,' said the Queen to her one day, 'you seem very fond of jackets. How is it that you always wear a jacket?' 'Well,' said little Alexandra, 'I like them; and then you see a jacket is so economical! You can wear different skirts with it, and I have very few gowns–having to make them all myself. My Sisters and I have no Lady's maid, and have been brought up to make all our own clothes. I made my own bonnet.' Bless her!

MRS. JANE WELSH CARLYLE, *Letters and Memorials*

1864

The Queen now wears a modified cap in Tulle or Crepe . . . like a Marie Stuart's cap, a little Point going back at the sides, with the hair combed back and frizzed out–it is most becoming, and she looks as nice as possible with her gowns not quite as high in the evenings and a diamond cross.

HON. ELEANOR STANLEY, *Twenty Years at Court*

1863–1868

1863. Compiègne–The Empress looked superb in a brown tulle over satin, looped up with brooches of diamonds. She had a diamond crescent in her hair like Diana.

1868. Visit to Compiègne–Here is the list of my dresses:

Morning Costumes:
   Dark-blue poplin, trimmed with plush the same colour, toque, muff to match.
   Black velvet, trimmed with braid, sable hat, sable tippet and muff.
   Brown cloth, trimmed with bands of sealskin, coat, hat, muff to match.
   Purple plush, trimmed with bands of pheasant feathers, coat, hat to match.
   Grey velvet, trimmed with chinchilla, chinchilla hat, muff and coat.
   Green cloth (hunting costume).
   Travelling suit, dark-blue cloth.

Evening Dresses:
   Light green tulle, embroidered in silver, and for my locks, what they call *une fantaisie*.
   White tulle, embroidered with gold wheat ears.
   Light-gray satin, quite plain, with only Brussels lace flounces.
   Deep pink tulle, with satin ruchings and a lovely sash of lilac ribbon.
   Black lace over white tulle, with green velvet twisted bows.
   Light-blue tulle with Valenciennes.

Afternoon Gowns:
   Lilac faille.
   Light café au lait, with trimmings of the same.
   Green faille faced with blue and a red Charlotte Corday sash (Worth's last gasp).
   Red faille, quite plain.
   Gray faille with light-blue facings.

Do you not think there is enough to last me as long as I live?

It is the fashion this year for ladies to wear lockets on a black-velvet ribbon round their necks. The more lockets you can collect and wear, the finer you are. Each locket represents an event, such as a birthday, a bet, an anniversary of any kind, and so forth. Any excuse is good for the sending of a locket. The Empress had seventeen beautiful ones to-day (I counted them). They have rather a cannibalish look, I think.

MRS. HEGERMANN-LINDENCRONE, *In the Courts of Memory*

## 1865

Crinoline at length is going out, thank goodness! In matters of costume, lovely woman rarely ceases to make herself a nuisance, and the length of her skirt now is almost as annoying as, a while ago, its width was. . . . Well-nigh as many accidents will be met with by these trains as by those upon our railways, and we really hardly know which of the two may prove more dangerous. For ourselves, having the welfare of our little ones at heart, we always try to tread upon as many dresses as we can, and to do them all the damage that hobnailed boots can perpetrate.

*Punch*

## 1870's

In designing his dresses my father followed the same method that had proved so successful with cloaks. He considered the feminine figure and saw to it that the bodices were better fitted, took care that the direction of the weave of the material for the various parts of a garment is cut either on the bias or straight, so that the warp will always lie in the direction taken by the principal movements of the body–to give the figure the maximum of elegance. . . .

We made dresses for Lady Sykes to wear at Epsom, the biggest race course in England, that today would be too gorgeous even for a ball. For instance, she had one princess gown, made of alternating breadths of apple green and white embroidered as exquisitely as any Louis XV dress, and with a train two metres long. This was duplicated in copper-coloured satin with four wide black and four tan *crevés*.

JEAN-PHILLIPE WORTH, *A Century of Fashion*

## 1871

False hair was worn more generally than ever. We learn from some interesting and curious statistics that 51,816 kilogrammes of false hair were sold in France in 1871; 85,959 in 1872; and 102,900 in 1873. These figures were probably surpassed in 1874 and the succeeding years.

A. CHALLAMEL, *The History of Fashion in France*

1876

Parisian Gossip—It is not the colour, nor the material, nor the trimmings, which now constitutes the elegance of a lady's dress; it is the *cut* of the dress. It has, indeed, become quite an art to cut a lady's skirt so that she may be elegant, fashionable, and to some extent, modest. Each time that I write to you I am compelled to state that dresses are tied still 'tighter' round the figure, and I have still tighter to write this month. Our skirts are now so tight that our sitting and walking are seriously inconvenienced; and the sleeves of bodies are so closely fitting to the arms that we can hardly raise them, even to half their usual height. In a word, exaggeration is still the order of the day. Unfortunately, also, these very tight dresses are more frequently disadvantageous to the greater portion of the ladies than they are becoming. . . . Long trains, even for ordinary walking purposes, are universally worn. These must be held up with one hand, or they may be thrown *à l'Amazone* over one arm. For demi-long skirts, hold them up; for quite long trains, throw them over the arm.

*The Ladies' Treasury*

1879–1882

1879. Paris—At the Théâtre Français they wear the most magnificent dresses I ever saw in my life. All the long ones have princesse backs, many of them with long basques and pockets in front, cut steel buttons, jet fringes on the tablier, etc. I see that café-au-lait coloured silk is worn again. Skirts are made so scant and short as to require very little material.

1880. The white damask, cut out thoughtfully and slowly by myself, is a perfect beauty; the whole front covered with white bead braid and bead fringes, which gleam and shine and move and give an altogether effect. The enclosed picture is the design I followed for the front, taking the other part from a white satin wedding-dress in another number of the Bazar.

1882. Tomorrow my dressmaker finishes her engagement with me and I hope my satin dress. I couldn't have believed a dyed dress could have turned out so well; I cheerfully bear witness to Miss Watson's wisdom, upon which I am happy to say I acted at the time. Just before she called four years ago, I had been looking at a dress length of splendid black satin sent home from the shop. 'Why didn't you buy it white first, and get the good of a white satin?' she asked. 'You could so easily have dyed it black.' Happy thought! They consented to change it for me at the shop, it did admirably as a white dinner dress, then, dyed a pretty red; and now it comes out once more ever beautiful and new, black! Even the way it was made at first, very full princess with a set in the train, suits for the present panier style.

LADY JEBB, *With Dearest Love to All*

1880's

There were many visitors to the house, amongst whom were the beautiful Mrs. Langtry and Mrs. Wheeler, both friends of my still beautiful mother. I well remember their curious concertina-shaped bustles and little pork-pie hats decorated with silk pom-poms, and their tippets, either of fur or eiderdown, which barely covered their shoulders. My mother once showed me a hat which had been sent her as a present by the late Duke of Fife; it was made of a ptarmigan, the head of which stuck out in front so that when she put it on her head it gave the impression of the bird sitting on a nest.

GEORGE CORNWALLIS-WEST, *Edwardian Hey-Days*

*The Ranavala Toilette*

PART FOUR

Twentieth Century
1890-1930

1903

# 1890-1908

Although the fact was at first hardly discernible, the fitted skirt and blouse of 1890 introduced a new phase in dress design. Women were becoming more independent. For the few who were launching out into the professions, and the many more who were taking up active outdoor sports, the costume, with its plain skirt and loose blouse was for those days a practical outfit. However, the end of the nineteenth century and the beginning of the twentieth was also a time of great economic prosperity, both in England and France, and a period of luxury and leisure not only for the women of high society but for many from the middle class as well. Subtlety of cut and a multitude of trimmings transformed the simple blouse and skirt into one of the most seductive and feminine of all dresses.

## 1890–1898

The corset was now very long-bodied and the seaming straighter so that the bust was more sharply defined and not quite so rounded as hitherto. The front spoon busk and the excessively small waist produced well-rounded hips, behind, and stomach. The size of the waist in relation to that of the bust and hips was much smaller in the 1890's and early 1900's than at any other time. From the point of view of silhouette and of cut the focus of interest was now from the waist downwards. The skirt fitted smoothly below the waist, and from wide hips the sides and back fell in folds to the ground. The heavy materials and foundations of the 1880's continued to be worn for a while into the 1890's, and these kept the silhouette sharp and rather severe.

Except for the shirt blouse styles, all bodices and blouses were still cut as before and were mounted on to a firm lining with all seams boned. As a contrast to the plain skirt they were usually very much decorated. There were yokes of various shapes, drapery, or gathered front, or the separate plastron front. Until c. 1898, however, the fullness was always kept taut to the foundation. From c. 1893, wide revers tapering in to the waist, and epaulettes or shoulder frills, emphasized the growing spread of the sleeves and the smallness of the waist. The small gigot sleeve of 1890 expanded and was enormous by 1895; in the following year it began to

227

contract. The sleeves were similar to those of the 1830's. They were cut from the cross-way of the material with one seam, often with extra top fullness pleated into the seam just below the armhole. Sometimes they were gathered at the elbow on to a fitted lower sleeve. They were always mounted on a two-piece fitting foundation sleeve, and set high on the shoulders. Suit jackets were often basqued, but from *c.* 1892 the bolero or the Zouave or Eton jacket was more customary with the dressmaker style of costume. The tailored jacket was still cut like the foundation lining with two back seams each side running in to the armhole, an underarm seam, and front darts; the shorter bolero style often had only the underarm seam, or one back seam each side into the armhole. All day dresses had high collars. Very ornate blouses of silk, lace, etc. were worn with black silk or satin skirts for dress occasions. The more simple shirt blouse, with a yoke, was unlined and sometimes hung outside the skirt, being held in to the waist by a belt. The bodice of the evening dress was very low-necked and tight-fitting, with either drapes or deep flounces round the neckline. The sleeve was usually a short but wide puff.

The 1890 skirt was the foundation skirt of the late 1880's, and for two more years, until the new line developed, often retained the front drape. When shorn of its drape this skirt was rather straight and dull. The cut was either slight gores with extra hip darts or quite unshaped except for hip darts, and both styles had the extra fullness closely gathered centre back. Artificial pads were no longer worn except where nature was deficient. Soon, in order to balance the expanding sleeve the bottom of the skirt began to widen as well. Two main types of cut emerged–the new gored skirt and the umbrella skirt; in addition there was a bell skirt. In order to widen the base the gores of the new skirt were cut at a much more acute angle, especially the side ones. The centre back was now always gored as well, for a fashionable skirt, and the back fullness gathered, but from *c.* 1893 it was more usually arranged in inverted pleats centre back. In more practical skirts the centre back might still be on the straight of the material. In order to fit over the well-rounded hips and into the small waist the top of each gore had to be slightly curved. This shaping replaced the earlier darts. The gores were sewn cross to straight, except in the bell skirt, which was usually two-piece, having a straight centre front and centre back but with both front and back pieces gored at the sides. The number of gores varied a good deal, being as a rule from five to nine, but occasionally even more. The umbrella skirt–the one-piece unseamed skirt–was now cut circular, or rather about three-eighths of a circle. The centre front was on the straight, the centre back on the cross, and the skirt was fitted to the waist by a series of radiating hip darts. The material was kept fairly straight to the figure in the front, and began to drop on to the cross from the sides. This skirt also had inverted centre back pleats. As this cut necessitated very wide material another version, where narrow widths were used, had an extra slightly-gored panel inserted centre front so that the selvedge join, necessary to give the width, came lower down the centre back seam and was not so obvious. Day skirts were ground length, but evening ones had a train.

Owing to the enormous sleeves coats were not possible wear, so capes–elbow length, three-quarter length, plain or tiered, etc.–were very fashionable. These also might be cut gored or circular and fitted with shoulder darts. They had very high-standing Medici collars. See plates 57–60; Diagrams LVII, LVIII, LVIX, LX, LXI.

## 1898–1908

Towards the end of the 1890's, dress materials became softer and more fluid and the silhouette more supple, reflecting the sinuous flowing lines of *l'art nouveau*. In order to allow full play to the new textures the fitted lining of bodice and skirt were now made up separately.

In 1900 the new straight-fronted corset appeared. It began lower down, thus dropping the bust line. Suspenders, now attached to the bottom of the corset, kept the centre front straight and taut, but as the waist was still small the hips, sides and back swelled out as much as before.

By 1898, though the back of the bodice fitted closely, the front fullness became softer and looser and began to pouch over the waistline. The front of this bodice was cut on the straight, waist length at the sides, but dipping towards the centre several inches below waist level. The resulting fullness was gathered or pleated on to the fitted lining, this 'kangaroo' pouch becoming more pronounced when worn with the new straight-fronted corset.

After its collapse in 1896, the sleeve for a few years retained some fullness at the top–a puff, or flounces, etc.–but the rest of the sleeve was tight-fitting all down the arm, its severity often relieved by ruching or tucking. By the end of the 1890's the top fullness had gone, and the shoulder line became smooth and fitting. In the early 1900's, repeating the line of the bodice and skirt, the sleeve began to pouch from the elbow and was gathered into a wrist-band, or cuff. Sometimes it was a slight pagoda with a separate full under-sleeve. Such sleeves were cut on the straight of the material. The evening bodice was very low, usually with shoulder straps, and the sleeve close-fitting to just above the elbow, ending in flounces cut straight or circular.

The bodice continued to become looser and fuller, and by 1904 was pouched all round. It was mounted on to a fitted foundation which, however, was now usually made of lighter silk and gradually the bones were being eliminated. More tailored styles might still have the boned lining, and some older women preferred this type for many years to come. Sleeves again became fuller at the top and were gathered below the elbow, with frills, or cuff, or fitted lower sleeve.

The more fluid line of the late 1890's was especially noticeable in the skirt. From 1898 onwards the umbrella skirt was fitted closer to the limbs, to just below knee level, and a circular flounce was added–in the early 1900's sometimes two or three flounces. Or there were many variations of circular flounces which, very cleverly cut, were usually low in front, curving up in various shapes round the sides and becoming higher at the back. In gored skirts the seams were fitted to about knee level and then flared out on each side of the seam. Sometimes this lower fullness was achieved by inverted pleats starting from each seam, also from about knee level. In order to hold out this fluted base the skirts were cut long enough to rest on the ground, and had a train at the back. Such skirts required expert cutting and even more expert management. The more practical skirt, for walking, etc., was not as a rule flared, nor so long.

With the fuller bodice, *c.* 1904, the skirt also became fuller, and was no longer flared. The same cuts continued – gored, umbrella, and now also a full circle, or of several unshaped widths. The waist fullness was gathered, tucked, or pleated, and after 1903 was sometimes set on to a shaped hip yoke. These skirts were always made with a separate and more fitted foundation skirt, either gored or umbrella, with the waist fullness removed by hip darts. Skirt and foundation skirt were sewn together on to the waistband. Bodices and skirts were separate, and both as a rule fastened centre back.

The fullness of bodice and skirt was separated and emphasized by a deep tight-fitting waist belt. For dresses this was usually 'Swiss' style; that is, deeper centre front and centre back, made of soft material folded and supported by whalebones.

Boleros and Zouave jackets were still worn. The strictly tailored jacket was styled like the man's, the skirt being less fitted than in dresses, and clearing the ground. It was worn for walking, cycling, etc., and by the fashionable woman for shooting parties, and on the moors. Loose sack coats, some with raglan sleeves, and long dust coats were worn for travelling. In the early 1900's, a very long fitted coat trimmed with fur was fashionable winter wear.

Tea-gowns were loose and full, sometimes with 'Watteau' back pleats or the Empire line, and with long, hanging sleeves.

From the 1880's there had been attempts to revive the high waisted Empire line, but the average woman was not yet ready to accept such a drastic change of shape. The Empire line was used in tea-gowns and occasionally in evening gowns, when it was a transparent loose-hanging over-dress; but it was always worn over the fashionable tight-fitting bodice and skirt. The full bodice and skirt separated by a deep waist belt were reminiscent of the dresses of the late eighteenth century, so it is not surprising to find the fashion magazines calling these styles a 'Romney' or a 'Greuze'. Again, as at the end of the eighteenth century, this style gradually trained the eye to accept a higher waist level. From 1906 the deep waistband was being replaced by the corselet skirt. This was the gored skirt fitted in to the waist and continued several inches above waist level. Such skirts were boned round the waist to give a corset-like fit. Sometimes, in soft materials, the skirt hung straight from this new high waistline, but it would be mounted on to a corselet-shaped foundation skirt. The high waist was emphasized by a full bodice. Draped bretelles over the shoulders became a loose kimono over-blouse, worn with a fitted lining to which the high lace collar, yoke and under-sleeves were attached. The high waistline once admitted, the change to a slender silhouette followed rather rapidly. By the end of 1908 the easier fit and straighter line – the characteristic silhouette of the twentieth century – were at last established. See plates 61, 62; Diagrams LXII, LXIII, LXIV.

## MATERIALS, DECORATIONS, ETC

Materials in the early 1890's were still firm and stiff–cloth, serge, tweed, etc., for tailored styles, plush, velvet, heavy silk, damask, broché velvet, Duchess satin, etc. for dresses. Except for bands round the bottom, and sometimes braiding on the seams, skirts were rarely trimmed. Bodices, on the contrary, were heavily decorated. Sleeves, revers, epaulettes, etc., were often of a contrasting colour and material, usually velvet, over which there might also be heavy lace flounces and additional passementerie trimming. If the high collar and yoke were of lace, this was always backed with silk, and the collar had a stiff lining. Sometimes there was an additional collar–the 'collarette'–of velvet, silk, pleated chiffon, etc., with bows or pleated *choux* at the sides or back, or with jabot and frilling to hang down centre front.

The softer materials from the end of the 1890's were fine cloth, mohair, cashmere, tussore or linen for tailored styles, with surah, crêpe-de-chine, voile or muslin for day dresses, and usually flimsy materials for evening, such as net, chiffon, ninon, etc. As fine materials look poor when seamed, the fullness was reduced by pin tucks or gathering and the seaming disguised or replaced by insertions of lace or appliqué, etc. These were often applied in elaborate designs which were repeated on other parts of the dress. To hold out the fluted base the foundation skirt, at first of glacé silk and later of softer silk, had a circular or gathered flounce. Round the bottom of this was a pleated or gathered frill on the outside and another on the inside–the *balayeuse*. Sometimes there was an additional frill of finely kilted net, chiffon, etc., edged with lace or narrow ribbon, over the silk one. When the dress was of transparent material there was also an additional underskirt of chiffon, ninon, etc. trimmed with pleating, flounces, etc. The fuller skirts *c.* 1904 had softer silk foundations and fewer layers of frilling. The yokes and high necks were now of lace or net and backed with chiffon or net so that they were semi-transparent; the collar had whalebone, celluloid or fine wire supports. Lace, black, white or cream, was lavishly used, and was now much lighter in type–Cluny, Valenciennes, Brussels, etc.

To balance the frou-frou round the bottom of the skirt, long boas were worn. These were made from feathers, or ruffles of kilted net edged with narrow silk, satin or velvet ribbon, all with long stole ends.

Accordion pleating had been introduced in the late 1880's. It was very much used in the early 1900's for frillings, etc., while tea-gowns and circular skirts were often accordion pleated.

Short sealskin jackets, capes, fur collars and borders, stoles and muffs were popular.

With full evening dress there was always a magnificent display of jewels: tiaras, or diamond hair ornaments, necklaces, brooches, etc. The high neckline of the day dress was repeated in the deep 'dog-collar' of diamonds, pearls, etc. Long ropes of pearls were worn. The less affluent could buy dog-collars of diamanté and imitation pearls. The average women possessed at least one good brooch, usually of diamonds in the shape of a crescent or a star, also several rings of diamonds or other precious stones. For day wear, gold brooches of delicate floral or bird designs set with small pearls or semi-precious stones were worn. Long fine gold chains were popular, sometimes strung with small pearls or semi-precious stones, or hung with charms. They might also be used to carry a lorgnette, a muff, or a watch which was pinned to the left side of the bodice with a bow brooch. There were also gold lockets and small gold pendants, often in the shape of a heart, and chain bracelets from which hung charms. When the tailored skirt was worn with the full blouse the small waist was defined by a deep belt of silver plaques, or a leather, velvet, etc. belt with large ornate silver clasp centre front.

Fresh flower sprays were worn with dressy afternoon frocks and evening gowns. They were also pinned to muffs–carnations, malmaisons, lilies of the valley, parma violets, etc.

# 1908–1930

## 1908–1915

The looser and more relaxed silhouette that was emerging at the end of 1908 could be interpreted either very simply or more stylishly. In the latter case, more emphasis and fit was given to the high waist and long slender line.

To achieve this new slenderness the fashionable woman, who for years had been tight-lacing, had to change her corset style. The new corset, which began just above waist level, encased the limbs almost to the knees; it thickened the waist and subdued rounded contours. In its most exaggerated form it was so long that sitting down became almost an impossibility. For some years, however, a lighter and simpler corset had been manufactured which was originally designed for sports wear but was being increasingly worn by those who preferred comfort to fashion.

The new cut, which was to be the basis of the fundamental style of the twentieth century, was first seen *c.* 1908, when tailored coats became straighter and no longer fitted closely in to the waist. In order to hang well the material was now kept on the straight round the widest parts of the figure, that is, round the bust and hips. The fit was achieved in front by side seams which ran from the shoulders over the point of the bust and then moved slightly in to the waist and out again, an underarm seam, and two back seams which also ran from the shoulder seam slightly in to the waist and out again. The shoulder seams moved higher up. This cut was also used for the princess dress, the tailored day-dress, and styles where a closer fit was required.

By 1910 the bodice fullness had been reduced and bodices were simply and loosely cut. The two main styles were either the bodice with smoothly fitted sleeve and with side seams only (sometimes the front had shoulder tucks or a yoke), or the new side front and back seams with the side front cut on the straight of the material. The kimono cut with the sleeve in one with the bodice was becoming very popular. This was usually on the straight at the centre front and slightly off the straight centre back. Both bodices were gathered round the waist, with greater fullness arranged in the centre front. Most bodices still had a fitted lining. This was now simply

233

cut–sometimes still with front darts and usually only the underarm seam; it was now used not so much for fit but in order to pouch the dress bodice and keep the waist high. With the straight line the princess cut, which had only occasionally been used earlier, was now very frequent, as was also the semi-princess, which was a long panel centre front and another centre back but with bodice and skirt seamed at the side waist. By 1910, though the older woman still kept to a high collar, the neckline was round the base of the throat, often with a small frill or peter-pan collar; sometimes it was a slight V. Bodices of dressy afternoon frocks and evening dresses, when of transparent materials, as they usually were, might still be draped or pleated on the shoulders.

The fitted corselet skirt continued for a few years, but more frequently the skirt hung straight from the high waistline. The fitted foundation skirt became a corselet belt; later, and more usually, this was replaced by a petersham about four inches deep. Although the fashionable skirt was very much reduced in volume *c.* 1908 it was not until 1910 that the narrow skirt became general wear. The same cuts continued but with less material and with fewer and much straighter gores. The waist fullness was set into darts, or was gathered, or was pleated from the sides round to the back. The hem was faced with self material; lining skirts were less worn. Soft or transparent materials, often unshaped and gathered to the waist, were however always mounted on to a more fitted foundation skirt. In fashionable tailored styles, afternoon dresses and evening gowns, the skirt was trained until *c.* 1910, the seams straight but flaring from the knees–the 'mermaid' skirt. Very simple summer dresses, untrained of course, were known as 'tub' frocks. Tailored costumes were more fashionable during this period, both the classical type and the more dressmaker versions. In 1909 the high waist produced a Directoire suit. This had a long, cut-away coat with close-fitting sleeves, a false waistcoat, buttons and frilled jabot. It was usually worn with a slender skirt with mermaid train. Later styles were more severe, with the jacket well below hip level and the skirt easy and untrained. Dressmaker suits were more varied–the coats might have a separate basque, kimono sleeves, cut-away front, false waistcoat, etc. There were also long straight coats with revers and wrap-over front, and looser raglan and sack types for country wear and for travelling. Bodices and skirts were now joined, and usually fastened at the centre back.

In 1910–11 the skirt became very tight–the 'hobble' skirt. Sometimes the slight fullness at the bottom gathered into a deep band, sometimes the skirt was slit at the side. The silhouette was becoming rather uninspired when the French couturier Poiret, influenced by the oriental designs of the Russian ballet, gave subtlety to the straight skirt by draping it or adding a knee-level full tunic. The drapery was of the eastern type where the material is pulled tightly round the hips and caught up into folds in front. This new development, however, was arrested by the outbreak of war. During 1914 there was little change in dress styles but as women became increasingly involved in wartime activities clothes became simpler and more practical. See plates 63–6; Diagrams LXV, LXVI, LXVII.

## 1915–1930

The simple sports corset became general wear during this time and soon began from the waist and was little more than a hip belt. The low cut corset and lighter underwear brought in the brassière. This was cut to flatten the bust as the straighter bodice line developed.

The tunic lengthened to become a full skirt replacing the impractical narrow one. It was usually cut bell shape with two gored side seams, and was often fitted to a hip yoke. Sometimes the skirt was pleated. For more dress occasions the skirt was two- or three-tiered, and sometimes the whole skirt was covered with flounces. Skirts of this type were usually cut from material on the straight and gathered on to a two-piece foundation. Although the very high line had gone, the waist was still above normal level. The skirt was mounted on to a petersham about two inches deep. The day skirt was some seven or eight inches off the ground–shorter than it had ever been before. Suits were general wear, and to go with the fuller skirt the coat was either a loose sack or had a basque. A little later, a loose sack held in by a belt, with deep pockets, had a military air.

There was little change in bodice cut. Blouses were of the shirt type, with yoke or raglan sleeves and long narrow revers giving the new deep V neckline. Dress bodices were as before, with natural shoulder fit and long sleeves–or were kimono-shaped. The neckline was round, V-shape, or had a cross-over front. When either of these was very long the 'modesty' vest was worn. In 1916–17 a high standing collar at the back gave a military touch, and in 1916 the jumper appeared. This was a long loose blouse to hip level, held in to the waist by a belt or sash. It was soon followed by the coat-frock and the chemise dress. These were all-in-one frocks; that is, waistless with the fullness held in by a belt or sash and with only two side seams. Skirts were again becoming longer and narrower. The coat-frock usually had the long V neck, often with revers, and the chemise dress a rounded neckline. The evening bodice was a straight strip of unshaped light silk or satin material with shoulder straps and over it chiffon or net kimono drapery or just a little drapery. Jumpers and chemise style frocks slipped over the head without fastenings. Coats were long and loose; sack, raglan, trench coat, and other slightly military styles.

The chemise dress continued to be worn into the early 1920's–rather loose and down to the ankles again. When the war ended the French couturiers began to experiment with various styles to break the monotony of this loose chemise cut. The 'barrel' silhouette was obtained by knee-length tunics or side drapery or decoration on the hips, the bottom of the skirt tapering in, sometimes with an elastic threaded through the hem. The Chinese influence was a wide loose sleeve with deep armhole. The Renaissance style produced the 'tabard'–a long straight loose panel over the front and another over the back, the shoulders seamed and the panels caught together low on each hip. It was worn over a simple basic dress, often with knife-pleating at the sides. A shorter version of the tabard was to hip level and caught at the sides on the hip, often with long hanging bows of ribbon, thus achieving the barrel silhouette. The picture dress was an evening dress with loose sleeveless chemise top and a full skirt from the low hip line. By 1921 the waist was round the hips.

In spite of these variations, the freedom of the chemise dress and the simple suit with straight coat and skirt and jumper was more acceptable to the post-war generation of women. It was now the young girl, freed from centuries-old conventions of behaviour and dress, who was influencing the direction fashion was to take. The chemise dress remained, but by 1923 had achieved a style of its own. The skirt began to rise and by 1925 had reached the knees; all superfluous fullness was removed, as were sometimes the sleeves also, or they were long and tight-fitting. A youthful, simple dress emerged in which the sex appeal lay in the movements of long slender arms and legs instead of in static curves of breasts and hips.

The fashionable figure was flat and boyish. For women so unfortunate as to have curves, a straight foundation garment of heavy cotton enclosing bust and hips helped to give a more uniform line. Flatness required little fitting; shoulder seams and two side seams were all that were required. Sometimes, however, and especially with a large bust, the material had to be lifted so that it hung straight round the figure. This was accomplished by front shoulder gathers, tucks, or a dart—in the late 1920's this dart began to be taken from the bust into the side seam instead of in to the shoulder seam—sometimes a horizontal dart at hip level was all that was necessary. The dresses were cut either in one piece or with a skirt added to the low hip line. Interest was given to the severity of line by the variations which allowed for freedom of movement. For day wear and tailored styles there was usually pleating: inverted pleats, pleats all round, or inserted panels of pleating, etc. For dressy day and evening frocks in soft materials, there were godets, panels gathered or shirred, or handkerchief drapery panels. The fullness was at first usually concentrated centre front, apron-wise. In the late 1920's the design became more geometrical and asymmetrical: the skirt began to be cut circular, with an uneven hemline; in 1928 the panel drapes were longer at the sides; by 1929 they were long all round.

Another innovation of the late 1920's was the cutting of the straight chemise dress on the cross grain of the material so that it clung to the figure once more, outlining curves. After years of the utmost simplicity of cut, this use of the cross together with the longer skirt was to be the beginning of a new era, and once more a completely new fashion line was to be created. See plates 67–71; Diagrams LXVIII, LXIX, LXX, LXXI, LXXII, LXXIII, LXXIV, LXXV.

## MATERIALS, DECORATIONS, ETC.

By 1908 serges and tweeds were replacing face cloth for tailor-mades, which in summer were of linen, tussore, etc., with soft woollen or silk materials for dresses. Shirt blouses were of pleated Japanese silk and crêpe-de-chine, tub frocks of linen, cotton, shantung, etc. Very simply cut lingerie blouses and frocks of fine voile or muslin, delicately embroidered all over, were fashionable in the pre-war years, they often had lace insertions–Guipure, Valenciennes, Torchon, Irish crochet, etc. For evening dresses and elaborate afternoon frocks soft silks and especially satin, were used, also transparent materials such as ninon, chiffon, lace, net, etc., several layers of these being used in one dress. For example, ninon over ninon trimmed with lace over a silk foundation, or chiffon over chiffon embroidered with sequins over a satin foundation, etc. Bodices of evening gowns were diaphanous, the foundation being a strip of lace mounted on flesh-coloured chiffon with shoulder straps and a little light drapery. Trimmings for tailored styles were cords, flat braids, soutache braid, etc., for dresses, rouleaux and pipings of satin, small bows of satin, often made from rouleaux; beading and diamanté and many buttons of all sizes. There were jabots and frilling fronts to tailored coats. Hip-length golf jackets were of heavy knitted wool. Long fur coats were fashionable–sable, seal musquash, chinchilla, etc. and no costume was complete without a fur stole and muff. These had at first been lavishly festooned with heads and tails but later, with the straight line, long flat stoles and large pillow muffs were made from the smoother furs. In jewellery the pre-war oriental influence was seen in long ropes of pearls, amber, jade and other semi-precious stones.

From the end of the war plain matt surfaces were preferred: wool velour, gabardine, wool marocain, velvet, etc., crêpe-de-chine, silk and cotton georgettes, silk marocain, velvet, etc. Stockinette weaves became popular–silk and fine wool jersey for jumpers and dresses, and heavy wool knits for cardigan suits. Having become expert in knitting socks, balaclavas, etc. during the war, women now knitted their own jumpers, cardigans, and dresses. The Chinese influence, *c.* 1920, was seen in oriental motifs and bands of embroidery, also in long tassels. The Renaissance style was carried out in brocades. The early long loose chemise dress was heavily patterned with embroidery, with appliqué, painted, and beaded designs. The discovery of Tutankhamen's tomb in 1923 produced a wave of Egyptian motifs, carried out in earthy reds and dark blues. Rodier fabrics, especially the soft woollen kasha, often with beautifully designed woven patterns, were very much used in the 1920's. A great many of the chemise evening dresses were completely covered with designs carried out in sequins, beads, fringes, or just by rows of fringes, silk or beaded. All-over lace in various colours was used for afternoon and evening dresses, for the latter metallic lace, or lace embroidered with sequins, beads, etc. From the mid 1920's dresses began to be less decorated. Interest was given by using two or more shades of the one colour, or by fine tucking, shirring, pleating, flouncing, etc. In the late 1920's patterned chiffon was coming into fashion, and chiffon coats were worn over afternoon dresses. Fur coats were of kolinsky, moleskin, musquash, squirrel, etc., and fur collars and cuffs were added to coats. In 1922 monkey fur was used as trimming; from the early 1920's fox was the vogue, worn as a stole or for a coat collar. Costume jewellery relieved the severity of cropped heads and chemise topped dresses–long drop ear-rings, shoulder brooches, ropes of beads, a slave bangle worn on the upper arm, etc.

# Construction of
# Twentieth-century Dresses

In the early 1890's each piece of the bodice was mounted separately on to a similarly cut piece of lining material, then both were seamed together. Each seam was boned. The outside seam of the two-piece lining sleeve was first sewn, and then the dress material mounted on to it–the fullness at the top gathered and tacked on to the top of the lining sleeve. The sleeve and lining were then sewn together down the inside arm. From *c.* 1895, first the back seams of the bodice lining were stitched, and the front darts of the lining, and then the dress material for the back of the bodice was laid over the lining, the front over the front lining, and the two stitched together at the shoulders and side seams. This was done because the seaming of the outer material was being reduced to only two back side seams, or none, while the front usually had a gathered or plastron front. This latter was a piece of material mounted on a lining piece and then attached to the right side of the bodice lining. The bodice was fastened edge to edge at the centre front with hooks and eyes, and the plastron piece was hooked separately to the left side of the lining, the dress material folding over a little each side. This method was followed later for the looser bodices if they fastened centre front, the gathered front, now unlined, fastening separately on the left side. In the 1890's bodices fastened centre front, except in evening bodices, which sometimes fastened or were laced centre-back; from 1900 back fastening was more usual. The high collar of the 1890's was backed with stiff muslin, not boned. From *c.* 1900, when it was of lighter lace, net, etc., it was boned or had wire supports. In early bodices the lining was still of heavy striped cotton, but in better dresses heavy silk taffeta was used. Later bodices have a glacé silk or satin boned lining. From *c.* 1904 bodice linings, of softer silk and usually unboned, were made up separately. These might be fitted with front darts or just gathered, with an underarm seam and sometimes an additional back seam. With the high waistline, bodice and skirt were joined together and usually fastened at the centre back. As long as bodices were cut separately from the skirt and slightly pouched–that is, until *c.* 1917–they were mounted on a lining and were cut with only two side seams; though the lining became very light–jap silk or net. The waist fullness of bodice and skirt was gathered on to the petersham. Chemise dresses of wool usually have a bodice lining of jap silk but this is for neatness only. Elaborate evening

238

bodices were mounted on to a lining of Japanese silk or chiffon which fastened centre back. The outer material, often of two or more layers of chiffon, lace, etc., crossed over or were draped, each layer fastening separately in different places, as also often happened with the skirt, the fastenings being minute hooks and eyes and tiny press studs. From outside no opening was visible, and it required the services of a lady's maid to adjust these dresses successfully. Muslin and voile dresses and the tub frocks were usually unlined.

Umbrella skirts, without the centre front panel, had a selvedge join at the centre front. Except in the bell skirt, gored skirts were always joined cross to straight, the top of each gore being slightly curved in to the waist, and the top of the skirt slightly eased on to the waistband. Until about 1893 the extra back fullness was gathered tightly, and tapes were still attached to the side seams and tied round the back to hold the skirt straight to the figure. After 1893, the centre back fullness was usually arranged in inverted pleats. Until *c.* 1897 the lining was sewn in with the skirt and was of fine linen, though silk was beginning to be used:

1891. 'Glacé silk–more usually black–is now used for the inside lining, for the double purpose of making a good finish when the skirt is raised, and to create the fashionable *frou-frou*, without which no skirt is considered *à la mode*.'

In 1895 the wide skirts often had an extra stiffening to hold them out: 'Parisiennes are now using a very heavy linen or cord to fold up in the edge of the lining, and this addition to the stiff lining is universally employed in all dress skirts. This cord is indeed to all intents and purposes, an ordinary linen blind cord.'

By 1897 lining and material were cut alike but made up separately and then joined together on to the waistband:

1899. 'Very few skirts either plain or shaped, are now made without a separate foundation which is to all intents and purposes a petticoat when the dress is raised. Glacé silk has by no means gone out of fashion as a lining but the long fluted skirts require a soft foundation such as nun's veiling, merv, surah, or satin.'

Cloth and woollen skirts had a brush braid all round the bottom to catch the dust; the fluted skirt of the early 1900's, which rested on the ground, was weighted.

The high-waisted corselet skirts were boned round the waist.

1906. 'Directoire Skirts have the top lined to the hips–the seams require thin bones or steels to a depth of six inches. Seams are boned to about two inches below the waistline and the casing sewn on very loosely just at the waist, so that the bone is very light and curves well, to avoid wrinkles round the figure.'

By 1910 many dresses hung straight from the high waist but were held up by an inside corselet foundation. This latter had been earlier replaced by a deep petersham. Until about 1920 all dresses with separately cut bodice and skirt were mounted on a petersham. By 1909 skirts were no longer made with a separate lining, the hem alone being faced with self material.

This did not apply to afternoon and evening dresses of flimsy materials, which were often cut without shaping and required a fitted underskirt.

The variations of the skirt most usually seen from 1909 to 1914 were: the umbrella one-piece, less curved and slightly gored centre back; the two-piece, with narrow back panel and front gored to the back panel; the three-piece, with narrow front panel, slightly gored, and two side pieces with straight front and gored centre back; the four-piece, with narrow centre front and a narrow centre back panel, both slightly gored, and with two side gores straight in front and gored to back panel. Draped skirts usually had a narrow centre back panel and the two front pieces draped in various styles at centre front or to one side. A front foundation was sometimes added, and was useful in keeping the drapery in position.

From *c.* 1910 fullness in dresses was sometimes gathered on to piping cords. Later yokes and other seams were joined by faggot stitching. Handwork was popular:

1912. 'Probably there never has been a greater craze for all sorts of handwork than at the present time . . . no woman should consider her dress complete nowadays without at least some daintily embroidered blouses, dress accessories and pretty tub dresses bearing evidence of her own skilful fingers and good taste.'

In the 1920's drapes were picot-edged; necks and sleeveless armholes were finished by crossway binding: 'Bindings for sheer material, such as georgette, crepe, chiffon, and all the soft silks, are cut double and pressed. The two raw edges are stitched to the edge to be bound, then the binding is folded over the edge, and hemmed down on the wrong side. Binding for cloth and velvet should be cut single on the bias, as a double binding is too clumsy to be practical.'

Shirring was a series of rows of gathering using very small stitches. Godets were gores added to give fullness. The skirt was slit on the straight grain, and triangular gores were inserted. Later these gores became fuller—a quarter of a circle—with the top often rounded. Handkerchief drapes were so-called because they originated in the use of rectangular pieces of material such as a handkerchief square. One right-angle was attached to the skirt—the corner usually being cut off and the rest of the material hung free in folds, making a zig-zag edge. Or the long side of a rectangular piece was stitched part of the way, the ends then hanging free in the handkerchief drape. In the late 1920's more circular cuts were being used, on the same principle.

Many aids to dressmaking could be bought ready-made in the shops: foundation skirts, and *balayeuses* for foundation skirts; boned corselet belts to support the high-waisted Empire skirts; lining bodices with the high boned collar attached and the front trimmed with lace and net, and sometimes also with sleeves; lace yokes with high boned collars; boned collars alone; chemisettes, jabots, and false fronts to wear with tailored jackets.

There were firms specializing in embroidery, variations of pleatings, hem-stitching, picot-edging, etc.

59. 1895. Outdoor costume. *Le Salon de la Mode*
This shows the Leg o' Mutton sleeve at its fullest, making the shoulders a focal point for bows, frills, and wide collars. Below the skirts were gored or neatly darted over the hips. See Cutting Diagrams LVII, LVIII and LIX

58. 1895. Evening dresses. *The Queen*

60b. 1897. Outdoor costume. *Le Journal des Modes*
Worn with a severely tailored skirt, a pretty blouse appears even more feminine

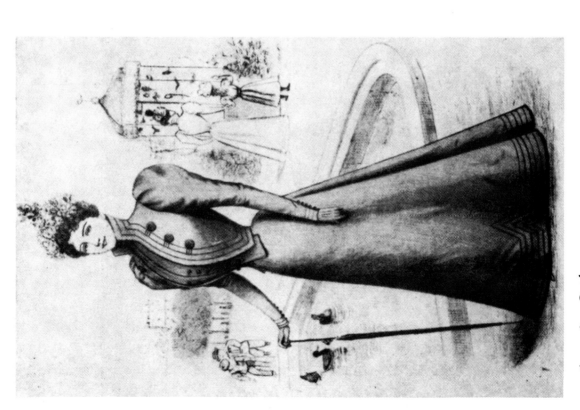

60a. 1897. Outdoor costume
The bolero jacket and matching skirt, with a sleeve shrinking back to a more standard size

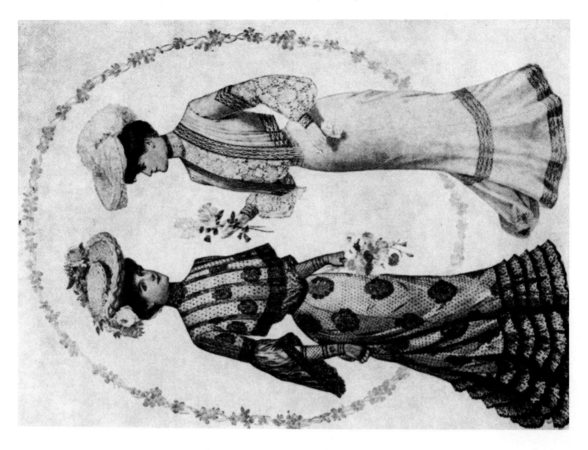

61. 1900 Outdoor costume. *Le Journal des Modes*

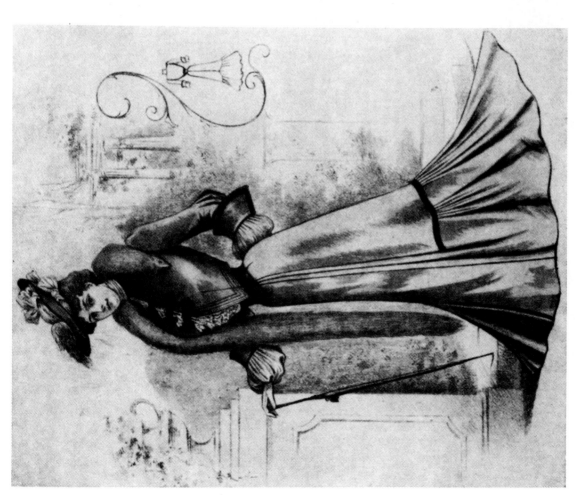

62. 1903. Outdoor costume. *Le Journal des Modes*

The straight-fronted corset has begun to alter the stance by throwing the upper part of the body forward. This is balanced by the deep curve at the back of the skirt being extended by means of the flounce to the ground. See Cutting Diagram LXII

63.  *c.* 1908. Afternoon dresses. "*Chic Parisien*"
There is a distinct rise in waistlines, and the full bodices with their wide kimono-like sleeves are worn over fitted linings to which the under sleeves, lace vests and high collar bands are attached.

64a. 1909. Day dress.

64b. 1909. Outdoor costume. *Journal des Demoiselles*

The new slender line. To attain this a long restricting corset reaching almost to the knees was necessary

JOURNAL DES DEMOISELLES

Suppl¹ au N° 12
15 Juin 1912

Parfumerie
HOUBIGANT
19, Faub⁷ S⁺ Honoré
Le Gérant: A. Bazard

Reproduction interdite

N° 5097
ALAIN THIÉRY Directeur
3, Rue du 4 Septembre
PARIS
Imp Fattorini & Crespin

65.  1912. Day dresses. *Journal des Demoiselles*
The waists are still high, and although bodices show little change in cut, the skirts
are being gathered into a confining narrowness at knee level. See Cutting
Diagrams LXV, LXVI and LXVII

a. 1914. Afternoon dress

b. 1914. Dinner dress (Worth)

66. *The Gazette du Bon Ton*
Plate a. shows dresses with kimino and
raglan-shaped sleeves. The figure on the
right is seen wearing a double skirt with
the lower one composed of narrow frills:
a prediction of Plate LXVII. See Cutting
Diagrams LXVIII and LXIX.
Plates b. and c. show skirts still confined
at the knee, but despite this, dresses
display a freedom which has not been
enjoyed for many years

c. 1914. Outdoor costume

67.  1916. Day Dress. *Gazette du Bon Ton*
A dress with a separate bodice which ends in a row of narrower scallops to
form a basque. The skirt is worn shorter and is typical of this date with its
many tiers of frills

257

68.  1917. Outdoor Costume
A semifitted tailored costume, with braided decoration

69.   1925. Coats and Dresses. *"Chic Parisien"*
The silhouette is slim and straight, and as narrow as possible at the hips. The freedom that is given to the short skirts is by close pleating or godets. See Cutting Diagram LXXIV

70. 1927–1928. Evening Dresses. *"Chic Parisien"*
In the asymmetrical design of these dresses one can perceive a new softness of line as the swathing is draped slightly on the cross about the waist and hips

71. 1929. Day Dresses. "*Chic Parisien*"
The dress on the right very clearly forecasting the complicated crossway cut of the
1930s. See Cutting Diagram LXXV

# Cutting Diagrams

For full explanation see Notes on the Cutting Diagrams, page 303

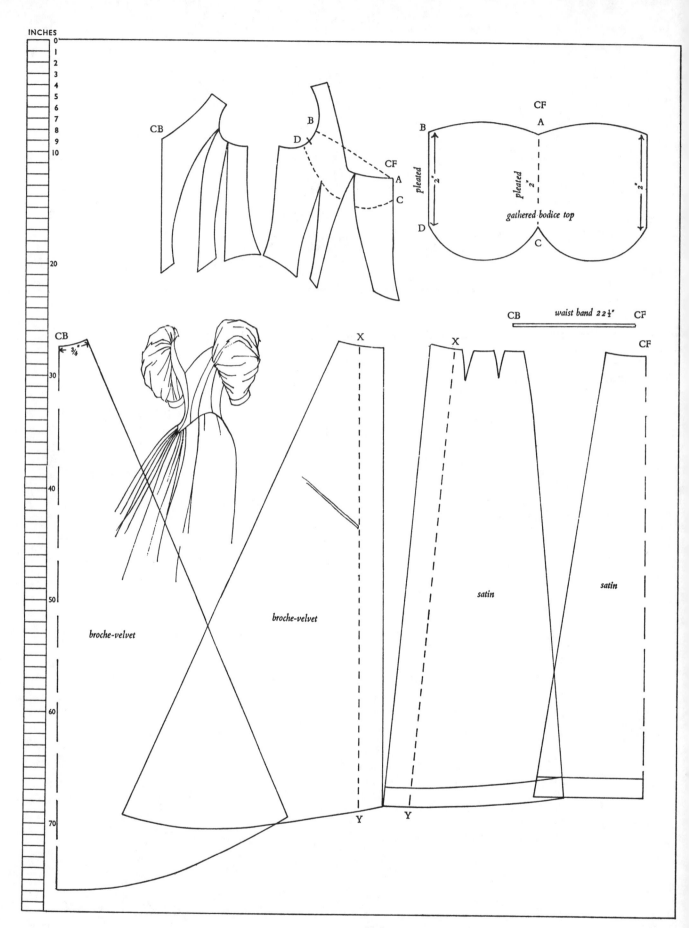

INCHES

CB

B
D
CF
A
C

CF
A
B
pleated
2'
pleated
2'
2'
D
C
gathered bodice top

waist band 22½"
CB
CF

CB
¾'
CF

X
X

broche-velvet
broche-velvet
satin
satin

Y
Y

DIAGRAM LVII

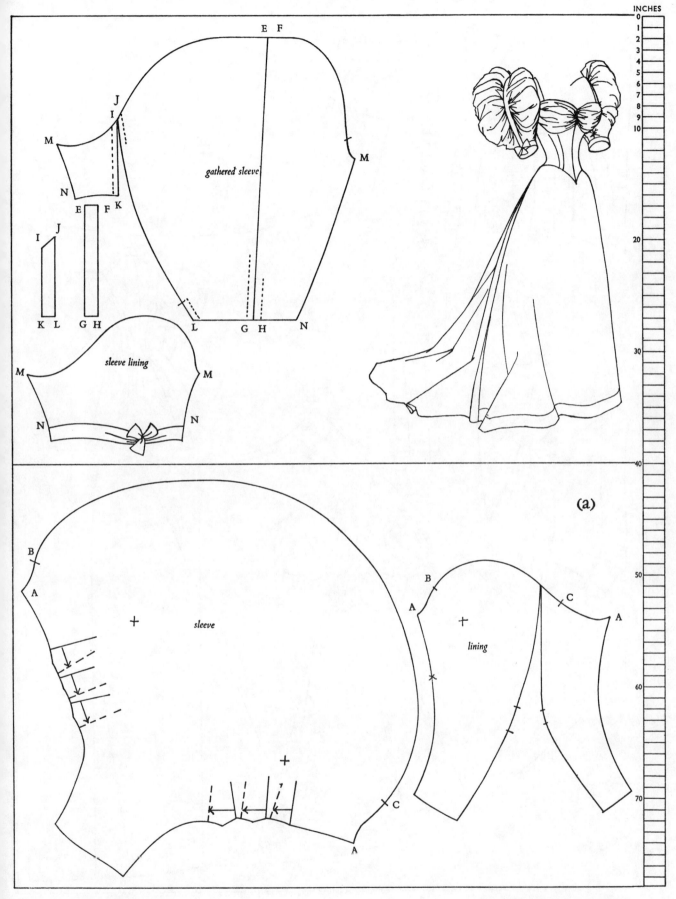

*gathered sleeve*

*sleeve lining*

*sleeve*

*lining*

(a)

DIAGRAM LVII (above)

DIAGRAM LVIII (below)

'LEG O' MUTTON' SLEEVE 1895

INCHES

INCHES

0
1
2
3 CB
4
5
6
7
8
9
10

20

30

40

50

60

70

F    A
CB    CF

F

CF

B

J

E

G

A    B

E

F

F

C    D

sleeve

H

H

I

I

I

H    H

J

sleeve lining

I    I

G

C    D

CB

24"

CF

DIAGRAM LIX

DAY DRESS *c. 1895. Privately owned*

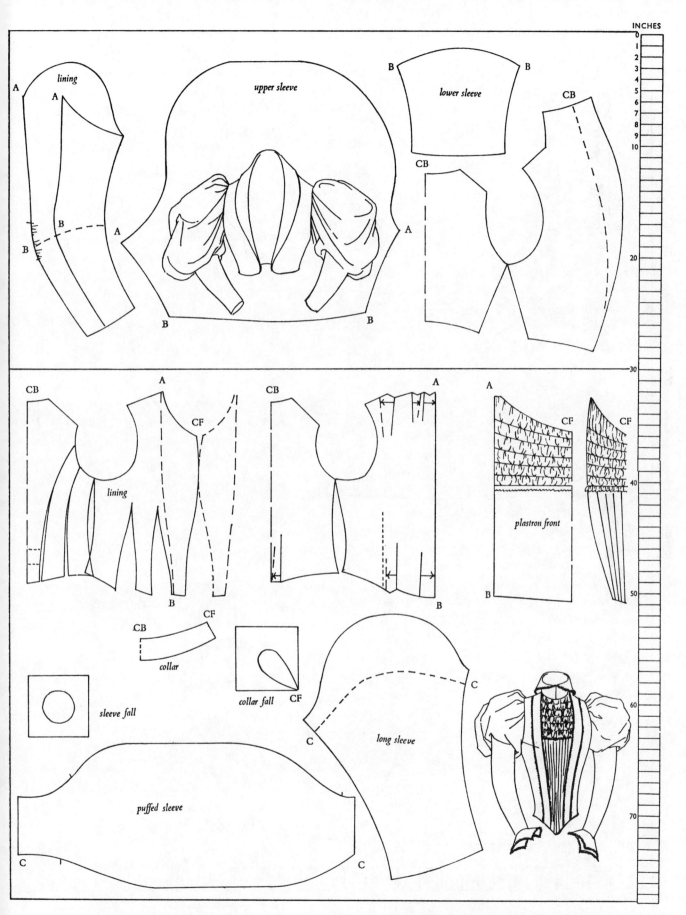

INCHES

0
1
2
3
4
5
6
7
8
9
10

20

30

40

50

60

70

*lining*

A

A

B

B

B

A

upper sleeve

B

B

B

lower sleeve

B

CB

CB

CB

A

CB

A

CF

*lining*

B

CB

A

B

A

CB

CF

collar

CB

CF

collar fall

CF

sleeve fall

puffed sleeve

C

C

C

long sleeve

C

C

A

CF

CF

*plastron front*

B

DIAGRAM LX (above)

BOLERO *c.* 1895. *Privately owned*

DIAGRAM LXI (below)

BLOUSE *c.* 1898. *Central School of Art and Design, London*

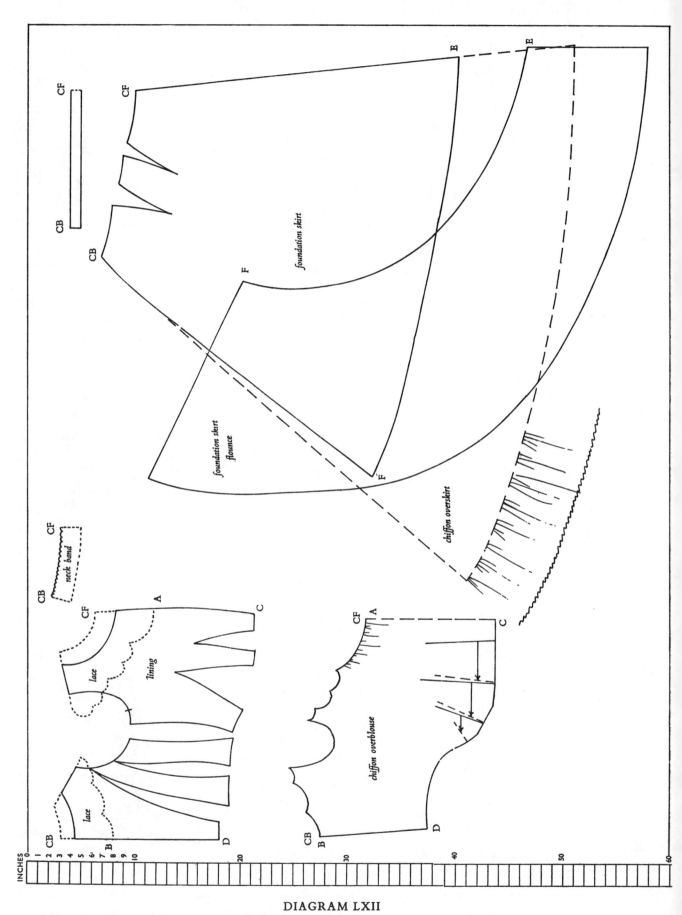

DIAGRAM LXII

AFTERNOON DRESS *c.* 1901. *Central School of Art and Design, London*

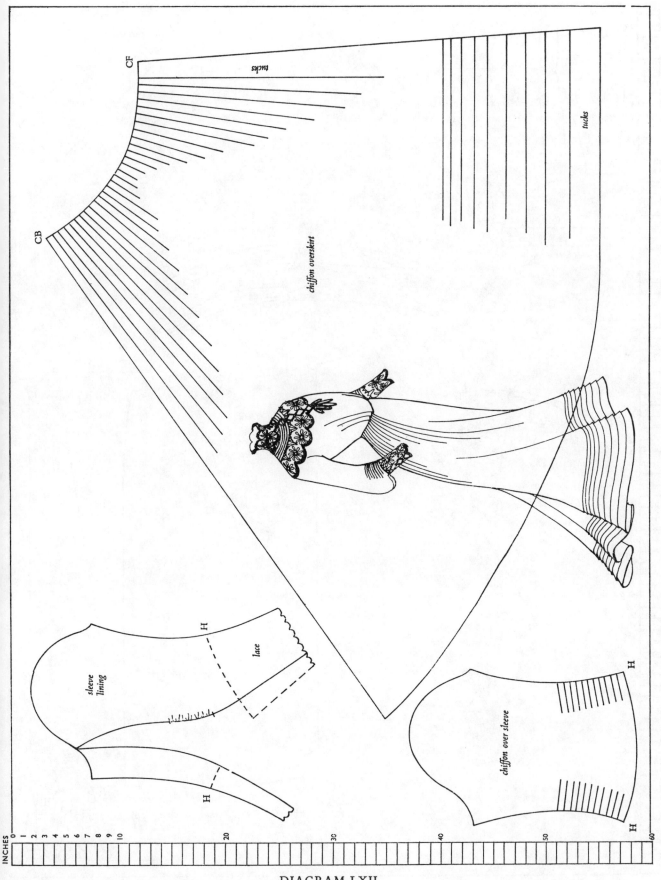

CF

tucks

CB

chiffon overskirt

tucks

sleeve
lining

lace

H

H

chiffon over sleeve

H

H

H

INCHES

0 1 2 3 4 5 6 7 8 9 10     20     30     40     50     60

DIAGRAM LXII

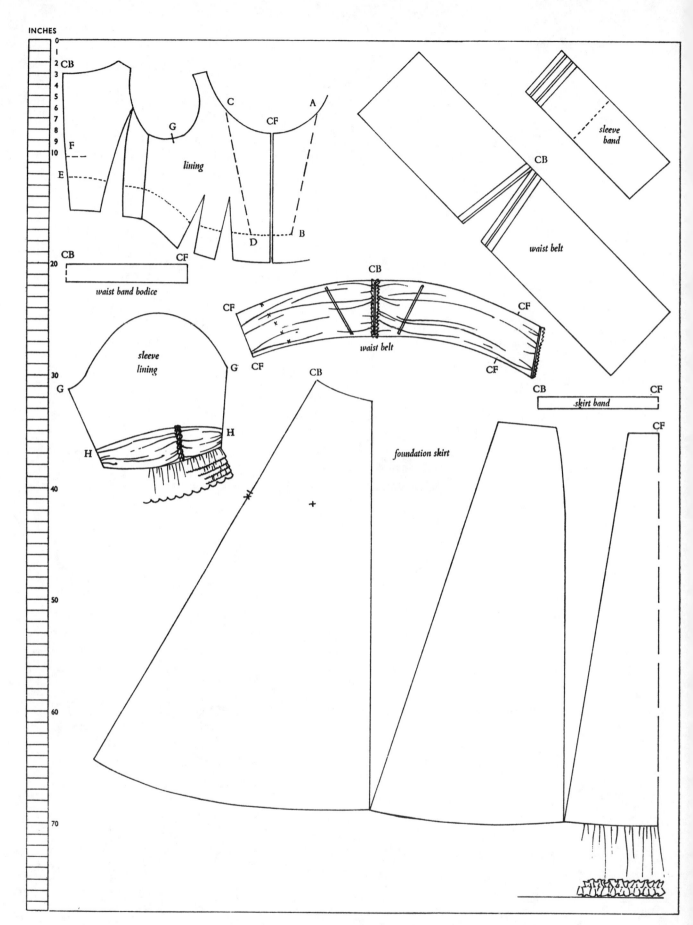

INCHES

CB

lining

CF

C

A

G

CF

F

E

D

B

sleeve
band

CB

waist belt

CB
waist band bodice

CB

CF

CF

waist belt

CF

CF

skirt band

CB

CF

sleeve
lining

G

G

G

H

H

H

CB

foundation skirt

CF

DIAGRAM LXIII

EVENING DRESS 1905–6. *Central School of Art and Design, London*

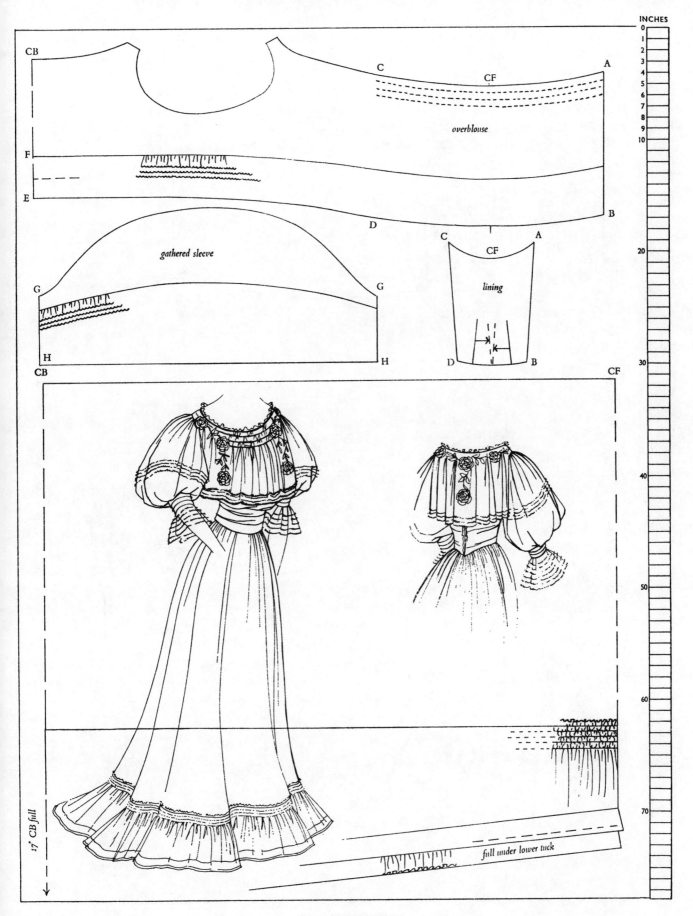

CB

C          CF                                    A

*overblouse*

F

E

D                                              B

*gathered sleeve*

C          CF          A

G                          G

*lining*

H                          H

CB                                              CF

D                          B

*17″ CB full*

*full under lower tuck*

INCHES
0
1
2
3
4
5
6
7
8
9
10

20

30

40

50

60

70

**DIAGRAM LXIII**

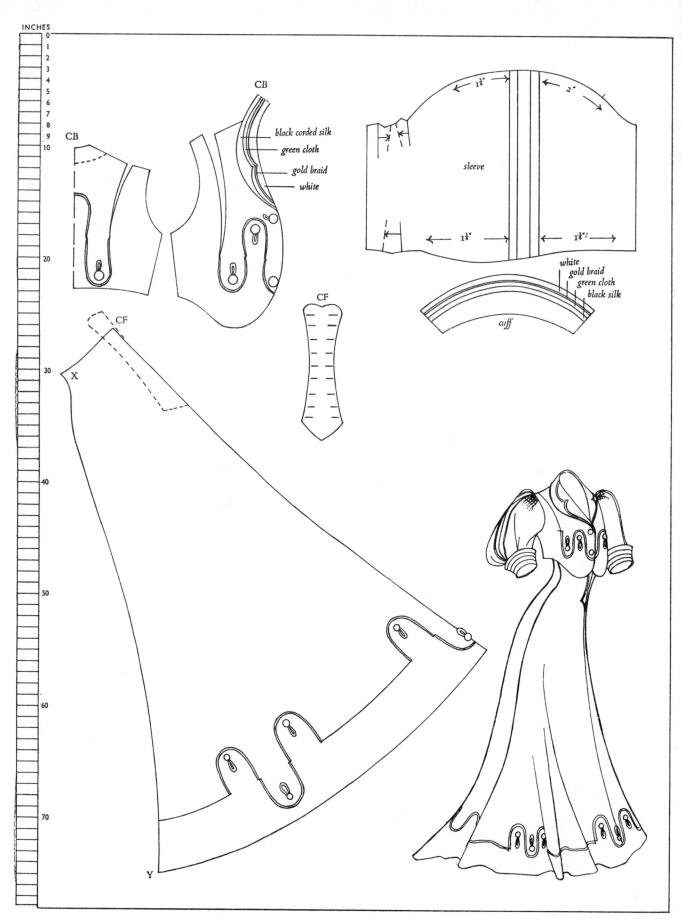

INCHES

CB

CB

CB

black corded silk
green cloth
gold braid
white

sleeve

$1\frac{3}{4}''$   2''

$1\frac{1}{4}''$   $1\frac{1}{4}''$

white
gold braid
green cloth
black silk

cuff

CF

CF

X

Y

DIAGRAM LXIV

BOLERO JACKET AND SKIRT 1906–7. *Victoria and Albert Museum*

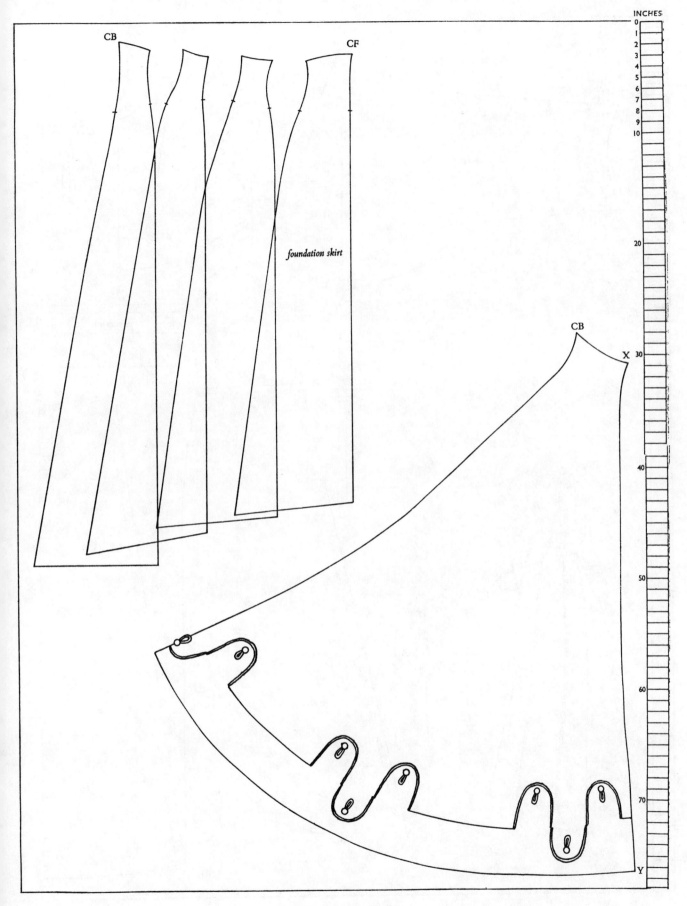

CB

CF

*foundation skirt*

CB

X

Y

INCHES

DIAGRAM LXIV

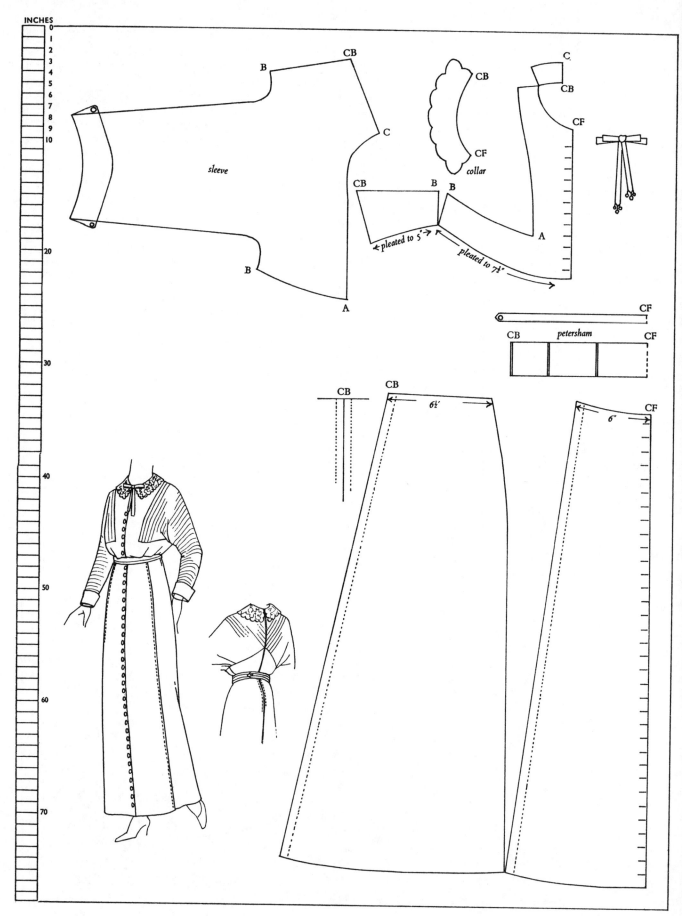

INCHES

sleeve

collar

CB

CF

B    CB

B    B

A

CB    B

pleated to 5"

pleated to 7½"

A

CF

CF

petersham

CB    CF

CB    CB

6½"

CF

6"

DIAGRAM LXV

TUB FROCK 1910–11. *Victoria and Albert Museum*

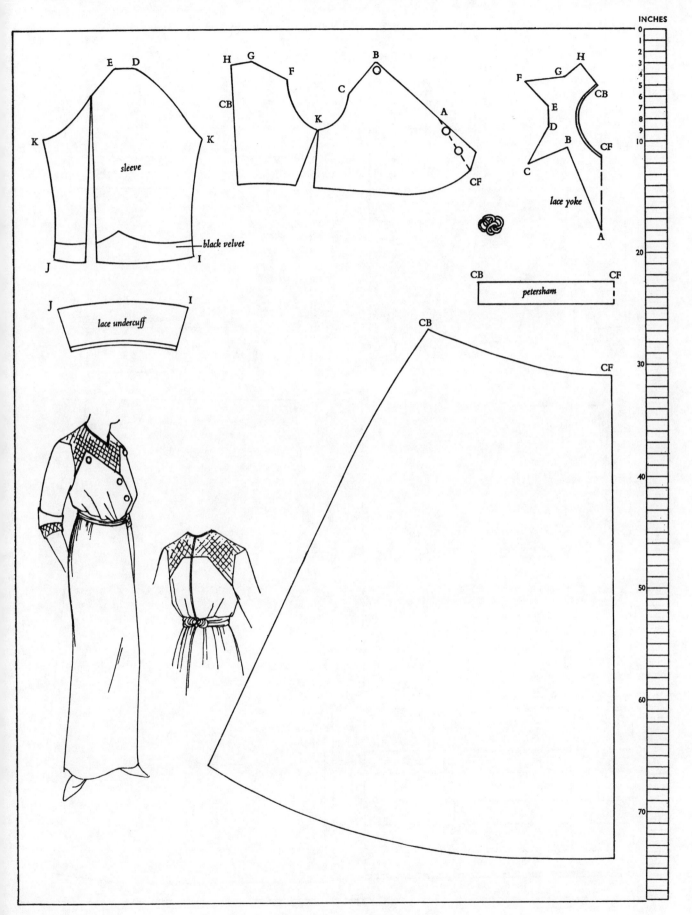

INCHES

sleeve

black velvet

lace undercuff

lace yoke

petersham

## DIAGRAM LXVI

AFTERNOON DRESS 1910–11. *London Museum*

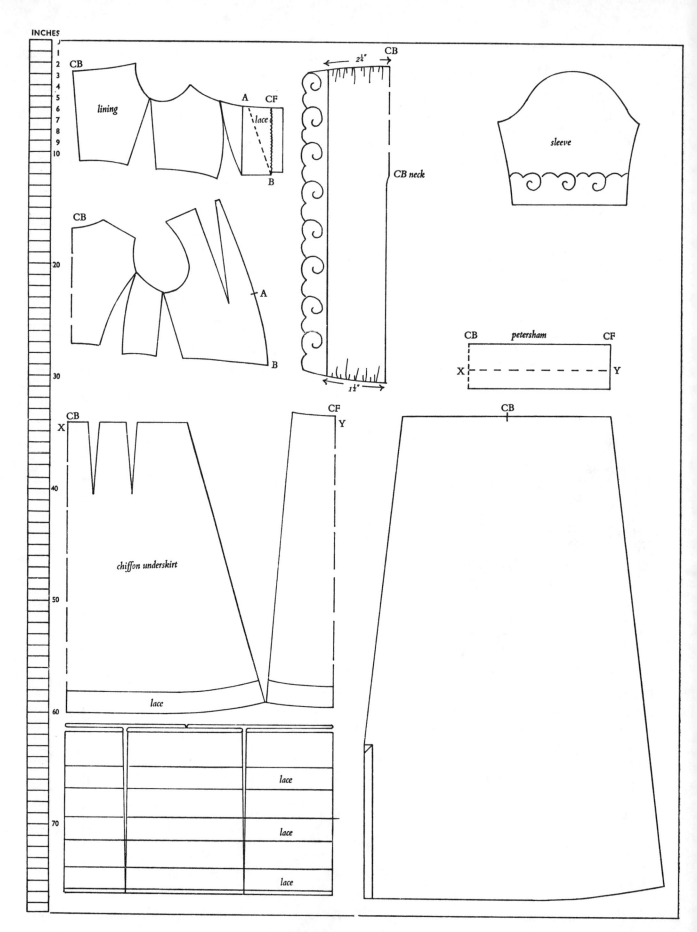

INCHES

CB

lining

A    CF

lace

B

CB

A

B

2¼"

CB

CB neck

1¼"

sleeve

CB    petersham    CF

X ---- Y

CB    X

CF    Y

chiffon underskirt

lace

lace

lace

lace

CB

DIAGRAM LXVII

AFTERNOON DRESS (LUCILE) 1911–12. *London Museum*

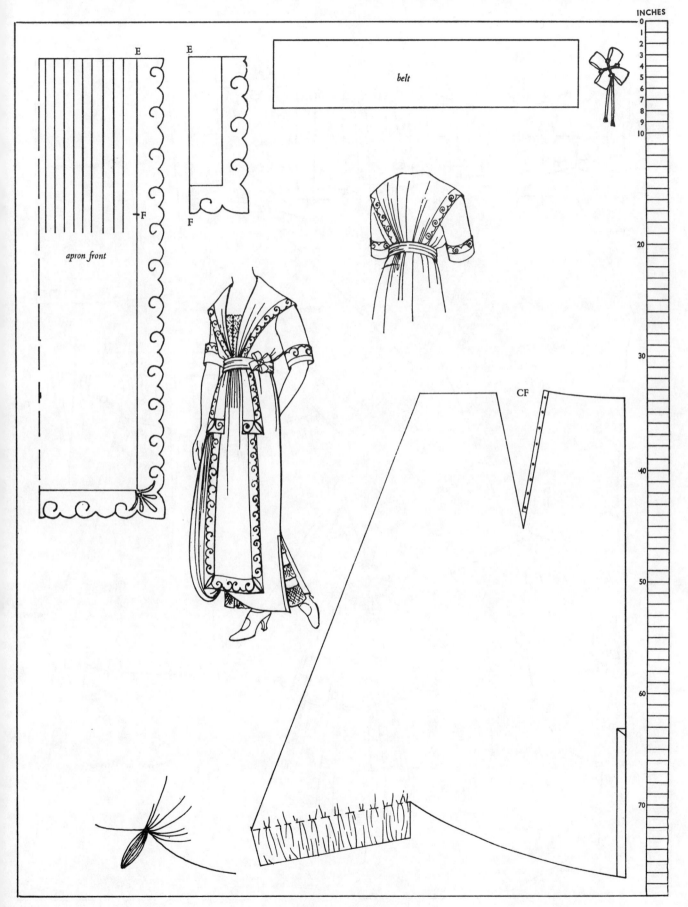

E    E

belt

INCHES
0
1
2
3
4
5
6
7
8
9
10

F

F

apron front

20

30

CF

40

50

60

70

DIAGRAM LXVII

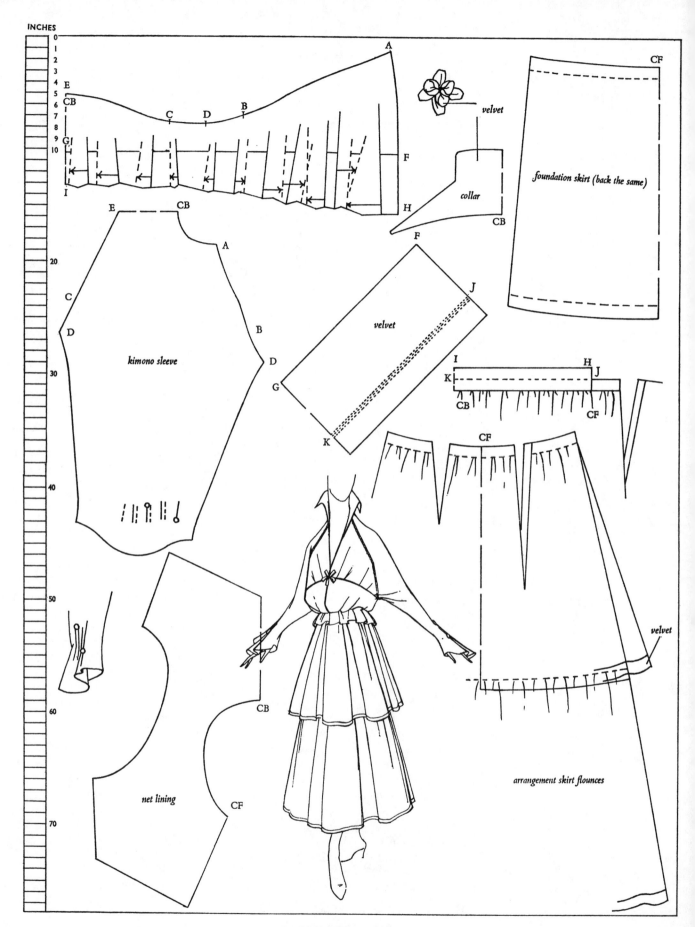

INCHES

0 1 2 3 4 5 6 7 8 9 10

20

30

40

50

60

70

A

E
CB

C    D    B

G
I

F

H

velvet

collar

CB

CF

*foundation skirt (back the same)*

E    CB

A

C

D

B

D

*kimono sleeve*

G

F

J

*velvet*

K

I          H
K          J
CB        CF

CF

*velvet*

CB

*net lining*

CF

*arrangement skirt flounces*

**DIAGRAM LXVIII**

AFTERNOON DRESS 1916–17. *Privately owned*

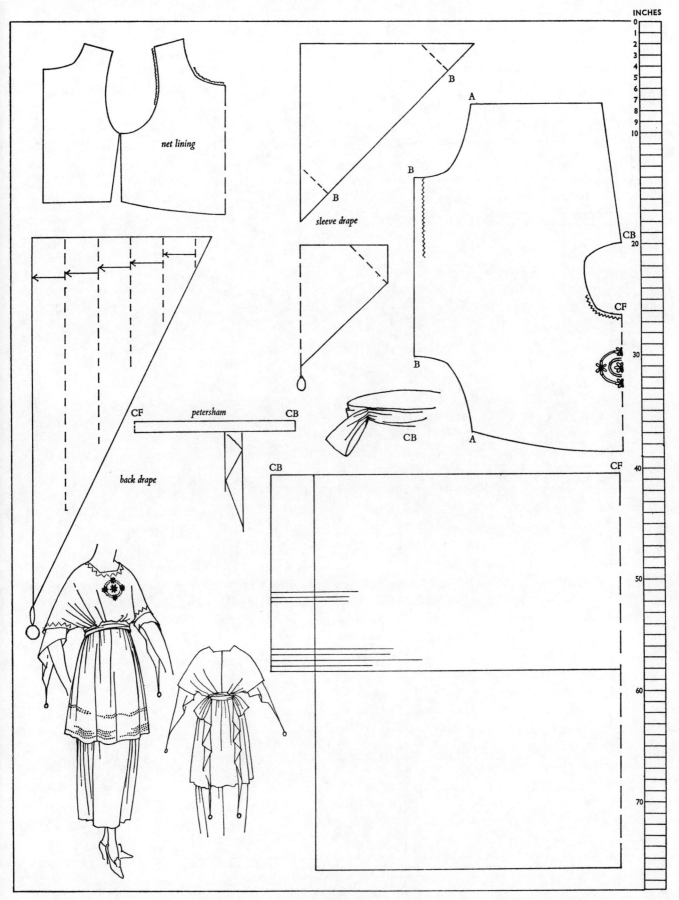

*net lining*

*sleeve drape*

*back drape*

*petersham*

A

B

B

B

B

B

CB

CF

CB

CF

CB

CB

A

CF

CB

CB

CF

0
1
2
3
4
5
6
7
8
9
10

20

30

40

50

60

70

DIAGRAM LXIX

AFTERNOON DRESS *c. 1918. London Museum*

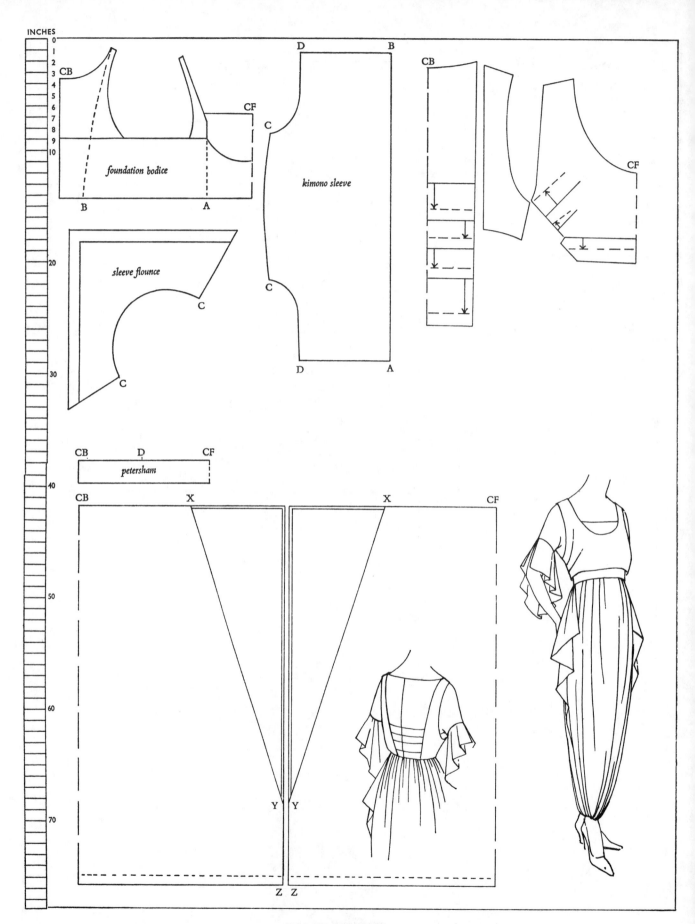

INCHES

CB

CF

foundation bodice

B                    A

D                    B

C

kimono sleeve

C

D                    A

CB

CF

sleeve flounce

C

C

C

CB          D          CF

petersham

CB                    X                              X                    CF

Y  Y

Z  Z

DIAGRAM LXX

EVENING DRESS 1920–1. *Privately owned*

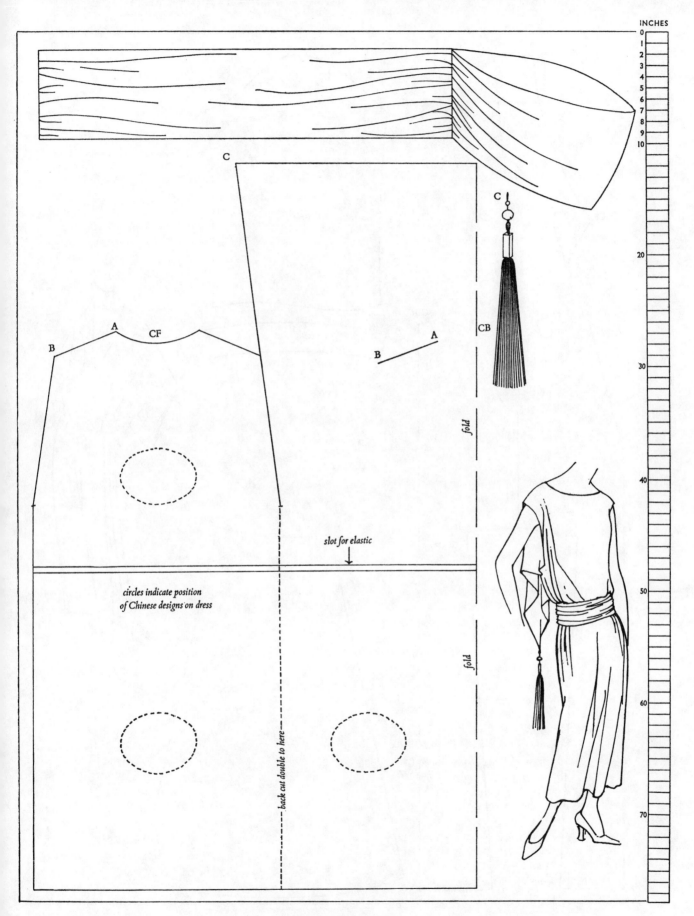

INCHES

C

C

CB

A

B

A

B

CF

*fold*

*slot for elastic*

*circles indicate position
of Chinese designs on dress*

*fold*

*— back cut double to here —*

DIAGRAM LXXI

EVENING DRESS (POIRET) 1922. *Centre de Documentation du Costume, Paris*

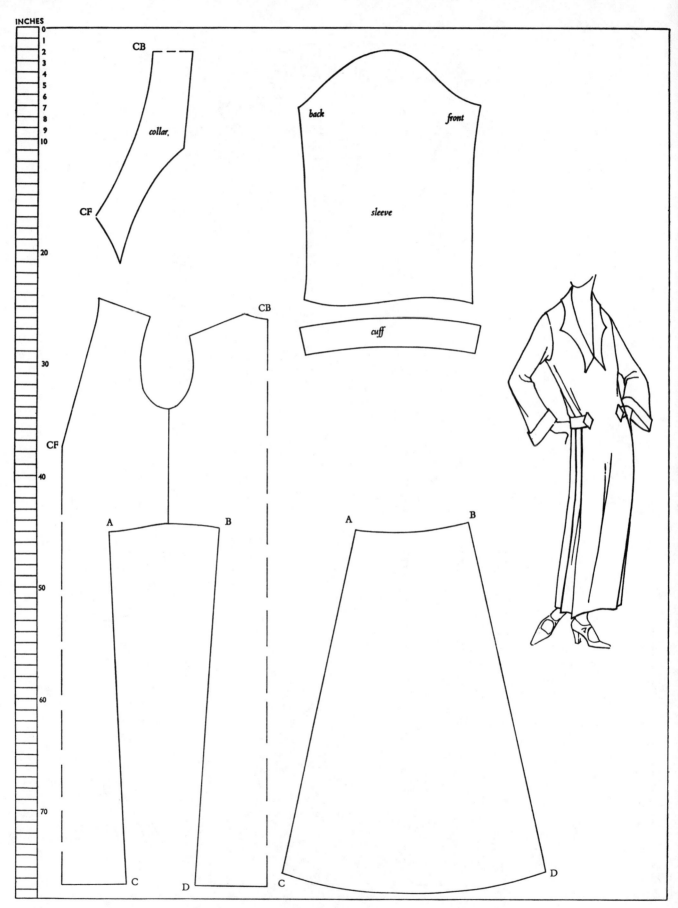

INCHES

0 1 2 3 4 5 6 7 8 9 10 20 30 40 50 60 70

CB

*collar*

CF

back    front

*sleeve*

*cuff*

CF

CB

A        B        A        B

C    D    C                    D

DIAGRAM LXXII

DAY DRESS (WELDONS) 1924. *Gallery of English Costume, Manchester*

DIAGRAM LXXIII

EVENING DRESS (VIONNET) 1925. *Centre de Documentation du Costume, Paris*

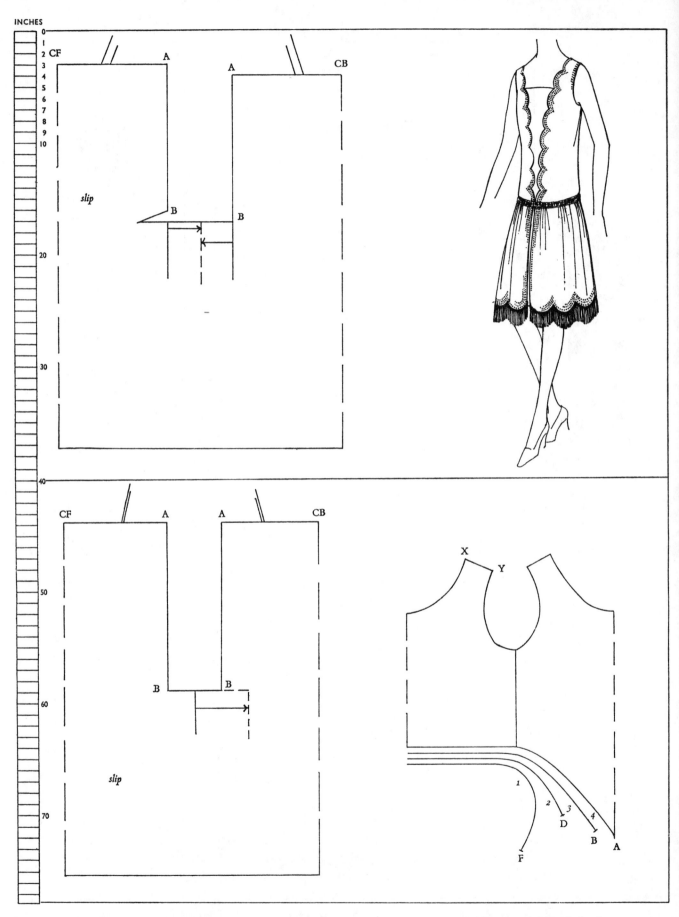

INCHES

0
1
2 CF
3
4
5
6
7
8
9
10

A

A                    CB

20

*slip*

B          B

30

40

CF          A          A          CB

50

B          B

60

*slip*

70

X
                    Y

1
2    3        4
      D
            B      A

F

DIAGRAM LXXIV (above)

EVENING DRESS *c.* 1926. *London Museum*

DIAGRAM LXXV (below)

EVENING DRESS 1925. *Privately owned*

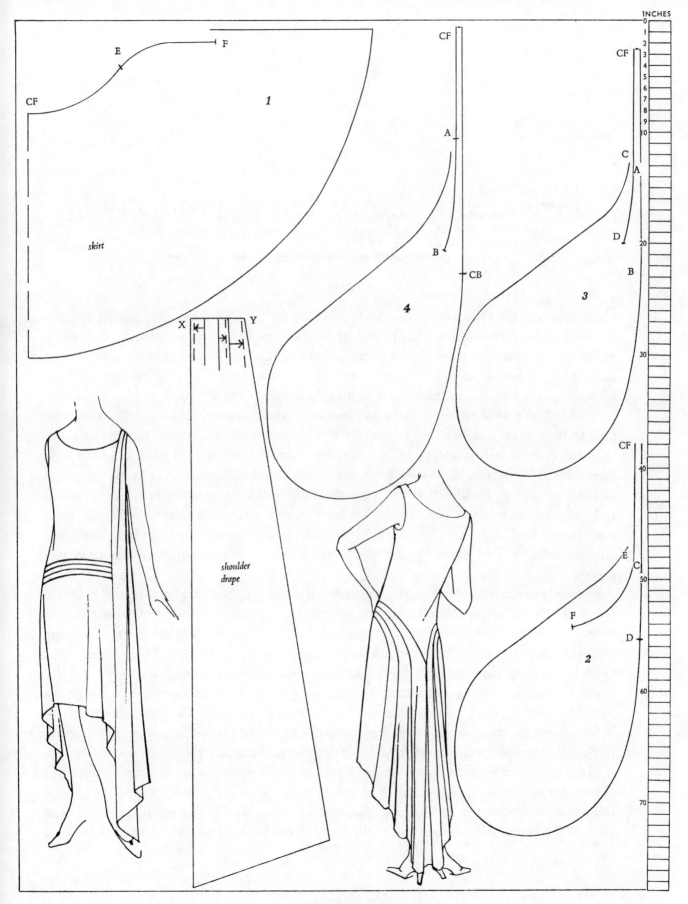

E    F

CF

*1*

*skirt*

CF

A

B

CB

*4*

INCHES

CF

C
A

D

B

*3*

CF

É
C

F

D

*2*

X    Y

*shoulder
drape*

**DIAGRAM LXXV**

# Twentieth-century Dress Production

Parisiennes call the early twentieth century *La Belle Époque*, and the extravagancies and elegance of women's dress during this period are seen at their best in the creations of the French couturiers. In London also, dress-designers had now their own houses, run on similar lines. Since the establishment of Haute Couture, from time to time a dress designer has appeared who is exceptionally sensitive to changing fashions in culture, art and social life and has the flair to create new lines for their interpretation. In pre-war days it was Poiret. He brought the silhouette back to the vertical and when that became dull, inspired by oriental art and the Russian ballet he transformed it with drapery, tunics, magyar sleeves, turbans, etc. In London at the same time Lady Duff Gordon–Lucile–became one of the first English designers to gain an international reputation. Lucile introduced no revolutionary change in cut or line, but her subtle and very feminine use of materials and colours gave a distinctive charm to the deceptive simplicity of the Empire line. Another feminine note, Lucile began to make underclothes of the same soft silks, chiffons, etc. as her dresses. It was Lucile, too, who inaugurated the mannequin parade.

Poiret's later interest in Greek costume produced dresses of great simplicity modelled on the Greek chiton. Although this influence can be seen in the chemise dress and in other post-war styles, Poiret's somewhat flamboyant, theatrical approach to dress design was out of keeping with the practical geometrical 'twenties. It was another woman designer, Mlle Chanel, who, again by choice of material, exquisite workmanship and attention to detail, gave style and chic to the chemise dress, achieving 'luxury through simplicity'. Then when women were getting tired of boyish figures it was another woman dress designer, Mme Vionnet, who broke the monotony of the straight line. Mme Vionnet had introduced the handkerchief drapes, and in the late 'twenties she was cutting the chemise dress from the cross grain of the material so that it clung to, instead of hung from, the body and, at first very subtly, again revealed feminine curves. Mme Vionnet is considered to be one of the most original designers and the greatest technician of modern Haute Couture. Through her understanding of the straight and cross weaves of material and their relation to the forms of the human body, she devised an intricate system of cutting which was to dominate the 'thirties but which already by 1929 had dealt a death blow to the sack-like chemise.

Haute Couture was for the very wealthy, for actresses and, later, film stars. Though there were still many women who preferred to have their clothes made by high-class dressmakers, the development of the large shops was attracting an ever-increasing number of customers. In the early 1900's the average woman was now buying her best clothes from the shops. These were usually specially made for her in their workrooms. For simpler dresses she still had a good dressmaker, and for alterations, remaking, and for her children's clothes there was always the 'little dressmaker'. Although at first it was still considered not quite the thing to buy ready-mades, the easier-fitting styles that were being introduced as the century progressed made it possible to buy a dress that would fit with or without alterations – and every store ran an excellent alteration department. Until 1908, partly ready-mades – that is, a finished skirt with extra material for bodice and sleeves – were still being sold. By 1910 shops were advertising 'ready-to-wear except joining back seam of Skirt', or 'Unmade Skirt Foundation (well-shaped) to match Robe'. After the war there was no longer a stigma attached to ready-mades, the loose chemise had solved the problem of fitting, and by the 1920's shops could offer a wide selection of styles and price ranges from which to choose.

This increase in bought clothes, the simplicity of cut, and the growing number of jobs available to women, led in England, though not in France, to the gradual, though not quite complete, disappearance of the private dressmaker. Older women, and those with difficult figures, might still have their dresses made for them, but good private dressmakers were becoming rare. Simplicity of cut also meant a revival of home dress making, especially by young girls with limited incomes. Paper patterns had improved, and the few pieces required to make a dress were quite comprehensible and easily assembled. Pre-war paper patterns, consisting as they did of innumerable pieces of thin brown tissue paper without any markings, had been a mystery and a jigsaw puzzle to be solved only by the most expert and experienced of dressmakers.

From 1890 onwards the paper pattern industry developed rapidly. The new fitted skirt lent itself to much more straightforward cutting than did the earlier draped bustle styles. At the turn of the century, in addition to firms specializing in paper patterns, such as McCalls, Weldons, etc. with their own pattern books, many of the numerous women's magazines continued the pattern service that had been begun in the previous century, but which was less prevalent later. Two of these magazines which still exist are *The Lady* and *Vogue*. *The Lady*, which was first issued in 1885, ran an excellent pattern service from its beginning until 1935. The 'Dressmaking Notes' in its issues during this period are illustrated by the design of a dress together with a diagram of some of the pattern pieces, and instructions as to how the pattern should be cut out and the dress constructed. They provide a continuous guide to changing methods of cut and construction. *Vogue*, which first appeared in America in 1892, also included patterns in its early numbers. During the twentieth century, when most of the other high class magazines were dropping their pattern service, *Vogue* developed this branch and the standard of their styling rose to such a high quality that Vogue Paper Patterns were being sold in high-class shops all over the world, and eventually a *Vogue Pattern Book* was published as well as the journal. British *Vogue* was founded in 1916, and the English *Vogue Pattern Book* in 1927.

From the 1880's, when tailored styles became fashionable wear, the tailors' system of drafting patterns on the flat was being increasingly applied to cut women's clothes. It was cleverly adapted to cut the more fanciful versions of coat and skirt that became so popular from the 1890's onwards. More technical books were being published. As well as those giving sewing instructions there were many on tailoring, each with its own variation of drafting systems. The diagrams given in some early women's tailoring books were as a rule simple basic shapes, as their emphasis was on technique rather than on style. The *Tailor & Cutter* publications are, however, an exception. Although usually associated with men's clothes, the *Tailor & Cutter* has always included women's dress in their cutting systems, technical books and magazines, and ran a separate journal *The Ladies' Tailor*. The text is, of course technical, giving drafting and construction methods, but the diagrams, often illustrated, show a great variety of fashionable styling and are another interesting guide to the evolution of cut from the 1890's down to the present day.

Drafting is not a system to produce a revolutionary change in fashion line but it is a practical and accurate way of making a pattern. It is eminently suitable for coats, suits, and simple dresses, and of course for mass production.

The private dressmaker now relied almost entirely on paper patterns for cut, and if she was skilful she adapted them to fit her customer. Some of the more expert cut direct on a dummy, or dress stand. This method is more personal and individual, and is essential in designing dresses where fullness and draping is required. The proportion and balance of a design also can be better judged when it is cut in the round. Sometimes the first sketch is cut in cotton material, the pattern of the dress being made from this *toile*. The use of actual materials is more inspiring as the pattern, texture, weight and hang suggest the treatment. Every dress designer has, of course, his own method of creating his new models, and it is this, not a woman's fickle whim, which has given the ever-changing, infinite variety to women's clothes.

# Twentieth-century
# Tailors' and Dressmakers' Patterns

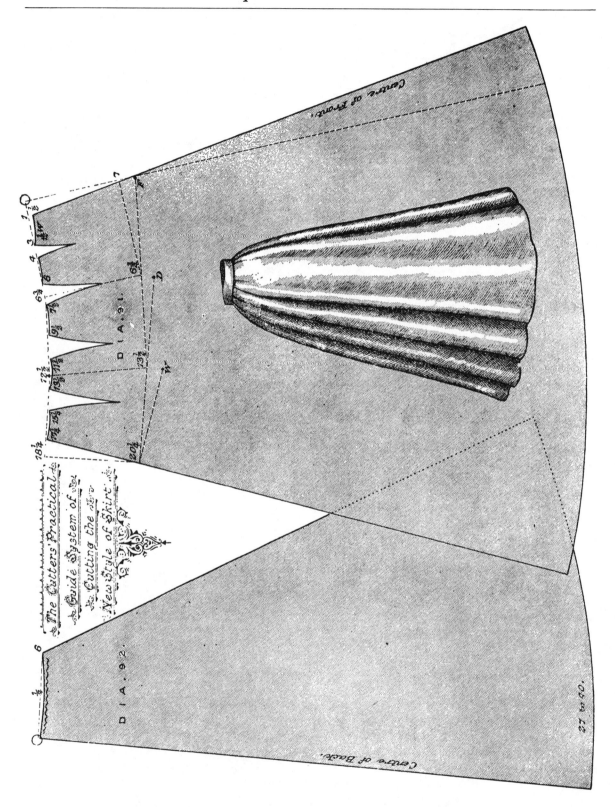

34. *The Cutters' Practical Guide,* W. D. F. Vincent, *c.* 1893
New Style of Skirt—All Skirts are now being made lined throughout, a facing put
round the bottom 5 or 6 inches deep, and in many cases braid is added just on the
edge.

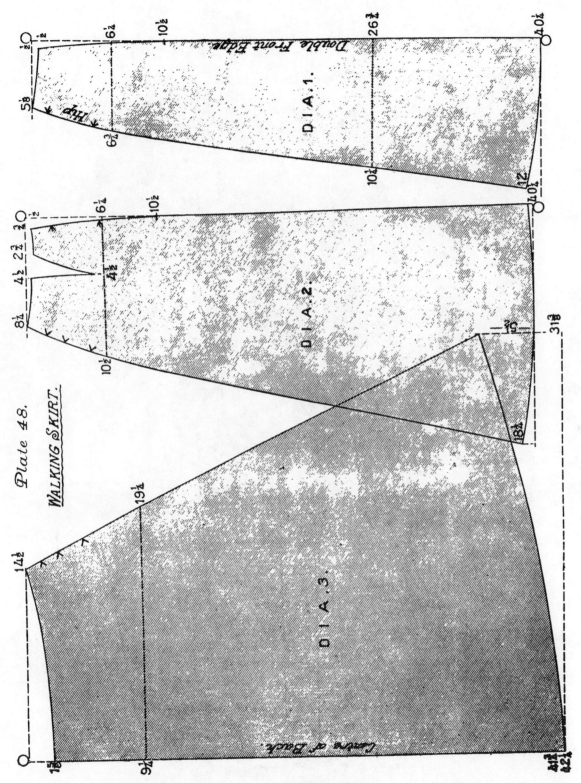

35. *The Direct System of Ladies' Cutting*, T. H. Holding, 1897
Walking Skirts are cut with sufficient fulness, or spring, as to sit round the hip
with scarcely any V's, or darts, and the bottom bells out to something like 3½ yards
or more.

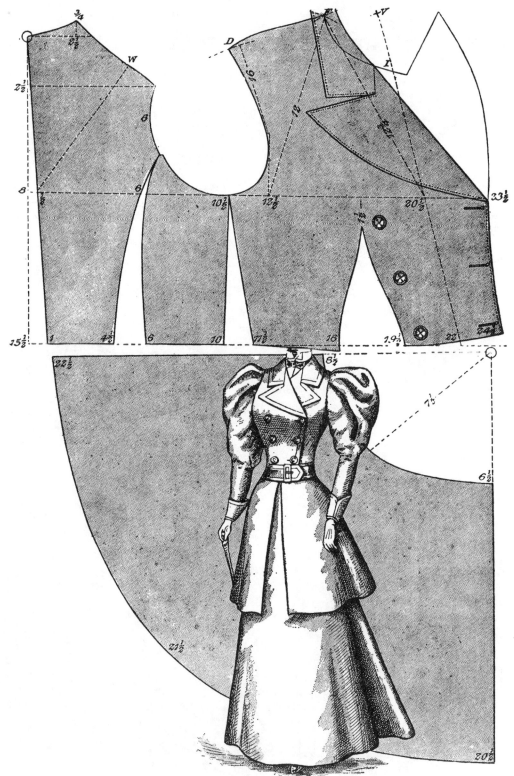

DIA. 4. : FIG. 14.

**36.** *The Cutters' Practical Guide*, W. D. F. Vincent, *c.* 1893

The latest novelty is the Skirted Jacket—it can be made double or single breasted according to the season of the year. The back is a decided variation from the style worn years ago—there is only one sidepiece instead of two.

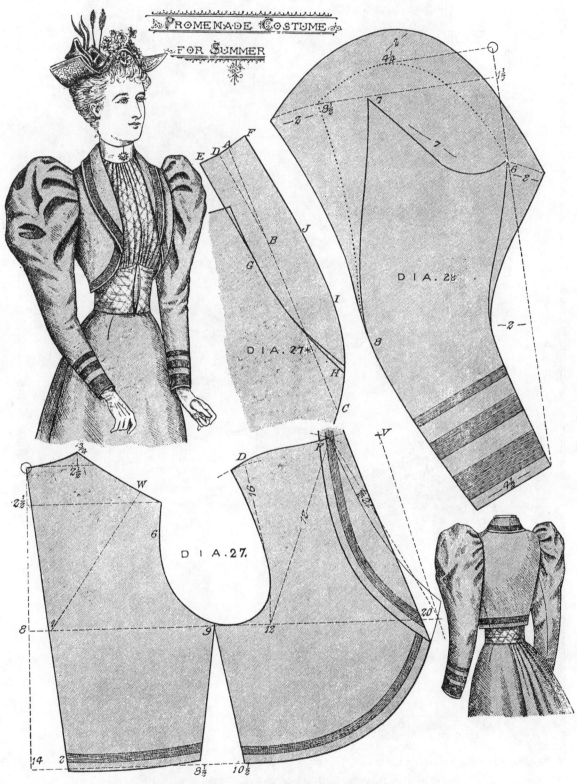

**37.** *The Cutters' Practical Guide*, W. D. F. Vincent, c. 1893
Zouave Jackets one of the most noticeable features last season, are mostly natty
little garments, giving an amount of freedom for the various movements of the
body without hiding the outline of the figure.

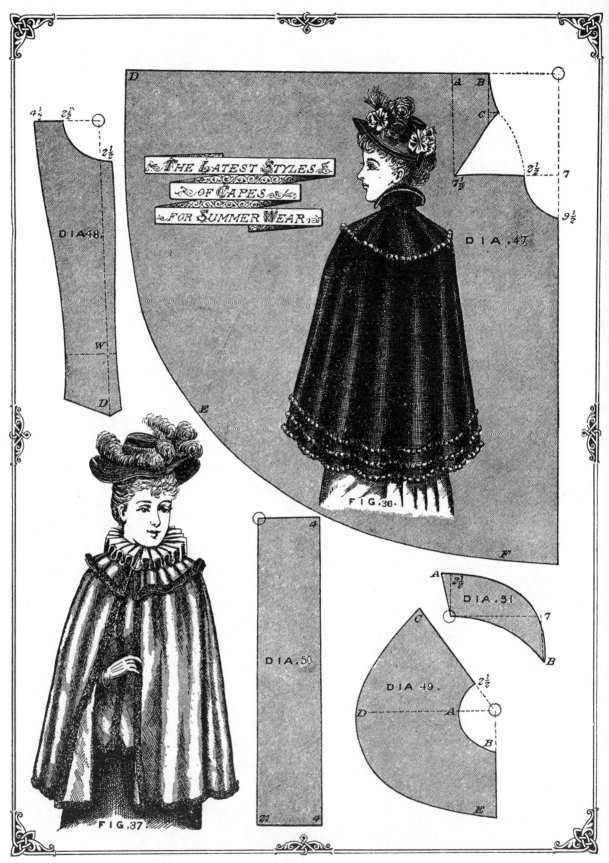

38. *The Cutters' Practical Guide*, W. D. F. Vincent, *c.* 1893

Cape with additional Short Full Cape—Dia. 47 the cape; Dia. 49 the short full cape; Dia. 36 the Medici collar; Dia. 37 the ruffle to go round the neck; Dia. 48 the vest, which can be sewn to the shoulders and neck seam and fastened round the waist by a piece of elastic.

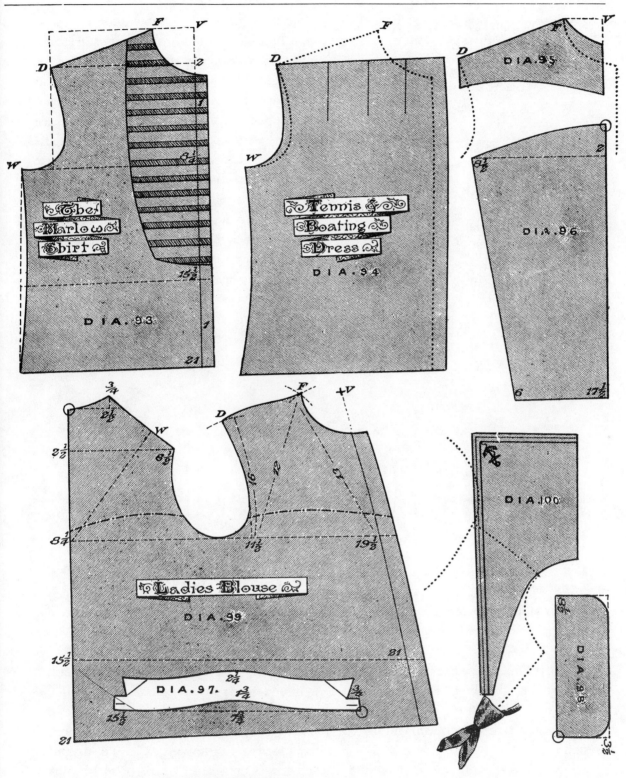

39. *The Cutters' Practical Guide*, W. D. F. Vincent, c. 1893

Dia. 93–98 the Marlow Shirt, usually in cambric, very popular amongst the frequenters of the Thames Valley in the Summer time, as well as at those fashionable seaside resorts such as Brighton, Hastings, etc. A tape is placed at the waist, and a drawing-tape run through it, thus enabling the fulness to be equally distributed all round the waist. Dia. 99 Lady's Blouse. The dot and dash line across the front and back illustrate the plan adopted when a yoke is desired, the lower part being often fulled on this line. Dia. 100 Sailor Collar.

## A PRETTY BODICE FOR SPRING COSTUME.

40. *The Ladies' Gazette*, 1896
A Pretty Blouse for Spring. An extract from one of the little magazines of this period—it cost 1d.

The smart little bodice shown in the illustration heading this lesson may be made in any material constituting the whole costume, or in striped silk trimmed with plain silk or satin and lace; the trimming round edges being lace appliquéd on, or embroidered, and three pretty buttons put on each side of the fronts as ornaments. The following instructions are for the completion of a whole costume in one of the new mohair materials. It will require 7 yards of material for the whole dress, the skirt of which must be cut first, and from this there will be some good pieces towards the bodice. The epaulettes and cuffs should be of satin, or merv to match the light shade in the material, and for this ⅝ths of a yard will be required; also the same quantity of soft silk for the front, and a quarter of a yard of either

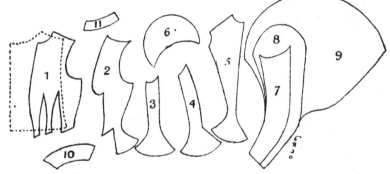

1, Front; 2, Upper front; 3, Under side piece; 4, Side piece; 5, Back; 6, Epaulette
7, 8, 9, Sleeve; 10, Cuff; 11, Half-collar.

the silk or satin for collar trimming and small waistband; 2 yards of lace for the waterfall. The design fastens down the front, hooking edge to edge, the gathered lace being sewn to each edge.

**To Cut it Out.**—First cut the linings for Nos. 1, 3, 4, 5, 7, and 8 portions, and then either canvas or linings for No. 2 pieces. These may be in lining, with a strip of stiffening tacked in the front edges, as that is not quite so warm as if stiffened all across although for thin figures the latter is decidedly the better plan. Cut the material to match except for Nos. 1 and 8. The dotted lines on former show the full front, and the material for latter is shown by No. 9 of diagram. The cuffs and epaulettes must be lined with French canvas or wireen, which (latter) I think I mentioned in a previous lesson as being particularly nice for stiffening purposes as well as open, which must be cooler wear than any of the thick closely-woven stiffenings used.

**Arranging Front Fulness.** – The darts are stitched in the lining only, and the silk drawn in at the waist over them. It may be taken in with the back dart, or carried a little further back and hemmed down; the latter is almost best, as there is then no possibility of the lining showing. A tack should be run (or a pencil line marked) down each side where silk has to spread across to, and may be carried from about 2 inches from armhole end, on shoulder line, to one inch at the back of back dart, at waist, as shown by dotted lines on No. 1 of diagram.

**Front Fastening.** – The front edge of silk must be put to the lining fully an inch short, so that the latter is very much eased to former, especially down towards the waist. A half inch turning should be allowed outside the fitting lines down front, and when turned under, the fitting lines must be on the exact edge; then the hooks and eyes must be sewn on alternately, and so that they draw the edges quite close together, but do not make them overlap. This is not at all easy, and I think that a little trouble in the first place, of herringboning the turning firmly down to the lining, will be a great help in preventing the fastenings from pulling forward and causing a gap between the edges. It is sometimes better to bone each edge, just as one does for lacing up the middle of back. The row of stitching which is always put down to encase the bone, keeps the edge so nice and firm, and without a bone, the stitching is not permissible. The upper pieces of fronts should be quite separate at front edges from the under part, and should be faced with small pieces of silk or satin, which may be gleaned from the cuttings, as also may that required for basque, although it may be necessary to get an extra quarter of a yard for latter. Under the facing in each case should be a strip of stiffening, as already explained, to prevent its creasing and getting out of condition soon. The front edge of under arm seam should be stretched as much as possible, as this will greatly improve the set of fronts. The epaulettes and cuffs must be stiffened, and may be lined with either silk or material, whichever is the more convenient.

**Sleeve.** – The sleeve uppers may be stiffened or not, according to taste, as at present they are worn equally stiffened or limp, although the fashion is supposed to be steadily decreasing the size and stiffness that has so long been in them. Where the edge bulges out from edge of lining just above the elbow, on the outer line of No. 9, the material must be gathered to lining and continued up to the top. A number of dressmakers are putting a frill of stiffening into the armhole at shoulders just to keep the fulness out a little, which is a very good compromise between the two extremes. The epaulettes are best slip-stitched on after being made quite neat all round edge.

**Boning.** – Every seam should be boned, and each bone be carried an inch or two below waist, but not longer; the remainder of the basque being stiffened. The buttons may be sewn right through to keep the upper fronts from slipping and creasing round front of armhole.

**The Band** is arranged so that the left half is loose and hooks over under edge of left upper front; this and the collar drapery must be on the cross of material. The latter hooks edge to edge, or it may fasten over like the band if preferred. Pattern Bodice, 1s. o½d.

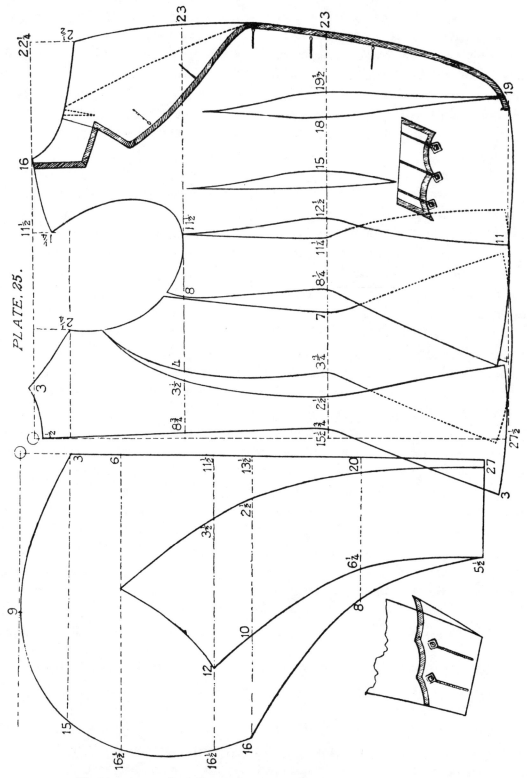

41. *The Direct System of Ladies' Cutting*, T. H. Holding, 1897
Highland Jacket—not only is it suitable for the purpose for which it originated—
that of shooting and walking in the Highlands for ladies who took to the gun and
sports of that ilk, but it is, as a coat, extremely nice for cycling and home use. The
coat has a leather binding half an inch wide backstitched on raw.

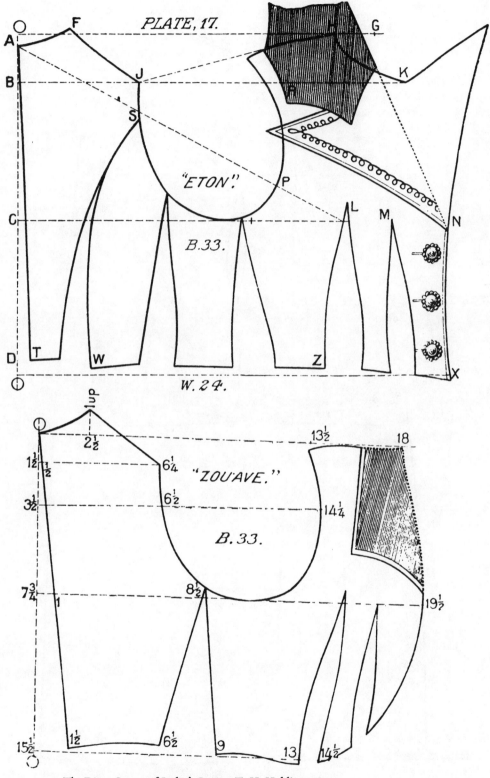

9. *The Direct System of Ladies' Cutting*, T. H. Holding, 1897
Eton Jacket. A great number of them are not made to button at all, but simply
hang as boy's Eton jackets, as snugly to the figure as possible.
The Zouave—at present they are cut without sideseams, though there is no im-
movable law why they should not have them.

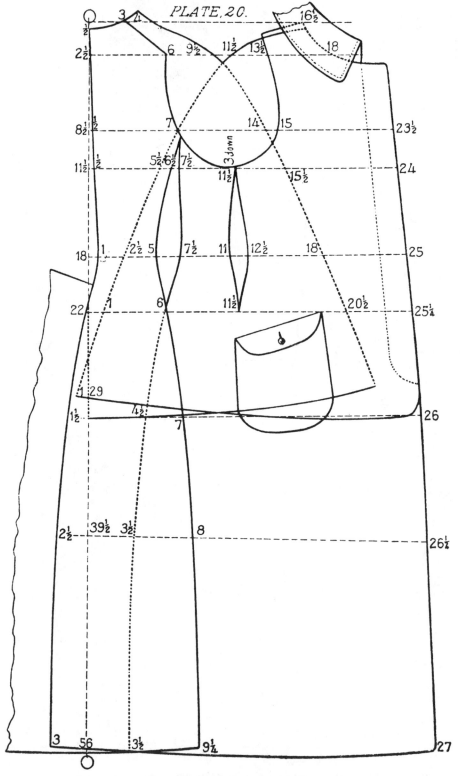

43. *The Direct System of Ladies' Cutting*, T. H. Holding, 1897
The Deerstalker—cut to fit the comparatively full sleeves still worn.

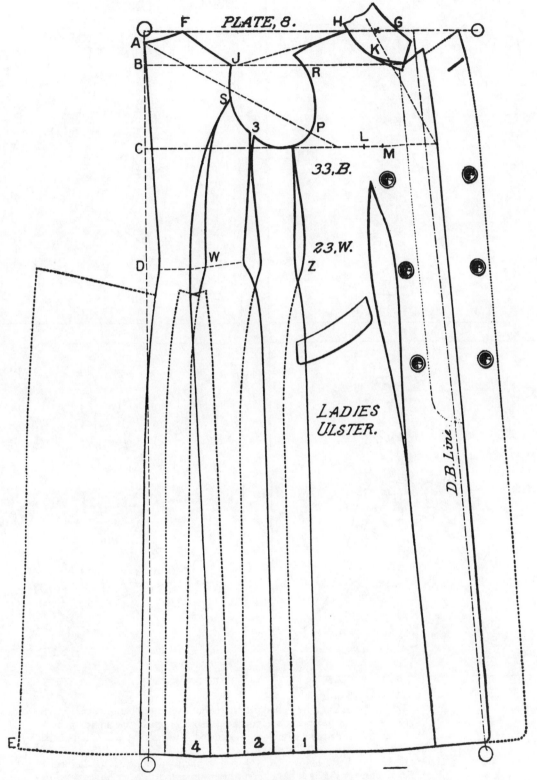

**44.** *The Direct System of Ladies' Cutting*, T. H. Holding, 1897
Ladies' Ulster. A lady despises, so far as tailor-made garments are concerned, any
name or designation which borders on the feminine. The more like men's
garments the names we give their garments, the better they like it.

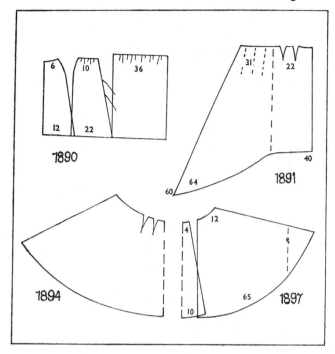

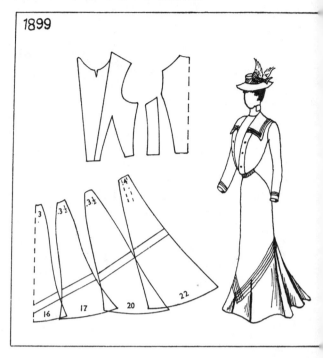

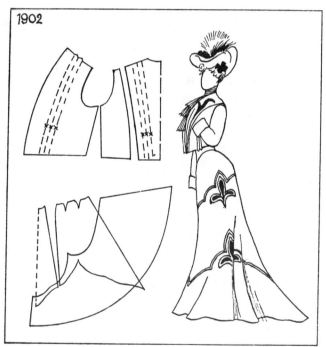

45. *The Lady,* 1891–1913

This magazine ran a very good pattern service over a number of years. In each issue there was an article on 'Home Dressmaking' which gave advice on how some of their patterns should be constructed, illustrated by the design of the dress and portions of the pattern.

1891. 'The latest innovation is a daring one, and opposed to all former traditions; for the back has hitherto been straight, no matter how shaped or gored the front.'

1894. The new Umbrella Skirt.

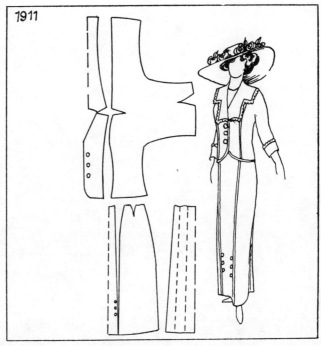

1907. The pleated bodice which led to the kimona cut.

1913. The dotted lines give the position of the centre front, when the extension is laid on its marked folds, the draped portion lies over the front only. The remainder of the skirt—the centre front panel and left side—are shewn in reduced size in diagram. The simplest plan for the amateur is to cut a plain lining for the skirt, and arrange the material and draped front over it.

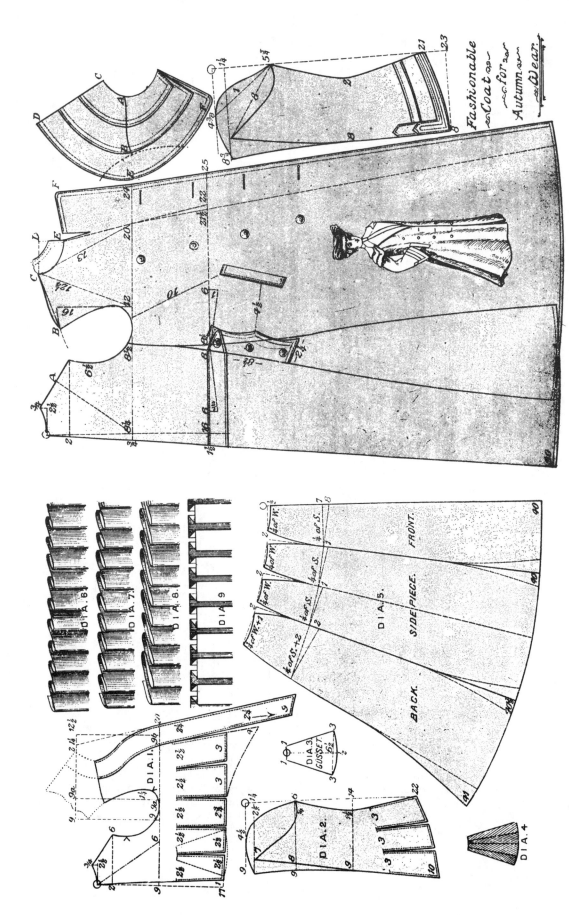

Fashionable Coat for Autumn Wear.

Long coat.

DIA.6.  DIA.7.  DIA.8.  DIA.9

DIA.1.

DIA.2.

DIA.3. GUSSET.

DIA.4.

DIA.5.

BACK.  SIDEPIECE.  FRONT.

46. *The Ladies' Tailor (The Tailor & Cutter)*, 1903.
Bolero and gored skirt.

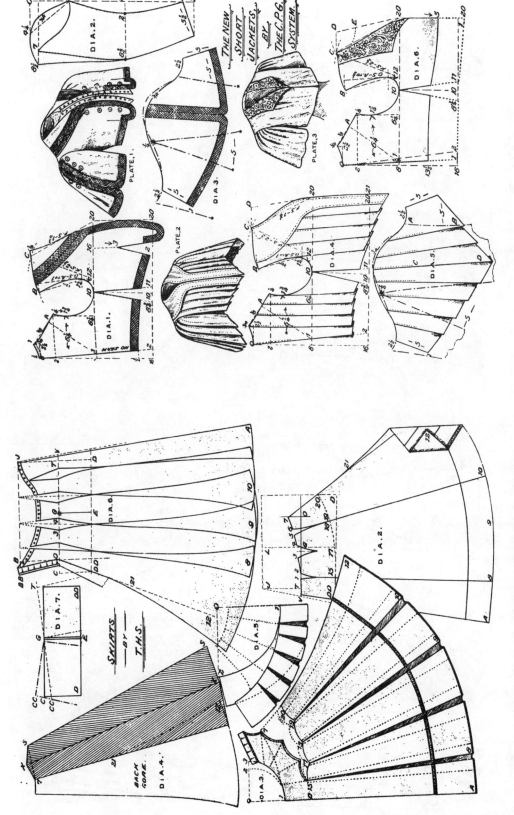

46. (cont.). *The Ladies Tailor* (*The Tailor & Cutter*), 1906.
Dia. 6 is the new Corselet Skirt.

The short boleros usually worn with the corselet skirt.

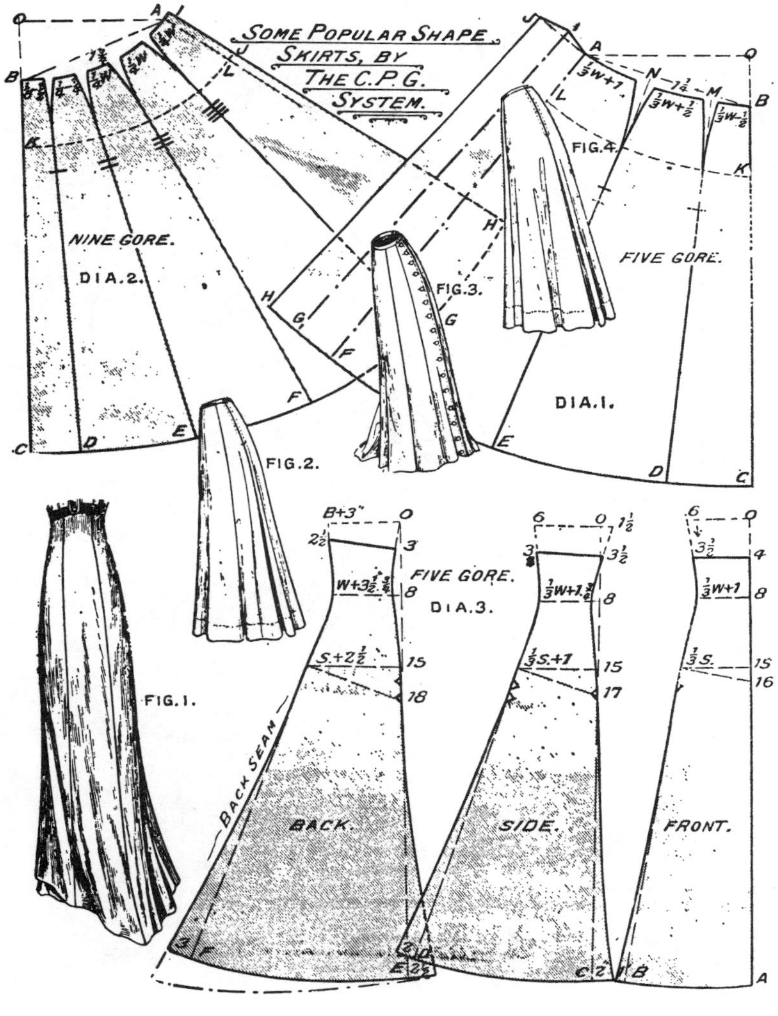

ÀTOUT. 1909

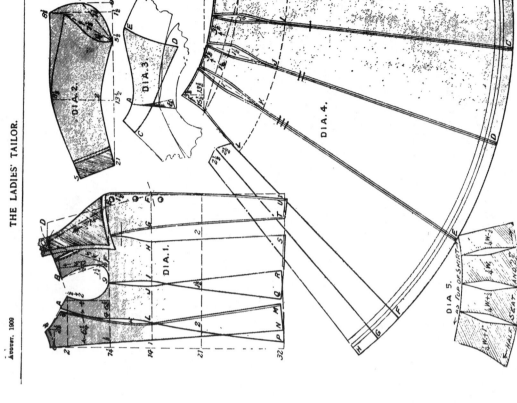

DIA. 1.

DIA. 2.

DIA. 3.

DIA. 4.

DIA. 5.

PLATE 37.

MAY, 1909

SOME POPULAR SHAPE SKIRTS, BY THE C.P.G. SYSTEM.

FIVE GORE.

NINE GORE.

DIA. 1.

DIA. 2.

DIA. 3.

FRONT.

SIDE.

BACK.

BACK SEAM.

FIG. 1.

FIG. 2.

FIG. 3.

FIG. 4.

PLATE 22.

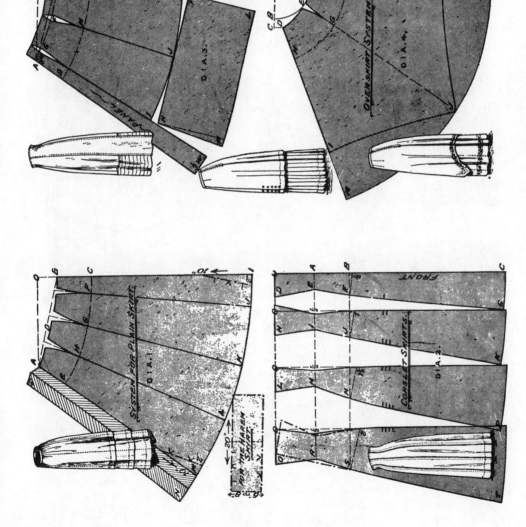

47. *The Ladies' Tailor* (*The Tailor & Cutter*), 1909, 1911

Plate 22. Skirt variations.

Plate 37. Costume with corselet skirt and straight coat.

(*left*) 1911. More skirt variations.

Dia. 1 for the Harem Skirt – the diagram shows by dot and dash line how the back and front are both cut away 2 inches at the bottom to 10 inches up, and then the shape and size of the leg portion with balance marks, are also shown. From the centre of back to centre of front is from 6 to 8 inches, so that when the legs are brought together, as when in natural pose, only the small opening is visible; but when the legs are open, as in the act of striding, the trouser-like form is fully displayed.

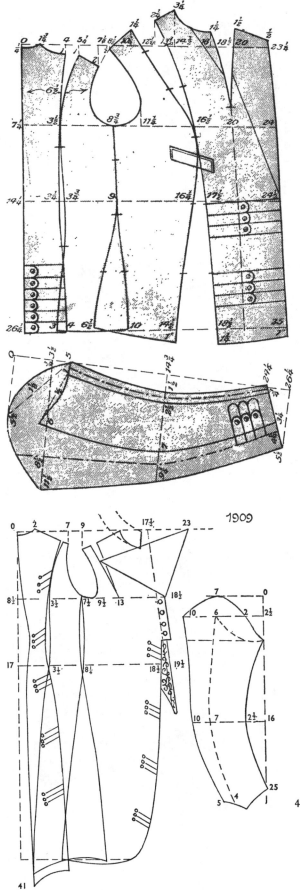

1909

49. *The Ladies' Tailor* (*The Tailor & Cutter*), 1911
The straight-line costume.

48. *The Ladies' Tailor* (*The Tailor & Cutter*), 1909
'The Coat of the Season'. This design is inspired
by the fashionable Directoire styles.

50. *The Ladies' Tailor (The Tailor & Cutter)*, 1915

Kimona Promenade Costume. 'The kimona is finding abundant patronage. Early
in the year the style of skirts suddenly changed from the narrow pegtop design to
the full skirt of from 2½ to 3½ yards wide, or more. At the present time yoked
skirts are being worn by those who follow the trend of fashion. The skirt is best
only lined through the yoke part.'

Ladies' Military Jacket. The war made military styles popular.

LADIES' MILITARY JACKET.

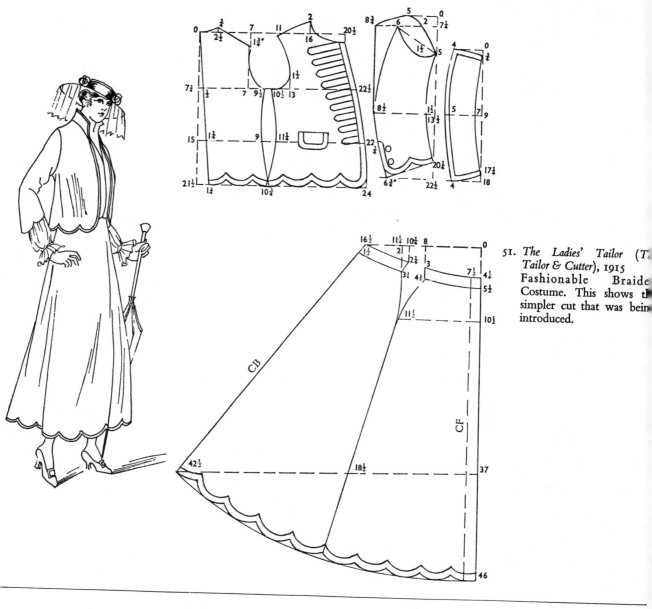

51. *The Ladies' Tailor (T. Tailor & Cutter)*, 1915 Fashionable Braide Costume. This shows th simpler cut that was bein introduced.

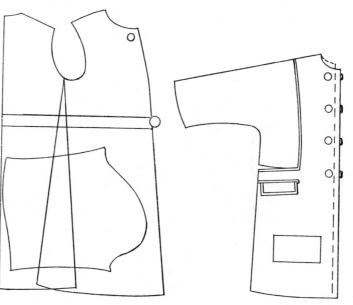

52. *The Ladies' Tailor (The Tailor & Cutter)*, 1923 Coat with sleeves. Coat with Magyar sleeves.

**53.** *The Ladies' Tailor (The Tailor & Cutter),* 1921
A Smart Russian Costume. 'Patch pockets may be placed on each hip, and this, together with collar, cuffs, and bottom edge of coat, may be trimmed with fur, which usually gives a touch of beauty to the finished garment. If desired gathers may be made at back of skirt, and covered with a belt, or it may be made to fit quite plainly without a belt.'
Magyar Coat—'there is a large demand for such garments.'
Coat Frock.

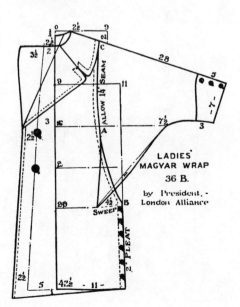

LADIES' MAGYAR WRAP 36 B.

by President.- London Alliance

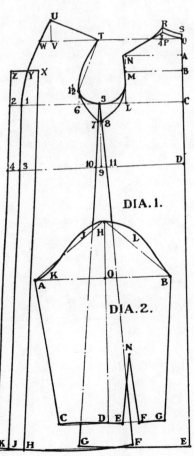

DIA. 1.

DIA. 2.

323.

1925　　　　　　　　　1926

1927　　　　　　　　　1928

1929

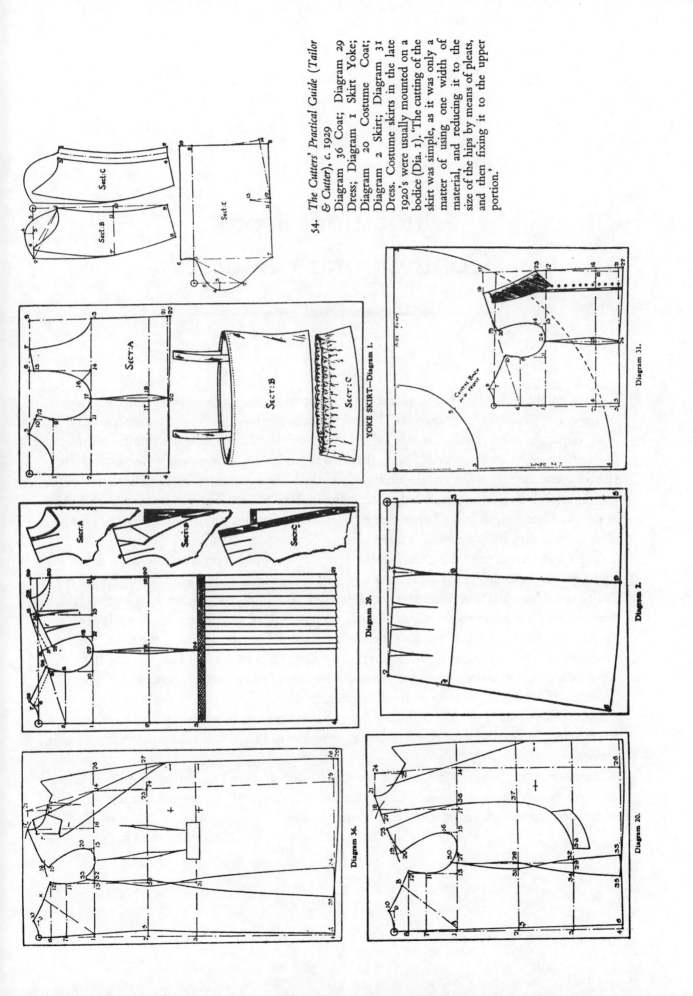

54. *The Cutters' Practical Guide (Tailor & Cutter)*, c. 1929
Diagram 36 Coat; Diagram 29 Dress; Diagram 1 Skirt Yoke; Diagram 20 Costume Coat; Diagram 2 Skirt; Diagram 31 Dress. Costume skirts in the late 1920's were usually mounted on a bodice (Dia. 1). 'The cutting of the skirt was simple, as it was only a matter of using one width of material, and reducing it to the size of the hips by means of pleats, and then fixing it to the upper portion.'

YOKE SKIRT—Diagram 1.

Diagram 31.

Diagram 29.

Diagram 2.

Diagram 36.

Diagram 20.

# Quotations from Contemporary Sources

———————————

1890's

The thought of the discomfort, restraint and pain, which we had to endure from our clothes, makes me even angrier now than it did then; for in those days nearly everyone accepted their inconveniences as inevitable. Except for the most small-waisted, naturally dumb-bell-shaped females, the ladies never seemed at ease, or even quite as if they were wearing their own clothes. For their dresses were always made too tight, and the bodices wrinkled laterally from the strain; and their stays showed in a sharp ledge across the middles of their backs. And in spite of whale-bone, they were apt to bulge below the waist in front; for, poor dears, they were but human after all, and they had to expand somewhere. . . .

Skirts were more tiresome than painful, but they could be very tiresome indeed. By the time I was eighteen my skirts came right down to the ground, and Sunday dresses had to have little trains behind. It was difficult to walk freely in the heavy tweed 'walking skirts', which kept on catching between the knees. Round the bottom of these skirts I had, with my own hands, sewn two and a half yards of 'brush braid', to collect the worst of the mud; for they inevitably swept the roads, however carefully I might hold them up behind; and the roads were then much muddier than the tarred roads are now. Afterwards the crusted mud had to be brushed off, which might take an hour or more to do.

Hair in the 'nineties was worn all in coils and plaits, and was often very prettily arranged. In the nineteen hundreds it had to be puffed out in hideous lumps and bumps, over cushions or frames. . . .

However, obviously, less favoured ladies did use powder, with discretion; but never young girls. And never, never, rouge or lipstick. That was definitely only for actresses, or 'certain kinds of women', or the wickedest sort of 'fashionable' lady.

GWEN RAVERAT, *Period Piece*

1890's

I remember the fine subscription evenings at the 'Gymnase' and the 'vaudeville', when all the bourgeoise and all the financial powers listened to *Viveurs*, or *Nos Bons Villageois* or *Amants*. The women kept on their hats, they were little bonnets, with or without strings and plaited with velvet flowers, Parma violets or geraniums. Then the parterre really was a flower garden. And furthermore, there were leg of mutton sleeves that did not match but were cut from another stuff than the dress itself, and in the foyer, during the intervals, the rustling skirts that swept the waxed parquet with their ruches and their bouillonnés, which were also called sweepers (*balayeuses*).

PAUL POIRET, My First Fifty Years

1899

You ought to see the skirts, not a wave of fullness anywhere, but such round proportions as these French women show! No artificial tournure required. The dress is held tightly with one hand across the lower back to keep the slight train off the ground, and the sight is one for gods and men. I indulge a constant grin.

LADY JEBB, With Dearest Love to All

Early 1900's

Furs were largely worn, but the most exclusive and popular of them were sables and ermine. Mink had not yet come into its own. Fur stoles replaced the one-time fashionable shawls and girls wore little fur tippets round their necks, fastened with the actual head of the little beast who had owned the fur in the first place. In winter women carried muffs, and that was a charming fashion. They varied too, large and small, round and oblong, all sorts of materials but mostly fur and often astrakhan, but it depended largely on the main set of furs. They were supported round the neck by cords or sometimes muff chains, made of metal, gold or silver (or imitation thereof) and very delightful to see. In the summer, when furs were not worn, they were replaced by feather boas–long strips of feathers of all sorts which were worn according to fashion, sometimes round the neck, sometimes over the shoulders but most fashionably half-way down the back and supported by the elbows. That must have been quite a knack. . . .

Women wore a tremendous amount of underclothes, as compared with today. They wore many petticoats, fringed with lace which formed an enchanting foam around their ankles, their corsets were formidable affairs, whalebone covered in silk and other material and laced up the back. . . .

The sight of an Edwardian lady, stepping out of her brougham, her victoria, or landau outside a Regent Street shop was a spectacle which cannot be seen today. . . . The lady swept across the pavement like a queen, like a procession of one, for she knew how to move and carry herself. She had balance and poise, she had elegance and she was one hundred per cent feminine. She paid no attention to the world around, to the envious glances of her less favoured sisters but she proceeded like a ship in full sail, a gracious galleon into the harbour of the favoured emporium.

W. MACQUEEN-POPE, *Goodbye Piccadilly*

Early 1900's

During the Ascot meetings we Gaiety Girls led the fashions, trailing the lawns wearing gorgeous creations of crêpe-de-chine, chiffon or lace over petticoats of rustling silk edged with hundreds of yards of fine Valenciennes lace threaded with narrow velvet ribbon. Every stitch sewn by hand and no couturier of repute would have dreamed of copying a model gown.

Individuality of fashion was the keynote of the era. Our precious hats, graceful shapes of fine crinoline straw, trimmed with lancer plumes, wide rich satin ribbon from Paris, or real lace, were exquisite. Occasionally we wore small toques made entirely of fresh flowers to match our gowns. Our gloves, shoes and stockings always matched, and we carried dainty parasols of ruched chiffon, feathers or lace with the most beautiful handles of carved ivory, mother-of-pearl or hand-painted porcelain. We were indeed the cynosure of all eyes, and brought much trade to the dress designers of our day.

On Ascot Sunday, at Boulter's Lock, Maidenhead, crowds lined the banks watching the famous Girls being poled up and down the river by their elegant escorts. We girls would be in punts on vari-coloured cushions, wearing enchanting summer frocks in white or pastel shades of silk, muslin, tussore silk or broderie Anglaise, our hats of leghorn trimmed with wide velvet ribbons and flowers. We were not allowed to tan and we never used make-up off stage, so our natural pink-and-white or cream complexions had to be protected by large silk sunshades.

RUBY MILLER, *Champagne from my Slipper*

Early 1900's

Many of our clothes were far from comfortable or convenient. Country tweeds were long and trammeling. Imagine the discomfort of a walk in the rain in a sodden skirt that wound its wetness round your legs and chapped your ankles. Even our lawn-tennis dresses, usually like nurserymaid's wear, made of white piqué, were so long that it was impossible to take a step back without treading on them. Walking about the London streets trailing clouds of dust was horrid. I once found I had carried into the house a banana skin which had got caught up in the unstitched hem of my dress! I hated the veils that, worn twisted into a squiggle under my chin, dotted my vision with huge spots like symptoms of liver trouble. They flattened even my short eyelashes. Our vast hats which took the wind like sails were painfully skewered to our heads by huge ornamental hatpins, greatly to the peril of other people's eyes. I couldn't endure the high choking collars with boned supports that dug red dints in my neck, so I wore low square-necked blouses long before these became the fashion–a nonconformity for which I was severely criticised. . . . My opaque stockings, never other than black, brown or white, were darned, darned, darned. My underclothes were unglamorously sensible. Though, thank goodness, the days of tight-lacing were over, it still behoved one to have a small waist, so even at the cost of bulging hips, nearly every girl did have a small, if no longer wasp-like waist. . . .

Feather boas were regrettably in fashion, and in these if you couldn't afford a new one you soon looked like poultry in very poor condition. The alternative neckwear was a still more perishable tulle ruffle.

Country house visiting–A large fraction of our time was spent in changing our clothes, particularly in winter when you came down to breakfast ready for church in your 'best dress', made probably of velvet if you could afford it, or velveteen if you couldn't. After church you went into tweeds. You always changed again before tea, into a 'tea-gown' if you possessed that special creation; the less affluent wore a summer day-frock. However small your dress allowance, a different dinner dress for each night was considered necessary.

Thus a Friday to Monday party meant taking your 'Sunday Best', two tweed coats and skirts with appropriate shirts, three evening frocks, three garments suitable for tea, your 'best hat'– probably a vast affair loaded with feathers, flowers, fruit or corn–a variety of country hats and caps, as likely as not a riding-habit and billycock hat, rows of indoor and outdoor shoes, boots and gaiters, numberless accessories in the way of petticoats, shawls, scarves, ornamental combs and wreaths, and a large bag in which to carry your embroidery about the house. All this necessitated at least one huge domed trunk, called a 'Noah's Ark', an immense hat-box and a heavy dressing-case.

In one respect we were all humiliatingly dependent on help, most of the dresses we were for ever changing being so constructed that it was a physical impossibility to get in or out of them unassisted. Either they laced up at the back, or they fastened with quite ungetatable intricacies of hooks and eyes. One way or another, dressmakers seemed bent on setting their customers insoluble problems.

Not even my clothes escaped my mother's kindness of heart, for unfortunately for me a charming sometime lady's maid of hers had set up as a dressmaker–the kind of dressmaker whom, whatever her size and bulk, one always calls–in the hope, I suppose, that her bills will be light–a 'Little Woman'. Needless to say a large proportion of my clothes had to be made by this 'Little Woman' who had no models, but only paper patterns. Even my seventeen-year-old unsophisticated eye could see that her clothes were not 'right'.

CYNTHIA ASQUITH, *Remember and be Glad*

1906

*Show Day at Lucile's Ltd.*

June–One of the latest society functions was inaugurated at 23, Hanover Square. In this aristocratic quarter a series of living pictures partaking of the order of tableaux vivants, was displayed as suggestions for costumes, dresses and gowns for the present season. The salons of Lucile, Ltd., are admirably adapted for an afternoon meeting, and to the accompaniment of a string band, the events of the day passed off in a most successful manner.

The idea of displaying the latest suggestions of the artist on living figures, graceful in form and outline, instead of on the lay models usually associated with the customers' show-rooms, was, in this instance, a most pronounced success. . . .

A small platform was arranged at one end of the large salon, and a simultaneous entrance was made by two ladies, each wearing a different design of costume or dress, and equipped with sunshades, hat, or bonnet, and gloves to match. Then, standing in a well chosen position, the audience had time to take in the general effect from one point of view, after which the living models exchanged positions, so that another view was presented. This method of displaying each costume or dress might have sufficed for the ordinary observer, but in order to admit of a more detailed examination of the styles and materials, the ladies descended from the stage and walked through the salon, and again returned to the starting point. . . .

The exhibition was arranged in a series which represented the various purposes and materials which make up the sum and substance of some ladies' lives. Coats and skirts were introduced in brown cloth, rose tweed, various shades of blue serges, white serge, plum cloth and faded scarlet. The last named was one of the most striking of the range, a yoked cape, extending down back and front, with fullness at the shoulders, being a perfect figure. Another range included blue voiles and crepons, green alpaca and black cloth. These were summer-like and useful, the bodices being short and of the Bolero or Zouave character, while the skirts showed the *gaugeing* round the waist, which was one of the leading suggestions offered by this exhibition. . . .

The Ascot dresses suggested many emotions, such as the pink foulard 'Love and Delight', a yellow-stripe 'Eternal Spring', a blue poplin 'Dreamy Longing', and a pink check 'My Sweetheart'. A great many of these were dainty on account of their simplicity, but one of the features seemed to be a short back waist and lengthy skirt, while fancy waist-belts and streamers were also shown on others.

Tea-gowns and high evening dress introduced us to the region of flimsy gauzes, taffetas and nets, as well as poplins and silks, and akin to these were many gorgeous dinner dresses. A flame satin caused quite a sensation, and was termed by the artist 'A Madness of Colour'; but the cardinal and magenta shades seemed to grow in favour as the afternoon progressed, until one became quite accustomed to pink and cherry colours as a likelihood for the coming season.

*The Ladies' Tailor*

*c.* 1908

It was still the age of the corset. I waged war upon it. The last representative of this abominated apparatus was called the *Gache Sarraute*. It divided the wearer into two distinct masses: on one side there was the bust and bosom, on the other, the whole behindward aspect, so that the lady looked as if she were hauling a trailer. It was almost a return to the bustle. Like all great revolutions, that one had been made in the name of Liberty–to give free play to the abdomen: it was equally in the name of Liberty that I proclaimed the fall of the corset and the adoption of the brassière which, since then, has won the day. Yes, I freed the bust but I shackled the legs. You will remember the tears, the cries, the gnashings of teeth caused by this ukase of fashion. Women complained of being no longer able to walk, nor get into a carriage. All their jeremiads pleaded in favour of my innovation. Are their protestations still heard?–Everyone wore the tight skirt.

When I began to do what I wanted to do in dress-designing there were absolutely no tints left on the palette of the colourists. The taste for the refinements of the eighteenth century had led all the women into a sort of deliquescence, and on the pretext that it was 'distinguished', all vitality had been suppressed. Nuances of nymph's thigh, lilacs, mauves, tender hortensia blues, niles, maizes, straws, all that was soft, washed-out, and insipid, was held in honour. I threw into this sheepcote a few rough wolves; reds, greens, violets, royal blues, that made all the rest sing aloud. I had to wake up the good people of Lyons, whose stomach is a bit heavy, and put a little gaiety, a little new freshness, into their colour schemes. There were orange and lemon crêpe-de-chines which they would not have dared to imagine.

PAUL POIRET, My First Fifty Years

*c.* 1909

Even when a Directoire style came into vogue and a leg could be glimpsed through a slashed skirt, only a few ultra-smart women attempted it. Many wore the style which was most becoming, but eschewed the slash. . . . The fashion was introduced from a musical comedy at Daly's Theatre–the stage set the fashions then–called *Les Merveilleuses*. . . . I remember my wife–we were engaged then–had a Directoire dress. It was of tobacco brown, with no belt, and had a little coat or bolero, I suppose, with black revers, and the buttons were black too. It was charming. But her skirt, needless to say, had no slash. At one time there was an attempt to introduce what was called a 'harem skirt'–which died a sudden death–men called it the 'harem-skarem' and derided this attempt at female trousers.

W. MACQUEEN-POPE, Goodbye Piccadilly

1909

### A Directoire Frock

*Long languid lines unbroken by a frill,*
*Superfluous festoons reduced to nil,*
*A figure like a seal reared up on end*
*And poking forward with a studied bend;*

*A shortish neck imprisoned in a ruff,*
*Slim-fitting sleeves that show a stint of stuff,*
*A waist promoted half-way up the back,*
*And not a shred that's comfortably slack;*

*A multitude of buttons, row on row,*
*Not there for business–merely made for show,*
*A skirt whose meagre gores necessitate*
*The waddle of a Chinese Lady's gait;*

*A 'busby' toque extinguishing the hair*
*As if a giant hand had crushed it there–*
*Behold the latest mode! and write beneath,*
*'A winter blossom bursting from its sheath'.*

*Punch*

c. 1909–1910

I was particularly anxious to have a department for beautiful underclothes, as I hated the thought of my creations being worn over the ugly nun's veiling or linen-cum-Swiss embroidery which was all that the really virtuous woman of those days permitted herself. . . . So I started making underclothes as delicate as cobwebs and as beautifully tinted as flowers, and half the women of London flocked to see them, though they had not the courage to buy them at first.

It seems so silly now that we have just got over wearing skirts above our knees and showing backbone below the waist to think that those demure little morning dresses and diaphanous tea-gowns I made were once considered by many people 'too daring', but they were. . . . I took it as a compliment, for in those days virtue was too often expressed by dowdiness, and I had no use for the dull, stiff, boned-bodice brigade. I had a message for the women I dressed. I was the first dressmaker to bring joy and romance into clothes. I was a pioneer. I loosed upon a startled London, a London of flannel underclothes, woollen stockings and voluminous petti-coats, a cascade of chiffons, of draperies as lovely as those of Ancient Greece, of softly-rounded breasts (I brought in the brassière in opposition to the hideous corset of the time, which was distorting women's figures) and draped skirts which opened to reveal slender legs.

Incidentally I made history as far as dressmaking is concerned. The evolution of the mannequin was brought about in my grey salons in Hanover Square (1906). . . . The first parade of mine, in addition to the mannequins, originated another custom which has been in use ever since – the naming of different models. . . . How they made my audience smile as they were called out one by one – 'When Passion's Thrill is O'er', 'The Sighing of Lips Unsatisfied', 'Red Mouth of a Venomous Flower', 'The Meaning of Life is Clear', etc.

King Alphonse often accompanied the Queen to a fitting and took as much interest in it as she did . . . once I remember I had words with him on the subject of a dress. . . . The Queen had chosen a model, which had a slit at one side so that as the wearer walked the drapery opened to give just the most fleeting glimpse of the legs. The Queen loved it and said so at once, and I, knowing how well it would suit her, began arranging details immediately. Then King Alphonso put his foot down. 'I am sorry, my dear,' he said, 'but you cannot possibly wear that skirt. Not in Spain.' The Queen was dreadfully disappointed, and I began to argue with him. Not for anything in the world would I alter and spoil this model I said. . . . Of course I gave in, and finally we arrived at a happy compromise. The dress opened like the original model, but only to show a lovely cascade of lace underskirt. It really was very pretty and the Queen wrote saying that it had been much admired in Spain.

The largest sums of all were spent on hats, for the craze of ospreys and other valuable plumage was at its height, and women would go about with the equivalent of hundreds of pounds on their heads.

I was the first designer to abolish the high-boned collar, then disfiguring the neck of every woman who wore it. No woman who has not worn one can possibly imagine how horrible it was to have one's throat scarred by sharp collar supports made of either whalebone or steel, which ran into one with every movement, so that the head had to be kept rigidly in a most unnatural position. . . . When I arrived in Paris every good Parisienne was encased to the ears in a collar of net or chiffon, heavily boned, and they all looked rather askance at the beautifully rounded and untrammelled throats of my mannequins, but before long I was sufficiently an accepted fact to be taken seriously and followed. They came to choose their new dresses found the low necks on all of them, demurred a bit – they gave in, tried the experiment of a low collar – and never wore anything else from that day. Triumphantly I launched the 'Quaker Girl Collar', and the 'Peter Pan neck' and saw each in turn become the rage.

LADY DUFF GORDON (Lucile), *Discretions and Indiscretions*

*c.* 1912

We were now approaching the era of the 'hobble-skirt'; the exiguous waist had disappeared and I was extremely fortunate in never being required to wear a boned corset. Nevertheless the evening-dresses, deeply cut out low in front, were so tight that one had to hold one's breath while the hooks were being fastened at the back. Before every ball, Madame Adi from Pessl's, the Court hairdresser, came to the house hours earlier to do my hair, marcel-waving it in front and piling it in coils, which she nailed to my head with innumerable hairpins. My mother had to admit that my natural pallor made me look ghastly in evening dress, so she rubbed some pink tooth-powder on my cheeks!

Between noon and one o'clock you could meet everybody you knew walking in the Graben and the Kärntnerstrasse. Everybody was *dressed*. . . . Everything one wore was most elaborate, hats decorated with feathers, artificial flowers and fruit; tailor-made suits trimmed with braid and velvet facings, fountains of lace flowing out as jabots; walking shoes with silver buckles, like those of a French abbé, which had to be made by Herring, the Court shoemaker, who also specialized in very pointed evening shoes, covered with steel embroidery. It would have been quite impossible to buy anything ready-made (except those exquisite blouses of thin batiste, embroidered and inserted with hand-made lace, which were a Viennese speciality), or to wear under-garments which had not been made by hand. It was very expensive to be well-dressed according to the standards of the time, but there can be no doubt that the prevailing fashions were ungraceful and over-elaborate.

NORA WYDENBRUCK, *My Two Worlds*


1919

Mamma presented me at one of their Majesties' Summer Courts. . . . My presentation dress came from Reville and Rossiter, in Hanover Square, and was made of pale pink tulle, with a brocade and silver train. To the envy of my girl-friends, Mr. Reville prevailed on Mamma to let me have hardly any sleeves. Up till then, we all had draped bits of net, or chiffon, or the stuff the dress was made of, concealing the outline of the shoulders. The rest of the dress was plain and, as far as possible, flat-chested, with my bosom kept within Spartan bounds underneath it by a broad band of satin ribbon. This restriction was essential as, at that time, we all tried to obliterate our feminine curves, in antithesis to the fashion about twelve years earlier, when every woman had to accentuate them.

1920. Wedding—My going-away dress was of pale blue marocaine, with a skirt cut in petals, topped by a black velvet coat with a grey fox collar, and a grey velvet cap trimmed with ospreys.

SONIA KEPPEL, *Edwardian Daughter*

1914

But even the War could not make women forget the fashions. . . . Their men were going to fight for them, they wanted themselves to represent everything that was most feminine. So they put on frills and laces and big hats and ribbon bows to gladden the hearts of the returning warriors. . . . Later, as the struggle became far graver than anyone had imagined, the fashions changed again—tailor-made suits replaced the bouffant skirts, hats became plain; fashions became almost like the uniforms the men were wearing. The war ended and once more the fashions reflected the reaction. This time there was no apparent logic in the change. The only definite idea seemed in favour of discarding the old institutions. Women took off their corsets, reduced their clothing to the minimum tolerated by conventions and wore clothes which wrapped round them rather than fitted. Dresses slipped on and off without fastenings, unrestrained hips wobbled in the freedom of the new barbaric jazz movements; some people were shocked; others, grown wise, shrugged their shoulders over a passing phase. The revolt came in the austerity of the new 'boyish ideal' established by the dressmakers; slender figures were dressed with the simplicity of the Greek tunics. . . .

The old standard of extravagant dressing had gone for ever; it passed away with the days of the great courtesans, whose whims and follies had so delighted the Parisians in 1912. Even the women who were noted as the best dressed in Europe had cut down their dressmakers' bills to half the previous amounts. . . . The Rue de la Paix is nothing if not resourceful and it brought in the ideal of the 'boyish woman'. Here was the perfect solution of the problem. Slight figures covered with three yards of material, skirt ending just below the knees, tiny cloche hat trimmed with a band or ribbon. No woman, at least no woman in civilization, could cost less to clothe! And best of all the women were delighted with the new presentation of themselves. They improvised on the idea, shingled their hair, adopted boyish mannerisms and slang and flew to the cocktail bar (long, silk-stockinged legs looked so well dangling from a high stool).

LADY DUFF GORDON (Lucile), *Discretions and Indiscretions*

1920's

One of the brightest stars the dressmaking world has ever known was Gabrielle Chanel. Her enormous vogue came after the war with the low-waisted, brief-skirted, and infinitely graceless chemise frock. . . . Her jersey dresses, her sweaters, the magnificent jewels worn with the simplest of sports clothes, the rich, delicious scents that emanated from her salon, and which she also sold, created tremendous talk and became very popular. When the war ended and she enlarged her business her simple chiffon evening dresses with their petal skirts, deep-cut backs and low sashes were worn by smart women around the world. . . .

Chanel had flair and she was a super-saleswoman, if not a creator in the sense that Poiret was, and she was by no means an artist to equal Vionnet, who in my opinion was unique, perhaps the only true creator in our time in the art of the couture. Vionnet invented a way of cutting, a way of sewing pieces of material together that was infinitely complex, but which once mastered had a scientific purity of line. She was an artist in fabric, as Picasso is in paint.

EDNA WOOLMAN CHASE and ILKA CHASE, *Always in Vogue*

1926

*Mothers advice, and Father's fears,*
*Alike are voted just a bore,*
*There's negro music in our ears,*
*The World is one huge dancing floor.*
*We mean to tread the Primrose Path*
*In spite of Mr Joynson-Hicks,*
*We're People of the Aftermath,*
*We're girls of 1926.*

*In greedy haste, on pleasure bent,*
*We have no time to think or feel,*
*What need is there for sentiment*
*Now we've invented Sex-Appeal?*
*We've silken legs and scarlet lips,*
*We're young and hungry, wild and free,*
*Our waists are round about the hips,*
*Our skirts are well above the knee.*

*We've boyish busts and Eton crops,*
*We quiver to the saxaphone,*
*Come, dance before the music stops,*
*And who can bear to be alone?*
*Come drink your gin, or miff your 'snow',*
*Since Youth is brief, and Love has wings.*
*And time will tarnish, 'ere we know,*
*The brightness of the Bright Young Things.*

JAMES LAVER, *Women's Dress in the Jazz Age*

# Notes on the Cutting Diagrams

i Gown, *c*. 1600. *Victoria and Albert Museum.*
A gown with hanging sleeves, of dark claret broché velvet with a small design of pinks and pomegranates. The top is mounted on a small foundation yoke of lighter claret taffeta, part of which is quilted on to a canvas lining. The epaulettes, collar and sleeves are also interlined with canvas. The collar and sleeves are faced with claret taffeta, that of the sleeves having a spot pinking. The sleeves are open down the front and just caught together at T. Threads indicate where metal braid and spangles have been removed down the edge of the front panels, shoulder seams, around armholes, collar, epaulettes and down each edge of the hanging sleeves. The two holes indicated at the centre back of the collar are probably lace holes for securing the ruff.

ii Embroidered Jacket, *c*. 1610. *London Museum.*
A jacket of linen embroidered in black with an all-over pattern of flowers, fruit and acorns.

iii Embroidered Jacket, 1625–30. *Victoria and Albert Museum*. ref. 324–19.
A jacket of white linen. The fabric has an open squared design obtained by drawn thread work and decorated with sequins. There is a $\frac{1}{2}''$ lace decorating the edge of the neck and centre front opening. Around the bottom of the jacket is a lace $1\frac{3}{4}''$ deep also patterned with sequins. The sleeve fullness is gathered into tape at the wrists with the ends left for tying. Each piece of the garment has been narrowly hemmed all round before making up.

iv Bodice, 1635. *London Museum.*
A cream damask bodice lined with fine linen, and stiffened with canvas. The sleeves are lined with a mixture of cotton and linen.

v Bodice, 1650–60. *London Museum.*
A bodice of pale blue watered silk, mounted on thick cotton and heavily boned.

vi Dress, 1660's. *Museum of Costume, Bath.*
A dress with a separate bodice and skirt of silver tissue, trimmed with needlepoint lace, through which a design has been threaded, using a fine cord made from a narrow strip of kid

$\frac{1}{16}$" wide and wound round with cream silk. The bodice is mounted on a fully boned linen foundation and laces up the centre back. It has a slot centre front for a busk. The sleeves are lined with cotton and have extra stiffening at the top, with the fullness gathered into fine cartridge pleats top and bottom. The skirt is also set in cartridge pleats of $\frac{1}{4}$" each at the waist and held in position to a depth of $2\frac{1}{4}$", the top edge being cut raw and bound. It is unlined, but has a wide linen facing up the centre front and around the hem.

vii Bodice, 1650–60. *Victoria and Albert Museum.*
A black velvet bodice mounted on a linen interlining stiffened with whalebone. The sleeves, oversleeves and epaulettes are also interlined with linen. All the seams are outlined with a narrow black braid and the neck edge is bound. There is also a basque made up of small tabs joined together, but this is too perished to give an accurate pattern, therefore its length must be conjectural.

viii Bodice, 1670–80. *Mrs P. Anthony.*
A bodice of peach coloured velvet, embroidered with coloured silks in a pomegranate design, using long and short stitches. The three centre front, and two centre back tabs are covered with the same velvet and bound with green ribbon, but the side tabs are covered with turquoise blue satin and bound with yellow corded ribbon. The neck edge is also bound with the yellow ribbon. The velvet is mounted on a lightly boned foundation of white silk, which has a centre front and centre back lacing, the eyelet holes being concealed by the velvet covering. There are two large brass hooks on the outside at the centre back.

**PART TWO**

ix Mantua, *c.* 1700. *Metropolitan Museum, New York.*
A dress and petticoat of grey wool, striped in indigo blue and henna, and unlined. It is generously embroidered in silver gilt with a floral and scroll pattern. The stomacher is stiffened, and trimmed with metallic lace. The petticoat has the stripe running horizontally. It is 124" wide and unshaped, 36" long centre front, 49" long centre back, and has the waist fullness arranged in 13 pleats on either side.

x Casaque, *c.* 1735–40. *London Museum.* ref. 39–106.
A casaque of stiff pink silk with a silver floral motif, lined with a light pink silk. The front pleats are held in position on either side at XXX with a tape 2" long. There is no firm foundation lining.

xi Robe Battante (sack), 1725–35. *Centre de Documentation du Costume, Paris.*
A sack or robe battante of emerald lampas satin with a large floral design in rich colours, beautifully shaded. The bodice is lined with coarse terracotta canvas, and in each cuff there is stitched a weight.

xii  Mantua, 1735–40. *London Museum.*
A trained mantua of heavy pink silk damask. The long skirt appears to have been draped by having each side panel folded outwards and in towards the centre back, then the long train folded up inside the back of the gown and lightly tacked or pinned into position. The sides are then draped on either hip by taking the silk cord loops coming from underneath the gown and fastening them over the buttons which are placed in the same position but on the outside of the skirt. To ensure the damask was facing right side out when draped, panels X, Y and Z are made up on the wrong side with all their adjoining seams turned outwards. The petticoat has 7 widths of 21″ wide damask and is arranged in pleats on either side of the waist, where it has been cut raw and bound leaving a slot across the back. It is 36″ long centre front, 47½″ side, and 39″ centre back.

xiii  Mantua (large panier), 1740. *Victoria and Albert Museum.* ref. T44–1910.
A bodice with a basque, and tail, and petticoat, of white figured silk with a floral motif, trimmed with green lace down side fronts, basque and sleeve flounces. The back and front of the petticoat are cut the same, except for the front waist being cut lower.

xiv  Mantua, 1740–50. *Victoria and Albert Museum.* ref. T34–1960.
A simple close bodied gown of heavy white damask. The skirt fullness is arranged in deep pleats about 1″ apart and meeting at each side waist with an inverted pleat.

xv  Sack Dress, 1740–1750. *London Museum.*
The sack and matching petticoat of rich silver brocade, with a floral pattern. The back of the bodice only is lined. The petticoat has six panels each 21″ wide, and is 35″ long centre front, and 38″ long at the sides and centre back. It is arranged in pleats at the waist except across the back, where it is slotted with a tape.

xvi  Mantua, 1740–50. *Leeds City Art Galleries.*
A close bodied gown of heavy blue damask. The side fronts are cut in one piece, without a completely severed waist, and it has the skirt fullness arranged in deep pleats on either side, meeting in the centre with an inverted pleat.

xvii  Mantua (large panier), 1750's. *London Museum.* ref. A6853.
A bodice with tail, and petticoat, in pale pink and silver brocade with a floral design. The front of the basque, sleeve flounces, neck edge, and bottom of the petticoat are trimmed with silver lace. There is a fine white silk lining to the petticoat.

xviii  Sack Dress, 1770's, *London Museum.*
A sack dress, with a petticoat, of plain terracotta silk decorated with puffs and flounces of self material, and terracotta tassels. The edges are trimmed with a narrow terracotta braid. The bodice front is boned and has a centre front lacing, which originally would have been covered with a highly decorated stomacher to match.

xix Sack Dress, 1755–60, *Leeds City Art Galleries.*
A sack dress of pale blue spitalfield silk broacade, with a small floral pattern, and trimmings of green pleated silk edged with narrow white lace. The bodice has a boned lining and a cord lacing across the stomacher (which is missing). The sides of the skirt from E to F are arranged in pleats. The ribbon bows on the sleeves are edged with lace and stiffened down the centre with a fine whalebone.

xx Sack Dress (large panier), late 1770's. *Victoria and Albert Museum.*
A sack dress and petticoat of heavy white satin, trimmed with puffs of self material and edged with a narrow silk braid and tassels. The bodice has a white linen lining which laces up the centre back. There are tapes and rings at the back XX and YY so that the sack can be caught up.

xxi Polonaise, late 1770's. *Victoria and Albert Museum.*
A polonaise of pale cream light silk, decorated with pleated edgings of lilac silk. Lilac cords outline the back seams each terminating in a lilac tassel, under which is concealed a covered button. There is a loop of fine braid attached to the inside of the polonaise at the same spot as the button for looping up the skirt. The bodice is lined with linen.

xxii Robe à l'Anglaise, 1775–80. *Leeds City Art Galleries.*
A robe à l'Anglaise (or close bodied gown), and petticoat of light silk taffeta with a plaid design in apple green and rose on a white ground, and decorated with green silk pleating around the neck and sleeves. Each piece of the bodice is lined separately with white cotton and seamed together as one piece of material, and a narrow whalebone is placed on either side of the three back seams. The skirt fullness is arranged in very close pleats. The petticoat is made from 4 widths of $22\frac{1}{2}''$ wide silk, $37''$ long centre front, $38''$ long at the sides, and $39''$ long centre back, and arranged in 14 pleats on either side of the waist moving from a wide inverted pleat centre front to a box pleat at centre back.

xxiii Polonaise style Jacket, early 1780's. *Leeds City Art Galleries.*
A polonaise of cream figured silk, bordered with a deep facing of green silk, the inner edge being a narrow pink ribbon. Green cord outlines the three back seams, and the long button loops which fasten across the bodice are also of green cord.

xxiv Pierrot Jacket, late 1780's. *London Museum.*
A striped jacket of soft satin edged with a fine silk fringe. The narrow stripes of the satin are in black, pale blue, tan and yellow, and the fringe which is $1\frac{1}{4}''$ deep is made up of small sections divided into the same colours. The bodice is lined with silk to the waist, the back seams having the lining and outer layer treated as one piece of material and sewn together. At the sides the satin only is pleated and then stitched down to the lining at the dotted lines. From the waist downwards it is unlined.

xxv Chemise Dress, c. 1785. *The Gallery of English Costume, Manchester.*
A robe in the style of the Chemise de la Reine, made of white muslin with a very small

woven lozenge design. The sleeves are of plain muslin. The dotted lines indicate where slots are stitched, and through which narrow white cords are threaded. These tie in the front, which is open. There is a narrow cotton fringe decorating the side fronts and the hem of the skirt. The bodice at the neck is gathered into a binding.

xxvi Robe à l'Anglaise, early 1790's. *London Museum.*
A robe à l'Anglaise of soft cream satin which has a $\frac{1}{2}''$ figured silk stripe alternating with a warp printed flowered satin stripe about 1″ wide. The bodice is decorated around the edge with a silk braid fringe everywhere but the back of the neck, which is left plain. The pierrot pleating is stitched to the bodice lining, which is of linen and there is a bone on either side of the three back seams. The skirt is set in small pleats and the side fronts edged with the silk braid fringe.

xvii Stays, mid-eighteenth century. *After Leloir.*

xviii Corsage of Marie Antoinette, 1780's. *M. Parguez, Paris.*
Corsage of Marie Antoinette, made of blue-green taffeta lined with cotton. It is unboned and the eyelet holes at the back are concealed. This is probably a tight fitting bodice that was worn with a polonaise or caraco. It was found attached to the account books of Madame Eloffe, milliner to Marie Antoinette.

xxix Corset of Lady Hamilton, 1790's. *Victoria and Albert Museum.*
A corset worn by Lady Hamilton, made of white silk and backed with cotton. The boning is on either side of the centre back and centre front.

xxx Jacket, 1760–70. *Gallery of English Costume, Manchester.* ref. 1948–77.
A jacket of brown silk trimmed with a matching silk fringe and fastened at the centre front with braided tabs. It is lined to the waist with linen and it has a lacing tab inside the centre front opening.

xxxi Riding Coat, 1750. *Victoria and Albert Museum.*
A jacket of brown camlet, lined to the waist only. This cut was often used for informal day wear, but then the neck was cut much lower.

**PART THREE**

xxxii Round Robe, *c.* 1795.
A round robe of very fine soft white muslin with frills of self material. The bodice lining is of firmer cotton, and the backs of both lining and bodice are cut the same. The bodice and skirt are sewn to the waistband, except the left side front, which from the centre front to the side opening is gathered into a narrow band $5\frac{1}{2}''$ long.

xxxiii Open Robe, *c.* 1797. *Museum of Costume, Bath.*
An open robe of fine white muslin, having a heavier woven stripe alternating with a delicately coloured seaweed, coral, and leaf design. The bodice and sleeves are lined with a slightly

thicker cotton. The front bodice lining is pinned in position and the dress front gathered on a cord to the centre front, and then extended to wrap over. The skirt is pleated on to the bodice round to I, and then gathered on a cord to the centre front, the front being left open.

xxxiv Open Gown, *c.* 1795. *Victoria and Albert Museum.* ref. T513–1902.
An open gown of pale yellow wool with a small white satin spot. The edges and back seams are outlined with a narrow red looped cord. The vest is of plain cream satin. The bodice and sleeves are lined with white linen, and the back seams have narrow bones on either side. The side fronts are held back in pleats on either side of the gown with a tab and button. The back panels are seamed down to the high waist level and then fall away in box pleats.

xxxv Robe with 'bib' front, *c.* 1803. *Cheltenham Museum.*
A robe with a bib or apron front, of very fine soft muslin decorated with delicate white embroidered panels. The back and sides of the bodice are lined with a heavier cotton. The back is attached to the bodice round to J, and the front to F. F to G is sewn to a narrow band and continues the apron front round towards the back.

xxxvi Bodice of Dress, *c.* 1810. *London Museum.*
A bodice of fine white muslin, trimmed with delicately embroidered flounces, also in white.

xxxvii Evening Dress, 1816–19. *The Gallery of English Costume, Manchester.* ref. 1947–1757.
A dress of transparent cream silk with a satin stripe, trimmed with rouleaux of white satin and net. At the neck edge the rouleaux decoration has net threaded through the loops, and there is also a drawstring. The skirt is decorated at the bottom with ovals of pleated net edged with satin ribbon and folded over, and between each of these there is an artificial rose.

xxxviii Day Dress, 1816–19. *Privately owned.*
A dress of firm white muslin with a fine cord stripe. The bodice front is gathered into a piping cord at the next edge, and the cuffs and waistband have a piping cord at the top and bottom. Around the armhole is also piped. The skirt ruching is of thinner muslin and has a cord sewn around the top edge.

xxxix Pelisse, *c.* 1820. *The Central School of Art and Design, London.*
A pelisse of saxe blue foulard, with decorative tabs and buttons in self material. All the tabs are bound with a very narrow binding and the bodice seams and belt are piped. The bodice, sleeves and back of the skirt are lined with cotton, but the fronts are faced with white silk. There is a triple row of padding round the hem.

xl Evening Dress, *c.* 1825. *The Gallery of English Costume, Bath.*
A dress of paper thin white satin. The neck, armhole, and side seams of the bodice are piped, and there is a drawstring at the neck and waist. The whole dress is lined with fine glazed cotton and the hem is padded. The pattern given for the outer sleeve is added as it was very typical for this type of dress to have such transparent oversleeves.

xli Day Dress, *c.* 1834. *Privately owned.*

A day dress of very fine muslin, with a delicate all-over seaweed design in tan and dark brown. The bodice, sleeves, and epaulettes are lined with white cotton, and the skirt is faced up to 18″ around the hem with the same. The neck, centre fronts, armholes, side seams, bottom of the sleeves, and edges of the epaulettes are all piped. The skirt is gathered to the bodice at the back as shown by the dotted line, and the apron front is gathered on to a narrow band 16″ long. Tapes tie inside the sleeves to keep the fullness from drooping over the forearm.

xlii Day Dress, *c.* 1837. *Museum of Costume, Bath.*

A dress of cream challis with a satin stripe, having a delicate leaf design in green between each stripe. The bodice and sleeves are lined with cotton and the skirt is faced up to 4″ around the hem. The drapery of the bodice comes from the shoulders with the fullness meeting centre back and centre front, where it has a narrow cord to disguise the join. There are no waist darts in the bodice and it fastens at the centre back with hooks and eyes.

xliii Bodice, *c.* 1839. *The Central School of Art and Design, London.*

A bodice made of challis with a floral design in bright colours. The neck, waist, armholes, back seams, and front darts all piped in apple green. The bertha is made from crossway strips of the material which overlap, mounted on to a net foundation. There is a whalebone up the centre front.

xliv Bodice, early 1840's. *The Central School of Art and Design, London.*

A bodice of satin with $\frac{1}{2}$″ stripes in plum and scarlet. The neck, waist, the bottom edge of the jockeys and long sleeves have a crossway binding of self material. The bodice and long sleeves are lined with glazed cotton and it is boned at the centre front, side and back seams. It has a centre back fastening. The skirt is 7 widths of $18\frac{1}{2}$″ satin, 36″ long at the centre front and 39″ at the centre back, this is also lined with glazed cotton and has the fullness finely gauged into the waist.

xlv Evening Dress, 1840's. *Privately owned.*

A dress of cream silk taffeta. The armholes and waist are piped, and it has a fine muslin edging at the neck and sleeves. The front of the bodice is pleated on to the lining, but the back bodice and its lining are cut the same. It is boned at the centre front darts and side seams. The skirt is lined with glazed cotton and finely gauged on to the bodice at the waist, where the gauging is deeper at the back. The bottom is edged with a round braid.

xlvi Summer Dress, *c.* 1850's. *The Central School of Art and Design, London.*

A simple dress of very fine muslin with a delicate pattern of roses and black ribbon. The bodice is lined with white cotton and fastens centre front. The foundation skirt is of 4 widths each 32″ wide. The flounces are 12″ deep and contain 6 widths each 32″ wide.

xlvii Carriage Dress, late 1850's. *London Museum.* ref. 62–20/I.

A carriage dress of dove grey taffeta, the flounces having wide bands in a plaid design of white grey and black. Strips of this are also used to trim the pagoda sleeves, and jockey sleeves. The bodice is decorated with grey braid froggings and tassels. The sleeves are open as far up as the jockey sleeves and are lined with white silk. Both bodice and skirt are lined and the skirt has a 10″ band of stiff muslin around the hem. It is pleated to the waistband at the front and sides but gauged at the centre back. The foundation skirt has 5 widths of 21½″ plain grey taffeta, and the flounces are each 19″ deep, the top flounce has 6 widths each 21½″ wide, and the bottom 7 widths, each 21″ wide. The bodice and skirt are separate garments, the bodice having bones at all waist seams except centre front.

xlviii  Evening Dress, early 1860's. *The Central School of Art and Design, London.*
A white moire dress trimmed with black Maltese lace. The bertha is of black spotted net, trimmed with the black lace and a narrow pleated paper thin white satin ribbon. This same decoration is used on the skirt. The sleeves have two flounces of chiffon 2½″ deep. The bodice is lined with white cotton and has fine boning at all seams. The skirt is lined with stiff muslin and its fullness taken in at the waist by deep inverted pleats centre front, and two large double box pleats at each side of the centre back.

xlix  Afternoon Dress, c. 1868–9. *Privately owned.*
A dress of tan moire, trimmed with crossway bands of dark brown velvet. The flounce at the back and sides of the skirt is 18½″ deep and is arranged in box pleats, the tops of these are caught down to show the velvet facing. The skirt is unlined but it has a 9″ facing of stiff muslin at the bottom.

l  Bishop Sleeve, c. 1863.
A bodice made of checked silk with yellow and white lines on a green ground, and decorated with bands of black lace over white satin.

li  Late 'Pagoda' Sleeve.
A pagoda sleeve decorated with black velvet bands and bow.

lii  Evening Dress (bustle), c. 1870. *The Central School of Art and Design, London.*
An evening dress of lightweight shot taffeta in lilac pink, and edged with cream lace. The bodice is piped at all seams and edges, and is lined with cotton. It is boned at the darts and the centre front opening. The pannier is also lined with cotton and is gathered from A to centre back. The bodice, skirt, and pannier are all separate.

liii  Day Dress (bustle), c. 1873. *Cheltenham Museum.*
A day dress of cream alpaca with chine spots in mauve, and bound with crossway bands in mauve. The back pannier is pleated (meeting in a box pleats centre back) on to a small band which is under the back bodice pleats, and tapes are sewn on the inside at X and Y looping the skirt up to the centre back, with side tapes tying across the back. The skirt is separate and pleated on to a waistband. The flounces on the skirt are cut on the cross of the material and are of cream alpaca, as also are the bands. All are edged with a narrow crossway binding. The dress is unlined.

liv Afternoon Dress (bustle), *c.* 1878. *The Central School of Art and Design, London.*
A dress of cream taffeta, with a scarf drapery of cream silk in an open lace pattern. The bodice is lined with white cotton to the hips and boned at the centre back ($21\frac{1}{2}''$), underarm ($6\frac{1}{2}''$), and centre front ($10\frac{1}{2}''$). The skirt is faced with net around the bottom, graduating from a depth of 12″ at centre front to 25″ at centre back. There is also an extra band of stiff muslin $7\frac{1}{2}''$ deep at the hem. The drape of self silk (90″ long and 21″ wide with a $2\frac{1}{2}''$ crossway binding at one edge) is set in pleats to the side back seam at C D. It falls down across the front and is pleated into the side back seam at A B. The longer scarf drapery with the lace pattern (118″ long and 21″ wide, and attached along the dotted line), is also pleated at C D and falls over the lower drape round the front, and is arranged in pleats at E F, under the bow, from where it falls freely. The decorative pleating at the hem of the skirt is of self silk and underneath there is a balayeuse of fine kilted muslin edged with lace 1″ deep. The sleeves are edged with crossway bands of cream taffeta below which is a kilted net frill.

lv Afternoon Dress (bustle), *c.* 1883. *The Gallery of English Costume, Manchester.*
A dress of pale blue ottoman silk, decorated with crossway bands of black velvet, black lace, and black velvet buttons. The bodice is lined with heavy striped cotton and boned at the seams, with the fronts piped and the lower edge of the jacket trimmed with a narrow black lace. The vest is mounted on cotton and is of ruched silk, fastening at centre back neck, and with ties at the waist. The skirt is also of silk with the front ruched and held with bands of black velvet; the back is bordered at the hem with kilted frills. The back drape is pleated and caught to the sides at W, X, Y, and Z. There is a balayeuse of kilted muslin edged with lace.

lvi Day Dress (bustle), *c.* 1888. *Victoria and Albert Museum.* ref. T69–1937.
A day dress of heavy terracotta grosgrain. The bodice buttons on to a plastron of pleated grey satin which bears a small pattern in terracotta velvet. The collar and cuffs are of plain terracotta velvet. The lining of the bodice is of striped cotton and the seams are boned. It has a foundation skirt of terracotta alpaca with two slots at the back for steels and there is a 9″ facing of black linen at the bottom. The overskirt is of double box pleated silk and is attached as shown from the dotted line. It is faced 7″ up with black linen and the pleats are held in position at the back by two rows of tapes, one 7″ up and the other 14″. The back drape is caught into loops at centre back.

PART FOUR

lvii Evening Dress, 1893–4. *Privately owned.*
An evening dress of ivory broché velvet and ivory satin. The bodice, front drape, and sleeve bands are of the cut velvet, with the full sleeves of ivory satin. Both bodice and sleeves are lined with white taffeta. The front of the skirt is of ivory satin lined with cotton and bordered with a band of cut velvet, and the two back panels which overlap at the sides are of cut velvet, lined with satin and interlined with stiff muslin. The bodice which is boned at the seams, fastens at the centre front, and the skirt, which is separate, is bound with satin at the waist and fastens at the centre back.

lviii  'Leg o' Mutton' Sleeve pattern, 1895.

lix  Day Dress, *c.* 1895. *Privately owned.*
A dress of black satin with the plastron front, epaulettes, collar and cuffs of black satin with a
black velvet stripe. The bodice is boned at the darts and side seams and is lined with striped
cotton, as also are the sleeves. The upper sleeves have a lining of stiff muslin. The skirt has a
lining of black linen and a black corded braid at the bottom edge. The bodice buttons at the
centre front and there is a large hook and eye at the waist. The skirt is separate and fastens at
the centre back.

lx  Bolero, *c.* 1895. *Privately owned.*
A bolero of purple taffeta with narrow purple velvet ribbing, and lined with purple taffeta.

lxi  Blouse, *c.* 1898. *The Central School of Art and Design, London.*
A blouse of pale green taffeta with a pink pin stripe and a light floral design, trimmed at the
edges with a fine white lace. The lining of striped cotton fastens at the centre front, above
which the plastron front hooks over to the left.

lxii  Afternoon Dress, *c.* 1901. *The Central School of Art and Design, London.*
An afternoon dress of pale blue voile with a lace yoke and cuffs. The bodice is gathered and
pleated at the centre front to a white taffeta lining and set into a waist belt which fastens at the
centre back. The voile skirt is pin tucked to fit around the waist and had 9 graduated tucks
around the bottom. There are two underskirts, the lower of white taffeta with a circular
flounce, and the upper of chiffon with a gathered frill.

lxiii  Evening Dress, 1905–6. *The Central School of Art and Design, London.*
A dress of ivory chiffon with 1″ satin stripes alternating with a fancy stripe 3″ wide, and
trimmed with rows of narrow valenciennes lace. The waist belt and sleeve bands are of soft
white satin. The bodice and skirt foundations are of soft ivory silk. The bodice is gathered
into a lining which fastens at the centre front, but the front of the chiffon bodice is gathered
to an extra lining centre front which fastens on the left side from A to B. The dress skirt has a
frill 1½″ deep around the bottom and over that the deeper flounce is gathered and edged with
two crossway bands of ivory satin. The foundation skirt has a flounce and ruchings of self
material. The belt only is boned.

lxiv  Bolero Jacket and Skirt, 1906–7. *Victoria and Albert Museum.*
A bolero jacket and matching skirt of apple green face cloth decorated with loops, buttons
and tabs. The tabs are outlined with a narrow fold of black silk. The cloth skirt has a centre
front busk which protrudes above the waist line, and there is a foundation skirt of apple green
taffeta with small bones supporting the high waist.

lxv  Tub Frock, *c.* 1910. *Victoria and Albert Museum.*  ref. T24–1960.
A tub frock of lilac linen with raglan sleeves in narrow lilac and white striped cotton. The

buttons and belt are also of the striped cotton. The bodice and skirt are attached to the top of a deep petersham waistband and fastened centre back. The buttoned front is false. There is a slip of lilac silk which is darted at the waist.

lxvi Afternoon Dress, 1910–11. *London Museum.*
A dress of grey silk gaberdine with a narrow black velvet stripe ½″ apart. The yoke and cuffs are of white lace covered with black chiffon and edged with a black velvet piping, and the buttons are of corded silk. The bodice and skirt from sides to back are gathered on to the top of a deep petersham waistband.

lxvii Afternoon Dress (Lucile). 1911–12. *London Museum.*
A dress by Lucile of soft blue satin, with shoulder drapes and apron front of cream chiffon with embroidered borders. The bodice and sleeves are backed with white chiffon and the bodice is lined with white satin. The skirt is slit on the left side and gathered on the right, where it is looped up and caught to the underslip. The underslip is of chiffon with a box pleated flounce of machine made lace bands. The back of the bodice and the top of the skirt are sewn to the top of the petersham, but the underslip is attached at a lower line. The dress opens centre front, and the narrow belt of folded blue satin fastens on the left side with an ornamental bow.

lxviii Afternoon Dress. 1916–17. *Privately owned.*
A dress of navy blue taffeta. The kimono sleeves are attached to the bodice with faggoting, each edge having first been rolled over a narrow piping cord. The foundation skirt is the same back and front and is attached at the waist to the middle of the petersham. The two flounces are 20½″ deep and 74″ round, with crossway bands at the bottom edges. The bodice, which has a net lining, has a small lap over at the centre front, and the skirt fastens to the left side.

lxix Afternoon Dress, c. 1918. *London Museum.*
A dress of pale pink crepe de chine, patterned at the centre front, neck, sleeves and hem with tiny white china beads. The sleeves and back drapes are of pale pink georgette and the bobbles are pads covered with silk and beaded. It has a belt of black velvet. The bodice is mounted on a net lining with its fullness arranged at the waist in small pleats. The overskirt and underskirt are both gathered into the waist.

lxx Evening Dress. 1920–1. *Privately owned.*
An evening dress with a dark blue charmeuse satin skirt, its side drapes bound with gold ribbon, and the overblouse of blue and gold brocade with a side fastening. The kimono sleeves are of dark blue net over blue chiffon, and the sleeve flounces are of single net picot edged. The foundation bodice is of dark blue satin with a flesh coloured chiffon top, the centre front being covered with a layer of blue net. There is a centre back fastening and elastic is threaded through the hem to draw it in at the ankles.

lxxi Evening Dress (Poiret), *c. 1922. Centre de Documentation du Costume, Paris.*
A dress designed by Poiret for his wife. It is of black crepe de chine, and has one seam only on the left-hand side. The ovals indicate the positions of Chinese motifs printed in bright colours. A heavy tassel hangs from the corner drape. The sash is of emerald green georgette 36″ deep. There is a slot at the low waistline for elastic.

lxxii Day Dress (Weldons), *c. 1924. The Gallery of English Costume, Manchester.* Pattern no. 70618.
A Weldons' dress pattern, with suggested materials of gaberdine or serge for day wear and, for smart afternoon occasions and theatre going, in maroon crepe de chine, or satin with ninon sleeves and beaded decoration.

lxxiii Evening Dress (Vionnet), *c. 1925. Centre de Documentation du Costume, Paris.*
A dress by Vionnet of ivory morocain. The lines indicate rows of handmade ivory silk fringe.

lxxiv Evening Dress, *c. 1926. London Museum.*
A dress of beige georgette with scalloped edges, decorated with rows of green beads and a bronze and green fringe. The skirt has two panels at the front and one at the back and all are gathered to a low waist. The underslip is also of beige georgette.

lxxv Evening Dress, *c. 1929. Privately owned.*
A pale green georgette dress and slip. The drapes are top stitched around the waist and the bottom of the skirt, and the shoulder drape is picot edged. There is a narrow binding at the neck edge and armholes.

# Glossary of Materials

ALPACA. A material of plain weave with a lustrous quality, having a cotton warp and a wool weft.

BARÈGE, BARREGE. A gauze fabric, with a silk warp and a wool weft. Semi-transparent and sometimes used for head coverings at religious ceremonies.

BATISTE. A very fine quality fabric of French origin, and woven from ecru coloured cotton yarns or grey yarn when flax is used.

BEAVER. An overcoating cloth, heavily milled, with one face sheared and a nap raised finish. Soft to handle and woven from fine grade wool. Also used for hats.

BLONDE LACE. Silk lace of two threads in hexagonal meshes. Originally of raw silk colour, now white or black.

BOMBAZINE. A black fabric of open twill weave, with a silk warp and a worsted weft. Usually worn for mourning.

BOOK MUSLIN. A very light cotton fabric of gauze weave. Stiffly finished.

BROADCLOTH. A stout wool cloth, soft and silky to the touch, with an even satin nap finish. A term sometimes used to describe clerical clothes.

BROCADE (from the Spanish 'bro cade' to figure). Originally a silk fabric with a pattern produced by extra weft threads of gold or silver, and later developing into a material with the ground of a simple weave and the figuring weft threads of different colours. Cotton brocade usually having only one colour warp and one colour weft, and silk brocade with several wefts of silk yarn in different colours.

BROCHÉ VELVET. A figured silk material with an additional velvet pattern.

BRODÉRIE ANGLAISE. White linen or cotton embroidered in white thread to produce an all-over openwork pattern. The design is made by cutting small holes into the fabric and then overcasting the edges to prevent fraying.

BUCKRAM. A strong linen fabric of plain open weave, stiffened with flour paste, china clay and glue.

315

CALICO, CALLICOE. A term applied to any plain cotton heavier than muslin. Originally it applied to a rather coarse printed cotton.

CAMBRIC. A very fine white linen.

CAMLET. Introduced into England by the Dutch it was then woven from camel or goat's hair, but later mixed with silk or wool.

CANVAS. An open mesh fabric, usually of linen, though Dress canvas is woven with a linen warp and a cotton weft.

CASHMERE. At first woven entirely from the wool of the Cashmere goat, but later woven with a mixture of cotton, or cotton and wool weft.

CHALLIS, CHALY. A fine material similar to a muslin delaine and printed in colours. Originally woven with a silk warp and a worsted weft, and later of all wool.

CHAMOIS. A soft pliable leather from the wild mountain antelope. A term applied to any soft leather from sheep, goat or deer.

CHENILLE. This fancy weft is made by first weaving a fabric on an ordinary loom which has a gauze mounting, and then cutting the material into strips. These strips are used as weft threads in shawls, tablecovers, etc.

CHIFFON (from the French 'chiffe' meaning rag or flimsy cloth). A plainly woven fabric of silk. Very soft and flimsy. Semi-transparent.

CHINTZ. Plural for 'Chint', the Eastern name for a printed cotton.

CLOTH. A term used for any woven fabric, but more particularly with reference to closely woven woollen material of fine quality.

COTTON. Of the cotton plant, and woven in many thicknesses and qualities, the chief varieties being—American, Brazilian, African, East Indian, Egyptian, Peruvian and Sea Island.

CRAPE, CRÊPE. A puckered and crinkled semi-transparent fabric, which is usually dyed black. Hard twisted yarns are used and when the fabric is washed a permanent crinkle is produced by the shrinkage of certain threads.

CRÊPE DE CHINE. A very soft china silk crêpe, it can be plain, figured or printed, and is easy to drape. Woven from a fine silk warp and a tightly twisted worsted weft.

CREPON. A soft fabric, similar to crêpe de chine, but thicker.

CRINOLINE. Material woven from horsehair and cotton yarns and used for the making of stiff petticoats in the mid-nineteenth century.

DAMASK. A fabric woven in geometrical or floral patterns. The designs are produced by interchanging the warp and weft threads in satin and twill weaves, and it is the reflection of light on the material that brings out the pattern.

DIMITY. A firm cotton fabric with raised cords forming stripes. Sometimes printed.

FAILLE. A corded silk, similar to grosgrain but softer and finer.

FELT. Not a woven fabric. A material produced by the matting and pressing together of woollen fibres.

FERRANDINE, FERRENTINE. A stout fabric of silk and wool.

FLORENCE. An open mesh fabric, similar to barège, but with a corded appearance.

FOULARD. A very soft lightweight silk of twilled weave.

FRIEZE. A type of woollen cloth or baize, with a napped face the right side having a surface of little burrs.

FUSTIAN. Early term for a coarse napped cotton of drab colour. Later describes a class of cottons which include corduroy and Bedford cord.

GABARDINE. A fabric woven with a cotton warp and a worsted weft. Usually waterproofed and used for rainwear.

GEORGETTE. A semi-transparent material with a crêpe weave. Woven from either silk, or fine Egyptian cotton yarns.

GIMP. Originally a yarn with a central wire thread and a silk yarn twisted round it, but later with a core of any hard twisted yarn bound by a soft one.

GLACÉ SILK. A plain weave silk with a lustrous quality. Sometimes having a warp and weft of different colours giving the fabric a shot effect.

GOLD, Cloth of. A material woven either, entirely of gold thread or gold thread with silk.

GROSGRAIN, GROGORINE. A sturdy silk with a corded weft, giving a firm ribbed appearance. The corded weft thread can be of cotton or silk.

HOLLAND. A fine linen fabric of plain weave, bleached or left grey.

HOMESPUN. A coarse cloth of tweed character, the yarn spun and then woven in the home. Of simple tabby weave and dyed one colour.

ITALIAN CLOTH. A firm fabric with a cotton warp and a botany weft, woven with a satin weft face and dyed black. Woven in imitation from all cotton.

JEAN. A twilled cotton dyed or bleached and used for boot and shoe linings, corsets, etc.

KASHA. A soft silky fabric of wool and goat's hair with a twill weave.

LAMA, LLAMA. Fabric woven from the wool of the Llama.

LAWN. An exceptionally fine linen.

LINEN. The yarn is made from the flax plant. Woven in many qualities it is strong and endurable and can be bleached a pure white. Unlike silk or wool it has no elasticity.

LUSTRING. A paper thin silk with a lustrous quality.

LUTESTRING. A thin finely corded silk with a glossy surface.

MAROCAIN. A crêpe fabric, of silk or wool or both.

MERINO. A fine quality twilled cloth woven from the fleece of the Merino sheep.

MERV. A satin fabric often used for trimmings.

MOHAIR. A fine camlet woven from the hair of the Angora goat.

MOIRÉ. A term referring to the watered effect given to fabrics by the pressure of engraved rollers which displace and flatten the threads. Usually processed on to a silk grosgrain.

MOIRÉ, ANTIQUE. A water mark applied on to a figured and satin striped grosgrain.

MUSLIN. A light open fabric used for summer dresses. Also a term used for all thin cotton varieties of lawn, mull and cambric.

NANKEEN. A cloth woven from a cotton yarn with a natural yellow tint. Now woven and dyed yellow. Used for pocket linings.

NINON. A plain weave sheer fabric, slightly heavier than chiffon and woven from a variety of yarns.

NUN'S VEILING. A very thin soft woollen material woven from fine yarns of very good quality.

OTTOMAN. A stout silk with a thickly corded weft.

PADUASOY. A plain stout silk with a fine smooth texture.

PETERSHAM. A strongly corded silk ribbon.

PETERSHAM CLOTH. A heavy woollen overcoating dyed dark blue.

PIQUÉ. A firm fabric woven with a raised rib. Usually of cotton.

PLUSH. A fine quality pile fabric, the pile of silk and the ground of high grade cotton.

POPLIN. A fine material, smooth and strong, either with a plain silk warp and a coarse silk weft, or made entirely of cotton.

PRINT. A term used for a plain fabric which has a printed design on one or both sides.

RODIER FABRICS. Exclusively designed fabrics woven in France. The Rodiers were the original creators in the middle of the nineteenth century of the modern lightweight tweeds and other materials woven from new fibres.

SARCENETT, SASNET, SCARCENET. A thin silk, plain or twilled.

SATEEN. A cotton material with a satin surface, often used for linings.

SATIN. A silk cloth with the warp predominating over the weft. The weft threads are completely covered to achieve a fine glossy warp face.

SERGE. A cloth woven in twill weaves with a warp of worsted and a weft of wool. Cheap imitations can be of cotton. A superior quality silk serge is also woven.

SHANTUNG. A plain, rough cloth of wild silk.

SILK. One of the most beautiful of fibres. Produced from the silk-worm cocoons. The filaments are drawn off in pairs and twisted together, using as many as ten or twelve pairs to make one thread. Its characteristics are strength, lustre and elasticity. It is woven in a great variety of ways, and dyes easily while retaining its luminous quality.

STOCKINETTE. A knitted material with an elastic quality, produced in a variety of yarns.

STUFF. A term originally used to describe a plain woollen cloth.

SURAH SILK. A soft but strong Indian silk.

TABBY, TABI. A coarse silk taffeta, shiny and watered. The term tabby is also used to describe a plain weave.

TAFFETA. A thin glossy silk of plain weave.

TARLATAN. A very fine open muslin with a stiff finish.

TIFFANY. A gauze-like silk.

TRICOT. Originally a hand knitted fabric of wool, but later applied to knitted ribbed fabrics of silk, cotton and rayon.

TULLE. A gossamer net fabric made from silk yarns.

TUSSORE. A term originally used to describe a cotton fabric woven from mercerized yarns in a light brown colour range. Later the term was applied to a raw silk fabric which was the same natural colour.

TWEED. A cloth woven from soft woollen yarns, and originally made by the banks of the river Tweed. It is open and elastic in texture and of a plain or twilled weave.

VELOUR, WOOL. A heavy woollen cloth with a soft pile.

VELVET. A closely woven fabric with a short dense pile on the upper surface. Velvet has a cotton back of twofold yarn and a silk pile, but it can also be woven entirely of silk.

VELVETEEN. A fabric woven from cotton in imitation of a silk velvet.

VOILE. A light open textured fabric woven plain from hard twisted yarns. Can be either all wool or all cotton.

# Bibliography

ADBURGHAM, Alison, *Shops and Shopping 1800-1914*

BOEHN, Max von, *Modes and Manners*

BOUCHER, Francois, *Histoire du Costume en Occident de l'Antiquité à nos Jours*

BUCK, Anne M., *Victorian Costume and Costume Accessories*

CHALLAMEL, Augustin, *The History of Fashion in France*

CUNNINGTON, C. Willett, *Englishwomen's Clothing in the Nineteenth Century; Englishwomen's Clothing in the Present Century*

CUNNINGTON, C. Willett & Phillis, *Handbook of English Costume in the Seventeenth Century; Handbook of English Costume in the Eighteenth Century; Handbook of English Costume in the Nineteenth Century*

DAVENPORT, M., *The Book of Costume*

FAIRHOLT, F. W., *Costume in England*

HOLLAND, Vyvyan, *Fashion Plates*

KELLY, F. and SCHWABE, R., *Historic Costume*

LANGLEY MOORE, Doris, *The Woman in Fashion*

LATOUR, Anny, *Kings of Fashion*

LAVER, James, *Taste and Fashion; Women's Dress in the Jazz Age*

LINTHICUM, M. Channing, *Costume in Elizabethan Drama*

LELOIR, Maurice, *Histoire du Costume, VIII, IX, X, XI, XII*

NIENHOLDT, Eva, *Kostümkunde*

QUICHERAT, J., *Costume en France*

RUPPERT, F., *Le Costume*

## Technical Books

1589 ALCEGA, Juaan de, *Libro de Geometrica Practica y Traca*

1618 LA ROCHA BURGUEN, F. de, *Geometrica y Traca*

1688 HOLME, Randle, *Academy of Armory*

1769 GARSAULT, F. A., *Description des Arts et Métiers, 'L'Art du Tailleur'*

1771 DIDEROT, *Encyclopédie, Tome IX, Tailleur d'Habits*

1787 PANCKOUCKE, *Encyclopedie*

1796 *The Taylor's Complete Guide*

1822 WYATT, J., *The Tailors' Friendly Instructor*

1833 HEARN, W., *The Art of Cutting Ladies Riding Habits, Pelisses, Gowns, Frocks, etc.*

1845 HOWELL, Mrs. M. J., *The Handbook of Dressmaking*

1855 WHITELEY, Mrs. T., *A New and Complete Method of Dressmaking*

1870 HIRTZ, E., *Méthode de Coupe et de Confection pour Vêtements de Femmes et d'Enfants*

1875 WHITELEY, Mrs. T., *The Complete Dressmaker*

1893 VINCENT, W. D. F., *The Cutters' Practical Guide*

1897 BROUGHTON, Mrs. J., *Practical Dressmaking for Students*

1897 HOLDING, T. H., *Direct System for Ladies' Garments*

1896 BROWNE, M. Prince, *New and Simplified System of Dress Cutting, Drafting and Tailoring;* 1902, *Dress Cutting, Drafting and French Pattern Modelling;* 1907, *Up-to-date Dress Cutting and Drafting*

1909 ROBERTS, M. E., *The Cutters' Guide*

1910 SHORT, Isabella, *Practical Home Sewing and Dressmaking*

1912 MERWIN, Pearl, *American System of Dressmaking*

1916 BALDT, Laura, *Clothing for Women*

1926 MANNING & DONALDSON, *Fundamentals of Dress Construction*

1930 TAILOR & CUTTER, *Cutters' Practical Guide*

## Selection of Journals

1770–1837 *Lady's Magazine*

1778–1787 *La Galerie des Modes*

1794–1803 *Heideloff's The Gallery of Fashion*

1798–1832 *Lady's Monthly Museum*

1806–1868 *La Belle Assemblée*

1809–1828 *The Repository of Arts*

1822–1865 *Petit Courier des Dames*

1823-1888   *Townsend's Parisian Costumes*
1829-1892   *Le Follet*
1833-1904   *Le Journal des Desmoiselles*
1841-19-    *Punch*
1852-1877   *Englishwoman's Domestic Magazine*
1854-19-    *Der Bazar*
1858-1895   *The Ladies' Treasury*
1860-19-    *La Mode Illustrée*
1861-19-    *The Queen*
1865-19-    *Die Modenwelt*
1866-19-    *Tailor & Cutter*
1875-1893   *Myra's Journal of Dress and Fashion*
1880-19-    *L'Art et la Mode*
1885-19-    *The Lady*
1892-19-    *Vogue*
1901-1940   *The Ladies' Tailor*
1916-19-    *British Vogue*

# Index

All items listed under a sub-heading are cross referenced, i.e., APRON, gauze, 26, *see also* GAUZE, Apron; with the exception of items listed under a main heading in date order, i.e., PETTICOAT (SKIRT)

*Italic numerals refer to plates*

A la giraffe, 216–*see also* HAIR
A la Titus, 214–*see also* HAIR
A tour, 112–*see also* HAIR
Accordion, pleating, 231–*see also* PLEATING
Aigrette, *frontispiece, 2,* 71
Alexandra, Princess of Wales, 141, 219
Allowance, for tucks, 186–*see also* TUCKS
Alpaca, 296, 310
Amber, 237–*see also* JEWELLERY
Amethyst, 138–*see also* JEWELLERY
Andrienne, 66, 113
Apron,
    embroidered, 26, 71, 124
    front, 132; (for riding habit) 133
    gauze, *5,* 26, *26*
    knee-length, 67
    lawn, 26, 71
    linen (linnen), 52, 74
    long, *5, 26,* 133
    short, 138
    silk (silke), 52
    tucked, 126
Artificial, pads, 228–*see also* PADS
Astrakan, muff, 293–*see also* MUFF

Back, pleating (18th Cent.), *23–24, 30, 32–33, 75,* 76, 124–*see also* PLEATING

Balayeuse, 231–*see also* BOUILLONNES
    muslin, 145
    ready-made, 240
Ball, fringe, 147–*see also* FRINGE
Band, *frontispiece, 1, 4,* 26, 43, 111
    falling, 52, 55
Barège, 188
Basque
    bodice, *frontispiece, 1, 6, 8, 9, 15, 17, 28,* 28–30, *49,* 69, 133, 141, 275
    circular, *frontispiece, 1, 23*
    Dressmaker suit, 234
    jacket, *3a, b, 5,* 25–6, *48, 51a, 57a, b,* 66, 67, 140, 228
    princess dress, 222
    riding coat, 70, 73
    suit, 235
    Swiss, 136, 141, 142
    waistcoat, 66
Batiste, 126, 300
Beaded
    braid, 142, 222
    embroidery, 257
Bearers, 45–*see also* HIPPADS; PADS
Beaver
    hat, 52, 121
    jacket, 147, 231
Bed gown, 70–*see also* GOWN
Bell
    hoop, *23,* 123
    skirt, *58,* 228, 239

Belle epoque, la, 264
Belt, *2, 46–47, 53,* 232
    corselet, *60b–63,* 234, 240
    gold, 214
    hip, 235
    mantua, *18–20, 22,* 65
    shirt blouse, 228
    Swiss, 136, 141, 142
Bertha, *47–8, 50b, 51b,* 137, 139, 140
Bertin, Rose, 103, 124
Betsie (ruff), *44a, b,* 47, 133–*see also* COLLAR, RUFF
Bib, 67, 74
    front, *43,* 132
Bishop, sleeve, *44c, 47, 49, 50a, b,* 140, 141–*see also* SLEEVES
Blonde, lace, 124, 126, 127, 214–*see also* LACE
    cap, 128
    collar (cherusque) 142
Blouse
    embroidered, 240
    full, *61,* 232
    jumper, 235
    kimono, 230
    muslin, 141
    revers, 227
    shirt, 227, 228, 235, 236
    Viennese, 300
Blue-striped, stays, 111–*see also* STAYS

323

Ninon, 231, 237
Nun's Veiling, 239, 298

'Officer' Collar, *59*, 145–*see also* COLLAR
Opal, 147–*see also* JEWELLERY
Open
  robe (gown), *1, 4, 7, 17–20, 22, 24–27, 29, 31–38, 40, 42a, c, 55*, 132, 133
  ruff, *56*
  skirt, *1, 4, 7, 14, 17–20, 22–24, 29, 31–37, 23, 45*
  sleeve, *7, 45*
Oriental Influenced, 237–*see also* JEWELLERY; EMBROIDERY
Osprey, Plumage, 299, 300–*see also* PLUMAGE
Ostrich Feather, fringe, *1, 2, 21, 34, 37–38, 40–41, 44a, c, 45–46, 48–49, 50a, 53–54, 56, 57a, b, 59, 60, 62–63, 65*, 147–*see also* FRINGE
  Fan, *1, 70*
Ottoman, silk, 146–*see also* SILK
Oval, neckerchief, 29
Over
  skirt, *1, 4, 14, 16, 27a, 29, 31–38, 40, 42a, 51a, b, 52, 55–56, 65, 66a, 31, 32*, 132, 144, 146
  sleeve, *2, 5, 7, 35–36, 38, 40, 44b, c, 57b, 62–63*, 137

Padded
  hem, *44b, d, 45*, 148
  roll, *4, 23*, 138
  sleeve, *4, 6, 23, 27, 45*
Pads
  artificial, 228
  bearers, *45*
  bum roll, 23, 54
  bustle, 136, 138
  cork rump, 68
  cotton wool, 149
  cul de Paris, 23, 68
  cul postiche, 23
  down filled, 137
  false bums, 68
  farthingale roll, *4, 58*
  hip, *24, 28*, 67, 68, 72, 113
  horsehair, 146, 149

rowl, *45*
rump, 121, 126
Paduasoy, 115
Pagoda, sleeve, *50a, b, 51a*, 140, 141, 142, 144, 229–*see also* SLEEVES
Pair (of bodies), 23–*see also* BODY
Palatine (Tippet), *22*, 67, 103, 112
Paletot (Victoria), 199
Pamela, bonnet, 217–*see also* BONNET
Panier, 68, 69, 102, 115, 133, 144–*see also* HOOP PETTICOAT
  kidney shaped, *27a, b, 28*, 68
  style, 222
Paper patterns–*see* PATTERNS
Parasol, *44b, 49, 50a, 51a, 52, 54, 56, 57a, b, 59–61, 64b, 68*, 294
Partlet, *5, 9, 15, 26, 29*
Parure, 71, 134, 142
Passementerie, 147, 231
Patches, *20, 22, 59*, 114, 116
Patinet, 215–*see also* LACE
Patterns–paper: (1840), 183; (from 1825), 185, 187, 188, 189; (1860), 219; (from 1908), 265
  scale drafting, 185, 266
  service, 266
Peake, *6, 7, 10, 11, 14–16, 18, 20, 22, 27–28, 44*
Pearls, *1, 2, 5, 7–9, 13–16, 29, 32, 52, 54, 61*, 214, 231–*see also* JEWELLERY
  buttons, *55*
Pelerines, fichu, 138–*see also* FICHU
Pelisse (Plisse),
  cape, 110
  dress, *42c, 44a*, 133, 136, 138, 148
  mantle, 142
Peplos, *41, 132*
Peridots, 147–*see also* JEWELLERY
Perriwig, *21, 52*, 60, 61, 114
Perruques, 60–*see also* HAIR
Persian, silk 112–*see also* SILK
Pet en l'air (Casaquin), *23b*, 68, 70, 73 *see also* GOWN; JACKET
Petal, skirt, 300, 301–*see also* SKIRT
Peter Pan, collar, 234, 299–*see also* COLLAR

Petersham, *234, 235, 238, 239*
Petticoat (skirt)
  seventeenth century: *1, 4, 7, 14–17, 23, 25, 27, 28, 29, 31, 32, 45, 46, 54, 55, 56, 57, 60, 61*
  eighteenth century: *18–20, 22–27, 29, 31–38a*, 67, 69, 70, 72, 73, 76, 102, 103, 111, 113, 115, 120, 124, 127, 128
  nineteenth century: *40, 132*, 212, 214, 215
Petticoat (undergarment), 23
  circular, 217
  criardes, 67
  hooped (panier), *27b*, 66, 68, 69, 102, 115, 133, 144
  horsehair (crin), 139, 140
  lace, 293
  maker, 102
  quilted, 70, 111, 113
  satin (sattin), 60, 61, 111
  trained, 143
Pheasant plumage, 220–*see also* PLUMAGE
Picot edging, 240
Pierrot, *38*, 73, 124, 126
Pin tucks, *frontispiece, 1, 29, 30, 231*–*see also* TUCKS
Pinchbeck, 134, 147–*see also* JEWELLERY
Pinking, 26, 29, 74, 76, 118
Piping, 136, 148, 149, 186, 237
Pique, 141, 294
Plaid, silk, 219–*see also* SILK
Plain, ruffles, *6, 14–15, 25–26, 43*–*see also* RUFFLES
Plastron, *54–56, 57b*, 145, 227, 238
Pleating,
  accordion, 231
  back (eighteenth century), *23b, 24, 30, 32–33*, 69, 75, 76, 124
Plumage, *frontispiece, 1, 2, 34, 37–38, 40–41, 44a, c, 45–46, 49, 50a, 53–57b, 59, 60b, 61–65, 66c*, 67, 70, 111, 119, 120, 121, 124, 133, 202, 293, 295
  osprey, 299, 300
  pheasant, 220
Plush, 146, 220, 231